The Welfare State Reader

Third Edition

Edited by
**Christopher Pierson,
Francis G. Castles and
Ingela K. Naumann**

polity

First edition published in 2000 by Polity Press
Second edition published in 2006 by Polity Press
This third edition first published in 2014 by Polity Press

Polity Press
65 Bridge Street
Cambridge CB2 1UR, UK

Polity Press
350 Main Street
Malden, MA 02148, USA

ISBN-13: 978-0-7456-6368-5
ISBN-13: 978-0-7456-6369-2(pb)

A catalogue record for this book is available from the British Library.

Typeset in 10 on 12 pt Stempel Garamond
by Toppan Best-set Premedia Limited
Printed and bound in Great Britain by Clays Ltd, St Ives plc

The publisher has used its best endeavours to ensure that the URLs for external websites referred to in this book are correct and active at the time of going to press. However, the publisher has no responsibility for the websites and can make no guarantee that a site will remain live or that the content is or will remain appropriate.

Every effort has been made to trace all copyright holders, but if any have been inadvertently overlooked the publisher will be pleased to include any necessary credits in any subsequent reprint or edition.

For further information on Polity, visit our website: www.politybooks.com

Contents

Contents

Editors' Note

An ellipsis within square brackets indicates an omission from the original publication, thus: [. . .]. Where more than a paragraph has been excluded, a line space appears above and below such ellipses. Apart from minor amendments (e.g. capitalization, British rather than American spellings and the presentation of reference material), the few editorial interventions necessitated by publishing these extracts in a single volume also appear in square brackets. The authors' opinions are, of course, those held at the time of writing; dates of original publication are reflected in the Notes to each reading.

Editors' Introduction to the Third Edition

Hard times for people are hard times for the welfare state. In periods of prolonged economic hardship, people look to the state as the one agency with the resources and the will to protect them against the worst effects of a world of bewildering complexity and indifference. At the same time, the resources which make that state work seem to be in ever shorter supply and plenty of voices are raised to tell us that the problems that we now face are the consequences of an excess of state largesse in the past. What we need is not more, but (still) less. In the Western world, at least, we seem to be living through such times. This makes it even more important that we should really understand what welfare states are, what they can and cannot do and how we can change them smartly. These concerns are reflected in this the third edition of our *Welfare State Reader*.

We begin, as in the earlier editions, with a series of contributions which give us a sense of where welfare states have come from and of the sorts of disagreements about their purposes that have been with us now for more than a hundred years. These longstanding disputes continue to resonate in the arguments of the present, even if they often go unacknowledged. These sorts of basic questions – about how best to minimize poverty and promote equality, what sorts of policy intervention produce the best results and the extent to which state intervention for welfare purposes is compatible with other desired goals of modern societies – remain central preoccupations of the disciplines of social theory and social policy and have informed a large part of the analytical content of both political science and sociology throughout these disciplines' existence. They are, moreover, questions that have become ever more salient and of even greater practical policy relevance as the governments of democratic states having once responded to popular demands and new social and economic problems by extending the scope of the caring state have now entered into a phase in which these commitments seem to be increasingly contested. Today, the state spends more on welfare than on all other purposes combined and anyone who is interested in and concerned about the size and expenditure of the contemporary state is, whether they like it or not, concerned with the operations of the welfare state.

The content of this third edition of our reader reflects this changing climate. Part I retains its focus upon classical understandings of the welfare state project. Part II is re-cast as a discussion of welfare regimes *under threat* and assesses a series of constraints and challenges. Here we deal not only with Esping-Andersen's classic typology of the 'Three Worlds of Welfare Capitalism' and Paul Pierson's characterization of 'The New Politics of the Welfare State' but also with some alternative perspectives (including Manow and van Keesbergen's emphasis upon the longstanding impact of religious affiliation upon the character of welfare states). We consider anew the impact of processes of globalization, convergence and Europeanization. We confront the intensifying challenges presented by ageing, low fertility, migration and other forms of demographic change. As well as considering the logic and logistics of new social risks, we also give due weight to the perhaps unprecedented duress brought to bear upon mature welfare states by (ongoing) global economic crisis.

Part III shifts our attention towards emerging ideas and emergent forms. Many of the contributions here are also new to this third edition. They include evaluations of the ideas of the 'big society' and the 'social investment state', a characterization of the challenges of governing under increasing economic uncertainty and a short piece that considers the impact of climate change upon the social policy environment. Finally, the section on emergent forms discusses the new gender dispensation of contemporary welfare states, the new shape of poverty and tries to get at the politics of happiness that lies behind the politics of welfare. Our new selection ends with a magisterial piece by Jürgen Habermas that assesses what the politics of welfare should look like in a post-democratic European order.

Overall, our comprehensively revised third edition of *The Welfare State Reader*, in which Parts II and III are made up overwhelmingly of material new to this collection, provides an up-to-date user's guide to the politics of welfare in dark times. The choices may have become harder but, as ever, they are unavoidable and critical to the possibility of our all living decent lives in civilized societies.

Part I

Approaches to Welfare

In this first part, we bring together a series of 'classic' contributions to the literature of the welfare state. Thomas Paine is our sole representative of thinking about welfare *before* the rise of the modern welfare state. Writing more than two hundred years ago, many of Paine's thoughts have a strikingly contemporary resonance. His views on the interaction of poverty, criminality, indolence and employment are often simply a more elegant and direct expression of the kinds of arguments that go on today. It is as well to remember that thinking about welfare did not begin in 1945.

It used to be said that we lacked any serious theoretical account of where welfare states came from and what they are for. The business of the welfare state was social administration: the mundane tasks of mopping up poverty and improving public services. This was always, in part, a caricature. There have always been sharp and insightful critics of this dreary-but-worthy view of the welfare state. But we now have a wealth of competing theoretical accounts of the welfare state to choose from and the principal aim of Part I of the reader is to offer a representative survey of the best and the most influential of this literature. We begin with a series of writings from the years immediately following the end of the Second World War. These are not, for the most part, the years in which welfare states were founded. The origins of welfare states among most developed states actually lie in the twenty-five years *preceding* the First World War. But the postwar period was one of unprecedented and, at least to some extent, consensual growth in welfare states. It is also the time that gave us the most authoritative and enduring social democratic accounts of welfare and state. Here we have included three 'Classical' statements of the social democratic approach drawn from the work of Asa Briggs, T. H. Marshall and Richard Titmuss. The views of social democratic writers on the welfare state have always been vulnerable to misrepresentation, especially as they have so often been glossed as holding a rather simple-minded and wholly benign view of both the state and the human condition, a view which it is difficult to reconcile with a *careful* reading of what they actually said. But certainly these authors stand at the fount of a view of the welfare state which sees it as essentially a 'good thing', capable of forging a new and stable reconciliation between the seemingly competing claims of economic efficiency and social justice. Much of the rest of the literature on the welfare state is a more or less explicit engagement with these positions.

In Perspectives on the Left, we bring this more theoretical approach forward towards our own time. The view here is not straightforwardly social democratic. Indeed, Claus Offe is quite explicitly critical of a form of political compromise which he sees to be unsustainable in the medium term. The view that he expresses here suggests that capitalist welfare states are vulnerable to a series of deep-seated contradictions which make them politically quite unstable. By contrast, the selections from the Institute for Public Policy Research's *Justice Gap* represents an attempt to refashion social democratic impulses under the duress of changing (and more difficult) circumstances.

The views represented in Responses from the Right have been extraordinarily influential upon welfare debates over the past forty years. Friedrich von Hayek probably remains the most sophisticated representative of the view that welfare state institutions are essentially irreconcilable with a social order premised on the value of human freedom. In von Hayek's wake has come a vast array of critics who have condemned the welfare state, variously, as uneconomic, unproductive, inefficient, ineffective, despotic and inconsistent with freedom. Two of the most influential spokespersons for a tradition which has always been at its strongest in the Anglo-Saxon world (above all, in North America) are Charles Murray and Lawrence Mead. Murray has become strongly identified with the idea that welfare state institutions tend to produce a social 'underclass' wedded to criminality, while Mead is similarly associated with the idea that welfare generates new forms of poverty and dependency in which the appeal to rights swamps any corresponding sense of social obligations. The views of both authors are given characteristically robust expression in the articles chosen here.

Among the most influential interventions in re-shaping the entire debate about the politics of welfare over the past thirty years have been the contributions of feminist authors. Starting (at least in its contemporary form, since there are many precursors) with Elizabeth Wilson's 1977 book *Women and the Welfare State*, the intervening period has seen the growth of a literature which has challenged the very terms upon which all previous discussions of state and welfare had proceeded. Although a diverse literature, feminist writers have consistently sought to show how the nature of welfare states and, within them, of the interplay of public and private institutions and of formal and informal labour markets, voluntary and family care and so on, have generated welfare regimes which can be seen to be very clearly gendered in their structures and outcomes. At the same time, they argue that this aspect of gender within the welfare state is effectively concealed, often under the rubric of the universality of citizenship. Carole Pateman's piece on 'The Patriarchal Welfare State' is an outstanding example of this approach. Helga Maria Hernes's chapter (first published in 1987), in some ways by contrast, discusses the ways in which a sort of 'state feminism' embedded in welfare state institutions may actually work to empower women.

The First Welfare State?

Thomas Paine

[. . .]

When, in countries that are called civilized, we see age going to the work-house and youth to the gallows, something must be wrong in the system of government. It would seem, by the exterior appearance of such countries, that all was happiness; but there lies hidden from the eye of common observation, a mass of wretchedness that has scarcely any other chance than to expire in poverty or infamy. Its entrance into life is marked with the presage of its fate; and until this is remedied, it is in vain to punish.

Civil government does not consist in executions; but in making that provision for the instruction of youth, and the support of age, as to exclude, as much as possible, profligacy from the one, and despair from the other. Instead of this, the resources of a country are lavished upon kings, upon courts, upon hirelings, impostors and prostitutes; and even the poor themselves, with all their wants upon them, are compelled to support the fraud that oppresses them.

Why is it, that scarcely any are executed but the poor? The fact is a proof, among other things, of a wretchedness in their condition. Bred up without morals, and cast upon the world without a prospect, they are the exposed sacrifice of vice and legal barbarity. The millions that are superfluously wasted upon governments are more than sufficient to reform those evils, and to benefit the condition of every man in a nation, not included within the purlieus of a court.

[. . .]

In the present state of things, a labouring man, with a wife and two or three children, does not pay less than between seven and eight pounds a year in taxes. He is not sensible of this, because it is disguised to him in the articles which he buys, and he thinks only of their dearness; but as the taxes take from him, at least, a fourth part of his yearly earnings, he is consequently disabled from providing for a family, especially, if himself, or any of them, are afflicted with sickness.

The first step, therefore, of practical relief, would be to abolish the poor rates entirely, and in lieu thereof, to make a remission of taxes to the poor of double the amount of the present poor-rates, viz. 4 millions annually out of the surplus taxes. By this measure, the poor will be benefited 2 millions, and the housekeepers 2 millions.

[. . .]

I proceed to the mode of relief or distribution, which is,

To pay as a remission of taxes to every poor family, out of the surplus taxes, and in room of poor-rates, four pounds a year for every child under fourteen years of age; enjoining the parents of such children to send them to school, to learn reading, writing and common arithmetic; the ministers of every parish, of every denomination, to certify jointly to an office, for that purpose, that this duty is performed.

The amount of this expense will be,
For six hundred and thirty thousand children,
at four pounds *per ann.* each, — — — — — — — — £2,520,000

By adopting this method, not only the poverty of the parents will be relieved, but ignorance will be banished from the rising generation, and the number of poor will hereafter become less, because their abilities, by the aid of education, will be greater. Many a youth, with good natural genius, who is apprenticed to a mechanical trade, such as a carpenter, joiner, millwright, shipwright, blacksmith, &c. is prevented getting forward the whole of his life, from the want of a little common education when a boy.

I now proceed to the case of the aged.

I divide age into two classes. First, the approach of age beginning at fifty. Secondly, old age commencing at sixty.

At fifty, though the mental faculties of man are in full vigour, and his judgement better than at any preceding date, the bodily powers for laborious life are on the decline. He cannot bear the same quantity of fatigue as at an earlier period. He begins to earn less, and is less capable of enduring wind and weather; and in those more retired employments where much sight is required, he fails apace, and sees himself, like an old horse, beginning to be turned adrift.

At sixty his labour ought to be over, at least from direct necessity. It is painful to see old age working itself to death, in what are called civilized countries, for daily bread.

[. . .]

[I propose] To pay to every such person of the age of fifty years, and until he shall arrive at the age of sixty, the sum of six pounds *per ann.* out of the surplus taxes; and ten pounds *per ann.* during life after the age of sixty. The expense of which will be,

Seventy thousand persons at £6 *per ann.*	420,000
Seventy thousand ditto at £10 *per ann.*	700,000
	£1,120,000

This support, as already remarked, is not of the nature of a charity, but of a right. Every person in England, male and female, pays on an average in taxes, two pounds eight shillings and sixpence *per ann.* from the day of his (or her) birth; and, if the expense of collection be added, he pays two pounds eleven shillings and sixpence; consequently, at the end of fifty years he has paid one hundred and twenty-eight pounds fifteen shillings; and at sixty, one hundred and fifty-four pounds ten shillings. Converting, therefore, his (or her) individual tax into a tontine, the money he shall receive after fifty years is but little more than the legal interest of the net money he has paid; the rest is made up from those whose circumstances do not require them to draw such support, and the capital in both cases defrays the expenses of government. It is on this ground that I have extended the probable claims to one third of the number of aged persons in the nation. Is it then better that the lives of one hundred and forty thousand aged persons be rendered comfortable, or that a million a year of public money be expended on any one individual, and him often of the most worthless or insignificant character?

[. . .]

After all the above cases are provided for, there will still be a number of families who, though not properly of the class of poor, yet find it difficult to give education to their children; and such children, under such a case, would be in a worse condition than if their parents were actually poor. A nation under a well-regulated government should permit none to remain uninstructed. It is monarchical and aristocratical government only that requires ignorance for its support.

Suppose then four hundred thousand children to be in this condition, which is a greater number than ought to be supposed, after the provisions already made, the method will be,

To allow for each of those children ten shillings a year for the expense of schooling, for six years each, which will give them six months schooling each year and half a crown a year for paper and spelling books.

The expense of this will be annually   £250,000

There will then remain one hundred and ten thousand pounds.

Notwithstanding the great modes of relief which the best instituted and best principled government may devise, there will be a number of smaller cases, which it is good policy as well as beneficence in a nation to consider.

Were twenty shillings to be given immediately on the birth of a child, to every woman who should make the demand, and none will make it whose circumstances do not require it, it might relieve a great deal of instant distress.

There are about two hundred thousand births yearly in England, and if claimed, by one fourth,

The amount would be   £50,000

And twenty shillings to every new-married couple who should claim in like manner. This would not exceed the sum of £20,000.

Also twenty thousand pounds to be appropriated to defray the funeral expenses of persons, who, travelling for work, may die at a distance from their friends. By relieving parishes from this charge, the sick stranger will be better treated.

I shall finish this part of the subject with a plan adapted to the particular condition of a metropolis, such as London.

[. . .]

First, To erect two or more buildings, or take some already erected, capable of containing at least six thousand persons, and to have in each of these places as many kinds of employment as can be contrived, so that every person who shall come may find something which he or she can do.

Secondly, To receive all who shall come, without enquiring who or what they are. The only condition to be, that for so much, or so many hours work, each person shall receive so many meals of wholesome food, and a warm lodging, at least as good as a barrack. That a certain portion of what each person's work shall be worth shall be reserved, and given to him, or her, on their going away; and that each person shall stay as long, or as short time, or come as often as he choose, on these conditions.

If each person stayed three months, it would assist by rotation twenty-four thousand persons annually, though the real number, at all times, would be but six thousand. By establishing an asylum of this kind, persons to whom temporary distresses occur would have an opportunity to recruit themselves and be enabled to look out for better employment.

Allowing that their labour paid but one half the expense of supporting them, after reserving a portion of their earnings for themselves, the sum of forty thousand pounds additional would defray all other charges for even a greater number than six thousand.

The fund very properly convertible to this purpose, in addition to the twenty thousand pounds, remaining of the former fund, will be the produce of the tax upon coals, so iniquitously and wantonly applied to the support of the Duke of Richmond. It is horrid that any man, more especially at the price coals now are, should live on the distresses of a community; and any government permitting such an abuse deserves to be dismissed. This fund is said to be about twenty thousand pounds *per annum*.

I shall now conclude this plan with enumerating the several particulars, and then proceed to other matters.

The enumeration is as follows:

First, Abolition of two million poor-rates.

Secondly, Provision for two hundred and fifty-two thousand poor families.

Thirdly, Education for one million and thirty thousand children.

Fourthly, Comfortable provision for one hundred and forty thousand aged persons.

Fifthly, Donation of twenty shillings each for fifty thousand births.

Sixthly, Donation of twenty shillings each for twenty thousand marriages.

Seventhly, Allowance of twenty thousand pounds for the funeral expenses of persons travelling for work, and dying at a distance from their friends.

Eighthly, Employment, at all times, for the casual poor in the cities of London and Westminster.

By the operation of this plan, the poor laws, those instruments of civil torture, will be superseded, and the wasteful expense of litigation prevented. The hearts of the humane will not be shocked by ragged and hungry children, and persons of seventy and eighty years of age begging for bread. The dying poor will not be dragged from place to place to breathe their last, as a reprisal of parish upon parish. Widows will have a maintenance for their children, and not be carted away, on the death of their husbands, like culprits and criminals; and children will no longer be considered as increasing the distresses of their parents. The haunts of the wretched will be known, because it will be to their advantage; and the number of petty crimes, the offspring of distress and poverty, will be lessened. The poor, as well as the rich, will then be interested in the support of government, and the cause and apprehension of riots and tumults will cease. – Ye who sit in ease, and solace yourselves in plenty, and such there are in Turkey and Russia, as well as in England, and who say to yourselves, 'Are we not well off', have ye thought of these things? When ye do, ye will cease to speak and feel for yourselves alone.

[. . .]

Note

Thomas Paine's *Rights of Man* was first published in London by J. S. Jordan in 1791–2. The same publisher produced several new editions in quick succession. The extract reproduced here is from the Penguin Classics reprint of 1985 (with introduction by Eric Foner and notes by Henry Collins), pp. 218, 240–48.

'Classical'

The Welfare State in Historical Perspective

Asa Briggs

[. . .]

A welfare state is a state in which organized power is deliberately used (through politics and administration) in an effort to modify the play of market forces in at least three directions – first, by guaranteeing individuals and families a minimum income irrespective of the market value of their work or their property; second, by narrowing the extent of insecurity by enabling individuals and families to meet certain 'social contingencies' (for example, sickness, old age and unemployment) which lead otherwise to individual and family crises; and third, by ensuring that all citizens without distinction of status or class are offered the best standards available in relation to a certain agreed range of social services.

The first and second of these objects may be accomplished, in part at least, by what used to be called a 'social service state', a state in which communal resources are employed to abate poverty and to assist those in distress. The third objective, however, goes beyond the aims of a 'social service state'. It brings in the idea of the 'optimum' rather than the older idea of the 'minimum'. It is concerned not merely with abatement of class differences or the needs of scheduled groups but with equality of treatment and the aspirations of citizens as voters with equal shares of electoral power.

Merely to define the phrase welfare state in this way points to a number of historical considerations, which are the theme of this article. First, the conception of 'market forces' sets the problems of the welfare state (and of welfare) within the context of the age of modern political economy. In societies without market economies, the problem of welfare raises quite different issues. Within the context of the age of modern political economy an attempt has been made, and is still being made, to create and maintain a self-regulating system of markets, including markets in the fictitious commodities, land, money and labour. The multiple motives lying behind the attempt to control these markets require careful and penetrating analysis.

Second, the conception of 'social contingencies' is strongly influenced by the experience of industrialism. Sickness, old age and death entail hardships in any kind of society. Ancient systems of law and morality include precepts designed to diminish these hardships, precepts based, for example, on the obligations of sons to support their parents or on the claims of charity, *obsequium religionis*. Unemployment, however, at least in the form in which it is thought of as a social contingency, is a product of industrial societies, and it is unemployment more than any other social contingency which has determined the shape and timing of modern welfare legislation. Before the advent of mass unemployment, 'unemployability', the inability of individuals to secure their livelihood by work, was a key subject in the protracted debates on poor law policy. The existence of 'chronic unemployment', structural or cyclical, has been a powerful spur from the nineteenth century onwards leading organized labour groups to pass from concentration on sectional interests to the consideration of 'social rights' of workers as a class; to philanthropic businessmen wishing to improve the 'efficiency' and strengthen the 'social justice' of the business system; and to politicians and governments anxious to avoid what seemed to be dangerous political consequences of unemployment. The memories of chronic unemployment in the inter-war years and the discovery of what it was believed were new techniques of controlling it reinforced welfare state policies in many countries after the Second World War.

Third, the idea of using organized power (through politics and administration) to determine the pattern of welfare services requires careful historical dating. Why not rely for welfare on the family, the church, 'charity', 'self help', 'mutual aid' (guild, trade union, friendly society) or 'fringe benefits' (business itself)? Whole philosophies of welfare have been founded on each of these ideas or institutions: often the philosophies and the interests sustaining them have been inimical to the suggestion that the state itself should intervene. The possibility of using governmental power has been related in each country to the balance of economic and social forces; estimates of the proper functions and, true or false, of the available resources of the state; effective techniques of influence and control, resting on knowledge (including expert knowledge); and, not least, the prevalence (or absence) of the conviction that societies can be shaped by conscious policies designed to eliminate 'abuses' which in earlier generations had been accepted as 'inevitable' features of the human condition.

Not only does the weighting of each of these factors vary from period to period, but it also varies from place to place. It was Bentham, scarcely distinguished for his historical sense, who in distinguishing between *agenda* (tasks of government) and *sponte acta* (unplanned decisions of individuals) wrote that 'in England abundance of useful things are done by individuals which in other countries are done either by government or not at all . . . [while] in Russia, under Peter the Great, the list of *sponte acta* being a blank, that of *agenda* was proportionately abundant.'[1] This contrast was noted by many other writers later in the nineteenth century, just as an opposite contrast between Britain and the United States was often noted after 1945.

If the question of what constitutes welfare involves detailed examination of the nature and approach to 'social contingencies', the question of why the state rather than some other agency becomes the main instrument of welfare involves very detailed examination of a whole range of historical circumstances. The answer to the question is complicated, moreover, by differences of attitude in different countries, to the idea of 'the state' itself. Given these differences, a translation of basic terms into different languages raises difficulties which politicians and journalists may well have obscured. For example, is the term *Wohlfahrtsstaat* the right translation of welfare state? British and German approaches to 'the state' have been so different that they have absorbed the intellectual energy of generations of political scientists. In the nineteenth century there were somewhat similar difficulties (although on a smaller scale) surrounding the translation of the British term 'self help'. A French translator of Samuel Smiles's book of that title (1859) said that the term 'self help' was 'à peu près intraduisible'.

Fourth, the 'range of agreed social services' set out in the provisional definition of 'welfare state' is a shifting range. Policies, despite the finalism of much of the post-1945 criticism, are never fixed for all time. What at various times was considered to be a proper range shifts, as Dicey showed, and consequently must be examined historically. So too must changing areas of agreement and conflict. Public health was once a highly controversial issue in European societies: it still is in some other societies. The 'sanitary idea' was rightly regarded by the pioneers of public health as an idea which had large and far-reaching chains of consequences. It marked an assault on 'fate' which would be bound to lead to other assaults. Public health, in the administrative sphere of drains, sewers and basic 'environmental' services, has been taken outside the politics of conflict in Britain and other places, but personal health services remain controversial. There is controversy, very bitter indeed in the United States, not only about the range of services and who shall enjoy them but about the means of providing them. The choice of means influences all welfare state history. Welfare states can and do employ a remarkable variety of instruments, such as social insurance, direct provision in cash or in kind, subsidy, partnership with other agencies (including private business agencies) and action through local authorities. In health policy alone, although medical knowledge is the same in all countries of the West and the same illnesses are likely to be treated in much the same kind of way, there is a remarkable diversity of procedures and institutions even in countries which make extensive public provision for personal health services.

Fifth, there are important historical considerations to take into account in tracing the relationship between the three different directions of public intervention in the free (or partially free) market. The demand for 'minimum standards' can be related to a particular set of cumulative pressures. Long before the Webbs urged the need in 1909 for government action to secure 'an enforced minimum of civilized life', the case for particular minima had been powerfully advocated. Yet the idea of basing social policy as a whole on a public commitment to 'minimum' standards did not become practical politics in Britain until the so-called 'Beveridge revolution' of the Second World War. The third direction of 'welfare' policy, and the distinctive direction of the welfare state, can be understood only in terms of older logic and more recent history. The idea of separating welfare policy from 'subsistence' standards (the old minima, however measured) and relating it to 'acceptable' standards ('usual work income') provides an indication of the extent to which 'primary poverty' has been reduced in 'affluent societies'. It may be related, however, to older ideas of equality, some of which would lead direct not to state intervention in the market but to the elimination of the market altogether, at least as a force influencing human relationships. A consideration of the contemporary debate is more rewarding if it is grounded in history. . . .

German experience in the nineteenth century was in certain important respects different from that of Britain. If before 1900 factory legislation was more advanced in Britain than in any other European country, Germany had established a 'lead' in social security legislation which the British Liberal governments of 1906 to 1914 tried to wipe out. Bismarck's reforms of the 1880s – laws of 1882, 1884 and 1889 introducing compulsory insurance against sickness, accidents, old age and invalidity – attracted immense interest in other European countries. Just as British factory legislation was copied overseas, so German social insurance stimulated foreign imitation. Denmark, for instance, copied all three German pension schemes between 1891 and 1898, and Belgium between 1894 and 1903. Switzerland by a constitutional amendment in 1890 empowered the federal government to organize a system of national insurance. In Britain itself a friendly observer noted in 1890 that Bismarck had 'discovered where the roots of social evil lie. He has declared in words that burn that it is the duty of the state to give heed, above all, to the welfare of its weaker members'.[2]

More recently Bismarck's social policy has been described by more than one writer as the creation of a welfare state.[3] The term is very misleading.

Bismarck's legislation rested on a basic conservatism which Oastler himself would have appreciated and was sustained by a bureaucracy which had no counterpart in Britain except perhaps in Chadwick's imagination. The Prussian idea and history of the state and the British idea and history of the state diverged long before the 1880s, and it is not fanciful to attribute some of the divergences to the presence or absence a century before of 'cameralism', the idea of the systematic application to government of administrative routines.

Equally important, the history of political economy in the two countries diverged just as markedly. The development of a school of historical economics provided a powerful academic reinforcement in Germany for *Sozialpolitik*. The refusal of historical economists to 'isolate' economic phenomena, including 'economic man', their distrust of 'laws of political economy' covering all ages and all societies, their critique of the motives and institutions of contemporary capitalism and their underlying belief in a 'social order' distinguished them sharply from classical political economists in Britain. Their influence was considerable enough for Schmoller (1838–1917), the most important figure in the history of the school, to argue forcefully that no Smithian was fit to occupy an academic chair in Germany.[4]

Even among the 'precursors' of the historical school and among economists who stayed aloof from Schmoller and his circle, there was a powerful tradition linking social reform with conservative views of society.[5] J. K. Rodbertus (1805–75) was a conservative monarchist who combined dislike of the 'class struggle' and belief in state socialism. Adolf Wagner (1835–1917), who stayed aloof from Schmoller and admired Ricardo as the outstanding economic 'theorist', acknowledged his debt to Rodbertus when he gave a warm welcome to Bismarck's legislation.

According to Wagner Germany had entered a 'new social period', characterized by new economic ideas, new political views and new social programmes. National economy (*Volkswirtschaft*) had to be converted into state economy (*Staatswirtschaft*): the foundation of the new economy would have to be welfare. The idea of regarding 'labour power' as a commodity and wages as its price was 'inhuman' as well as 'unchristian'. Wagner proposed a number of practical measures, some of which went further than those introduced by Bismarck. Schmoller, too, advocated policies aiming at 'the re-establishment of a friendly relation between social classes, the removal or modification of injustice, a nearer approach to the principles of distributive justice, with the introduction of a social legislation which promotes progress and guarantees the moral and material elevation of the lower and middle classes.'[6]

Bismarck, for whom the idea of insurance had a particular fascination both in his domestic and foreign policies, did not envisage a social policy which would go anywhere near as far as some of the 'socialists of the chair' would have wished. He objected, for example, to the limitation by law of the hours of women and children in factories and he was at least as stubborn as any mill-owner of the Manchester School when 'theorists' talked of state officials interfering with private concerns in agriculture or industry. He also disliked extensions of direct taxation. He wanted the state, however, to be actively involved in the financing and administering of the insurance schemes which he proposed and he defended the introduction of these schemes – against both right-wing and left-wing opposition – in terms of 'the positive advancement of the welfare of the working classes'. 'The state', it was laid down in the preamble to the first and unsuccessful bill of 1881, 'is not merely a necessary but a beneficent institution.' Bismarck disagreed with Theodor Lohmann, who drafted his first social insurance legislation, about whether the state should contribute directly to the costs of insurance. Bismarck got his way that it should, but the political parties objected and his first attempts at legislation foundered. It was a measure of his recognition of political realities that the idea of state contributions was dropped in 1884 when his accident insurance bill was introduced. The law of 1889, providing for disability and old age pensions, did entail a flat-rate contribution from the imperial treasury of fifty marks for each person receiving a pension, but this was a small element in the total cost and fell far short of the amount Bismarck had originally envisaged.

Many of Bismarck's critics accused him, not without justification, of seeking through his legislation to make German workers 'depend' upon the state. The same charges have been made against the initiators of all welfare (and earlier, of poor law) policy often without justification, yet it was Bismarck himself who drew a revealing distinction between the degrees of obedience (or subservience) of private servants and servants at court. The latter would 'put up with much more' than the former because they had pensions to look forward to. Welfare soothed the spirit, or perhaps tamed it. Bismarck's deliberate invocation of 'subservience' is at the opposite end of the scale from the socialist invocation of 'equality' as the goal of the welfare state. It is brutally simple, too, when compared with sophisticated liberal attempts to define the conditions in which liberty and equality may be made to complement each other.[7] The invocation was, of course, bound up with conscious political calculation. Bismarck was anxious to make German social democracy less attractive to workingmen. He feared 'class war' and wanted to postpone it as long as possible. His talks with Lassalle in 1863 had ranged over questions of this kind,[8] and in 1884 he argued explicitly that if the state would only 'show a little more Christian solicitude for the workingman', then the social democrats would 'sound their siren song in vain'. 'The thronging to them will cease as soon as workingmen see that the government and legislative bodies are earnestly concerned for their welfare.'[9] It has been suggested that Bismarck was influenced by Napoleon III's successful handling of social policy as an instrument of politics. He certainly spent time seeking an 'alternative to socialism' and it was this aspect of his policy which gave what he did contemporary controversial significance throughout Europe.

His policy also provided a definite alternative to liberalism. During the last years of his life when he was prepared to contemplate insurance against unemployment and when he talked of the 'right to work' as enthusiastically as any Chartist, he was reflecting that sharp reaction against economic liberalism which could be discerned, in different forms, in almost every country in Europe. Disraeli's social policy in his ministry of 1874–80 had somewhat similar features. It also had the added interest of appearing to realize hopes first formulated by Disraeli in the age of Oastler and the Chartists. In 1874 also a royalist and clerical majority in the French National Assembly carried a factory act, limiting hours of work of children below the age of twelve, which went further than a law of 1848 on the same subject. A later and more comprehensive act of 1892 was the work of Conservative Republicans. The nineteenth century closed with a British Moneylenders Act which, Professor Clapham has argued, in effect revived the medieval law of usury, the last remnants of which had been swept away, it was thought for ever, in 1854.[10]

Medieval attitudes to welfare were echoed most strongly in Christian apologetics. Papal encyclicals, notably *Rerum Novarum* (1891), were not only manifestos in crusades against liberalism or socialism but were also important documents in the evolution of *Sozialpolitik*. De Mun, Von Ketteler and Von Vogelsang were writers who advocated particular or general welfare policies: so did Heinrich Pesch, who has been singled out for special treatment by Schumpeter. Among Protestants also there was renewed call for a 'social gospel'. It is not without interest that Lohmann, who had advised Bismarck and went on to advise William II in the formulation of the far-reaching Labour Code of 1891, was a deeply religious man, the son of a Westphalian Lutheran pastor. Canon W. L. Blackley (1830–1902), the pioneer of old-age pensions schemes not only in Britain but in other parts of the world and the founder of the National Providence League, was an honorary canon of Winchester Cathedral. On the Liberal side – and there was a close association in Britain between religious nonconformity and political liberalism – Seebohm Rowntree (1871–1954), one of the first systematic investigators of the facts of poverty, was a Quaker. The whole attack on the limitations of the poor law was guided, though not exclusively, by men of strong religious principles.

The complexity of the nineteenth-century background contrasts at first sight with the simplicity of the twentieth-century story. For a tangle of tendencies we have a 'trend', a trend culminating in greater 'order' and simplification. In fact, however, the twentieth-century story has its own complexities, which are now in the process of being unravelled. Professor Titmuss has shown, for instance, that Lloyd George's national health insurance legislation of 1911, a landmark in 'trend' legislation, was the culmination of a long and confused period in which doctors had been engaged in a 'Hobbesian struggle for independence from the power and authority exercised over their lives, their work and their professional values by voluntary associations and private enterprise'. He has maintained that the legislation of 1911 can only be understood if it is related, as so much else in the twentieth century must be related, to the history of hidden pressures from established interests and a sectional demand for an 'enlargement of professional freedom'.[11] Many of the complexities of twentieth-century history certainly lie buried in the records of the network of private concerns and of professional groups which came into existence in the nineteenth century. There can be no adequate historical explanation which concerns itself in large terms with the state alone. Just as the administration of welfare is complicated in practice and can be understood only in detail, so the outline of welfare state legislation only becomes fully intelligible when it ceases to be an outline, and when it looks beyond parliamentary legislation to such crucial twentieth-century relationships as those between governments and pressure groups and 'experts' and the 'public'.

Yet there are five factors in twentieth-century welfare history (other than warfare, one of the most powerful of factors) which are beyond dispute and dominant enough to need little detailed research. They are, first, the basic transformation in the attitude towards poverty, which made the nineteenth-century poor law no longer practicable in democratic societies; second, the detailed investigation of the 'social contingencies' which directed attention to the need for particular social policies; third, the close association between unemployment and welfare policy; fourth, the development within market capitalism itself of welfare philosophies and practices; and fifth, the influence of working-class pressures on the content and tone of welfare legislation.

The first and second of these five factors can scarcely be studied in isolation. The basis of the nineteenth-century British Poor Law of 1834 was economic logic. That logic was strained when empirical sociologists, like Charles Booth (1840–1916) and Rowntree, showed that a large number of poor people were poor through no fault of their own but because of tendencies within the market system. They pitted statistics against logic by attempting to count how many people were living in poverty and by surveying the various forms that the poverty assumed.[12] Prior to Booth's 'grand inquest', Beatrice Webb wrote, 'neither the individualist nor the socialist could state with any approach to accuracy what exactly was the condition of the people of England'.[13] Once the results of the 'inquest' had been published 'the net effect was to give an entirely fresh impetus to the general adoption of the policy of securing to every individual, as the very basis of his life and work, a prescribed natural minimum of the requisites for efficient parenthood and citizenship.'

Booth's thinking about economics was far less radical than his thinking about welfare, but Rowntree, who drew a neat distinction between 'primary' and 'secondary' poverty, the former being beyond the control of the wage-earner, went on to advocate specific welfare policies, ranging from old-age pensions to family allowances, public-provided housing to supervised welfare conditions in factories. The policies which he urged at various stages of his long life were, indeed, the main constituent policies of the welfare state.[14] Like the welfare state, however, Rowntree stopped short of socialism. He separated questions of welfare from questions of economic power, and remained throughout his life a 'new Liberal'. The main tenet of his liberalism was that the community could not afford the 'waste', individual and social, which was implied in an industrial society divided 'naturally' into 'rich' and 'very poor'. Poverty was as much of a social problem as 'pauperism'. The roots of poverty were to be found not in individual irresponsibility or incapacity but in social maladjustment. Poverty, in short, was not the fault of the poor: it was the fault of society. Quite apart from 'socialist pressure', society had to do something about poverty once it was given facts about its extent, its incidence (Rowntree drew attention to the cycle of poverty in families), its ramifications and its consequences. All facts were grist to the mill. They included facts not only about wages but about nutrition: subsistence levels could only be measured when nutritional criteria were taken into account.

Sharp turns of thought about poverty were by no means confined to people in Britain. There were signs of fundamental rethinking, allied [. . .] to 'feeling',[15] both in Europe and the United States at the end of the nine-teenth and the beginning of the twentieth century.[16] The survey method, which Booth and Rowntree depended upon, was capable of general applicability.[17] The limitations of systematic 'charity' were noted at least as generally as the limitations of unsystematic charity had been at the begin-ning of the industrial age. It is no coincidence that in Britain and Sweden, two countries with distinct welfare histories, there was keen debate about the Poor Law at almost exactly the same time. In Sweden the Poor Relief Order of 1871, with its checks on poor relief, was criticized by the Swedish Poor Relief Association which was formed at the first General Swedish Poor Law Congress in 1906. A year later the government appointed a committee to draw up proposals for fresh legislation govern-ing poor relief and the treatment of vagrants. In Britain the Royal Commission on the Poor Laws, which was appointed in 1905 and reported in 1909, covered almost all topics in social policy. The issues were clearly stated and both the social contingencies and the necessary policies of social control were carefully examined. Although new direct legislation was slow to come in both countries, there was much indirect legislation and in both countries there were demands for what Beatrice Webb called 'an enforced minimum of civilized life'.[18]

The main threat to that minimum in the later twentieth century came from 'mass involuntary unemployment'. This, of course, was a world phenomenon which strained poor law and social service systems in most countries and presented a threat – or a challenge – to politicians and administrators. In Britain, which was the first country to introduce compulsory unemployment insurance (1911; greatly extended in 1920), the system of relief broke down under the stresses of the 1930s. Insurance benefits, linked to contributions, were stringently restricted, and while tussles about the 'means test' were leading to extreme differences of outlook between socialists and their opponents, an Unemployment Assistance Board, founded in 1934, was providing a second-line income maintenance service, centrally administered. In Europe there was an extension of unemployment aid schemes, whether by insurance (the Swedes, for example, introduced state-subsidized unemployment insurance in 1934), 'doles' or in certain cases 'positive' state-run schemes of 'public works'. In the United States and Canada, where there had been entrenched resistance to government intervention in welfare provision, new legislation was passed,[19] while in New Zealand, which had long lost its reputation as a pioneer of welfare, there was a remarkable bout of state intervention after the return of a Labour government to power in 1935. The Social Security Act of 1938 contained a list of health services and pensions benefits which, while resting on previous legislation, were everywhere hailed as a bold and daring experiment. The Minister of Finance anticipated later welfare legislators in other countries by arguing unequivocally that 'to suggest the inevitability of slumps and booms, associated as they are with affluence for a limited number during a period, and followed by unemployment, destitution, hardship and privation for the masses, is to deny all conscious progressive purpose'.[20] According to the International Labor Office, the 1938 New Zealand Act 'has, more than any other law, determined the practical meaning of social security, and so has deeply influenced the course of legislation in other countries'.[21]

Twentieth-century social security legislation raises many interesting general issues – the relevance of the insurance principle, for example, the relationship between 'negative' social policy and 'positive' economic policy, and, underlying all else, the nature and extent of the responsibilities of the state. Insurance principles, actuarially unsound though they may be and inadequate though they have proved as instruments of finance at moments of crisis, have been historically significant. They removed the stigma of pauperism from a social service, reconciled 'voluntary' and 'compulsory' approaches to provision, and facilitated 'public approval' of state expenditures which otherwise would have been challenged. They thus served as a link between old ways of thinking ('self help' and 'mutual help') and new. 'Positive' economic policy was in the first instance, as in Roosevelt's America, the child of improvisation: its systematic justification had to await revolutions in political economy (Keynes and after) which accompanied shifts in social power. The difference in tone and content between two books by William Beveridge – his *Unemployment* (1909) and his *Full Employment in a Free Society* (1944) – is one of the best indications of the change in the world of ideas between the early and middle periods of the twentieth century. 'Beveridgism', an important British phenomenon during the Second World War, had sufficient popular appeal to show that the world of ideas and the world of practical politics were not very far apart. For the intellectuals and for the public the magnification of governmental power – and the enormous increase in government expenditure financed from taxation – were taken for granted.

The fourth and fifth factors are also related to each other. In all advanced industrial countries in the twentieth century there has been a movement towards welfare in industry – 'industrial betterment' it was originally called – which has been accompanied by the emergence of philosophies of 'human relations', 'welfare management' and industrial and labour psychology.[22] The movement has to be explained in terms of both economics and politics. A 'managerial revolution', limited though it may have been in its economic effects, has accelerated the tendencies making for 'welfare capitalism'. The need to find acceptable incentives for workers, to avoid labour disputes and to secure continuous production, to raise output in phases of technical change and (more recently) to hold labour 'permissively' in a period of full employment has often driven where 'human relations' philosophies have failed to inspire. Welfare, a word which was often resented by workers, when it was applied within the structure of the firm, was, indeed, used in a business context before it began to be applied to a new kind of state. Within state schemes of welfare employers have made, and are expected to make, sizeable contributions. In France and Italy, in particular, obligatory social charges as a percentage of assessable wages constituted the main source of welfare expenditure.[23] In the United States business rather than the state was, and is, expected directly to provide a network of welfare services. As in all such situations, the provision of welfare varies immensely from one firm (giant businesses are at one end of the scale) to another.

> In contrast to these countries, such as Great Britain, which appear to regard government (for reasons which have been stated above) merely as the most effective of several possible institutions for the administration of income security programs or the provision of services, [. . .] a society like the United

States that distrusts its government is likely to seek to organize its social security services in such a way as to keep government activity to a minimum.[24]

United States experience, in contrast to the experience described in other countries, shows that this likelihood has been converted into fact.

It is not accidental that the labour movement in the United States has showed little interest in socialism and that its leaders have chosen of their own volition to bargain for 'fringe benefits' at the level of the plant. In most European countries, particularly in Britain and in Scandinavia, there has been a tendency for working-class pressures to lead to greater state intervention. In Britain nineteenth-century patterns of 'mutual depend-ence' through 'voluntary action', which impressed so many observers from Tocqueville onwards, have become less dominant, except in the field of industrial relations where they have very tenaciously survived.[25]

As we have seen, the demand for state action has been related to the rights of citizenship, to equality as well as to security. During the critical period between the two World Wars, when economic and social condi-tions were very difficult, welfare measures were demanded and provided 'piecemeal' with varying conditions of regulation and administration, 'a frightening complexity of eligibility and benefit according to individual circumstances, local boundaries, degrees of need and so forth'.[26] The Second World War, which sharpened the sense of 'democracy', led to demands both for 'tidying up' and for 'comprehensiveness'. It encouraged the move from 'minima' to 'optima', at least in relation to certain specified services, and it made all residual paternalisms seem utterly inadequate and increasingly archaic. It was in the light of changes in working-class life within a more 'equal community' that postwar writers noted the extent to which the social services of the earlier part of the century had been shaped by assumptions about the nature of man, 'founded on outer rather than on inner observation', on the 'norms of behavior expected by one class from another'.[27] This period of criticism has already ended. The assumptions which shaped the welfare state have themselves been criti-cized,[28] and radical political slogans have concentrated more and more on differences of income between 'mature' and 'underdeveloped' countries rather than on differences within 'mature' countries themselves.

It may well be that in a world setting the five twentieth-century factors discussed in this article will be considered less important than other factors – the total size of the national income in different countries, for example, and the share of that income necessary for industrial (as, or when, distinct from social) investment, or even, on a different plane, the nature of family structure. Is not the making of the industrial welfare state in part at least the concomitant of the decline of the large, extended 'welfare family'? How far has the pressure of women (or just the presence of women voters) in industrial societies encouraged the formulation of welfare objectives? The historian does well to leave such large questions to be answered rather than to suggest that all or even the most important part of the truth is already known.

Notes

Abridged from *European Journal of Sociology*, 2, 1961, by permission of Archives Européennes de Sociologie.

1   J. Bentham, *Works*, ed. J. Bowring, 1843, vol. III, p. 35. Cf. J. M. Keynes's view of the 'agenda' of the state in *The End of Laissez Faire* (1926).
2   W. H. Dawson, *Bismarck and State Socialism* (1890), p. ix.
3   S. B. Fay, 'Bismarck's Welfare State', *Current History*, vol. XVIII (1950).
4   J. A. Schumpeter, *History of Economic Analysis* (1954), p. 765.
5   The pre-history of this approach leads back to Sismondi who has important links with Mill and the English utilitarians. He is a seminal figure in the critique of industrialism and the demand for welfare legislation.
6   A. Wagner, *Rede über die soziale Frage* (1872), pp. 8–9. G. von Schmoller, *Über einige Grundfragen des Rechts und der Volkswirtschaft* (1875), p. 92.
7   For the background of these attempts, see M. Ginsberg, 'The Growth of Social Responsibility', in M. Ginsberg, ed., *Law and Opinion in England in the Twentieth Century* (1959), pp. 3–26.
8   See G. Mayer, *Bismarck und Lassalle* (1927).
9   Dawson, op. cit., p. 35. This remark was made in 1884. Five years earlier the emperor, referring to the anti-socialist law of 1878, had said, 'a remedy cannot alone be sought in the repression of socialistic excesses; there must be simultaneously the positive advancement of the welfare of the working classes' (quoted ibid., p. 110).
10   J. H. Clapham, *An Economic History of Modern Britain*, vol. III (1938), p. 445.
11   R. M. Titmuss, 'Health', in Ginsberg, op. cit., p. 308. Cf. p. 313: 'The fundamental issue of 1911 was not [. . .] between individualism and collectivism, between contract and status; but between different forms of collectivism, different degrees of freedom; open or concealed power.'
12   C. Booth, *Life and Labour of the People in London*, 17 vols (1892–1903); B. S. Rowntree, *Poverty: A Study of Town Life* (1901).
13   B. Webb, *My Apprenticeship* (1926), p. 239.
14   For Booth, see T. S. and M. B. Simey, *Charles Booth, Social Scientist* (1960); for Rowntree, see A. Briggs, *Seebohm Rowntree* (1961). See also B. S. Rowntree and G. R. Lavers, *Poverty and the Welfare State* (1951).
15   'In intensity of feeling', Booth wrote, 'and not in statistics, lies the power to move the world. But by statistics must this power be guided if it would move the world aright.' *Life and Labour, Final Volume, Notes on Social Influences and Conclusion* (1903), p. 178.
16   See *inter alia* C. L. Mowat, *The Charity Organisation Society*; K. De Schweinitz, *England's Road to Social Security* (1943); C. W. Pitkin, *Social Politics and Modern Democracies*, 2 vols (1931), vol. II being concerned with France; R. H. Bremner, *From the Depths: The Discovery of Poverty in the United States* (1956).
17   See M. Abrams, *Social Surveys and Social Action* (1951); P. V. Young, *Scientific Social Surveys and Research* (1950); D. C. Caradog Jones, *Social Surveys* (1955).

18 The British controversy is well described in U. Cormack, 'The Welfare State', *Loch Memorial Lecture* (1953). For Sweden, see The Royal Social Board, *Social Work and Legislation in Sweden* (1938).
19 J. C. Brown, *Public Relief 1929–39* (1940); E. A. Williams, *Federal Aid for Relief* (1939); P. H. Douglas, *Social Security in the United States* (1939 edn).
20 Quoted in W. K. Hancock, *Survey of British Commonwealth Affairs*, vol. II (1940), p. 275.
21 International Labor Office, *Social Security in New Zealand* (1949), p. 111.
22 See A. Briggs, 'The Social Background', in H. Clegg and A. Flanders, eds, *Industrial Relations in Great Britain* (1955); L. Urwick and E. F. L. Brech, *The Human Factor in Management 1795–1943* (1944); E. D. Proud, *Welfare Work, Employers' Experiments for Improving Working Conditions in Factories* (1916); E. T. Kelly, ed., *Welfare Work in Industry* (1925); PEP, 'The Human Factor in Industry', *Planning* (March 1948).
23 PEP, 'Free Trade and Security', *Planning* (July 1957); 'A Comparative Analysis of the Cost of Social Security', in *International Labour Review* (1953).
24 E. M. Burns, *Social Security and Public Policy* (1956), p. 274.
25 For the nature of the nineteenth-century pattern, see J. M. Baernreither, *English Associations of Working Men* (1893). For industrial relations, see Clegg and Flanders, op. cit.
26 R. M. Titmuss, *Essays on the Welfare State* (1958), pp. 21–2.
27 Ibid., p. 19.
28 See A. Peacock, 'The Welfare Society', *Unservile State Papers* (1960); R. M. Titmuss, 'The Irresponsible Society', *Fabian Tracts* (1960); J. Saville, 'The Welfare State', *The New Reasoner*, no. 3 (1957).

Citizenship and Social Class
T. H. Marshall

[. . .]

I propose to divide citizenship into three parts. [. . .] I shall call these three parts, or elements, civil, political and social. The civil element is composed of the rights necessary for individual freedom – liberty of the person, freedom of speech, thought and faith, the right to own property and to conclude valid contracts, and the right to justice. The last is of a different order from the others, because it is the right to defend and assert all one's rights on terms of equality with others and by due process of law. This shows us that the institutions most directly associated with civil rights are the courts of justice. By the political element I mean the right to participate in the exercise of political power, as a member of a body invested with political authority or as an elector of the members of such a body. The corresponding institutions are parliament and councils of local government. By the social element I mean the whole range, from the right to a modicum of economic welfare and security to the right to share to the full in the social heritage and to live the life of a civilized being according to the standards prevailing in the society. The institutions most closely connected with it are the educational system and the social services. [. . .]

By 1832 when political rights made their first infantile attempt to walk, civil rights had come to man's estate and bore, in most essentials, the appearance that they have today.[1] 'The specific work of the earlier Hanoverian epoch', writes Trevelyan, 'was the establishment of the rule of law; and that law, with all its grave faults, was at least a law of freedom. On that solid foundation all our subsequent reforms were built.' This eighteenth-century achievement, interrupted by the French Revolution and completed after it, was in large measure the work of the courts, both in their daily practice and also in a series of famous cases in some of which they were fighting against parliament in defence of individual liberty. The most celebrated actor in this drama was, I suppose, John Wilkes, and, although we may deplore the absence in him of those noble and saintly qualities which we should like to find in our national heroes, we cannot complain if the cause of liberty is sometimes championed by a libertine.

In the economic field the basic civil right is the right to work, that is to say the right to follow the occupation of one's choice in the place of one's choice, subject only to legitimate demands for preliminary technical training. This right had been denied by both statute and custom; on the one hand by the Elizabethan Statute of Artificers, which confined certain occupations to certain social classes, and on the other by local regulations reserving employment in a town to its own members and by the use of apprenticeship as an instrument of exclusion rather than of recruitment. The recognition of the right involved the formal acceptance of a fundamental change of attitude. The old assumption that local and group monopolies were in the public interest, because 'trade and traffic cannot be maintained or increased without order and government', was replaced by the new assumption that such restrictions were an offence against the liberty of the subject and a menace to the prosperity of the nation. [. . .]

By the beginning of the nineteenth century this principle of individual economic freedom was accepted as axiomatic. You are probably familiar with the passage quoted by the Webbs from the report of the Select Committee of 1811, which states that:

> no interference of the legislature with the freedom of trade, or with the perfect liberty of every individual to dispose of his time and of his labour in the way and on the terms which he may judge most conducive to his own interest, can take place without violating general principles of the first importance to the prosperity and happiness of the community.[2] [. . .]

The story of civil rights in their formative period is one of the gradual addition of new rights to a status that already existed and was held to appertain to all adult members of the community – or perhaps one should say to all male members, since the status of women, or at least of married women, was in some important respects peculiar. This democratic, or universal, character of the status arose naturally from the fact that it was essentially the status of freedom, and in seventeenth-century England all men were free. Servile status, or villeinage by blood, had lingered on as a patent anachronism in the days of Elizabeth, but vanished soon afterwards. This change from servile to free labour has been described by Professor Tawney as 'a high landmark in the development both of economic and political society', and as 'the final triumph of the common law' in regions from which it had been excluded for four centuries. Henceforth the English peasant 'is a member of a society in which there is, nominally at least, one law for all men'.[3] The liberty which his predecessors had won by fleeing into the free towns had become his by right. In the towns the terms 'freedom' and 'citizenship' were interchangeable. When freedom became universal, citizenship grew from a local into a national institution.

The story of political rights is different both in time and in character. The formative period began, as I have said, in the early nineteenth century, when the civil rights attached to the status of freedom had already acquired sufficient substance to justify us in speaking of a general status of citizenship. And, when it began, it consisted, not in the creation of new rights to enrich a status already enjoyed by all, but in the granting of old rights to new sections of the population. [. . .]

It is clear that, if we maintain that in the nineteenth century citizenship in the form of civil rights was universal, the political franchise was not one of the rights of citizenship. It was the privilege of a limited economic class, whose limits were extended by each successive Reform Act. [. . .]

It was, as we shall see, appropriate that nineteenth-century capitalist society should treat political rights as a secondary product of civil rights. It was equally appropriate that the twentieth century should abandon this position and attach political rights directly and independently to citizenship as such. This vital change of principle was put into effect when the Act of 1918, by adopting manhood suffrage, shifted the basis of political rights from economic substance to personal status. I say 'manhood' deliberately in order to emphasize the great significance of this reform quite apart from the second, and no less important, reform introduced at the same time – namely the enfranchisement of women. [. . .]

The original source of social rights was membership of local communities and functional associations. This source was supplemented and progressively replaced by a Poor Law and a system of wage regulation which were nationally conceived and locally administered. [. . .]

As the pattern of the old order dissolved under the blows of a competitive economy, and the plan disintegrated, the Poor Law was left high and dry as an isolated survival from which the idea of social rights was gradually drained away. But at the very end of the eighteenth century there occurred a final struggle between the old and the new, between the planned (or patterned) society and the competitive economy. And in this battle citizenship was divided against itself; social rights sided with the old and civil with the new. [. . .]

In this brief episode of our history we see the Poor Law as the aggressive champion of the social rights of citizenship. In the succeeding phase we find the attacker driven back far behind his original position. By the Act of 1834 the Poor Law renounced all claim to trespass on the territory of the wages system, or to interfere with the forces of the free market. It offered relief only to those who, through age or sickness, were incapable of continuing the battle, and to those other weaklings who gave up the struggle, admitted defeat, and cried for mercy. The tentative move towards the concept of social security was reversed. But more than that, the minimal social rights that remained were detached from the status of citizenship. The Poor Law treated the claims of the poor, not as an integral part of the rights of the citizen, but as an alternative to them – as claims which could be met only if the claimants ceased to be citizens in any true sense of the word. For paupers forfeited in practice the civil right of personal liberty, by internment in the workhouse, and they forfeited by law any political rights they might possess. This disability of defranchisement remained in being until 1918, and the significance of its final removal has, perhaps, not been fully appreciated. The stigma which clung to poor relief expressed the deep feelings of a people who understood that those who accepted relief must cross the road that separated the community of citizens from the outcast company of the destitute.

The Poor Law is not an isolated example of this divorce of social rights from the status of citizenship. The early Factory Acts show the same tendency. Although in fact they led to an improvement of working conditions and a reduction of working hours to the benefit of all employed in the industries to which they applied, they meticulously refrained from giving this protection directly to the adult male – the citizen *par excellence*. And they did so out of respect for his status as a citizen, on the grounds that enforced protective measures curtailed the civil right to conclude a free contract of employment. Protection was confined to women and children, and champions of women's rights were quick to detect the implied insult. Women were protected because they were not citizens. If they wished to enjoy full and responsible citizenship, they must forgo protection. By the end of the nineteenth century such arguments had become obsolete, and the factory code had become one of the pillars in the edifice of social rights. [. . .]

By the end of the nineteenth century elementary education was not only free, it was compulsory. This signal departure from *laissez-faire* could, of course, be justified on the grounds that free choice is a right only for mature minds, that children are naturally subject to discipline, and that parents cannot be trusted to do what is in the best interests of their children. But the principle goes deeper than that. We have here a personal right combined with a public duty to exercise the right. Is the public duty imposed merely for the benefit of the individual – because children cannot fully appreciate their own interests and parents may be unfit to enlighten them? I hardly think that this can be an adequate explanation. It was increasingly recognized, as the nineteenth century wore on, that political democracy needed an educated electorate, and that scientific manufacture needed educated workers and technicians. The duty to improve and civilize oneself is therefore a social duty, and not merely a personal one, because the social health of a society depends upon the civilization of its members. And a community that enforces this duty has begun to realize that its culture is an organic unity and its civilization a national heritage. It follows that the growth of public elementary education during the nineteenth century was the first decisive step on the road to the re-establishment of the social rights of citizenship in the twentieth. [. . .]

Citizenship is a status bestowed on those who are full members of a community. All who possess the status are equal with respect to the rights and duties with which the status is endowed. There is no universal principle that determines what those rights and duties shall be, but societies in which citizenship is a developing institution create an image of an ideal citizenship against which achievement can be measured and towards which aspiration can be directed. The urge forward along the path thus plotted is an urge towards a fuller measure of equality, an enrichment of the stuff of which the status is made and an increase in the number of those on whom the status is bestowed. Social class, on the other hand, is a system of inequality. And it too, like citizenship, can be based on a set of ideals, beliefs and values. It is therefore reasonable to expect that the impact of citizenship on social class should take the form of a conflict between opposing principles. If I am right in my contention that citizenship has been a developing institution in England at least since the latter part of the seventeenth century, then it is clear that its growth coincides with the rise of capitalism, which is a system, not of equality, but of inequality. Here is something that needs explaining. How is it that these two opposing principles could grow and flourish side by side in the same soil? What made it possible for them to be reconciled with one another and to become, for a time at least, allies instead of antagonists? The question is a pertinent one, for it is clear that, in the twentieth century, citizenship and the capitalist class system have been at war. [. . .]

It is true that class still functions. Social inequality is regarded as necessary and purposeful. It provides the incentive to effort and designs the distribution of power. But there is no overall pattern of inequality, in which an appropriate value is attached, *a priori*, to each social level. Inequality therefore, though necessary, may become excessive. As Patrick Colquhoun said, in a much-quoted passage: 'Without a large proportion of poverty there could be no riches, since riches are the offspring of labour, while labour can result only from a state of poverty . . . Poverty therefore is a most necessary and indispensable ingredient in society, without which nations and communities could not exist in a state of civilization.'[4] [. . .]

The more you look on wealth as conclusive proof of merit, the more you incline to regard poverty as evidence of failure – but the penalty for failure may seem to be greater than the offence warrants. In such circumstances it is natural that the more unpleasant features of inequality should be treated, rather irresponsibly, as a nuisance, like the black smoke that used to pour unchecked from our factory chimneys. And so in time, as the social conscience stirs to life, class-abatement, like smoke-abatement, becomes a desirable aim to be pursued as far as is compatible with the continued efficiency of the social machine.

But class-abatement in this form was not an attack on the class system. On the contrary it aimed, often quite consciously, at making the class system less vulnerable to attack by alleviating its less defensible consequences. It raised the floor-level in the basement of the social edifice, and perhaps made it rather more hygienic than it was before. But it remained a basement, and the upper storeys of the building were unaffected. [. . .]

There developed, in the latter part of the nineteenth century, a growing interest in equality as a principle of social justice and an appreciation of the fact that the formal recognition of an equal capacity for rights was not enough. In theory even the complete removal of all the barriers that separated civil rights from their remedies would not have interfered with the principles or the class structure of the capitalist system. It would, in fact, have created a situation which many supporters of the competitive market economy falsely assumed to be already in existence. But in practice the attitude of mind which inspired the efforts to remove these barriers grew out of a conception of equality which overstepped these narrow limits, the conception of equal social worth, not merely of equal natural rights. Thus although citizenship, even by the end of the nineteenth century, had done little to reduce social inequality, it had helped to guide progress into the path which led directly to the egalitarian policies of the twentieth century. [. . .]

This growing national consciousness, this awakening public opinion, and these first stirrings of a sense of community membership and common heritage did not have any material effect on class structure and social inequality for the simple and obvious reason that, even at the end of the nineteenth century, the mass of the working people did not wield effective political power. By that time the franchise was fairly wide, but those who had recently received the vote had not yet learned how to use it. The political rights of citizenship, unlike the civil rights, were full of potential danger to the capitalist system, although those who were cautiously extending them down the social scale probably did not realize quite how great the danger was. They could hardly be expected to foresee what vast changes could be brought about by the peaceful use of political power, without a violent and bloody revolution. The 'planned society' and the welfare state had not yet risen over the horizon or come within the view of the practical politician. The foundations of the market economy and the contractual system seemed strong enough to stand against any probable assault. In fact, there were some grounds for expecting that the

working classes, as they became educated, would accept the basic principles of the system and be content to rely for their protection and progress
on the civil rights of citizenship, which contained no obvious menace to
competitive capitalism. Such a view was encouraged by the fact that one
of the main achievements of political power in the later nineteenth century
was the recognition of the right of collective bargaining. This meant that
social progress was being sought by strengthening civil rights, not by
creating social rights; through the use of contract in the open market, not
through a minimum wage and social security.

But this interpretation underrates the significance of this extension of
civil rights in the economic sphere. For civil rights were in origin intensely
individual, and that is why they harmonized with the individualistic phase
of capitalism. By the device of incorporation groups were enabled to act
legally as individuals. This important development did not go unchal-
lenged, and limited liability was widely denounced as an infringement of
individual responsibility. But the position of trade unions was even more
anomalous, because they did not seek or obtain incorporation. They can,
therefore, exercise vital civil rights collectively on behalf of their members
without formal collective responsibility, while the individual responsibility of the workers in relation to contract is largely unenforceable. These
civil rights became, for the workers, an instrument for raising their social
and economic status, that is to say, for establishing the claim that they, as
citizens, were entitled to certain social rights. But the normal method of
establishing social rights is by the exercise of political power, for social
rights imply an absolute right to a certain standard of civilization which
is conditional only on the discharge of the general duties of citizenship.
Their content does not depend on the economic value of the individual
claimant. There is therefore a significant difference between a genuine
collective bargain through which economic forces in a free market seek
to achieve equilibrium and the use of collective civil rights to assert basic
claims to the elements of social justice. Thus the acceptance of collective
bargaining was not simply a natural extension of civil rights; it represented
the transfer of an important process from the political to the civil sphere
of citizenship. But 'transfer' is, perhaps, a misleading term, for at the time
when this happened the workers either did not possess, or had not yet
learned to use, the political right of the franchise. Since then they have
obtained and made full use of that right. Trade unionism has, therefore,
created a secondary system of industrial citizenship parallel with and supplementary to the system of political citizenship. [. . .]

A new period opened at the end of the nineteenth century, conveniently
marked by Booth's survey of *Life and Labour of the People in London*
and the Royal Commission on the Aged Poor. It saw the first big advance
in social rights, and this involved significant changes in the egalitarian
principle as expressed in citizenship. But there were other forces at work

as well. A rise of money incomes unevenly distributed over the social classes altered the economic distance which separated these classes from one another, diminishing the gap between skilled and unskilled labour and between skilled labour and non-manual workers, while the steady increase in small savings blurred the class distinction between the capitalist and the propertyless proletarian. Secondly, a system of direct taxation, ever more steeply graduated, compressed the whole scale of disposable incomes. Thirdly, mass production for the home market and a growing interest on the part of industry in the needs and tastes of the common people enabled the less well-to-do to enjoy a material civilization which differed less markedly in quality from that of the rich than it had ever done before. All this profoundly altered the setting in which the progress of citizenship took place. Social integration spread from the sphere of sentiment and patriotism into that of material enjoyment. The components of a civilized and cultured life, formerly the monopoly of the few, were brought progressively within reach of the many, who were encouraged thereby to stretch out their hands towards those that still eluded their grasp. The diminution of inequality strengthened the demand for its abolition, at least with regard to the essentials of social welfare.

These aspirations have in part been met by incorporating social rights in the status of citizenship and thus creating a universal right to real income which is not proportionate to the market value of the claimant. Class-abatement is still the aim of social rights, but it has acquired a new meaning. It is no longer merely an attempt to abate the obvious nuisance of destitution in the lowest ranks of society. It has assumed the guise of action modifying the whole pattern of social inequality. It is no longer content to raise the floor-level in the basement of the social edifice, leaving the superstructure as it was. It has begun to remodel the whole building, and it might even end by converting a skyscraper into a bungalow. It is therefore important to consider whether any such ultimate aim is implicit in the nature of this development, or whether, as I put it at the outset, there are natural limits to the contemporary drive towards greater social and economic equality. [. . .]

The degree of equalization achieved [by the modern system of welfare benefits] depends on four things: whether the benefit is offered to all or to a limited class; whether it takes the form of money payment or service rendered; whether the minimum is high or low; and how the money to pay for the benefit is raised. Cash benefits subject to income limit and means test had a simple and obvious equalizing effect. They achieved class-abatement in the early and limited sense of the term. The aim was to ensure that all citizens should attain at least to the prescribed minimum, either by their own resources or with assistance if they could not do it without. The benefit was given only to those who needed it, and thus inequalities at the bottom of the scale were ironed out. The system operated in its simplest and most unadulterated form in the case of the Poor Law and old age pensions. But economic equalization might be accompanied by psychological class discrimination. The stigma which attached to the Poor Law made 'pauper' a derogatory term defining a class. 'Old age pensioner' may have had a little of the same flavour, but without the taint of shame. [. . .]

The extension of the social services is not primarily a means of equalizing incomes. In some cases it may, in others it may not. The question is relatively unimportant; it belongs to a different department of social policy. What matters is that there is a general enrichment of the concrete substance of civilized life, a general reduction of risk and insecurity, an equalization between the more and the less fortunate at all levels – between the healthy and the sick, the employed and the unemployed, the old and the active, the bachelor and the father of a large family. Equalization is not so much between classes as between individuals within a population which is now treated for this purpose as though it were one class. Equality of status is more important than equality of income. [. . .]

I said earlier that in the twentieth century citizenship and the capitalist class system have been at war. Perhaps the phrase is rather too strong, but it is quite clear that the former has imposed modifications on the latter. But we should not be justified in assuming that, although status is a principle that conflicts with contract, the stratified status system which is creeping into citizenship is an alien element in the economic world outside. Social rights in their modern form imply an invasion of contract by status, the subordination of market price to social justice, the replacement of the free bargain by the declaration of rights. But are these principles quite foreign to the practice of the market today, or are they there already entrenched within the contract system itself? I think it is clear that they are. [. . .]

I have tried to show how citizenship, and other forces outside it, have been altering the pattern of social inequality. [. . .] We have to look, here, for the combined effects of three factors. First, the compression, at both ends, of the scale of income distribution. Second, the great extension of the area of common culture and common experience. And third, the enrichment of the universal status of citizenship, combined with the recognition and stabilization of certain status differences chiefly through the linked systems of education and occupation. [. . .]

I asked, at the beginning, whether there was any limit to the present drive towards social equality inherent in the principles governing the movement. My answer is that the preservation of economic inequalities has been made more difficult by the enrichment of the status of citizenship. There is less room for them, and there is more and more likelihood of their being challenged. But we are certainly proceeding at present on the assumption that the hypothesis is valid. And this assumption provides the answer to the second question. We are not aiming at absolute equality. There are limits inherent in the egalitarian movement. But the movement is a double one. It operates partly through citizenship and partly through the economic system. In both cases the aim is to remove inequalities which cannot be regarded as legitimate, but the standard of legitimacy is different. In the former it is the standard of social justice, in the latter it is social justice combined with economic necessity. It is possible, therefore, that the inequalities permitted by the two halves of the movement will not coincide. Class distinctions may survive which have no appropriate economic function, and economic differences which do not correspond with accepted class distinctions. [. . .]

Notes

Originally delivered in Cambridge as the Marshall Lecture for 1949 and published in *Citizenship and Social Class and Other Essays*, ed. T. H. Marshall, Cambridge, Cambridge University Press, 1950, by permission of Pluto Press.

1 G. M. Trevelyan, *English Social History* (1942), p. 351.
2 Sidney and Beatrice Webb, *History of Trade Unionism* (1920), p. 60.
3 R. H. Tawney, *The Agrarian Problem in the Sixteenth Century* (1916), pp. 43–4.
4 P. Colquhoun, *A Treatise in Indigence* (1806), pp. 7–8.

Universalism versus Selection

Richard Titmuss

[. . .]

Universalist and Selective Social Services

In any discussion today of the future of (what is called) 'The Welfare State'
much of the argument revolves around the principles and objectives of
universalist social services and selective social services.

[. . .]

Consider, first, the nature of the broad principles which helped to shape
substantial sections of British welfare legislation in the past, and particularly the principle of universalism embodied in such postwar enactments
as the National Health Service Act, the Education Act of 1944, the
National Insurance Act and the Family Allowances Act.

One fundamental historical reason for the adoption of this principle
was the aim of making services available and accessible to the whole
population in such ways as would not involve users in any humiliating
loss of status, dignity or self-respect. There should be no sense of inferiority, pauperism, shame or stigma in the use of a publicly provided service;
no attribution that one was being or becoming a 'public burden'. Hence
the emphasis on the social rights of all citizens to use or not to use as
responsible people the services made available by the community in
respect of certain needs which the private market and the family were
unable or unwilling to provide universally. If these services were not
provided for everybody by everybody they would either not be available

at all, or only for those who could afford them, and for others on such terms as would involve the infliction of a sense of inferiority and stigma.

Avoidance of stigma was not, of course, the only reason for the development of the twin concepts of social rights and universalism. Many other forces, social, political and psychological, during a century and more of turmoil, revolution, war and change, contributed to the clarification and acceptance of these notions. The novel idea of prevention – novel, at least, to many in the nineteenth century – was, for example, another powerful engine, driven by the Webbs and many other advocates of change, which reinforced the concepts of social rights and universalism. The idea of prevention – the prevention and breaking of the vicious descending spiral of poverty, disease, neglect, illiteracy and destitution – spelt to the protagonists (and still does so) the critical importance of early and easy access to and use of preventive, remedial and rehabilitative services. Slowly and painfully the lesson was learnt that if such services were to be utilized in time and were to be effective in action in a highly differentiated, unequal and class-saturated society, they had to be delivered through socially approved channels; that is to say, without loss of self-respect by the users and their families.

Prevention was not simply a child of biological and psychological theorists; at least one of the grandparents was a powerful economist with a strongly developed streak of nationalism. As Professor Bentley Gilbert has shown in his [. . .] book *The Evolution of National Insurance: The Origins of the Welfare State*, national efficiency and welfare were seen as complementary.[1] The sin unforgivable was the waste of human resources; thus, welfare was summoned to prevent waste. Hence the beginnings of four of our present-day universalist social services: retirement pensions, the Health Service, unemployment insurance and the school meals service.

The insistent drumming of the national efficiency movement in those far-off days before the First World War is now largely forgotten. Let me then remind you that the whole welfare debate was a curious mixture of humanitarianism, egalitarianism, productivity (as we would call it today) and old-fashioned imperialism. The strident note of the latter is now, we may thank our stars, silenced. The Goddess of Growth has replaced the God of National Fitness. But can we say that the quest for the other objectives is no longer necessary?

Before discussing such a rhetorical question, we need to examine further the principle of universalism. The principle itself may sound simple but the practice – and by that I mean the present operational pattern of welfare in Britain [in the 1960s] – is immensely complex. We can see something of this complexity if we analyse welfare (defined here as all publicly provided and subsidized services, statutory, occupational and fiscal) from a number of different standpoints.

An Analytical Framework

Whatever the nature of the service, activity or function, and whether it be a service in kind, a collective amenity, or a transfer payment in cash or by accountancy, we need to consider (and here I itemize in question form for the sake of brevity) three central issues:

1 What is the nature of entitlement to use? Is it legal, contractual or contributory, financial, discretionary or professionally determined entitlement?
2 Who is entitled and on what conditions? Is account taken of individual characteristics, family characteristics, group characteristics, territorial characteristics or social-biological characteristics? What, in fact, are the rules of entitlement? Are they specific and contractual – like a right based on age – or are they variable, arbitrary or discretionary?
3 What methods, financial and administrative, are employed in the determination of access, utilization, allocation and payment?

Next we have to reflect on the nature of the service or benefit.

What functions do benefits, in cash, amenity or in kind, aim to fulfil? They may, for example, fulfil any of the following sets of functions, singly or in combination:

1 As partial compensation for identified disservices caused by society (for example, unemployment, some categories of industrial injuries benefits, war pensions, etc.). And, we may add, the disservices caused by international society as exemplified [. . .] by the oil pollution resulting from the Torrey Canyon disaster in 1967 costing at least £2 million.[2]
2 As partial compensation for unidentifiable disservices caused by society (for example, 'benefits' related to programmes of slum clearance, urban blight, smoke pollution control, hospital cross-infection and many other socially created disservices).
3 As partial compensation for unmerited handicap (for example, language classes for immigrant children, services for the deprived child, children handicapped from birth, etc.).
4 As a form of protection for society (for example, the probation service, some parts of the mental health services, services for the control of infectious diseases, etc.).
5 As an investment for a future personal or collective gain (education – professional, technical and industrial – is an obvious example here; so also are certain categories of tax deductibles for self-improvement and certain types of subsidized occupational benefits).
6 As an immediate and/or deferred increment to personal welfare or, in other words, benefits (utilities) which add to personal command-over-

resources either immediately and/or in the future (for example, sub-sidies to owner-occupiers and council tenants, tax deductibles for interest charges, pensions, supplementary benefits, curative medical care, etc.).

7   As an element in an integrative objective which is an essential charac-teristic distinguishing social policy from economic policy. As Kenneth Boulding has said, '. . . social policy is that which is centred in those institutions that create integration and discourage alienation'.[3] It is thus profoundly concerned with questions of personal identity whereas economic policy centres round exchange or bilateral transfer.

This represents little more than an elementary and partial structural map which can assist in the understanding of the welfare complex [. . .]. Needless to say, a more sophisticated (inch to the mile) guide is essential for anything approaching a thorough analysis of the actual functioning of welfare benefit systems. I do not, however, propose to refine further this frame of study now, nor can I analyse by these classifications the several hundred distinctive and functionally separate services and benefits actu-ally in operation in Britain [in the 1960s].

Further study would also have to take account of the pattern and opera-tion of means-tested services. It has been estimated by Mr M. J. Reddin, my research assistant, that in England and Wales today local authorities are responsible for administering at least 3,000 means tests, of which about 1,500 are different from each other.[4] This estimate applies only to services falling within the responsibilities of education, child care, health, housing and welfare departments. It follows that in these fields alone there exist some 1,500 different definitions of poverty or financial hardship, ability to pay and rules for charges, which affect the individual and the family. There must be substantial numbers of poor families with multiple needs and multiple handicaps whose perception [. . .] of the realities of welfare is to see only a means-testing world. Who helps them, I wonder, to fill out all those forms?

I mention these social facts, by way of illustration, because they do form part of the operational complex of welfare in 1967. My main purpose, however, in presenting this analytical framework was twofold. First, to underline the difficulties of conceptualizing and categorizing needs, causes, entitlement or gatekeeper functions, utilization patterns, benefits and compensations. Second, to suggest that those students of welfare who are seeing the main problem today in terms of universalism versus selec-tive services are presenting a naive and oversimplified picture of policy choices.

Some of the reasons for this simple and superficial view are, I think, due to the fact that the approach is dominated by the concept or model of welfare as a 'burden'; as a waste of resources in the provision of benefits for those who, it is said, do not need them. The general solution is thus deceptively simple and romantically appealing: abolish all this welfare complexity and concentrate help on those whose needs are greatest.

Quite apart from the theoretical and practical immaturity of this solution, which would restrict the public services to a minority in the population leaving the majority to buy their own education, social security, medical care and other services in a supposedly free market, certain other important questions need to be considered.

As all selective services for this minority would have to apply some test of need–eligibility, on what bases would tests be applied and, even more crucial, where would the lines be drawn for benefits which function as compensation for identified disservices, compensation for unidentifiable disservices, compensation for unmerited handicap, as a form of social protection, as an investment, or as an increment to personal welfare? Can rules of entitlement and access be drawn on purely 'ability to pay' criteria without distinction of cause? And if the causal agents of need cannot be identified or are so diffuse as to defy the wit of law – as they so often are [. . .] – then is not the answer 'no compensation and no redress'? In other words, the case for concentrated selective services resolves itself into an argument for allowing the social costs or diswelfares of the economic system to lie where they fall.

The emphasis [. . .] on 'welfare' and the 'benefits of welfare' often tends to obscure the fundamental fact that for many consumers the services used are not essentially benefits or increments to welfare at all; they represent partial compensations for disservices, for social costs and social insecurities which are the product of a rapidly changing industrial-urban society. They are part of the price we pay to some people for bearing part of the costs of other people's progress; the obsolescence of skills, redundancies, premature retirements, accidents, many categories of disease and handicap, urban blight and slum clearance, smoke pollution, and a hundred-and-one other socially generated disservices. They are the socially caused diswelfares; the losses involved in aggregate welfare gains.

What is also of major importance [. . .] is that modern society is finding it increasingly difficult to identify the causal agent or agencies, and thus to allocate the costs of disservices and charge those who are responsible. It is not just a question of benefit allocation – of whose 'Welfare State' – but also of loss allocation – whose 'Diswelfare State'.

If identification of the agents of diswelfare were possible – if we could legally name and blame the culprits – then, in theory at least, redress could be obtained through the courts by the method of monetary compensation for damages. But multiple causality and the diffusion of disservices – the modern choleras of change – make this solution impossible. We have, therefore, as societies to make other choices; either to provide social services, or to allow the social costs of the system to lie where they fall. The nineteenth century chose the latter – the *laissez-faire* solution – because it had neither a germ theory of disease nor a social theory of causality; an answer which can hardly be entertained today by a richer society equipped with more knowledge about the dynamics of change. But knowledge in this context must not, of course, be equated with wisdom.

If this argument can be sustained, we are thus compelled to return to our analytical framework of the functional concepts of benefit and, within this context, to consider the role of universalist and selective social services. Non-discriminating universalist services are in part the consequence of unidentifiable causality. If disservices are wasteful (to use the economists' concept of 'waste') so welfare has to be 'wasteful'.

The next question that presents itself is this: can we and should we, in providing benefits and compensation (which in practice can rarely be differentially provided), distinguish between 'faults' in the individual (moral, psychological or social) and the 'faults of society'? If all services are provided – irrespective of whether they represent benefits, amenity, social protection or compensation – on a discriminatory, means-test basis, do we not foster both the sense of personal failure and the stigma of a public burden? The fundamental objective of all such tests of eligibility is to keep people out; not to let them in. They must, therefore, be treated as applicants or supplicants; not beneficiaries or consumers.

It is a regrettable but human fact that money (and the lack of it) is linked to personal and family self-respect. This is one element in what has been called the 'stigma of the means test'. Another element is the historical evidence we have that separate discriminatory services for poor people have always tended to be poor quality services; read the history of the panel system under National Health Insurance; read Beveridge on workmen's compensation; Newsom on secondary modern schools; Plowden on standards of primary schools in slum areas; Townsend on Part III accommodations in *The Last Refuge*,[5] and so on.[6]

In the past, poor quality selective services for poor people were the product of a society which saw 'welfare' as a residual; as a public burden. The primary purpose of the system and the method of discrimination was, therefore, deterrence (it was also an effective rationing device). To this end, the most effective instrument was to induce among recipients (children as well as adults) a sense of personal fault, of personal failure, even if the benefit was wholly or partially a compensation for disservices inflicted by society.

The Real Challenge in Welfare

Today, with this heritage, we face the positive challenge of providing selective, high quality services for poor people over a large and complex range of welfare; of positively discriminating on a territorial, group or 'rights' basis in favour of the poor, the handicapped, the deprived, the coloured, the homeless, and the social casualties of our society. Universalism is not, by itself alone, enough: in medical care, in wage-related social security and in education. This much we have learnt in the past two decades from the facts about inequalities in the distribution of incomes and wealth, and in our failure to close many gaps in differential access to and effective utilization of particular branches of our social services.[7]

If I am right, I think that during the 1960s Britain was beginning to identify the dimensions of this challenge of positive, selective discrimination – in income maintenance, in education, in housing, in medical care and mental health, in child welfare, and in the tolerant integration of immigrants and citizens from overseas; of preventing especially the second generation from becoming (and of seeing themselves as) second-class citizens. We have continued to seek ways and means, values, methods and techniques, of positive discrimination without the infliction, actual or imagined, of a sense of personal failure and individual fault.

At this point, considering the nature of the search in all its ramifying complexities, I must now state my general conclusion. It is this. The challenge that faces us is not the choice between universalist and selective social services. The real challenge resides in the question: what particular infrastructure of universalist services is needed in order to provide a framework of values and opportunity bases within and around which can be developed socially acceptable selective services aiming to discriminate positively, with the minimum risk of stigma, in favour of those whose needs are greatest.

This, to me, is the fundamental challenge. In different ways and in particular areas it confronts the Supplementary Benefits Commission, the Seebohm Committee, the National Health Service, the Ministry of Housing and Local Government, the National Committee for Commonwealth Immigrants, the policy-making readers of the Newsom Report and the Plowden Report on educational priority areas, the Scottish Report, *Social Work and the Community*, and thousands of social workers and administrators all over the country wrestling with the problems of needs and priorities. In all the main spheres of need, some structure of universalism is an essential prerequisite to selective positive discrimination; it provides a general system of values and a sense of community; socially approved agencies for clients, patients and consumers, and also for the recruitment, training and deployment of staff at all levels; it sees welfare, not as a burden, but as complementary and as an instrument of change and, finally, it allows positive discriminatory services to be provided as rights for categories of people and for classes of need in terms of priority social areas and other impersonal classifications.

Without this infrastructure of welfare resources and framework of values we should not, I conclude, be able to identify and discuss the next steps in progress towards a 'Welfare Society'.

Notes

Lecture delivered at the British National Conference on Social Welfare, London, April 1967, and published in the *Proceedings of the Conference*. This extract from R. M. Titmuss, *Commitment to Welfare*, London, Allen and Unwin, 1968, pp. 128–37, by permission of the Literary Estate of Richard Titmuss and Professor Ann Oakley.

1 B. B. Gilbert, *The Evolution of National Insurance: The Origins of the Welfare State*, London, Michael Joseph, 1966.
2 *The Torrey Canyon*, Cmnd 3246, London, HMSO, 1967.
3 K. E. Boulding, 'The Boundaries of Social Policy', *Social Work*, vol. 12, no. 1, January 1967, p. 7.
4 This study is to be published by Mr M. J. Reddin as an *Occasional Paper on Social Administration*.
5 P. Townsend, *The Last Refuge*, London, Routledge, 1964.
6 See also R. M. Titmuss, *Problems of Social Policy*, London, HMSO, 1950.
7 See P. Townsend, *Poverty, Socialism and Labour in Power*, Fabian tract, 371, 1967, and R. J. Nicholson, 'The Distribution of Personal Income', *Lloyds Bank Review*, January 1967, p. 11.

Perspectives on the Left

What is Social Justice?

Commission on Social Justice

In deciding to develop a conceptual framework for thinking about social justice, the Commission made a big assumption, namely that there is such a thing as 'social justice'. Some people (particularly of the libertarian Right) deny that there is a worthwhile idea of *social* justice at all. They say that justice is an idea confined to the law, with regard to crime, punishment and the settling of disputes before the courts. They claim that it is nonsense to talk about resources in society being fairly or unfairly distributed. The free market theorist Friedrich von Hayek, for example, argued that the process of allocating wealth and property 'can be neither just nor unjust, because the results are not intended or foreseen, and depend on a multitude of circumstances not known in their totality to anybody'.

What libertarians really mean, however, is not that there is no such thing as social justice, but rather that there is only one criterion of a just outcome in society, namely that it should be the product of a free market. But this is not as simple as it may sound, because ideas of fairness (and not merely of efficiency) are themselves used in defining what counts as a free market. While it is often said that a given market competition is not fair because it is not being played 'on a level field', it is not clear what counts as levelling the field, as opposed to altering the result of the match. For example, antitrust laws can be seen as an interference in a free market, or a device for making the field level.

In fact, people in modern societies *do* have strong ideas about social justice. We all know this from daily conversation, and opinion polls regularly confirm it. We are confident that at least in our belief there is such a thing as 'social justice', we reflect the common sense of the vast majority of people. However, polls are not easy to interpret, and they make it clear that people's ideas about social justice are complex.

There is more than one notion associated with the term social justice. In some connections, for example, justice is thought to have something to do with *equality*. Sometimes it seems to relate to *need:* for example, it can seem notably unfair if bad fortune prevents someone from having something they really need, such as medical care, less unfair if it is something they just happen to want. Yet again, justice relates to such notions as *entitlement, merit* and *desert*. These are not the same as each other. For example, if someone wins the prize in the lottery, they are entitled to the money, and it would be unjust to take it away from them, but it has nothing to do with their merits, and they have done nothing to deserve it. Similarly, if talented people win prizes in an activity that requires no great practice or effort, they are entitled to the prize and get it on the strength of their merits (as opposed, for instance, to someone's getting it because he is the son of the promoter), but they may well have not done anything much to deserve it. People who are especially keen on the notion of desert may want there to be prizes only for effort; or, at least, think that prizes which command admiration (as the lottery prize does not) should be awarded only for effort. Humanity has shown so far a steady reluctance to go all the way with this view.

As well as being *complex* in this way, people's views about justice are also *indeterminate*. This means that it is often unclear what the just outcome should be – particularly when various considerations of social justice seem to pull in different directions, as they often do. Most people, for instance, think that inheritance is at least not intrinsically evil, and that parents are entitled to leave property to their children. But no one thinks that one can leave anything one likes to one's children – one's job, for instance – and almost everyone thinks that it can be just for the state to tax inheritances in order to deal with social injustice, or simply to help the common good.

The mere fact that people's ideas about justice are both complex and indeterminate has an important consequence for democratic politics. There is more than one step from general ideas to practical recommendations. There have to be *general* policies directed to social justice, and these are going to be at best an interpretation of people's ideas on such matters. General policies will hope to offer considerations which people can recognize as making sense in the light of their own experience and ideas (this need not exclude challenging some of those ideas). *Specific* policies, however, involve a further step, since they have to express general policies in a particular administrative form. A given scheme of taxation or social security is, in that sense, at two removes from the complex and indeterminate ideas that are its moral roots.

This is not to deny that some administrative practices may acquire a symbolic value of their own. In the 1940s, the death grant was a symbol of society's commitment to end paupers' funerals and ensure for every family the means to offer deceased relatives a proper burial. It is a matter of acute political judgement to decide whether one is dealing with an important example of such a value, as opposed to a fetish (in the more or less literal sense of an inert object that has been invested with value that does not belong to it in its own right). Not every arrangement that has been taken to be an essential embodiment of social justice is, in changing circumstances, really so.

Theories of Social Justice

There are important theories of social justice. The most ambitious give a general account of what social justice is, explain and harmonize the relations between the different considerations associated with it, do the same for the relations between justice and other goods, notably liberty, help to resolve apparent conflicts between different values, and in the light of all that, even give pointers to practical policies. The most famous such theory in modern discussion is that of John Rawls, which gives a very rich elaboration to a very simple idea: that the fair division of a cake would be one that could be agreed on by people who did not know which piece they were going to get.

Rawls invokes an 'Original Position', in which representatives of various parties to society are behind 'a veil of ignorance' and do not know what role each party will occupy in the society. They are asked to choose a general scheme for the ordering of society. The scheme that they would reasonably choose in these imagined circumstances constitutes, in Rawls's view, the scheme of a just society.

Rawls's theory, and others with similar aims, contains important insights, and anyone who is trying to think about these problems should pay attention to them. But there is an important question – one acknowledged by Rawls himself – of what relation such a theory can have to politics. Rawls thinks that his theory articulates a widely spread sense of fairness, but it is certain that the British public would not recognize in such a theory, or in any other with such ambitions, all its conflicting ideas and feelings about social justice. Even if the Commission, improbably, all agreed on Rawls's or some other such theory, we would not be justified in presenting our conclusions in terms of that theory. The Commission has a more practical purpose.

Our task is to find compelling ways of making our society more just. We shall be able to do so only if we think in ways that people can recognize and respect about such questions as how best to understand merit and need; how to see the effects of luck in different spheres of life; what is implied in saying, or denying, that health care is a morally special kind of good which makes a special kind of demand.

The Commission has to guard against all-or-nothing assumptions. It is not true that either we have a complete top-down theory, or we are left only with mere prejudice and subservience to polls. This particularly applies to conflict. Confronted, as will often be the case, with an apparent conflict within justice, or between justice and some other value, we may tend to assume that there are only two possibilities: the conflict is merely apparent, and we should understand liberty and equality (for instance) in such a way that they cannot conflict; or it is a real conflict, and then it can only be left to politics, majorities, subjective taste, or whatever. This will not do. Reflection may not eliminate all conflicts, but it can help us to understand them, and then arrive at policy choices.

The Equal Worth of Every Citizen

Social justice is often thought to have something specially to do with equality, but this idea, in itself, determines very little. A basic question is: equality of what? Furthermore, not all inequalities are unjust. For example, what people can do with money varies. Thus disabled people may well need more resources to reach a given quality of life than other people do, and if you are trying to be fair to people with regard to the quality of their life, unequal amounts of money is what fairness itself will demand. What this shows, as the philosopher and economist Amartya Sen has insisted, is that equality in one dimension goes with inequality in another. Since people have different capacities to turn resources into worthwhile activity (for instance because they are disabled), people will need different resources to be equally capable of worthwhile activity.

In fact, virtually everyone in the modern world believes in equality of *something*. All modern states are based on belief in some sort of equality and claim to treat their citizens equally. But what is involved in 'treating people equally'? Minimally, it implies political and civil liberties, equal rights before the law, equal protection against arbitrary arrest, and so forth. These things provide the basis of a 'civil society', a society of equal citizens.

However, these rights and freedoms cannot stand by themselves. More than this formal level of equality is needed if the minimal demands themselves are to be properly met. It is a familiar point that equality before the law does not come to much if one cannot afford a good lawyer. The 'equal freedom' of which modern democratic states boast should amount to more (as Anatole France observed) than the freedom to sleep on park benches and under bridges. Everyone needs the means to make use of their equal freedom, which otherwise would be hollow. Formal equalities have substantive consequences. Perhaps the most basic question about the nature of social justice in a modern society is what those substantive consequences are.

Meeting Basic Needs

People are likely to be restricted in what they can do with their freedom and their rights if they are poor, or ill, or lack the education which, to a greater extent today than ever before, is the basis of employment opportunities, personal fulfilment and people's capacities to influence what happens to them. These concerns define areas of *need*, and it is a natural application of the idea that everyone is of equal worth that they should have access to what they need, or at least to what they basically need.

Some basic needs are met by providing resources, or by helping people to save or acquire resources. This is the case with paid work; with financial security in old age; and with provisions for dealing with lack of resources, such as benefit in case of unemployment. In the case of health care and education, however, the most appropriate way of meeting needs seems to be not through money, but in kind; we think that someone who is ill has a right to access to treatment for their illness, but not that they have a right to funds which they can choose to spend on treatment or not. One way of expressing this commitment is that the state should itself provide the service. Another is that the state should provide means which command health care or education, but which cannot be converted into money. In the case of health, this may take the form of public insurance, though this can raise basic questions of fairness (with regard to individual risk) as well as of efficiency.

The case of health now raises a fundamental question which was not present fifty years ago. Health care has always seemed a very special good, in relation to social justice as in other respects. It involves our most basic interests, gives great power to certain professionals, and carries heavy symbolic value (brought out, for instance, in Richard Titmuss's famous discussion of blood donation *The Gift Relationship*). Treating health as one commodity, to be bought and sold like any other, is found offensive in most parts of the world (and Americans, though used to that attitude, seem to be turning against it). Our sentiments about health care merge with our sense of some very basic obligations: most people feel that resources should be used to save an identified person (as opposed to a merely statistical casualty) from death.

But today it is a fact that medicine's resources to extend life are expanding at an accelerating rate, and so is their cost. This raises hard questions not only about the distribution of resources devoted to health care (who gets the kidney machine?), but also about the amount of resources that should be devoted to health care at all. These hard questions are questions of justice, among other things. Confronted with the opportunity to save someone in the street from death, we will think that we should stop to save them even if the cost is not taking the children to school, but is it fair to save every saveable person from death at the cost of sending many children to quite inadequate schools?

To answer these questions, the Commission will need to consider what *sort* of goods we take health and health care to be. This was a less pressing question in the past, but it is now harder to avoid the issue of what we are distributing when we distribute medical care, and of what we most want it to do.

Education is also a good to which everyone has a right, because it is so closely tied to basic needs, to personal development, and to one's role in society. But it is also connected to equality in another way. Disadvantage is, notoriously, inherited, and an unfair situation in one generation tends to mean an unfair start for the next. Educational opportunity is still what it always has been, a crucial means for doing something about this unfairness.

This brings out a further point, that the ideal of 'equality of opportunity', which has often been thought by reformers to be a rather weak aspiration, is in fact very radical, if it is taken seriously. The changes required in order to give the most disadvantaged in our society the same life-chances as the more fortunate would be very wide-ranging indeed.

Opportunities and Life-Chances

Self-respect and equal citizenship demand more than the meeting of basic needs for income, shelter and so on. They demand the opportunities and life-chances central to personal freedom and autonomy. In a commercial society (outside monasteries, kibbutzim, etc.), self-respect standardly requires a certain amount of personal property. As Adam Smith remarked, a working man in eighteenth-century Scotland needed to own a decent linen shirt as a condition of self-respect, even though that might not be true of every man everywhere.

This does not mean that Adam Smith's man should be issued with a shirt. In a commercial society, his need is rather for the resources to buy a shirt of his choice. This is connected with his needing it as a matter of self-respect, which suggests something else, namely that where resources are supplied directly, for instance to those who are retired or who are caring for members of their families, it must be in ways which affirm their self-respect. But most people, for most of their lives, want the opportunities to earn the resources for themselves. The obvious question is whether everyone therefore has a right to a job, or the right to the means to gain a job.

The trouble, clearly, is that it may not be in the power of government directly to bring this about. Having a job, at least as the world is now, is closely connected with self-respect and hence with the equality of citizens, and for this as well as other reasons it must be a high priority for any government to create the circumstances in which there are jobs for those who want them. To insist, however, on a right to work – a right, presumably, which each person holds against the government – may not be the best way of expressing this aim. The Commission will therefore consider not only ways in which employment may be increased, but also what provision social justice demands for those who are unable to do paid work, or who are engaged in valuable unpaid work, or when significant levels of unemployment persist, even for a temporary period. Tackling unemployment is, of course, central to the realization of social justice.

There are questions here of how resources and opportunities can be extended to the unemployed. But there is a wider question as well, that extends to the provision for other needs: how opportunities may be created for the expression of people's autonomy and the extension of their freedom to determine their own lives. There is no doubt that advocates of social justice have often been insensitive to this dimension. The designers of the welfare state wanted to put rights in the place of charity: the idea of *entitlement* to benefit was meant to undercut any notion that the better-off were doing the worse-off a good turn. But the entitlement was often still understood as an entitlement to be given or issued with certain goods and services, the nature of which it was, in many cases, the business of experts to determine. There is a much greater awareness today that what people need is the chance to provide for themselves: [. . .] 'there is a limit to what government can do for people, but there is no limit to what they can be enabled to achieve for themselves'.

Relatedly, there is a stronger sense today that the aims of social justice are served not only by redistribution, by bringing resources after the event to people who have done badly. Social justice requires as well that structures should be adapted and influenced in ways that can give more people a better chance in the first place. That is why opportunities, and breaking down barriers to them, are so important.

There are, without doubt, conflicts between these various considerations. You cannot both encourage people's freedom to live their own lives as they choose, and guarantee that they will not suffer if they do not live them well. You cannot both allow people to spend money, if they wish, on their children's education – a right that exists in every democratic country – and also bring it about that everyone gets exactly the same education whether they pay privately for it or not. Here there are questions, too, of how far publicly supported provision to meet need should aim only at a minimal level, available to those without other provision, and how far it should seek to provide a high level of service for everyone. The view of most people is probably that the first answer applies to some needs and the goods and services that meet them, while in the case of health care and education, at least, no one should be excluded by disadvantage from a very high level of provision. Exactly how those different aims should now be conceived, and the extent to which they can realistically be carried out, are central questions for the Commission.

Unjustified Inequalities

Proponents of equality sometimes seem to imply that *all* inequalities are unjust (although they usually hasten to add that they are not in fact arguing for 'arithmetical equality'). We do not accept this. It seems fair, for instance, that a medical student should receive a lower income than the fully qualified doctor; or that experience or outstanding talent should be rewarded, and so on. Different people may have different views about what the basis of differential rewards should be; but most people accept, as we do, that some inequalities are just. There is, however, a question about the justifiable *extent* of an inequality, even if we accept that the inequality *per se* is not unjust.

Similarly, most people believe that it is fair for people to bequeath their property as they see fit, even though this means that some will inherit more than others. Nonetheless, it is also accepted that society may claim a share of an inheritance through the taxation of wealth or gifts, particularly when the estate is large. It is, after all, offensive to most ideas of social justice that a growing number of people own two homes while others have nowhere to live at all. This does not imply that one person's property should be confiscated to house another; but it does suggest the need for a fundamental reform of housing policy, an issue the Commission will certainly be addressing.

But if some inequalities are just, it is obviously the case that not all are so. It would, for instance, be unjust to allow people to inherit jobs from their parents: employment should be open to all, on the basis of merit. Inheritance of a family title offends many people's views about a classless society, but could not be said to deny somebody else something which they deserved. But inheritance of a peerage, in the UK, carries with it automatic entitlement to a seat and vote in the Second Chamber of Parliament: and that is an inequality of power which seems manifestly unjust.

Entitlement and Desert

Parents can, however, pass on intelligence, talent, charm and other qualities, as well as property or titles. Rawls in his theory rests a lot on the fact that a person's talents, and his or her capacity to make productive use of those talents, are very much matters of luck and are also, in some part, the product of society. Nobody, he has rightly insisted, *deserves* his or her (natural) talents. From this he has inferred that nobody, at a level of

basic principle, deserves the rewards of his or her talents. He argues that
no one has a right to something simply because it is the product of his or
her talents, and society has a right to redistribute that product in accord-
ance with the demands of social justice.

This is a very strong and surprising claim. Some people might agree that
no one deserves a reward that they get on the basis of some raw advantage,
without any investment of effort. (Of course, given the existing rules, that
does not mean that they are not entitled to it, or that it can merely be
taken away from them. It means that it would not necessarily be an injustice to change the rules.) But those who agree to this are very likely to
think that people who *do* invest effort deserve its rewards, at least up
to a certain point. But Rawls's argument applies just as much to effort as
to raw talent. First, it is practically impossible to separate the relative
contributions of effort and talent to a particular product. Moreover, the
capacity to make a given degree of effort is itself not equally distributed,
and may plausibly be thought to be affected by upbringing, culture and
other social factors. Virtually everything about a person that yields a
product is itself undeserved. So no rewards, in Rawls's view, are, at the
most basic level, a matter of desert.

Few people believe this. If someone has taken a lot of trouble in designing
and tending a garden, for instance, they will be proud of it and appropriately think of its success as theirs. The same applies to many aspects of life.
This does suggest that there is something wrong with the idea that basically
people never earn anything by their talents or labours – that in the last
analysis all that anyone's work represents is a site at which society has
achieved something. Yet, certainly, one does not 'deserve' the talents of
birth. It must be true, then, that one can deserve the rewards of one's talents
without deserving one's talents. As the American philosopher Robert
Nozick forcefully put it, why does desert 'have to go all the way down'?

What the various arguments about entitlement and desert suggest seems
to be something close to what many people believe: that there is basic
justice in people having some differential reward for their productive
activities, but that they have no right to any *given* differential of their
reward over others. It is not simply self-interest, or again scepticism about
government spending programmes (though that is certainly a factor), that
makes people resist the idea that everyone's income is in principle a
resource for redistribution; that idea also goes against their sense of what
is right. They rightly think that redistribution of income is not an aim in
itself.

At the same time, they acknowledge that the needs of the less fortunate
make a claim. Luck is everywhere, and one is entitled to some rewards of
luck, but there are limits to this entitlement when one lives and works with
other people. Even if one is entitled to some rewards from the product of
one's efforts and talents, there is the further point that in a complex enter-

prise such as a company or family, there is rarely a product which is solely and definitely the product of a given person's efforts and talents.

This is no doubt one reason why people are sceptical about vast rewards to captains of industry. It is also a question of the relation of one person's activity to that of others. Few people mind that Pavarotti or Lenny Henry are paid large sums – there is only one of them, and they are undoubtedly the star of the show. But in some cases, one person's reward can be another person's loss. The Nobel Prize winning economist Professor James Meade argued in a submission to the Commission that 'Keynesian full-employment policy . . . collapsed simply and solely because a high level of money expenditures came to lead not to a high level of output and employment but to a high rate of money wages, costs and prices . . . It is very possible that to absorb two million extra workers into employment would require a considerable reduction in real wage costs.'

This raises a crucial point, concerning the power to determine one's own rewards, and the relationship of that power to questions of justice and desert. In contrast to a simple focus on the distribution of rewards, this raises the question of the *generation* of rewards, the processes whereby inequalities are generated.

Unequal incomes are inherent in a market economy. Even if everyone started off with the same allocation of money, differences would soon emerge. Not all labour commands the same price; not all investments produce the same return; some people work longer hours, others prefer more leisure and so on. The resulting inequalities are not necessarily unjust – although the extent of them may be. In the real world, of course, people start off with very different personal and financial resources. The problem is that too many of these inequalities are exacerbated in the UK's system of market exchange.

But market economies are not all of a piece; different kinds of market produce different outcomes. For instance, Germany, Japan and Sweden all have more equal earnings distributions than the UK, where the gap between the highest and lowest paid is wider today than at any time since 1886. Social justice therefore has a part to play in deciding how a market is constructed, and not simply with the end result.

Fair Reward

Most people have some idea of a 'fair reward'. For example, it is clear to the vast majority of people that disadvantage and discrimination on grounds of sex or race or disability is unjust. However, once one gets beyond the general idea, there is less agreement on what fair rewards should be. Even if there were more agreement about this, it is very difficult, both practically and morally, to impose such notions on a modern economy. The very idea of a society that can be effectively managed from the top on the basis of detailed centralized decisions is now discredited. Moreover, our society does not stand by itself and happily does not have walls around it, and people can go elsewhere.

Ideas of social justice in this area are not, however, necessarily tied to the model of a command economy. It is often clear, at least, that given rewards in a market economy are not fair, because they are not being determined by such things as talent, effort and the person's contribution to the enterprise, but rather by established power relations. Real life does not conform to economic models: people are not paid for the 'marginal product' of their labour. They are paid, among other things, according to social norms. In one sense, such distortions are the product of the market: they are what we get if market processes, uncorrected, are allowed to reflect established structures and habits of power. Examples of this are the huge salaries and bonuses distributed to the directors of some large companies. [. . .] These salaries and bonuses are often quite unrelated to the performance of the company concerned, and are sometimes actually inversely correlated with company performance.

In another sense, unjust inequalities are themselves distortions of the market: it is not a fair market in talent and effort if it is not talent and effort that determine the outcome. This is most obviously demonstrated in the case of inequalities of pay between men and women. Although the 1970 Equal Pay Act eliminated overt pay inequities, it had a limited effect on the gap between men's and women's pay, which resulted in the main from job segregation and gender-biased views of what different jobs and different qualities were worth. Hence the concept of 'equal pay for work of equal value', which permits comparisons between two very different jobs performed for the same employer. Although designed to eradicate gender as a consideration in earnings, equal value claims may in practice require a complete transformation in an organization's pay-setting. Equal pay for work of equal value, after all, implies unequal pay for work of unequal value: thus, the basis for differentials has to be made explicit and justified.

Different organizations and people will have different views of what constitutes a fair basis for differentials: it should not be an aim of government to substitute its own view of fair wage settlements. It is, however, a legitimate aim of policy concerned with social justice to develop social institutions (of which equal value laws are one example) which will enable people to express their own ideas of a fair reward.

The Meaning of Social Justice: A Summary

In arriving at our principles of social justice, we reject the view, so fashionable in the 1980s, that human beings are simply selfish individuals, for whom there is 'no such thing as society'. People are essentially social creatures, dependent on one another for the fulfilment of their needs and potential, and willing to recognize their responsibilities to others as well as claiming their rights from them. We believe our four principles of social justice, based on a basic belief in the intrinsic worth of every human being, echo the deeply held views of many people in this country. They provide a compelling justification and basis for our work:

1 The foundation of a free society is the equal worth of all citizens.
2 Everyone is entitled, as a right of citizenship, to be able to meet their basic needs.
3 The right to self-respect and personal autonomy demands the widest possible spread of opportunities.
4 Not all inequalities are unjust, but unjust inequalities should be reduced and where possible eliminated.

[. . .]

Note

From Commission on Social Justice, *The Justice Gap*, London, Institute for Public Policy Research, 1993, pp. 4–16.

Some Contradictions of the Modern Welfare State

Claus Offe

The welfare state has served as the major peace formula of advanced capitalist democracies for the period following the Second World War. This peace formula consists, first, in the explicit obligation of the state apparatus to provide assistance and support (either in money or in kind) to those citizens who suffer from specific needs and risks which are characteristic of the market society; such assistance is provided as legal claims granted to the citizens. Second, the welfare state is based on the recognition of the formal role of labour unions both in collective bargaining and the formation of public policy. Both of these structural components of the welfare state are considered to limit and mitigate class conflict, to balance the asymmetrical power relation of labour and capital, and thus to overcome the condition of disruptive struggle and contradiction that was the most prominent feature of pre-welfare state, or liberal, capitalism. In sum, the welfare state has been celebrated throughout the postwar period as the political solution to societal contradictions.

Until [the 1970s], this seemed to be the converging view of political elites both in countries in which the welfare state is fully developed (e.g. Great Britain, Sweden) as well as in those where it is still an incompletely realized model. Political conflict in these latter societies, such as the USA, was centred not on the basic desirability and functional indispensability, but on the pace and modalities of the implementation of the welfare state model.

This was true, with very minor exceptions, up to the mid-1970s. From that point on we see that in many capitalist societies this established peace formula becomes itself the object of doubts, fundamental critique and political conflict. It appears that the most widely accepted device of political problem-solving has itself become problematic, and that, at any rate, the unquestioning confidence in the welfare state and its future expansion has rapidly vanished. It is to these doubts and criticisms that I will direct my attention in the following remarks. The point to start with is the observation that the almost universally accepted model for creating a measure of social peace and harmony in European postwar societies has itself become the source of new contradictions and political divisions in the 1970s.

Historically, the welfare state has been the combined outcome of a variety of factors which change in composition from country to country: Social Democratic reformism, Christian socialism, enlightened conservative political and economic elites and large industrial unions. They fought for and conceded comprehensive compulsory insurance schemes, labour protection legislation, minimum wages, the expansion of health and education facilities and state-subsidized housing, as well as the recognition of unions as the legitimate economic and political representatives of labour. These continuous developments in Western societies were often dramatically accelerated in a context of intense social conflict and crisis, particularly under war and postwar conditions. The accomplishments, which were won under conditions of war and postwar periods, were regularly maintained; added to them were the innovations that could be introduced in periods of prosperity and growth. In the light of the Keynesian doctrine of economic policy, the welfare state came to be seen not so much as a burden imposed upon the economy, but as a built-in economic and political stabilizer which could help to regenerate the forces of economic growth and prevent the economy from spiralling downward into deep recessions. Thus, a variety of quite heterogeneous ends (ranging from reactionary pre-emptive strikes against the working class movement in the case of Bismarck, to socialist reformism in the case of the Weimar Social Democrats; from the social-political consolidation of war and defence economies, to the stabilization of the business cycle) adopted identical institutional means which today make up the welfare state. It is exactly its multi-functional character, its ability to serve many conflicting ends and strategies simultaneously which made the political arrangement of the welfare state so attractive to a broad alliance of heterogeneous forces. But it is equally true that the very diversity of the forces that inaugurated and supported the welfare state could not be accommodated forever within the institutional framework which today appears to come increasingly under attack. The machinery of class compromise has itself become the object of class conflict.

The Attack from the Right

The sharp economic recession of the mid-1970s [gave] rise to a renaissance of neo-*laissez-faire* and monetarist economic doctrines of equal intellectual and political power. These doctrines amount to a fundamental critique of the welfare state, which is seen to be the illness of which it pretends to be the cure. Rather than effectively harmonizing the conflicts of a market society, it exacerbates them and prevents the forces of social peace and progress (namely the forces of the market place) to function properly and beneficially. This is said to be so for two major reasons. First, the welfare state apparatus imposes a burden of taxation and regulation upon capital which amounts to a *disincentive to investment*. Second, the welfare state grants claims, entitlements and collective power positions to workers and unions which amount to a *disincentive to work*, or at least to work as hard and productively as they would be forced to under the reign of unfettered market forces. Taken together, these two effects lead into a dynamic of declining growth and increased expectations, of economic demand over-load (inflation) as well as political demand overload (ungovernability) which can less and less be satisfied by the available output.

The reactionary political uses of this analysis are obvious, but it may well be that the truth of the analysis itself is greater than the desirability of its practical conclusions. Although the democratic left has often meas-ured the former by the latter, the two deserve at least a separate evaluation. In my view, at least, the above analysis is not so much false in what it says as in what it remains silent about.

To take up the first point of the conservative analysis: isn't it true that under conditions of declining growth rates and vehement competition on domestic and international markets, individual capitalists (at least those firms which do not enjoy the privileges of the monopolistic sector) have many good reasons to consider the prospects for investment and profits bleak, and to blame the welfare state, which imposes social security taxes and a great variety of regulations on them, for reducing profitability even further? Isn't it true that the power position of unions, which in turn is based on rights they have won through industrial relations, collective bar-gaining and other laws, is great enough as to make an increasing number of industrial producers unprofitable or to force them to seek investment opportunities abroad? And isn't it also true that capitalist firms will make investment (and hence employment) decisions according to criteria of expected profitability, and that they consequently will fail to invest when long-term profitability is considered unattractive by them, thus causing an aggregate relative decline in the production output of the economy?

No one would deny that there are causes of declining growth rates and capitalists' failure to invest which have nothing to do with the impact of the welfare state upon business, but which are rather to be looked for in inherent crisis tendencies of the capitalist economy such as overaccumula-tion, the business cycle or uncontrolled technical change. But even so, it still might make sense to alleviate the hardship imposed upon capital and therefore, by definition, upon the rest of society (within the confines of a capitalist society), by dropping some of the burdens and constraints of the welfare state. This, of course, is exactly what most proponents of this argument are suggesting as a practical consequence. But after all, as the fairly compelling logic of the argument continues, who benefits from the operation of a welfare state that undermines and eventually destroys the production system upon which it has to rely in order to make its own promises come true? Doesn't a kind of 'welfare' become merely nominal and worthless anyway if it punishes capital by a high burden of costs and hence everyone else by inflation, unemployment or both? In my view, the valuable insight to be gained from the type of analysis I have just described is this: the welfare state, rather than being a separate and autonomous source of well-being which provides incomes and services as citizen rights, is itself highly dependent upon the prosperity and continued profitability of the economy. While being designed to be a cure to some ills of capitalist accumulation, the nature of the illness is such that it may force the patient to refrain from using the cure.

A conceivable objection to the above argument would be that capitalists and conservative political elites exaggerate the harm imposed upon them by the welfare state arrangements. To be sure, in the political game they have good tactical reasons to make the welfare state burden appear more intolerable than it really is. The question boils down then to what we mean, and how we measure 'reality' in this context. In answering this question we must remember that the power position of private investors includes the power to *define* reality. That is to say, whatever they *consider* an intolerable burden *is* an intolerable burden which will *in fact* lead to a declining propensity to invest, at least as long as they can expect to effectively reduce welfare-state-related costs by applying such economic sanctions. The debate about whether or not the welfare state is 'really' squeezing profits is thus purely academic because investors are in a position to *create* the reality and the effects of 'profit squeeze'.

The second major argument of the conservative analysis postulates that the effect of the welfare state is a disincentive to work. 'Labour does not work!' was one of the slogans in the campaign that brought Mrs Thatcher into power. But again, the analytical content of the argument must be carefully separated from the political uses to which it is put. And again, this analytical argument can, often contrary to the intention of its proponents, be read in a way that does make a lot of empirical sense. For instance, there is little doubt that elaborate labour protection legislation puts workers in a position to resist practices of exploitation that would be applied, as a rule, in the absence of such regulations. Powerful and recognized unions can in fact obtain wage increases in excess of productivity increases. And extensive social security provisions make it easier, at least for some workers for some of the time, to avoid undesirable jobs. Large-scale unemployment insurance covering most of the working population makes unemployment less undesirable for many workers and thus partially obstructs the reserve army mechanism. In sum, the welfare state has made the exploitation of labour more complicated and less predictable. On the other hand, as the welfare state imposes regulations and rights upon the labour-capital exchange that goes on in production, while leaving the authority structure and the property relations of production untouched, it is hardly surprising to see that the workers are not, as a rule, intrinsically motivated to work as productively as they possibly can. In other words, the welfare state maintains the control of capital over production, and thus the basic source of industrial and class conflict between labour and capital; but it by no means establishes anything resembling 'workers' control'. At the same time, it strengthens workers' potential for resistance against capital's control, the net effect being that an unchanged conflict is fought out with means that have changed in favour of labour. Exploitative production relations coexist with expanded possibilities to resist, escape and mitigate exploitation. While the *reason* for struggle remained unchanged, the *means* of struggle increased for the workers. It is not surprising to see that this condition undermines the work ethic, or at least requires more costly and less reliable strategies to enforce such ethic.

My point so far has been that the two key arguments of the liberal-conservative analysis are valid to a large extent, contrary to what critics from the left have often argued. The basic fault in this analysis has less to do with what it explicitly states than with what it leaves out of its consideration. Every worthwhile political theory has to answer two questions: first, what is the desirable form of the organization of society and state, and how can we demonstrate that it is at all workable, i.e. consistent with our basic normative and factual assumptions about social life? This is the problem of defining a consistent *model* or goal of transformation. Second, how do we get there? This is the problem of identifying the dynamic forces and *strategies* that could bring about the transformation.

The conservative analysis of the welfare state fails on both counts. To start with the latter problem, it is extremely hard today in Western Europe to conceive of a promising political strategy that would aim at even partially eliminating the established institutional components of the welfare state, to say nothing about its wholesale abolition. That is to say, the welfare state has, in a certain sense, become an irreversible structure, the abolition of which would require nothing less than the abolition of political democracy and the unions, as well as fundamental changes in the party system. A political force that could bring about such dramatic changes is nowhere visible as a significant factor (right-wing middle-class populist movements that occasionally spring up in some countries notwithstanding). Moreover, political opinion research has shown that the fiercest advocates of *laissez-faire* capitalism and economic individualism show marked differences between their *general* ideological outlook and their willingness to have *special* transfers, subsidies and social security schemes abandoned from which they *personally* derive benefits. Thus, in the absence of a powerful ideological and organizational undercurrent in Western politics (such as a neo-fascist or authoritarian one), the vision of overcoming the welfare state and resurrecting a 'healthy' market economy is not much more than the politically impotent daydream of some ideologues of the old middle class. This class is nowhere strong enough to effect, as the examples of Mrs Thatcher and Ronald Reagan demonstrate, more than marginal alterations to an institutional scheme that they had to accept as given when taking office.

Even more significant, however, is the second failure of the conservative analysis, its failure to demonstrate that advanced capitalism *minus* the welfare state would actually be a workable model. The reasons why it is not, and consequently why the neo-*laissez-faire* ideology would be a very dangerous cure, *if* it could be administered, are fairly obvious. In the absence of large-scale state-subsidized housing, public education and health services, and extensive compulsory social security schemes, the working of an industrial economy would be inconceivable. Given the conditions and requirements of urbanization, large-scale concentration of labour power in industrial production plants, rapid technical, economic and regional change, the reduced ability of the family to cope with the difficulties of life in industrial society, the securalization of the moral order, and the quantitative reduction and growing dependence of the propertied middle classes, all of which are well known characteristics of capitalist social structures, the sudden disappearance of the welfare state would leave the system in a state of exploding conflict and anarchy. The embarrassing secret of the welfare state is that, while its impact upon capitalist accumulation may well become destructive (as the conservative analysis so emphatically demonstrates), its abolition would be plainly disruptive (a fact that is systematically ignored by the conservative critics). The contradiction is that while capitalism cannot coexist *with* the welfare state, neither can it exist *without* the welfare state. This is exactly the condition to which we refer when using the concept 'contradiction'. The flaw of the conservative analysis is in the one-sided emphasis it puts on the first side of this contradiction, and its silence about the second one.

This basic contradiction of the capitalist welfare state could of course be thought to be a mere dilemma which then would be solved or managed by a circumspect balancing of the two components. This, however, would presuppose two things, both of which are highly uncertain: first, that there *is* something like an 'optimum point' at which the order-maintaining functions of the welfare state are preserved while its disruptive effects are avoided; and second, if so, that political procedures and administrative practices will be sufficiently 'rational' to accomplish this precarious balance. Before I consider the prospects for this solution, let me first summarize some elements of the contending socialist critique of the welfare state.

The Critique from the Socialist Left

Although it would be nonsensical to deny that the struggle for labour protection legislation, expanded social services, social security and union recognition which has been led by the working-class movement for over a century now, and which has brought substantial improvements to the living conditions of most wage earners, the socialist critique of the welfare state is nevertheless a fundamental one. It can be summarized in three points which we will consider in turn: the welfare state is said to be (1) ineffective and inefficient, (2) repressive and (3) conditioning a false ideological understanding of social and political reality within the working class. In sum, it is a device to stabilize rather than a step in the transformation of capitalist society.

In spite of the undeniable gains in the living conditions of wage earners, the institutional structure of the welfare state has done little or nothing to alter the income distribution between the two principal classes of labour and capital. The huge machinery of redistribution does not work in a vertical direction but in a horizontal direction, namely *within* the class of wage earners. A further aspect of its ineffectiveness is that the welfare state does not *eliminate the causes* of individual contingencies and needs (such as work-related diseases, the disorganization of cities by the capitalist real estate market, the obsolescence of skills, unemployment, etc.) but *compensates for* some of the *consequences* of such events (by the provision of health services and health insurance, housing subsidies, training and retraining facilities, unemployment benefits and the like). Generally speaking, the kind of social intervention most typical of the welfare state is always 'too late', and hence its *ex post facto* measures are more costly and less effective than a more 'causal' type of intervention would allow them to be. This is a generally recognized dilemma of social policy making, the standard answer to which is the recommendation to adopt more 'preventive' strategies. It is also recognized that effective prevention would mean interference with the prerogatives of investors and management, i.e. the sphere of the market and private property which the welfare state has only very limited legal and *de facto* powers to regulate.

A further argument pointing to the ineffectiveness of the welfare state emphasizes the constant threat to which social policies and social services are exposed due to the fiscal crisis of the state, which in turn is a reflection of both cyclical and structural discontinuities of the process of accumulation. All West European countries [. . .] experienced a sharp economic recession in the mid-1970s, and we know of many examples of social policy expenditure cuts in response to the fiscal consequences of this recession. But even if the absolute and relative rise of social policy expenditures continues uninterrupted as a percentage of GNP, it is by no means certain, as Ian Gough and others before him have argued, that increases in the expenditures are paralleled by increases in real 'welfare'. The dual fallacy, known in technical literature as the 'spending service cliché', is this: first, a marginal increase in expenditures must not necessarily correspond to a marginal increment in the 'output' of the welfare state apparatus; it may well be used up in feeding the bureaucratic machinery itself. Second, even if the output (say of health services) *is* increased, a still larger increase in the level of risks and needs (or a qualitative change of these) may occur on the part of the clients or recipients of such services, so as to make the net effect negative.

The bureaucratic and professional form through which the welfare state dispenses its services is increasingly seen to be a source of its own inefficiency. Bureaucracies absorb more resources and provide less services than other democratic and decentralized structures could. The reason why the bureaucratic form of administering social services is maintained in spite of its inefficiency and ineffectiveness must therefore have to do with the social control function exercised by centralized welfare bureaucracies. This analysis leads to the critique of the *repressiveness* of the welfare state, its social control aspect. Such repressiveness, in the view of the critics, is indicated by the fact that in order to qualify for the benefits and services of the welfare state, the client must not only prove his or her 'need', but must also be a 'deserving' client, that is, one who complies to the dominant economic, political and cultural standards and norms of the society. The heavier the needs, the stricter these requirements tend to be defined. Only if, for instance, the unemployed are willing to keep themselves available for any alternative employment (often considerably inferior to the job they have lost) that is made available to them by employment agencies, are they entitled to unemployment benefits; and the claim for welfare payments to the poor is everywhere made conditional upon their conformity to standards of behaviour which the better-to-do strata of the population are perfectly free to violate. In these and other cases, the welfare state can be looked upon as an exchange transaction in which material benefits for the needy are traded for their submissive recognition of the 'moral order' of the society which generates such need. One important precondition for obtaining the services of the welfare state is the ability of the individual to comply with the routines and requirements of welfare bureaucracies and service organizations, an ability which is often inversely correlated to need itself.

A third major aspect of the socialist critique of the welfare state is its *politico-ideological* control function. The welfare state is seen not only as the source of benefits and services, but at the same time the source of false conceptions about historical realities which have damaging effects on working-class consciousness, organization and struggle. The welfare state creates the false image of two separated spheres of working-class life. On the one side is the sphere of work, the economy, production and 'primary' income distribution. On the other is the sphere of citizenship, the state, reproduction and 'secondary' distribution. This division of the socio-political world obscures the causal and functional links that exist between the two, and thus prevents the formation of a political understanding of society as a coherent totality to be changed. That is to say, the structural arrangements of the welfare state tend to make people ignore or forget that the needs and contingencies which the welfare state responds to are themselves constituted, directly or indirectly, in the sphere of work and production. The welfare state itself is materially and institutionally constrained by the dynamics of the sphere of production, and a reliable conception of social security does therefore presuppose not only the expansion of citizen rights, but of workers' rights in the process of production. Contrary to such insights, which are part of the analytical starting-points of any conceivable socialist strategy of societal transformation, the inherent symbolic indoctrination of the welfare state suggests the ideas of class co-operation, the disjunction of economic and political struggles, and an ill-based confidence in an ever continuing cycle of economic growth and social security.

The Welfare State and Political Change

What emerges from this discussion of the analysis of the welfare state by the right and the left are three points on which the liberal conservative and the socialist critic exhibit somewhat surprising parallels.

First, contrary to the ideological consensus that flourished in some of the most advanced welfare states throughout the 1950s and 1960s, the welfare state is no longer believed to be the promising and permanently valid answer to the problems of the socio-political order of advanced capitalist economies. Critics in both camps have become more vociferous and fundamental in their negative appraisal of welfare state arrangements. Second, neither of the two approaches to the welfare state could or would be prepared, in the best interests of their respective clientele, to abandon the welfare state, as it performs essential and indispensable functions both for the accumulation process as well as for the social and economic well-being of the working class. Third, while there is, on the conservative side, neither a consistent theory nor a realistic strategy about the social order of a non-welfare state (as I have argued before), it is evident that the situation is not much better on the left where one could possibly speak of a consistent theory of socialism, but certainly not of an agreed upon and realistic strategy for its construction. In the absence of the latter, the welfare state remains a theoretically contested, though in reality firmly entrenched fact, of the social order of advanced capitalist societies. In short, it appears that the welfare state, while being contested both from the right and the left, will not be easily replaced by a conservative or progressive alternative.

[. . .]

Note

From *Critical Social Policy*, 2, 2, 1982, pp. 7–14, copyright © *Journal of Critical Social Policy* 1982, by permission of the author and Sage Publications, conveyed through Copyright Clearance Center.

Responses from the Right

The Meaning of the Welfare State

Friedrich von Hayek

[. . .]

Unlike socialism, the conception of the welfare state has no precise meaning. The phrase is sometimes used to describe any state that 'concerns' itself in any manner with problems other than those of the maintenance of law and order. But, though a few theorists have demanded that the activities of government should be limited to the maintenance of law and order, such a stand cannot be justified by the principle of liberty. Only the coercive measures of government need be strictly limited. [. . .] There is undeniably a wide field for non-coercive activities of government and [. . .] a clear need for financing them by taxation.

Indeed, no government in modern times has ever confined itself to the 'individualist minimum' which has occasionally been described,[1] nor has such confinement of governmental activity been advocated by the 'orthodox' classical economists.[2] All modern governments have made provision for the indigent, unfortunate and disabled and have concerned themselves with questions of health and the dissemination of knowledge. There is no reason why the volume of these pure service activities should not increase with the general growth of wealth. There are common needs that can be satisfied only by collective action and which can be thus provided for without restricting individual liberty. It can hardly be denied that, as we grow richer, that minimum of sustenance which the community has always provided for those not able to look after themselves, and which can be provided outside the market, will gradually rise, or that government may, usefully and without doing any harm, assist or even lead in such endeavours. There is little reason why the government should not also play some role, or even take the initiative, in such areas as social insurance and education, or temporarily subsidize certain experimental developments. Our problem here is not so much the aims as the methods of government action.

References are often made to those modest and innocent aims of governmental activity to show how unreasonable is any opposition to the welfare state as such. But, once the rigid position that government should not concern itself at all with such matters is abandoned – a position which is defensible but has little to do with freedom – the defenders of liberty commonly discover that the programme of the welfare state comprises a great deal more that is represented as equally legitimate and unobjectionable. If, for instance, they admit that they have no objection to pure-food laws, this is taken to imply that they should not object to any government activity directed toward a desirable end. Those who attempt to delimit the functions of government in terms of aims rather than methods thus regularly find themselves in the position of having to oppose state action which appears to have only desirable consequences or of having to admit that they have no general rule on which to base their objections to measures which, though effective for particular purposes, would in their aggregate effect destroy a free society. Though the position that the state should have nothing to do with matters not related to the maintenance of law and order may seem logical so long as we think of the state solely as a coercive apparatus, we must recognize that, as a service agency, it may assist without harm in the achievement of desirable aims which perhaps could not be achieved otherwise. The reason why many of the new welfare activities of government are a threat to freedom, then, is that, though they are presented as mere service activities, they really constitute an exercise of the coercive powers of government and rest on its claiming exclusive rights in certain fields.

The current situation has greatly altered the task of the defender of liberty and made it much more difficult. So long as the danger came from socialism of the frankly collectivist kind, it was possible to argue that the tenets of the socialists were simply false: that socialism would not achieve what the socialists wanted and that it would produce other consequences which they would not like. We cannot argue similarly against the welfare state, for this term does not designate a definite system. What goes under that name is a conglomerate of so many diverse and even contradictory elements that, while some of them may make a free society more attractive, others are incompatible with it or may at least constitute potential threats to its existence.

We shall see that some of the aims of the welfare state can be realized without detriment to individual liberty, though not necessarily by the methods which seem the most obvious and are therefore most popular; that others can be similarly achieved to a certain extent, though only at a cost much greater than people imagine or would be willing to bear, or only slowly and gradually as wealth increases; and that, finally, there are others – and they are those particularly dear to the hearts of the socialists – that cannot be realized in a society that wants to preserve personal freedom.

There are all kinds of public amenities which it may be in the interest of all members of the community to provide by common effort, such as parks and museums, theatres and facilities for sports – though there are strong reasons why they should be provided by local rather than national authorities. There is then the important issue of security, of protection against risks common to all, where government can often either reduce these risks or assist people to provide against them. Here, however, an important distinction has to be drawn between two conceptions of security: a limited security which can be achieved for all and which is, therefore, no privilege, and absolute security, which in a free society cannot be achieved for all. The first of these is security against severe physical privation, the assurance of a given minimum of sustenance for all; and the second is the assurance of a given standard of life, which is determined by comparing the standard enjoyed by a person or a group with that of others. The distinction, then, is that between the security of an equal minimum income for all and the security of a particular income that a person is thought to deserve. The latter is closely related to the third main ambition that inspires the welfare state: the desire to use the powers of government to ensure a more even or more just distribution of goods. Insofar as this means that the coercive powers of government are to be used to ensure that particular people get particular things, it requires a kind of discrimination between, and an unequal treatment of, different people which is irreconcilable with a free society. This is the kind of welfare state that aims at 'social justice' and becomes 'primarily a redistributor of income'. It is bound to lead back to socialism and its coercive and essentially arbitrary methods.

Though *some* of the aims of the welfare state can be achieved *only* by methods inimical to liberty, *all* its aims *may* be pursued by such methods. The chief danger today is that, once an aim of government is accepted as legitimate, it is then assumed that even means contrary to the principles of freedom may be legitimately employed. The unfortunate fact is that, in the majority of fields, the most effective, certain and speedy way of reaching a given end will seem to be to direct all available resources towards the now visible solution. To the ambitious and impatient reformer, filled with indignation at a particular evil, nothing short of the complete abolition of that evil by the quickest and most direct means will seem adequate. If every person now suffering from unemployment, ill health or inadequate provision for [. . .] old age is at once to be relieved of his [or her] cares, nothing short of an all-comprehensive and compulsory scheme will suffice. But if, in our impatience to solve such problems immediately, we give government exclusive and monopolistic powers, we may find that we have been short-sighted. If the quickest way to a now visible solution becomes the only permissible one and all alternative experimentation is precluded, and if what now seems the best method of satisfying a need is made the sole starting-point for all future development, we may perhaps reach our present goal sooner, but we shall probably at the same time prevent the emergence of more effective alternative solutions. It is often those who are most anxious to use our existing knowledge and powers to the full that do most to impair the future growth of knowledge by the methods they use. The controlled single-channel development towards which impatience and administrative convenience have frequently inclined the reformer and which, especially in the field of social insurance, has become characteristic of the modern welfare state may well become the chief obstacle to future improvement.

If government wants not merely to facilitate the attainment of certain standards by the individuals but to make certain that everybody attains them it can do so only by depriving individuals of any choice in the matter. Thus the welfare state becomes a household state in which a paternalistic power controls most of the income of the community and allocates it to individuals in the forms and quantities which it thinks they need or deserve.

In many fields persuasive arguments based on considerations of efficiency and economy can be advanced in favour of the state's taking sole charge of a particular service; but when the state does so, the result is usually not only that those advantages soon prove illusory but that the character of the services becomes entirely different from that which they would have had if they had been provided by competing agencies. If, instead of administering limited resources put under its control for a specific service, government uses its coercive powers to ensure that men are given what some expert thinks they need; if people thus can no longer exercise any choice in some of the most important matters of their lives, such as health, employment, housing and provision for old age, but must accept the decisions made for them by appointed authority on the basis of its evaluation of their need; if certain services become the exclusive domain of the state, and whole professions – be it medicine, education or insurance – come to exist only as unitary bureaucratic hierarchies, it will no longer be competitive experimentation but solely the decisions of authority that will determine what men shall get.[3]

The same reasons that generally make the impatient reformer wish to organize such services in the form of government monopolies lead him also to believe that the authorities in charge should be given wide discretionary powers over the individual. If the objective were merely to improve opportunities for all by supplying certain specific services according to a rule, this could be attained on essentially business lines. But we could then never be sure that the results for all individuals would be precisely what we wanted. If each individual is to be affected in some particular way, nothing short of the individualizing, paternalistic treatment by a discretionary authority with powers of discriminating between persons will do.

It is sheer illusion to think that when certain needs of the citizen have become the exclusive concern of a single bureaucratic machine, democratic control of that machine can then effectively guard the liberty of the citizen. So far as the preservation of personal liberty is concerned, the division of labour between a legislature which merely says that this or that should be done[4] and an administrative apparatus which is given exclusive power to carry out these instructions is the most dangerous arrangement possible. All experience confirms what *is* clear enough from American as

> well as from English experience, that the zeal of the administrative agencies to achieve the immediate ends they see before them leads them to see their function out of focus and to assume that constitutional limitations and guaranteed individual rights must give way before their zealous efforts to achieve what they see as a paramount purpose of government.[5]

It would scarcely be an exaggeration to say that the greatest danger to liberty today comes from the men who are most needed and most powerful in modern government, namely, the efficient expert administrators exclusively concerned with what they regard as the public good. Though theorists may still talk about the democratic control of these activities, all who have direct experience in this matter agree that (as one [. . .] English writer put it) 'if the Minister's control . . . has become a myth, the control of Parliament is and always has been the merest fairy tale'.[6] It is inevitable that this sort of administration of the welfare of the people should become a self-willed and uncontrollable apparatus before which the individual is helpless, and which becomes increasingly invested with all the *mystique* of sovereign authority – the *Hoheitsverwaltung* or *Herrschaftstaat* of the German tradition that used to be so unfamiliar to Anglo-Saxons that the strange term 'hegemonic'[7] had to be coined to render its meaning.

Notes

From F. A. Hayek, *The Constitution of Liberty*, London, Routledge, and Chicago, University of Chicago Press, 1959, pp. 257–62, by permission of Taylor & Francis Books UK and the University of Chicago Press.

1   Cf., e.g., Henry Sidgwick, *The Elements of Politics*, London, 1891, ch. 4.

2   See on this particularly Lionel Robbins, *The Theory of Economic Policy*, London, 1952.

3   Cf. J. S. Mill, *On Liberty*, ed. R. B. McCallum, Oxford, 1946, pp. 99–100: 'If the roads, the railways, the banks, the insurance offices, the great joint stock companies, the universities, and the public charities, were all of them branches of the government; if, in addition, the municipal corporations and local boards, with all that now devolves on them, became departments of the central administration; if the employees of all these different enterprises were appointed and paid by the government, and looked to the government for every rise in life; not all the freedom of the press and popular constitution of the legislature would make this or any other country free otherwise than in name. And the evil would be greater, the more efficiently and scientifically the administrative machinery was constructed – the more skilful the arrangements for obtaining the best qualified hands and heads with which to work it.'

4   Cf. T. H. Marshall, *Citizenship and Social Class*, Cambridge, 1958, p. 59: 'So we find that legislation . . . acquires more and more the character of a declaration of policy that it is hoped to put into effect some day.'

5   Roscoe Pound, 'The Rise of the Service State and its Consequence', in *The Welfare State and the National Welfare*, ed. S. Glueck, Cambridge, MA, 1952, p. 220.

6   P. Wiles, 'Property and Equality', in *The Unservile State*, ed. G. Watson, London, 1957, p. 107.

7   See L. von Mises, *Human Action*, New Haven, 1949, pp. 196ff.

The Two Wars against Poverty

Charles Murray

[. . .]

When news reports cite percentages of 'people living in poverty', they are drawing from the official definition of the 'poverty line' established in 1964 by a task force in the Social Security Administration. The poverty line is, in effect, set at three times the cost of an adequate diet, and is adjusted for inflation, a variety of family characteristics and one's location (rural or non-rural).

This measure has been attacked as niggardly by some and as overly generous by others. Almost everyone agrees that it fails to capture the important differences in the quality of life between a family living at the poverty line in the South Bronx, for example, and a family with the same income that lives in a less punishing environment. But this measure of poverty has its merits nonetheless. It is widely known, it takes family size and inflation into account, and it provides a consistent measure for examining income over time. I will use it to discuss the history of three different 'types' of poverty: official poverty, net poverty and latent poverty [. . .].

The most widely used measure of poverty is the percentage of people with cash incomes that fall beneath the poverty line before taxes, but after taking cash income transfers from government into account. We shall call it *official poverty* because it is the measure reported by the Bureau of the Census.

Conventional wisdom has it that, at least according to this one measure, the 1960s and 1970s brought economic progress for the poor. The most widely shared view of recent events is that the United States entered the 1960s with a large population that had been bypassed during the prosperity of the Eisenhower years. The rich and the middle class gained but the poor did not. Then, after fits and starts during the Kennedy years, came the explosion in the number and size of social programmes under Johnson. The programmes were perhaps too ambitious, it is widely conceded, and perhaps some of the efforts were misdirected, but at least they put a big dent in the poverty problem; this can be seen, it is said, in the large reduction in poverty that occurred during LBJ's administration and thereafter. The Great Society reforms were seen to have produced results that Eisenhower's 'trickle-down' economics had not.

The essential assertion of this view is that poverty decreased during the War on Poverty and had not been decreasing as rapidly before this period. It is a simple assertion, for which the data are a matter of historical record, and it is only half right.

Poverty did indeed fall during the five Johnson years, from 18 per cent of the population in 1964 to 13 per cent in 1968, his last year in office. Yet this was scarcely an unprecedented achievement. Between 1949 and 1952, poverty had already begun to fall from 33 to 28 per cent. Under Eisenhower it fell to 22 per cent. Under Kennedy and Johnson it dropped to 18 per cent by 1964. In short, the size of the official 'impoverished' population dropped by twenty percentage points in twenty years, of which the five Johnson years accounted for precisely their fair share, five points.[1]

Then, after two decades of reasonably steady progress, improvement slowed in the late 1960s and stopped altogether in the 1970s. A higher percentage of the American population was poor in 1980, in terms of cash income, than at any time since 1968. The percentage dipped as low as 11.1 per cent in 1973, but by 1980 it stood at 13 per cent and was heading upward.

When this history of the official poverty level is placed alongside the history of social welfare expenditures, a paradox appears. Social welfare expenditures had been increasing at a steady rate through the Eisenhower, Kennedy and early Johnson years. But it was not until the budgets of 1967 and 1968 that the Johnson programmes were reaching enough people to have a marked impact on the budget; it was then that social welfare expenditures started to take off. So just at the time when the reforms of the mid-1960s were being implemented, progress in reducing poverty began grinding to a halt!

The paradox is even more pronounced when we remember what it is we are measuring. If the measure were of chronic joblessness, for example, the flattening curve [. . .] would be understandable: it often is harder to fix the last 10 per cent of a problem than the first 90 per cent. But in this case, 'official poverty' is simply a measure of cash income *after* taking government transfers into account. To eliminate official poverty, all we need do is mail enough cheques with enough money to enough people. Starting in the late 1960s, the number of cheques, the size of the cheques and the number of beneficiaries all began to increase. Even if we ignore increased in-kind expenditures such as housing, food stamps and medical care (which are not included in this definition), and discount administrative costs and the effects of inflation, the federal government increased its real cash-benefit payments for income maintenance programmes by more than two-thirds during the 1970s.

Furthermore, the anti-poverty programmes of the 1970s had a much smaller target population than those of earlier, smaller budgets. In 1950 there were an estimated 46 million people living beneath the poverty line (as it was subsequently defined); in 1960 there were 40 million, and in 1970 only 25 million. Given these conditions – more money and fewer people – progress begun during the 1950s and 1960s should have accelerated in the 1970s instead of slowing, stopping and then reversing.

Net Poverty

The official poverty statistic is based only on cash income. In-kind assistance – food programmes, housing, medical care – is not included. Yet this assistance has been the fastest-growing component of the social welfare budget, rising from $2.2 billion in 1965 to $72.5 billion in 1980. If the dollar value of these benefits is computed and added to cash income, this new measure may be called *net poverty*: the percentage of the population remaining beneath the poverty level after all resources – cash and in-kind, earned and unearned – are taken into account.[2]

In 1950, in-kind transfers were quite small, so the percentage of official poor (30 per cent) was nearly identical to the percentage of net poor. This situation continued into the early 1960s as net poverty decreased at roughly the same rate as official poverty. By 1968, the gap between official poverty (12.8 per cent) and net poverty (10.1 per cent) was quite small.

Unlike changes in official poverty, however, large decreases in net poverty continued into the early 1970s. Then, from 1972 until 1980, the trendline flattened, just as that for official poverty had a few years earlier. In 1980, net poverty stood at 6.1 per cent of the population, compared with 6.2 per cent in 1972, despite the fact that expenditures on in-kind assistance had tripled (in constant dollars) during the 1970s.

The concept of net poverty is ambiguous. Taken by itself, 6.1 per cent represents a near victory over poverty; it is a very small proportion of the population. But a citizen who lives in a black or Hispanic ghetto, for example, may be forgiven for arguing that poverty has not come within 6.1 percentage points of vanishing. We must consider what it really means to live at or near the poverty level through in-kind support.

It means, to begin with, living in housing projects or other subsidized housing. Given their cost, most of these units ought to provide decent, comfortable housing, but in practice public housing is among the most vandalized, crime-ridden and least livable housing in the country. It means relying on food stamps. In theory, food stamps can purchase the foods necessary for a nutritious diet, but in practice they can be misused in other ways. It also means paying for medical care through Medicaid or Medicare, which have concrete value only if the recipient is sick.

In short, having the resources for a life that meets basic standards of decency is not the same as actually living such an existence. Whether this is the fault of the welfare system or the recipient is not at issue; it is simply a fact that must be kept in mind when interpreting the small, encouraging figure of 6.1 per cent.

But the economic point remains: as of 1980, the many overlapping cash and in-kind benefit programmes made it possible for almost anyone to place themselves above the official poverty level. If the ultimate criterion of social welfare policy is eliminating net poverty, the War on Poverty has very nearly been won.

Latent Poverty

Of course, eliminating net poverty is not the ultimate criterion. Lyndon Johnson undertook the War on Poverty to end the dole, to enable people to maintain a decent standard of living by their own efforts. As he signed the initial anti-poverty bill he sounded the theme that formed the basis of the consensus for the Great Society:

> We are not content to accept endless growth of relief or welfare rolls. We want to offer the forgotten fifth of our population opportunity and not doles. . . . The days of the dole in our country are numbered.[3]

Johnson was articulating a deeply shared understanding among Americans as to how the welfare system is supposed to work – 'a hand, not a handout' was the slogan. Throughout American history, the economic independence of the individual and the family has been the chief distinguishing characteristic of good citizenship.

To measure progress along these lines we must calculate yet a third statistic. The poverty statistic with which I began, the one used by the government in its analyses, is cash income *after* the cash transfers from the government have been counted. Then I added the value of the non-cash, in-kind transfers in order to measure net poverty. Now I must ask: what is the number of poor before the cash and in-kind transfers are taken into account? How many people *would be* poor if it were not for government help? These may be called the *latent poor*. For practical purposes, they are the dependent population, those who were to be made independent as we eliminated the dole.

Latent poverty decreased during the 1950s. We do not know the precise level of decline, because 1965 is the first year for which the number of latent poor [was] calculated.[4] But we do know that the number of latent poor (pre-transfer poor) can be no smaller than the number of post-transfer poor; therefore, since the number of post-transfer poor stood at 30 per cent of the population in 1950, the percentage of latent poor had to have been somewhat larger (a conservative estimate is 32 per cent). As of 1965, the latent poor were 21 per cent of the population – a drop of about one-third. Put another way, dependency decreased during the years 1950–65. Increasing numbers of people were able to make a living that put them above the poverty level and progress was being made on the long-range goal of eliminating the dole.

The proportion of latent poor continued to drop through 1968, when the percentage was calculated at 18.2, but this [. . .] proved to be the limit of our success in the war against economic dependence. At some point during 1968–9, progress stopped; the percentage of latent poor then started to grow. It was 19 per cent by 1972, 21 per cent by 1976, and 22 per cent by 1980.[5] Once again, as in the case of official poverty, the shift in the trendline coincided with the advent of the programmes that were to eliminate poverty.

Again, how could it be that progress against official poverty and net poverty slowed or stopped when so much more money was being spent for cash and in-kind transfers? The data on latent poverty provide one of the most important answers: because latent poverty was increasing, it took more and more money in transfers just to keep the percentage of post-transfer poor stable. The social welfare system fell into the classic trap of having to run faster and faster to stay in the same place. The extremely large increases in social welfare spending during the 1970s were papering over the increase in latent poverty.

The three measures of poverty – official poverty, net poverty and latent poverty – reveal a pattern from 1950 to 1980 that has important implications for the American welfare state. For example, it explains a major element in the budget crisis. As of 1980, roughly the same proportion of people remained above the poverty line through their own earned incomes as did in the early 1960s. But in the early 1960s, our legislated spending obligations to those who earned less than that amount were comparatively small. Whether or not one approves of the spending obligations taken on since then, they cannot be sustained indefinitely in the face of increasing latent poverty. Latent poverty must be turned around, or the obligations must be slashed, or both.

Rising Tide, Sinking Ships

The poverty trendlines [. . .] are not widely publicized. Because it has not been recognized that the implementation of the Great Society reforms coincided with an end to progress in reducing poverty, there has been no debate over why this should be the case.

The best place to begin the debate is to examine the common view that the bright hopes of the 1960s dimmed in the 1970s due to a slowdown in the economy. According to this view, inflation and dislocations brought on by the Vietnam War, along with the revolution in energy prices, made the economy go sour. As the expansionist environment of the 1960s vanished, strategies and programmes of the War on Poverty had to be put aside. It is good that the entitlements and income transfer programmes were in place, runs this line of argument, or else the troubles in the economy would have been even more devastating on the poor.

What, if anything, do the data suggest about the merits of this economic explanation? As in the discussion of poverty, I must start with the simplest, most widely used measure of the state of the economy, growth in the GNP, and examine its relation to changes in the number of people living in poverty. The answer – perhaps surprisingly to those who have ridiculed 'trickle-down' as a way to help the poor – is that changes in GNP have a very strong inverse relation to changes in poverty. As GNP increases, poverty decreases. (The simple correlation coefficient for the period 1950–80 is –.69.[6]) The effects of economic growth did indeed trickle down to the lowest economic levels of the society. Economic growth during the 1950s and 1960s was strong, during the 1970s it was weak – and progress in reducing poverty ceased.

So it can be said that the fortunes of the economy explain recent trends in poverty. But the flip side of this finding is that social welfare expenditures did *not* have an effect on poverty. *Once the effects of GNP are taken into account, increases in social welfare spending do not account for reductions in poverty [since the 1950s].* The same analysis that supports the economic explanation for the failure in the 1970s gives scant support to remedies that would boost social welfare spending [. . .].

Conservatives generally recognize the role of economic growth in reducing poverty, but some feel this is not a sufficient explanation for the failures of the 1970s. It is not just that the social welfare reforms were ineffective in reducing poverty, they argue, but that the reforms actually made matters worse by emasculating the work ethic and creating 'work disincentives'. As people became less inclined to take low-paying jobs, hold onto them, and use them to get out of poverty, they became dependent on government assistance. The academic treatment of poverty has generally dismissed this conservative explanation out of hand. It has understandably been mistaken for curmudgeonly, mean-spirited and occasionally racist rhetoric. But the trendline for latent poverty – the key indicator of how people are doing without government help – offers a solid reason for concluding that the Great Society reforms exacerbated many of the conditions they sought to alleviate.

It is important to emphasize that the trend in latent poverty did not reverse direction when the economy went bad; it did not even wait until the official poverty and net poverty figures stabilized. Latent poverty started to increase while the other two measures of poverty were still going down. Most strikingly, progress on latent poverty stopped in 1968 while the economy was operating at full capacity (unemployment stood at 3.5 per cent in 1968–9, the lowest rate since the Korean War).

Welfare and Labour-Force Participation

The second half of the 1960s was a watershed in other ways as well. A number of social indicators began showing strange and unanticipated shifts during those years, and the onset of these changes had no discernible relation to the health of the economy. Together, the evidence is sufficiently provocative to make the conservative interpretation worth looking into.

One such indicator is *participation in the labour force*. By definition, participation in the civilian labour force means either being employed or intending to work, given the opportunity. Among the poor, participation in the labour force 'should' be very high, approaching 100 per cent, for able-bodied adults without childcare responsibilities. Conservatives argue that such participation has dropped because welfare benefits have become more extensive and more easily available. The statistics on labour-force participation – a standard measure calculated by the Bureau of Labor Statistics – are readily available, and they conform quite well to conservative expectations.

Consider the record of two populations of immediate comparative interest: black males, who are disproportionately poor relative to the entire population, and white males, who are disproportionately well off. In 1948 (comparable data for 1950 are not available), the participation rate for both groups was 87 per cent. This equivalence – one of the very few social or economic measures on which black males could claim parity with whites in the 1950s – continued throughout the decade and into the early 1960s. As late as 1965, only a percentage point separated the two groups. But by 1968, a gap of 3.4 percentage points in participation had opened up between black males and white males. By 1972, the gap was 5.9 percentage points. In 1980, 70.5 per cent of black males participated in the labour force compared with 78.6 per cent of white males; the gap had grown to 8.1 percentage points. To put it another way, during the period 1954–67, 1.4 black males dropped out of the labour force for every white male who dropped out; from 1968 to 1980, 3.6 black males dropped out for every white male who did.

The abrupt drop in the labour-force participation of black males cannot easily be linked to events in the economy at large. One of the most commonly cited popular explanations of why poor people drop out of the labour force is that they become discouraged – there are no jobs, so people quit looking. But the gap first opened up during the boom years of 1966–8, when unemployment was at a historic low. The 'discouraged worker' argument cannot be used to explain the drop-out rate during this period. Nor can the opposite argument be substituted: black males did not stop dropping out when the Vietnam boom cooled and unemployment rose. Whether unemployment was high or low, until 1967 black males behaved the same as whites; after 1967 they did not.

One may ask whether this is a racial phenomenon; it is nothing of the kind. Using the 1970 census data, participation for 1970 may be broken down by both race and economic status, and doing so reveals that the apparent racial difference is artificial. For males at comparable income levels, labour-force participation among black males was *higher* than among white males. The explanation of the gap is not race, but income. Starting in 1966, low-income males – white or black – started dropping out of the labour force. The only reason it looks as though blacks were dropping out at higher rates is that blacks are disproportionately poor. If trendlines are examined showing participation rates by income rather than race, the 1970 census data strongly suggest that middle- and upper-income males participated in the labour force at virtually unchanged rates since the 1950s, while the participation rate for low-income males decreased slowly until 1966, and plummeted thereafter.

This phenomenon needs explanation, for it was a fundamental change in economic behaviour – participation in the labour market itself. Once explanations based on unemployment fail, and once the racial discrepancy is shown to be artificial, the conservative hypothesis has considerable force. Without a doubt, *something* happened in the mid-1960s that changed the incentives for low-income workers to stay in the job market. The Great Society reforms constitute the biggest, most visible, most plausible candidate.

Welfare and Family Breakup (Revisited)

A second social indicator which links increases in latent poverty to the Great Society reforms is the decline in the intact husband–wife family unit, especially among blacks.

A racial difference in family composition has existed since statistics have been kept, but by the middle of this century the proportions for whites and blacks, while different, were stable. As of 1950, 88 per cent of white families consisted of husband–wife households, compared with 78 per cent of black families. Both figures had remained essentially unchanged since before the Second World War (the figures for 1940 were 86 and 77 per cent, respectively). In the early 1950s, the black proportion dipped slightly, then remained between 72 and 75 per cent until 1965. The figures for white families stayed in the 88 to 89 per cent range between 1958 and 1965, never varying by more than two-tenths of a percentage point from year to year.

The years 1966 and 1967 saw successive drops in the percentage of black husband–wife households, even though it remained in the 72–5 per cent range. Then, in a single year (1968), the percentage dropped to 69, the beginning of a steep slide that has not yet been arrested. By the end of 1980, the proportion of black husband–wife families had dropped to 54 per cent – a drop of 19 percentage points since 1965. The figure for whites dropped by four percentage points in the same period, from 89 to 85 per cent.

From a demographic perspective, a change of this magnitude is extraordinary, nearly unprecedented in the absence of war or some other profound social upheaval. Much is made of the social changes that swept America during the 1960s and 1970s, and discussions of the change in black family composition have discounted the phenomenon as a slightly exaggerated manifestation of this broader social transformation. But the data do not permit such an easy dismissal. In the rest of society the changes in family composition were comparatively modest.

As in the case of labour-force participation, we are witnessing a confusion between race and income, though not as severe. When husband–wife families are examined on the basis of income (using the 1970 census), the percentage of husband–wife families among blacks above the poverty level is found to be 82 per cent, very close to the overall rate for whites. This indicates that data based on income may be expected to show that the precipitous drop in intact families is concentrated among the low-income population, not exclusively (perhaps not even disproportionately) among blacks.

Why did low-income families start to disintegrate in the mid-1960s while higher-income families did not? As in the case of participation in the labour force, there is no obvious alternative to the conservatives' hypothesis: namely, during precisely this period, fundamental changes occurred in the philosophy, administration and magnitude of social welfare programmes for low-income families, and these changes altered – both directly and indirectly – the social risks and rewards, and the financial costs and benefits, of maintaining a husband–wife family. It should surprise no one that behaviour changed accordingly.

This hypothesis is not 'simplistic', as has been charged. It is plausible that the forces which changed welfare policy could have affected family composition even if welfare policy had not been changed. Those forces were surely various and complex. Still, these forces are not enough to explain the extraordinary change in family composition. If in the early

1960s one had foreseen the coming decade of sweeping civil rights legislation, an upsurge in black identity and pride, and a booming economy in which blacks had more opportunities than ever before, one would not have predicted massive family breakup as a result. The revolutionary change in black family composition went *against* the grain of many contemporaneous forces. Casual assertions that 'it was part of the times' are inadequate.

A Pyrrhic Victory?

The effect of the decline in labour-force participation, and of the breakup of the husband–wife family, were tragic and severe. In the case of the labour market, the nature of the effect is obvious: when low-income males drop out of the labour force and low-income females do not enter it, the size of the latent poor population will grow. This alone could explain why the proportion of latent poor increased even as the proportions of official poor and net poor were still declining.

The effects of family breakup are less obvious, but no less noteworthy. An analysis by the Bureau of the Census indicates that changes in family composition accounted for two million additional poor families in the 1970s.[7] For example, the analysis shows that if black family composition had remained the same as in 1971, the poverty rate for black families would have been 20 per cent in 1980 instead of 29 per cent. Other findings all lead to the same conclusion: the changes in family composition that started in the mid-1960s have raised poverty significantly above the levels that 'would have' prevailed otherwise. The Bureau's analysis actually *understates* the overall effect of the change in family composition on poverty – by 1971, the baseline for the analysis, much of the deterioration had already occurred.

These are some of the reasons behind the paradox of our failure to make progress against poverty in the 1970s despite the enormous increases in the amount of money that the government has spent to do so. There are other reasons as well – the large proportion of the social welfare budget spent on people above the poverty level being perhaps the most notable – but the preceding few will serve to convey a point that is too often missed in the debates over budget cuts in social welfare programmes. It is genuinely an open issue – intellectually as well as politically – whether we should be talking about spending cuts, or whether we should be considering an overhaul of the entire welfare system as conceived in the Great Society. If the War on Poverty is construed as having begun in 1950 instead of 1964, it may fairly be said that we were winning the war until Lyndon Johnson decided to wage it.

Notes

From *The Public Interest*, 69, 1982, pp. 4–16, by permission of the author.

1 Data for 1959–79 are taken from the figures published annually in the *Statistical Abstract of the United States*. Figures for 1949–58 are taken from 'Economic Report to the President: Combating Poverty in a Prosperous Economy', January 1969, reprinted in US Department of Health, Education and Welfare, *The Measure of Poverty*, ed. M. Orshansky, Technical Paper I, vol. 1 [n.d.], p. 349, chart 10. The percentage for 1980 was obtained directly from the Poverty Statistics Section of the Bureau of the Census.
2 The figures are taken from Timothy M. Smeeding, *Measuring the Economic Welfare of Low-Income Households and the Antipoverty Effectiveness of Cash and Noncash Transfer Programs*, PhD diss., Department of Economics, University of Wisconsin-Madison, 1975; Smeeding, 'The Antipoverty Effectiveness of In-Kind Transfers', *Journal of Human Resources*, 12, 1977, pp. 360–78; and Smeeding, 'The Anti-poverty Effect of In-Kind Transfers: A "Good Idea Gone Too Far?"', *Policy Studies Journal*, 10, 3, 1982, pp. 499–522.
3 Quoted in the *New York Times*, 21 August 1964, p. 1.
4 The figures for 1965–78 are taken from Sheldon Danziger and Robert Plotnick, 'The War on Income Poverty: Achievements and Failures', in *Welfare Reform in America*, ed. P. Sommers, Hingham, MA, Martinus Nijhoff, 1982, table 3.1, p. 40.
5 It should be noted that the measure of latent poverty excludes social security income. Since families headed by persons over the age of sixty-five make up nearly half of those in latent poverty, the percentages reported here may somewhat exaggerate the extent of the problem among those able to work. (Unfortunately, no figures on this point prior to 1976 have been published.) But even if it were possible to include social security – or exclude the elderly – in calculations over this period, this adjustment would not affect the steep *rise* in latent poverty we have observed. [. . .]
6 The variables are the first difference in real GNP per household and the first difference in percentage of population under the poverty line using the official measure of poverty.
7 Gordon Green and Edward Welniak, 'Measuring the Effects of Changing Family Composition during the 1970s on Black–White Differences in Income', unpublished manuscript, Bureau of the Census, 1982.

The New Politics of the New Poverty

Lawrence M. Mead

The poverty of today's underclass differs appreciably from poverty in the past: underclass poverty stems less from the absence of opportunity than from the inability or reluctance to take advantage of opportunity. The plight of the underclass suggests that the competence of many of the poor – their capacity to look after and take care of themselves – can no longer be taken for granted as it could in the past.

The changing nature of poverty has also ushered in a fundamental change in our politics, which formerly focused on class but now emphasizes conduct. Prior to the 1960s, in what I call the era of progressive politics, the overriding issue was how to help ordinary working Americans advance economically. The solutions of liberals and conservatives differed greatly, but both groups agreed that available opportunities would be seized by the poor. They disagreed in locating the barrier to opportunity: liberals blamed the unregulated economy, and conservatives blamed the government. As a result, liberals favoured greater government intervention, while conservatives hoped to reduce it. At issue were class inequalities and the need for economic redistribution: was the inequality meted out by the marketplace acceptable? How desirable were regulations of wages, hours and working conditions, along with the creation of social-insurance programmes to benefit workers and their families?

Anti-poverty strategy and politics differ greatly today, because poverty is rarely found among workers but is common among non-workers. In the new era, characterized by what I call dependency politics, the leading issue is how to handle the disorders of inner-city non-workers: conservatives usually want to enforce civilities, which liberals resist doing. For the most part, we spend less time debating whether the income of the working poor should be larger than we do discussing whether and how we can transform poor non-workers into workers.

Recent disagreements over tax hikes and budget cuts suggest that redistributive conflicts over the economy remain very much with us; economic inequality has increased, and Kevin Phillips's prediction of heightened conflict between rich and poor received much attention [in 1990]. Nevertheless, in the absence of economic collapse serious class conflict is unlikely. The politics of conduct, which focuses on dependency and disorder, is simply more salient than the politics of class. The problems of rising crime, welfarism, homelessness and declining schools (and the tax increases imposed to pay for them) are what chiefly concern most Americans; they worry far less about the income gap separating them from their employers. Most Americans doubt government's ability to solve the new social problems that confront us. Unless government better responds to them, it will receive no new mandate to tackle the older problem of unequal fortunes.

The public's focus on dependency and disorder has obviously damaged the American left, which is more comfortable dealing with issues of economic redistribution. The public's conservatism on social (as opposed to economic) issues largely explains why Republicans have controlled the White House and the national agenda for most of a generation. Democrats in presidential politics have paid a high price for their perceived softness on the question of 'values'. In the 1988 election, Michael Dukakis proposed new benefit programmes of the kind that used to win elections for Democrats. The Bush campaign easily defeated him by speaking of crime and Willie Horton.

But despite its electoral advantages, the anti-government right – like the redistributionist left – is uncomfortable with dependency politics. When the poor behave badly, bigger government becomes indefensible, because many of its beneficiaries are 'undeserving'. But smaller government is also questionable, because many believe that the poor could not cope without the many benefits and services that they receive. Distrust of the dysfunctional poor defeated the most ambitious plans to expand government during the Great Society. But concern for these same poor helps explain why Ronald Reagan was unable significantly to reduce the size of domestic government.

Working Class to Underclass

This political change was brought about by the appearance of an intractable type of poverty in American cities in the 1960s and early 1970s. Ironically, the same era witnessed the last great victories of old-style progressive politics. The victories were achieved by the civil-rights and feminist movements, which were largely composed of working people seeking expanded economic opportunities. Their demands, like those made in earlier decades by distressed farmers and organized labour, sought to increase the income of workers.

But in the same era, welfare rolls more than doubled, crime soared and riots broke out in the ghettos of major cities. These developments raised issues of order and propriety much more sharply than the earlier movements. By the end of the 1960s, the closely linked problems of poverty, welfare and the inner city dominated the domestic agenda. Since then, the claims of broader groups, including minorities and women, have not gone unnoticed, but they no longer command centre stage. Social-reform efforts now focus on welfare, education and criminal justice, not the economy. Even the recessions of the 1970s and early 1980s, the most serious since the Depression, failed to inspire major new efforts to help workers. Issues of dependency and dysfunction, not opportunity, now preoccupy us.

Some might say that dependency politics is not new, in that controversies about the 'undeserving' poor, and what to do about them, have often marked American history. But if the themes of dependency politics are not new, its prominence as 'welfare politics' before 1960 was largely a local affair. At the national level, the arena was always dominated by groups that were not dependent and were usually employed. Only in the recent era have dependent, mostly non-working groups captured the nation's political attention.

The employment issue, like no other, marks the boundary between the old politics and the new. The movements of the progressive era had weight above all because their members worked, or at least had a job history. The aggrieved might have been destitute, but they could make claims on the basis of desert. The recent poor seldom can do this. They are controversial, above all, because they usually do not work. Only 40 per cent of poor adults had any earnings at all in 1987, and only 9 per cent worked full-time year-round. That initially was why most of them were poor. Work effort among the poor has also dropped sharply. Only 47 per cent of the heads of poor families worked at all in 1987, down from 68 per cent in 1959.

Of course, only about half the poverty population is working-aged, and only about half remains in poverty for more than two years. The underclass, consisting of the poor with the most severe behavioural problems, is quite small: it includes no more than eight million people by various estimates. Yet persistent poverty is highly visible in cities, and it is central to all major urban problems – not only welfare, crime and homelessness, but troubled schools and a decaying economic base. So it gets more policy-making attention than the affairs of the vastly larger working and middle classes.

This new poverty created a new politics because the old politics found no answer to it. Neither of the traditional, competing progressive-era remedies – increasing or decreasing government intervention in the economy – seems an appropriate response to the passive poverty of the inner city. It is true that analysts wedded to progressive-era assumptions – whether liberal or conservative – continue to try to trace passive poverty to some social barrier that must be eliminated: liberals say that poor adults cannot earn enough to make work worthwhile, cannot find jobs or child care, or are barred from jobs by racial bias; conservatives claim that welfare 'pays' dependants not to marry or work. But the hard evidence mostly undercuts these explanations. Liberal claims notwithstanding, jobs usually are available to the unskilled; taking these jobs would generally move families in which both parents worked above the poverty line. The flood of new immigrants entering the job market is one clear sign that opportunity still exists. Working mothers can usually arrange child care informally and cheaply, and discrimination in any overt form has disappeared. But conservative claims notwithstanding, welfare disincentives are also too weak to explain the collapse of the family or the very low work levels typically found in the inner city today.

I do not mean that barriers are totally absent. Differences of opportunity certainly exist in America. Better-educated people, for example, are more likely to succeed. [Since the 1970s] the income disparity between low-skilled and high-skilled workers has increased. The progressive-era debate over whether and how to narrow these differences in wages remains alive.

Unequal opportunities, however, chiefly explain why some workers earn more than others. They usually do not explain the failure of non-workers to work steadily *at all*, which is in turn the cause of most poverty and dependency among working-aged people. Most Americans have responded to stagnant wages by working *more*; only the poor have worked less. Most Americans refuse to believe that society's failure to expand opportunity causes the poverty of non-workers who do not take and hold available jobs.

To explain most entrenched poverty, we must go back to what used to be called the 'culture of poverty'. Non-working adults apparently want to work, but they seldom do so consistently – some because the pay offered is unacceptable, others because they feel overwhelmed by the practical difficulties of employment. These reactions run strongest in the inner city, because of its isolation from workaday society, and among racial minorities who have traditionally faced discrimination. The greatest cause of today's poverty may simply be that the attempts [. . .] to equalize opportunity have failed to persuade many blacks and Hispanics that it is worth working.

But if non-work is rooted mostly in the demoralization of the poor, rather than impersonal impediments, then traditional reformism holds no answer for it. Passive poverty has defeated, in turn, the strategies of both larger and smaller governments. The Great Society invented wave after wave of new anti-poverty programmes, only to see the poverty level stagnate and welfare rise. The Reagan administration cut or curbed the growth of these programmes to reinvigorate the economy. But even the longest boom in American history could not reduce poverty below 13 per cent, because the poor are now substantially detached from the economy. Each in its own way, these strategies provided new chances to poor adults, but neither directly addressed the puzzling reluctance of the poor to do more to help themselves.

As a result, social policy has been driven away from structural reforms and towards paternalism. The drift is toward policies that address motivation by seeking to direct the lives of those dependent on government. Public institutions are taking over tutelary functions from weakened families. Social-service agencies are raising children, and schools are organizing the lives of students before and after class as well as during it. Homeless shelters and the criminal-justice system are managing the disordered lives of single men. Above all, recent welfare legislation requires rising numbers of employable recipients to participate in job placement or training on pain of cuts in their grants. Such measures violate the traditional prescriptions of liberals, who want benefits given without conditions, but also those of conservatives, who would prefer to see discipline applied by the private rather than the public sector. But they seem required by the changing nature of the social problem.

These trends are most advanced in the US, but they are appearing in Europe as well. An underclass, largely non-white, has grown up in British cities, while throughout Europe controversy rages over whether immigrants from the Third World are corrupting traditional mores. These racial and ethnic divisions now arouse more passion than the traditional conflicts of labour and business. The behaviour of 'outsiders' is far more controversial than economic claims. Crime, dependency and a failure to learn the national language are at issue, not working-class demands for higher wages and benefits. The West as a whole seems destined for a politics of conduct rather than class.

The New Agenda

Dependency politics and progressive-era politics differ substantially in content, even though there is much overlap in practice. I exaggerate the contrasts here for emphasis:

The old issues were economic; the new ones are social. Progressive-era politics debated the proper organization of society, especially the issue of government control of the economy. Liberals supported higher and more progressive taxation; public regulation of industries; union rights; the minimum wage and other protections for workers; pension, health and unemployment benefits: [. . .] [The right sought to] weaken or undo all these steps in the belief that only a revivified free market could really generate 'good jobs at good wages'.

In dependency politics, in contrast, the question is how to deal with the problems of basic functioning among the seriously poor. The social, more than the economic, structure of society is at issue. The focus is on troubled individuals or ethnic groups rather than industry, agriculture, or the relations of labour and management. Social problems are no longer seen to stem directly from injustice, nor are they obviously reformable. So social policy must focus on motivation and order rather than opportunity or equality.

Affluence helped produce this shift. Before the 1960s, working-class incomes were still low enough that many people were poor, even though they worked normal hours. That is much less common today, because the poverty line is constant in real terms while real wages have risen. The poor, who used to work more than the better-off, now commonly work less. Inevitably, the focus of the social agenda has shifted from the low wages that used to impoverish workers to the dysfunctions that keep the non-working poor out of the labour force.

In progressive-era politics the issue was government control of the economy; in dependency politics it is government supervision of behaviour. Progressive-era politicians disputed how far government should regulate the free market in the collective interest, how much it should spend on benefit programmes such as Social Security.

In dependency politics, however, the chief question is how far government should control the lives of dysfunctional people in their own interests. Do we require that people stay in school, obey the law, avoid drugs, and so on? Above all, do we require adults to work or prepare for work as a condition of receiving welfare? Proposals to do these things do not much change what government does for people. Rather, they demand that dependants do more for themselves in return.

Formerly it was local authorities who grappled with maintaining social order, while Washington managed the economy. But order issues have become federal, because national programmes are involved in all the key areas – welfare, education and criminal justice. It is now the main domestic challenge of presidents, as of mayors, to reduce crime and dependency and to raise standards in the schools. Presidents Nixon, Carter and Reagan all tried to reform welfare, and George Bush aspired to be an 'education president'.

The old issues concerned adults; the new issues concern children and youth. Progressive-era political claims were on behalf of adults, especially workers. The question was how to reorganize government or the economy so that adults could have influence and opportunity. In the dependency era, however, these issues are less salient than people's problems on the road to adulthood – illegitimacy, educational failure and crime. So dependency politics focuses heavily on the formative years. Reformism aims to improve family, neighbourhood and schools rather than the political or economic structure.

Daniel Patrick Moynihan says that social policy has entered a 'post-industrial' age. The main challenge is no longer to expand economic opportunity but to overcome social weaknesses that stem from the 'postmarital' family and the inability of many people to get through school. The inequalities that stem from the workplace are now trivial in comparison to those stemming from family structure. What matters for success is less whether your father was rich or poor than whether you knew your father at all.

A focus on youth is inevitable once the leading social problem changes from the poverty of workers to dysfunctional poverty. For if the source of poverty is behaviour rather than lack of opportunity, remedies must focus on youth, the stage of life at which behaviour is most malleable. Conversely, reform for adults must be structural because it must take personality largely as given.

The pressures in progressive-era politics arise from self-seeking behaviour; in dependency politics, they arise from passivity. Progressive-era politics debates the freedom that America allows people to make money and get ahead on their own. To conservatives, this prerogative is a right that government may not limit. To the left, it is a licence that government must restrain in the name of a broader social interest.

The poor and dependent, however, are not exploitative but inert. They are controversial mostly because they do so little to help themselves, not because they hurt others in the pursuit of advantage. Even when violent, they are unable to exert themselves effectively. They are not aggressive so much as *passive* aggressive. So in dependency politics, the issue is whether poor people should have to do more to help themselves. The question is how passive you can be and still be a citizen in full standing.

Formerly, the right defended property and the established order against public controls. Now it is the left that defends the status quo, by justifying passivity among the needy, while the right demands greater activity. Recent measures such as workfare or reformed schools are attempts to stimulate the poor, not to curb the rich. The point is to set a floor under self-advancement, not a ceiling above it. The hope is to make the poor more effectively self-seeking than they are.

Claims in progressive-era politics derived from strength; those in dependency politics arise from weakness. The chief players in the progressive era were unions, farmers, businesses and other economic interests that demanded some benefit or protection from government on a basis of desert. They were economically disadvantaged, but their demands were also made from a position of strength, because they had economic and political resources of their own. They could use these resources to get attention from politicians, but they could also survive on their own if rebuffed.

In dependency politics, the claimants usually have no such strength, as they lack any regular position in the economy. They are simply needy. Their main claim is precisely their vulnerability. It is not their own power that gets attention, but politicians' fear of a backlash from the better-off if the needy are left unprotected. Economic groups state their claims by speaking of troubled finances. The very poor state theirs by a disassembly of the personality – by failing to function in embarrassing ways that force society to take responsibility for them.

In dependency politics, the poor claim a right to support based on the injuries of the past, not on anything that they contribute now. Wounds are an asset today, much as a pay cheque was in progressive-era politics. One claims to be a victim, not a worker. The non-white poor, particularly, appeal to historic injustices. Even some policies that aid better-functioning minorities, such as affirmative action, require their beneficiaries to adopt the identity of victimhood to some extent – to exploit an appeal, as Shelby Steele says, based on 'suffering' rather than 'achievements'.

Poverty shifts the agenda from equality to citizenship. The question is no longer what the worst-off members of the community should receive. Now the question is who should be considered a bona fide member of the community in the first place. Who has the moral standing to make the demands for economic redress typically made in the progressive era? When dependency comes to dominate politics, class-oriented issues of equality for workers inevitably move off the agenda, while issues of identity and belonging replace them.

In Europe as well as the US, dependency concerns replaced progressive ones as motives for the reconsideration of the welfare state that began in the 1970s and 1980s. At first, the issues were economic, the fear that excessive spending on income and health programmes was overburdening the economy. Cuts were made to promote economic growth, the step conservatives always recommend in progressive-era politics. [In the 1990s], however, the greater concern has been declining social cohesion, as evidenced by rises in crime, single parenthood and chronic unemployment. The response, in Britain and Sweden as in the US, has been new steps to enforce child support and work effort among the dependent. The shift from the older, redistributive agenda to these new, more behavioural issues ushers in a new political age.

[. . .]

The Western Tradition

Today's efforts to respond to dependency face serious challenges. They may well not allay our social problems as fully as progressive policies resolved yesterday's economic disputes. The newer, paternalistic social programmes probably will do more to reduce poverty than the less demanding policies of the past: more authoritative schools are producing some results, and workfare programmes have been able to increase work effort (though they have not yet reduced dependency). But it is doubtful that even these programmes can do more than contain the social problem.

Even if they are effective, paternalistic measures raise serious political objections. The new structures reduce disorder, but at a cost to the autonomy of clients. This is particularly true if, as is likely, the chronic poor require direction on an on-going basis, not just temporarily. That is why, even now, government prefers to spend money on the dependent rather than try to tell them how to live. Benefits lack the power of public authority to change behaviour, but they do not violate our notions of a free society.

A more serious problem stems from our political traditions. Anti-dependency policies – and disputes about them – find no basis in the Western political tradition, which assumes that the individuals who compose society are competent to advance their own interests, if not society's. The traditional Western assumption is that politics arises from conflicting interests, as individuals and groups seek economic advantage. Government's task is to resolve these disputes in the general interest. It does not animate society, but rather responds to energy coming from below.

Historically, Western politics has been class-oriented: aristocratic elites, then bourgeois elements, then workers without property have advanced their own conceptions of how government and the economy should be organized. The dominant principles have become more democratic, then more collectivist, as government came to represent the mass of the populace and then to serve its needs. The contending visions may seem radically opposed, but from today's perspective they were remarkably alike: all assumed a working population, competent to advance its own interests.

This tradition is inapplicable to the problems posed by today's dysfunctional poor. But policy makers in [the US] and Europe are prone to respond to these problems by replaying the old scenarios. Today's liberals see history as a grand progression in which the rights of ordinary people have been expanded: first civil liberties, then representative government, then protections against the insecurities of capitalism were attained. Faced with passive poverty, the left can imagine no response other than providing some further entitlement, for example government jobs. The idea that dependants should have to function better seems like an attempt to deny benefits, and is thus anathema.

Anti-government conservatives, for their part, blame poverty on an excess of government, just as the left blames it on the lack of government intervention. They insist that cuts in spending and taxes will somehow liberate the energy of the poor, as they do that of entrepreneurs. The idea that competence is a prior and different problem, requiring perhaps more government rather than less, is unthinkable.

These liberal and conservative responses are doomed to fail. If the seriously poor had the initiative to respond to new opportunities, they would not be poor for very long in the first place. The Great Society and the Reagan era both failed to solve poverty, because each in a different way offered new chances to the poor without confronting the motivation problem. Neither could seriously address competence, because that problem fell outside the Western assumptions underlying their ideas of social reform.

But despite these conceptual failures, government has begun to do something about poverty: a new, paternalistic regime for the poor is emerging. Ronald Reagan's greatest domestic legacy, despite his tax cuts, was not to reduce government; it was to start changing welfare into workfare. But the new regime is accepted grudgingly, if at all. Politicians argue heatedly about the issues of responsibility and competence that it raises, but they seldom do so honestly. They mention the 'underclass' and the need for discipline, but they still talk as if they were offering the poor only 'freedom' or 'opportunity'.

We need a new political language that considers more candidly the questions of human nature that now underlie politics. The political contestants need to defend their positions on a philosophic level, rather than hide behind outmoded theories. Liberals need to show why poor people are blameless, therefore still deserving; conservatives need to show how the poor are competent and why they need to be held accountable, in spite of dysfunction. From such premises they could then erect consistent doctrines of social policy, comparable to the competing theories of economic management that framed the leading issues in the progressive era.

If anyone is writing this theory, it is not philosophers like John Rawls and his critics (who assume a rational economic psychology and thus remain wedded to the competence assumption) but social-policy experts who grapple concretely with poverty. They know too much of the hard evidence about barriers to pretend that nothing has changed. To explain poverty and justify any policy toward it, experts need a psychological doctrine that explains how personal degradation occurs in an affluent and open society.

Differing visions of human nature are what really divide Charles Murray, William Julius Wilson, myself and others. For Murray, poor adults are short-sighted calculators who are tempted into dysfunction by the disincentives of welfare. For Wilson, they are driven into disorder by a changing economy that denies them jobs that could support a family. My own view, articulated in *Beyond Entitlement: The Social Obligations of Citizenship* [1986], is that they are depressed but dutiful, willing to observe mainstream norms like work if only government will enforce them. But none of us has defended these premises in enough depth, or linked them clearly enough to our prescriptions.

Armed with theories like this, the political process might face more squarely the issues raised by dependency politics. It is more important that the positions be candid than that they agree. Progress requires that the fears of both sides be more fully aired, not that one side wins. The debate might finally generate the consensus needed to support the new paternalistic social policy that is already emerging. There could be agreement on the basic civilities that everyone is prepared to enforce. On that basis, the nation could grapple with passive poverty more successfully.

Note

From *The Public Interest*, 103, 1991, pp. 3–20; fuller version in Lawrence M. Mead, *The New Politics of Poverty*, New York, Basic Books, 1992, by permission of the author.

Feminism

The Patriarchal Welfare State

Carole Pateman

[. . .]

Theoretically and historically, the central criterion for citizenship has been 'independence', and the elements encompassed under the heading of independence have been based on masculine attributes and abilities. Men, but not women, have been seen as possessing the capacities required of 'individuals', 'workers' and 'citizens'. As a corollary, the meaning of 'dependence' is associated with all that is womanly – and women's citizenship in the welfare state is full of paradoxes and contradictions. [. . .] Three elements of 'independence' are particularly important for present purposes, all related to the masculine capacity for self-protection: the capacity to bear arms, the capacity to own property and the capacity for self-government.

First, women are held to lack the capacity for self-protection; they have been 'unilaterally disarmed'.[1] The protection of women is undertaken by men, but physical safety is a fundamental aspect of women's welfare that has been sadly neglected in the welfare state. From the nineteenth century, feminists (including J. S. Mill) have drawn attention to the impunity with which husbands could use physical force against their wives,[2] but women/wives still find it hard to obtain proper social and legal protection against violence from their male 'protectors'. Defence of the state (or the ability to protect your protection, as Hobbes put it), the ultimate test of citizenship, is also a masculine prerogative. The anti-suffragists in both America and Britain made a great deal of the alleged inability and unwillingness of women to use armed force, and the issue of women and combat duties in the military forces of the warfare state was also prominent in the [. . .] campaign [of the 1980s] against the Equal Rights Amendment in the United States. Although women are now admitted into the armed forces and so into training useful for later civilian employment, they are prohibited from combat duties in Britain, Australia and the United States.

Moreover, past exclusion of women from the warfare state has meant that welfare provision for veterans has also benefited men. In Australia and the United States, because of their special 'contribution' as citizens, veterans have had their own, separately administered welfare state, which has ranged from preference in university education (the GI bills in the United States) to their own medical benefits and hospital services, and (in Australia) preferential employment in the public service.

In the 'democratic' welfare state, however, employment rather than military service is the key to citizenship. The masculine 'protective' capacity now enters into citizenship primarily through the second and third dimensions of independence. Men, but not women, have also been seen as property owners. Only some men own material property, but as 'individuals', all men own (and can protect) the property they possess in their persons. Their status as 'workers' depends on their capacity to contract out the property they own in their labour power. Women are still not fully recognized socially as such property owners. To be sure, our position has improved dramatically from the mid-nineteenth century when women as wives had a very 'peculiar' position as the legal property of their husbands, and feminists compared wives to slaves. But today, a wife's person is still the property of her husband in one vital respect. Despite recent legal reform, in Britain and in some of the states of the United States and Australia, rape is still deemed legally impossible within marriage, and thus a wife's consent has no meaning. Yet women are now formally citizens in states held to be based on the necessary consent of self-governing individuals. The profound contradiction about women's consent is rarely if ever noticed and so is not seen as related to a sexually divided citizenship or as detracting from the claim of the welfare state to be democratic.

The third dimension of 'independence' is self-government. Men have been constituted as the beings who can govern (or protect) themselves, and if a man can govern himself, then he also has the requisite capacity to govern others. Only a few men govern others in public life – but all men govern in private as husbands and heads of households. As the governor of a family, a man is also a 'breadwinner'. He has the capacity to sell his labour power as a worker, or to buy labour power with his capital, and provide for his wife and family. His wife is thus 'protected'. The category of 'breadwinner' presupposes that wives are constituted as economic dependants or 'housewives', which places them in a subordinate position. The dichotomy breadwinner/housewife, and the masculine meaning of independence, were established in Britain by the middle of the nineteenth century; in the earlier period of capitalist development, women (and children) were wage-labourers. A 'worker' became a man who has an economically dependent wife to take care of his daily needs and look after his home and children. Moreover, 'class', too, is constructed as a patriarchal category. 'The working class' is the class of working *men*, who are also full citizens in the welfare state.

[T. H. Marshall first presented his influential account of citizenship in 1949, at the height of the optimism in Britain about the contribution of the new welfare state policies to social change. He referred specifically to . . .] the universal, civil right to 'work', that is, to paid employment. The democratic implications of the right to work cannot be understood without attention to the connections between the public world of 'work' and citizenship and the private world of conjugal relations. What it means to be a 'worker' depends in part on men's status and power as husbands, and on their standing as citizens in the welfare state. The construction of the male worker as 'breadwinner' and his wife as his 'dependant' was expressed officially in the census classifications in Britain and Australia. In the British Census of 1851, women engaged in unpaid domestic work were 'placed . . . in one of the productive classes along with paid work of a similar kind'.[3] This classification changed after 1871, and by 1911 unpaid housewives had been completely removed from the economically active population. In Australia an initial conflict over the categories of classification was resolved in 1890 when the scheme devised in New South Wales was adopted. The Australians divided up the population more decisively than the British, and the 1891 Census was based on the two categories of 'breadwinner' and 'dependant'. Unless explicitly stated otherwise, women's occupation was classified as domestic, and domestic workers were put in the dependant category.

The position of men as breadwinner-workers has been built into the welfare state. The sexual divisions in the welfare state have received much less attention than the persistence of the old dichotomy between the deserving and undeserving poor, which predates the welfare state. This is particularly clear in the United States, where a sharp separation is maintained between 'social security', or welfare-state policies directed at 'deserving workers who have paid for them through "contributions" over their working lifetimes', and 'welfare' – seen as public 'handouts' to 'barely deserving poor people'.[4] Although 'welfare' does not have this stark meaning in Britain or Australia, where the welfare state encompasses much more than most Americans seem able to envisage, the old distinction between the deserving and undeserving poor is still alive and kicking, illustrated by the popular bogey-figures of the 'scrounger' (Britain) and the 'dole-bludger' (Australia). However, although the dichotomy of deserving/undeserving poor overlaps with the divisions between husband/wife and worker/housewife to some extent, it also obscures the patriarchal structure of the welfare state.

Feminist analyses have shown how many welfare provisions have been established within a two-tier system. First, there are the benefits available to individuals as 'public' persons by virtue of their participation, and accidents of fortune, in the capitalist market. Benefits in this tier of the system are usually claimed by men. Second, benefits are available to the 'dependants' of individuals in the first category, or to 'private' persons, usually women. In the United States, for example, men are the majority of 'deserving' workers who receive benefits through the insurance system to which they have 'contributed' out of their earnings. On the other hand, the majority of claimants in means-tested programmes are women – women who are usually making their claims as wives or mothers. This is clearly the case with AFDC (Aid to Families with Dependent Children), where women are aided because they are mothers supporting children on their own, but the same is also true in other programmes: '46 per cent of the women receiving Social Security benefits make their claims as wives'. In contrast: 'men, even poor men, rarely make claims for benefits solely as husbands or fathers'.[5] In Australia the division is perhaps even more sharply defined. In 1980–81, in the primary tier of the system, in which benefits are employment-related and claimed by those who are expected to be economically independent but are not earning an income because of unemployment or illness, women formed only 31.3 per cent of claimants. In contrast, in the 'dependants group', 73.3 per cent of claimants were women, who were eligible for benefits because 'they are dependent on a man who could not support them, . . . [or] should have had a man support them if he had not died, divorced or deserted them'.[6]

Such evidence of lack of 'protection' raises an important question about *women's* standard of living in the welfare state. As dependants, married women should derive their subsistence from their husbands, so that wives are placed in the position of all dependent people before the establishment of the welfare state; they are reliant on the benevolence of another for their livelihood. The assumption is generally made that all husbands are benevolent. Wives are assumed to share equally in the standard of living of their husbands. The distribution of income *within* households has not usually been a subject of interest to economists, political theorists or protagonists in arguments about class and the welfare state – even though William Thompson drew attention to its importance as long ago as 1825 [in a book entitled *Appeal of One Half the Human Race, Women, against the Pretensions of the Other Half, Men*] – but past and present evidence indicates that the belief that all husbands are benevolent is mistaken. Nevertheless, women are likely to be better off married than if their marriage fails. One reason why women figure so prominently among the poor is that after divorce, as recent evidence from the United States reveals, a woman's standard of living can fall by nearly 75 per cent, whereas a man's can rise by nearly half.[7]

The conventional understanding of the 'wage' also suggests that there is no need to investigate women's standard of living independently from men's. The concept of the wage has expressed and encapsulated the patriarchal separation and integration of the public world of employment and the private sphere of conjugal relations. In arguments about the welfare state and the social wage, the wage is usually treated as a return for the sale of *individuals'* labour power. However, once the opposition breadwinner/housewife was consolidated, a 'wage' had to provide subsistence for several people. The struggle between capital and labour and the controversy about the welfare state have been about the *family wage*. A 'living wage' has been defined as what is required for a worker as breadwinner to support a wife and family, rather than what is needed to support himself; the wage is not what is sufficient to reproduce the worker's own labour power, but what is sufficient, in combination with the unpaid work of the housewife, to reproduce the labour power of the present and future labour force.

[. . .]

Women's Work and Welfare

Although so many women, including married women, are now in paid employment, women's standing as 'workers' is still of precarious legitimacy. So, therefore, is their standing as democratic citizens. If an individual can gain recognition from other citizens as an equally worthy citizen only through participation in the capitalist market, if self-respect and respect as a citizen are 'achieved' in the public world of the employment society, then women still lack the means to be recognized as worthy citizens. Nor have the policies of the welfare state provided women with many of the resources to gain respect as citizens. Marshall's social rights of citizenship in the welfare state could be extended to men without difficulty. As participants in the market, men could be seen as making a public contribution, and were in a position to be levied by the state to make a contribution more directly, that *entitled* them to the benefits of the welfare state. But how could women, dependants of men, whose legitimate 'work' is held to be located in the private sphere, be citizens of the welfare state? What could, or did, women contribute? The paradoxical answer is that women contributed – welfare.

The development of the welfare state has presupposed that certain aspects of welfare could and should continue to be provided by women (wives) in the home, and not primarily through public provision. The 'work' of a housewife can include the care of an invalid husband and elderly, perhaps infirm, relatives. Welfare-state policies have ensured in various ways that wives/women provide welfare services gratis, disguised as part of their responsibility for the private sphere. A good deal has been written about the fiscal crisis of the welfare state, but it would have been more acute if certain areas of welfare had not been seen as a private, women's matter. It is not surprising that the attack on public spending in the welfare state by the Thatcher and Reagan governments [went] hand-in-hand with praise for loving care within families, that is, with an attempt to obtain ever more unpaid welfare from (house) wives. The Invalid Care Allowance in Britain has been a particularly blatant example of the way in which the welfare state ensures that wives provide private welfare. The allowance was introduced in 1975 – when the Sex Discrimination Act was also passed – and it was paid to men or to single women who relinquished paid employment to look after a sick, disabled or elderly person (not necessarily a relative). Married women (or those cohabiting) were ineligible for the allowance.

The evidence indicates that it is likely to be married women who provide such care. In 1976 in Britain it was estimated that two million women were caring for adult relatives, and one survey in the north of England found that there were more people caring for adult relatives than mothers looking after children under sixteen.[8] A corollary of the assumption that women, but not men, care for others is that women must also care for themselves. Investigations show that women living by themselves in Britain have to be more infirm than men to obtain the services of home helps, and a study of an old people's home found that frail, elderly women admitted with their husbands faced hostility from the staff because they had failed in their job.[9] Again, women's citizenship is full of contradictions and paradoxes. Women must provide welfare, and care for themselves, and so must be assumed to have the capacities necessary for these tasks. Yet the development of the welfare state has also presupposed that women necessarily are in need of protection by and are dependent on men.

The welfare state has reinforced women's identity as men's dependants both directly and indirectly, and so confirmed rather than ameliorated our social exile. For example, in Britain and Australia the cohabitation rule explicitly expresses the presumption that women necessarily must be economically dependent on men if they live with them as sexual partners. If cohabitation is ruled to take place, the woman loses her entitlement to welfare benefits. The consequence of the cohabitation rule is not only sexually divided control of citizens, but an exacerbation of the poverty and other problems that the welfare state is designed to alleviate. In Britain today

when a man lives in, a woman's independence – her own name on the weekly giro [welfare cheque] – is automatically surrendered. The men become the claimants and the women their dependents. They lose control over both the revenue and the expenditure, often with catastrophic results: rent not paid, fuel bills missed, arrears mounting.[10]

It is important to ask what counts as part of the welfare state. In Australia and Britain the taxation system and transfer payments together form a tax-transfer system in the welfare state. In Australia a tax rebate is available for a dependent spouse (usually, of course, a wife), and in Britain the taxation system has always treated a wife's income as her husband's for taxation purposes. It is only relatively recently that it ceased to be the husband's prerogative to correspond with the Inland Revenue about his wife's earnings, or that he ceased to receive rebates due on her tax payments. Married men can still claim a tax allowance, based on the assumption that they support a dependent wife. Women's dependence is also enforced through the extremely limited public provision of childcare facilities in Australia, Britain and the United States, which creates a severe obstacle to women's full participation in the employment society. In all three countries, unlike Scandinavia, childcare outside the home is a very controversial issue.

Welfare-state legislation has also been framed on the assumption that women make their 'contribution' by providing private welfare, and, from the beginning, women were denied full citizenship in the welfare state. In America 'originally the purpose of ADC (now AFDC) was to keep mothers out of the paid labor force. . . . In contrast, the Social Security retirement program was consciously structured to respond to the needs of white male workers.'[11] In Britain the first national insurance, or contributory, scheme was set up in 1911, and one of its chief architects wrote later that women should have been completely excluded because 'they want insurance for others, not themselves'. Two years before the scheme was introduced, William Beveridge, the father of the contemporary British welfare state, stated in a book on unemployment that the 'ideal [social] unit is the household of man, wife and children maintained by the earnings of the first alone. . . . Reasonable security of employment for the breadwinner is the basis of all private duties and all sound social action.'[12] Nor had Beveridge changed his mind on this matter by the Second World War; his report, *Social Insurance and Allied Services*, appeared in 1942 and laid a major part of the foundation for the great reforms of the 1940s. In a passage now (in)famous among feminists, Beveridge wrote that 'the great majority of married women must be regarded as occupied on work which is vital though unpaid, without which their husbands could not do their paid work and without which the nation could not continue'.[13] In the National Insurance Act of 1946 wives were separated from their husbands for insurance purposes. (The significance of this procedure, along with Beveridge's statement, clearly was lost on T. H. Marshall when he was writing his essay on citizenship and the welfare state.) Under the act, married women paid lesser contributions for reduced benefits, but they could also opt out of the scheme, and so from sickness, unemployment and maternity benefits, and they also lost entitlement to an old age pension in their own right, being eligible only as their husband's dependant. By the time the legislation was amended in 1975, about three-quarters of married women workers had opted out.[14]

A different standard for men and women has also been applied in the operation of the insurance scheme. In 1911 some married women were insured in their own right. The scheme provided benefits in case of 'incapacity to work', but, given that wives had already been identified as 'incapacitated' for the 'work' in question, for paid employment, problems over the criteria for entitlement to sickness benefits were almost inevitable. In 1913 an inquiry was held to discover why married women were claiming benefits at a much greater rate than expected. One obvious reason was that the health of many working-class women was extremely poor. The extent of their ill health was revealed in 1915 when letters written by working women in 1913–14 to the Women's Cooperative Guild were published. The national insurance scheme meant that for the first time women could afford to take time off work when ill – but from which 'work'? Could they take time off from housework? What were the implications for the embryonic welfare state if they ceased to provide free welfare? From 1913 a dual standard of eligibility for benefits was established.[15] For men the criterion was fitness for work. But the committee of inquiry decided that, if a woman could do her housework, she was not ill. So the criterion for eligibility for women was also fitness for work – but unpaid work in the private home, not paid work in the public market that was the basis for the contributory scheme under which the women were insured! This criterion for women was still being laid down in instructions issued by the Department of Health and Social Security in the 1970s.[16] The dual standard was further reinforced in 1975 when a non-contributory invalidity pension was introduced for those incapable of work but not qualified for the contributory scheme. Men and single women were entitled to the pension if they could not engage in paid employment; the criterion for married women was ability to perform 'normal household duties'.[17]

Wollstonecraft's Dilemma

So far, I have looked at the patriarchal structure of the welfare state, but this is only part of the picture; the development of the welfare state has also brought challenges to patriarchal power and helped provide a basis for women's autonomous citizenship. Women have seen the welfare state as one of their major means of support. Well before women won formal citizenship, they campaigned for the state to make provision for welfare, especially for the welfare of women and their children; and women's organizations and women activists have continued their political activities around welfare issues, not least in opposition to their status as 'dependants'. In 1953 the British feminist Vera Brittain wrote of the welfare state established through the legislation of the 1940s that 'in it women have become ends in themselves and not merely means to the ends of men', and their 'unique value as women was recognised'.[18] In hindsight, Brittain was clearly overoptimistic in her assessment, but perhaps the opportunity now exists to begin to dismantle the patriarchal structure of the welfare state. In the 1980s the large changes in women's social position, technological and structural transformations within capitalism, and mass unemployment meant that much of the basis for the breadwinner/dependant dichotomy and for the employment society itself was being eroded (although both are still widely seen as social ideals). The social context of Hegel's two dilemmas is disappearing. As the current concern about the 'feminization of poverty' reveals, there is now a very visible underclass of women who are directly connected to the state as claimants, rather than indirectly as men's dependants. Their social exile is as apparent as that of poor male workers was to Hegel. Social change has now made it much harder to gloss over the paradoxes and contradictions of women's status as citizens.

However, the question of how women might become full citizens of a democratic welfare state is more complex than may appear at first sight, because it is only in the current wave of the organized feminist movement that the division between the private and public spheres of social life has become seen as a major *political* problem. From the 1860s to the 1960s women were active in the public sphere: women fought not only for welfare measures and for measures to secure the private and public safety of women and girls, but for the vote and civil equality; middle-class women fought for entry into higher education; and the professions and women trade unionists fought for decent working conditions and wages and maternity leave. But the contemporary liberal-feminist view, particularly prominent in the United States, that what is required above all is 'gender-neutral' laws and policies, was not widely shared. In general, until the 1960s the focus of attention in the welfare state was on measures to ensure that women had proper social support, and hence proper social respect, in carrying out their responsibilities in the private sphere. The problem is whether and how such measures could assist women in their fight for full citizenship. In 1942 in Britain, for example, many women welcomed the passage in the Beveridge Report that I have cited because, it was argued, it gave official recognition to the value of women's unpaid work. However, an official nod of recognition to women's work as 'vital' to 'the nation' is easily given; *in practice*, the value of the work in bringing women into full membership in the welfare state was negligible. The equal worth of citizenship and the respect of fellow citizens still depended on participation as paid employees. 'Citizenship' and 'work' stood then and still stand opposed to 'women'.

The extremely difficult problem faced by women in their attempt to win full citizenship I shall call 'Wollstonecraft's dilemma'. The dilemma is that the two routes toward citizenship that women have pursued are mutually incompatible within the confines of the patriarchal welfare state, and, within that context, they are impossible to achieve. For three centuries, since universal citizenship first appeared as a political ideal, women have continued to challenge their alleged natural subordination within private life. From at least the 1790s they have also struggled with the task of trying to become citizens within an ideal and practice that have gained universal meaning through their exclusion. Women's response has been complex. On the one hand, they have demanded that the ideal of citizenship be extended to them, and the liberal-feminist agenda for a 'gender-neutral' social world is the logical conclusion of one form of this demand. On the other hand, women have also insisted, often simultaneously, as did Mary Wollstonecraft, that *as women* they have specific capacities, talents, needs and concerns, so that the expression of their citizenship will be differentiated from that of men. Their unpaid work providing welfare could be seen, as Wollstonecraft saw women's tasks as mothers, as women's work *as citizens*, just as their husbands' paid work is central to men's citizenship.

The patriarchal understanding of citizenship means that the two demands are incompatible because it allows two alternatives only: either women become (like) men, and so full citizens; or they continue at women's work, which is of no value for citizenship. Moreover, within a patriarchal welfare state neither demand can be met. To demand that citizenship, as it now exists, should be fully extended to women accepts the patriarchal meaning of 'citizen', which is constructed from men's attributes, capacities and activities. Women cannot be full citizens in the present meaning of the term; at best, citizenship can be extended to women only as lesser men. At the same time, within the patriarchal welfare state, to demand proper social recognition and support for women's responsibilities is to condemn women to less than full citizenship and to continued incorporation into public life as 'women', that is, as members of another sphere who cannot, therefore, earn the respect of fellow (male) citizens.

The example of child endowments on family allowances in Australia and Britain is instructive as a practical illustration of Wollstonecraft's dilemma. It reveals the great difficulties in trying to implement a policy that both aids women in their work and challenges patriarchal power while enhancing women's citizenship. In both countries there was opposition from the right and from *laissez-faire* economists on the ground that family allowances would undermine the father's obligation to support his children and undermine his 'incentive' to sell his labour power in the market. The feminist advocates of family allowances in the 1920s, most notably Eleanor Rathbone in Britain, saw the alleviation of poverty in families where the breadwinner's wage was inadequate to meet the family's basic needs as only one argument for this form of state provision. They were also greatly concerned with the questions of the wife's economic dependence and equal pay for men and women workers. If the upkeep of children (or a substantial contribution toward it) was met by the state outside of wage bargaining in the market, then there was no reason why men and women doing the same work should not receive the same pay. Rathbone wrote in 1924 that 'nothing can justify the subordination of one group of producers – the mothers – to the rest and their deprivation of a share of their own in the wealth of a community'.[19] She argued that family allowances would, 'once and for all, cut away the maintenance of children and the reproduction of the race from the question of wages'.[20]

But not all the advocates of child endowment were feminists – so that the policy could very easily be divorced from the public issue of wages and dependence and be seen only as a return for and recognition of women's private contributions. Supporters included the eugenicists and pronatalists, and family allowances appealed to capital and the state as a means of keeping wages down. Family allowances had many opponents in the British union movement, fearful that the consequence, were the measure introduced, would be to undermine the power of unions in wage bargaining. The opponents included women trade unionists who were suspicious of a policy that could be used to try to persuade women to leave paid employment. Some unionists also argued that social services, such as housing, education and health, should be developed first, and the TUC adopted this view in 1930. But were the men concerned, too, with their private, patriarchal privileges? Rathbone claimed that 'the leaders of working men are themselves subconsciously biased by prejudice of sex. . . . Are they not influenced by a secret reluctance to see their wives and children recognised as separate personalities?'[21]

By 1941 the supporters of family allowances in the union movement had won the day, and family allowances were introduced in 1946 as part of the government's wartime plans for postwar reconstruction. The legislation proposed that the allowance would be paid to the father as 'normal household head', but after lobbying by women's organizations, this was overturned in a free vote, and the allowance was paid directly to mothers. In Australia the union movement accepted child endowment in the 1920s (child endowment was introduced in New South Wales in 1927, and at the federal level in 1941). But union support there was based on wider redistributive policies, and the endowment was seen as a supplement to, not a way of breaking down, the family wage.[22] In the 1970s, in both countries, women's organizations again had to defend family allowances and the principle of redistribution from 'the wallet to the purse'.

The hope of Eleanor Rathbone and other feminists that family allowances would form part of a democratic restructuring of the wage system was not realized. Nevertheless, family allowances are paid to women as a benefit in their own right; in that sense they are an important (albeit financially very small) mark of recognition of married women as independent members of the welfare state. Yet the allowance is paid to women as *mothers*, and the key question is thus whether the payment to a mother – a private person – negates her standing as an independent citizen of the welfare state. More generally, the question is whether there can be a welfare policy that gives substantial assistance to women in their daily lives *and* helps create the conditions for a genuine democracy in which women are autonomous citizens, in which we can act *as women* and not as 'woman' (protected/dependent/subordinate) constructed as the opposite to all that is meant by 'man'. That is to say, a resolution of Wollstonecraft's dilemma is necessary and, perhaps, possible.

The structure of the welfare state presupposes that women are men's dependants, but the benefits help to make it possible for women to be economically independent of men. In the countries with which I am concerned, women reliant on state benefits live poorly, but it is no longer so essential as it once was to marry or to cohabit with a man. A considerable moral panic has developed in recent years around 'welfare mothers', a panic that obscures significant features of their position, not least the extent to which the social basis for the ideal of breadwinner/dependant has crumbled. Large numbers of young working-class women have little or no hope of finding employment (or of finding a young man who is employed). But there is a source of social identity available to them that is out of the reach of their male counterparts. The socially secure and acknowledged identity for women is still that of a mother, and for many young women, motherhood, supported by state benefits, provides 'an alternative to aimless adolescence on the dole' and 'gives the appearance of self-determination'. The price of independence and 'a rebellious motherhood that is not an uncritical retreat into femininity'[23] is high, however; the welfare state provides a minimal income and perhaps housing (often substandard), but childcare services and other support are lacking, so that the young women are often isolated, with no way out of their social exile. Moreover, even if welfare state policies in Britain, Australia and the United States were reformed so that generous benefits, adequate housing, health care, child care and other services were available to mothers, reliance on the state could reinforce women's lesser citizenship in a new way.

Some feminists have enthusiastically endorsed the welfare state as 'the main recourse of women' and as the generator of 'political resources which, it seems fair to say, are mainly women's resources'.[24] They can point, in Australia for example, to 'the creation over the decade [1975–85] of a range of women's policy machinery and government subsidized women's services (delivered by women for women) which is unrivalled elsewhere'.[25] However, the enthusiasm is met with the rejoinder from other feminists that for women to look to the welfare state is merely to exchange dependence on individual men for dependence on the state. The power and capriciousness of husbands is being replaced by the arbitrariness, bureaucracy and power of the state, the very state that has upheld patriarchal power. The objection is cogent: to make women directly dependent on the state will not in itself do anything to challenge patriarchal power relations. The direct dependence of male workers on the welfare state and their indirect dependence when their standard of living is derived from the vast system of state regulation of and subsidy to capitalism – and in Australia a national arbitration court – have done little to undermine class power. However, the objection also misses an important point. There is one crucial difference between the construction of women as men's dependants and dependence on the welfare state. In the former case, each woman lives with the man on whose benevolence she depends; each woman is (in J. S. Mill's extraordinarily apt phrase) in a 'chronic state of bribery and intimidation combined'.[26] In the welfare state, each woman receives what is hers by right, and she can, potentially, combine with other citizens to enforce her rightful claim. The state has enormous powers of intimidation, but political action takes place collectively in the public terrain and not behind the closed door of the home, where each woman has to rely on her own strength and resources.

Another new factor is that women are now involved in the welfare state on a large scale as employees, so that new possibilities for political action by women also exist. Women have been criticizing the welfare state in recent years not just as academics, as activists, or as beneficiaries and users of welfare services, but as the people on whom the daily operation of the welfare state to a large extent depends. The criticisms range from its patriarchal structure (and, on occasions, especially in health care, misogynist practices), to its bureaucratic and undemocratic policy-making processes and administration, to social work practices and education policy. Small beginnings have been made on changing the welfare state from within; for example, women have succeeded in establishing Well Women Clinics within the NHS in Britain and special units to deal with rape victims in public hospitals in Australia. Furthermore, the potential is now there for united action by women employees, women claimants and women citizens already politically active in the welfare state – not just to protect services against government cuts and efforts at 'privatization' (which has absorbed much energy recently), but to transform the welfare state. Still, it is hard to see how women alone could succeed in the attempt. One necessary condition for the creation of a genuine democracy in which the welfare of *all* citizens is served is an alliance between a labour movement that acknowledges the problem of patriarchal power and an autonomous women's movement that recognizes the problem of class power. Whether such an alliance can be forged is an open question.

Despite the debates and the rethinking brought about by mass unemployment and attack on the union movement and welfare state by the Reagan and Thatcher governments, there are many barriers to be overcome. In Britain and Australia, with stronger welfare states, the women's movement has had a much closer relationship with working-class movements than in the United States, where the individualism of the predominant liberal feminism is an inhibiting factor, and where only about 17 per cent of the workforce is now unionized. The major locus of criticism of authoritarian, hierarchical, undemocratic forms of organization since about 1970 has been the women's movement. The practical example of democratic, decentralized organization provided by the women's movement has been largely ignored by the labour movement, as well as in academic discussions of democracy. After Marx defeated Bakunin in the First International, the prevailing form of organization in the labour movement, the nationalized industries in Britain and in the left sects has mimicked the hierarchy of the state – both the welfare and the warfare state. To be sure, there is a movement for industrial democracy and workers' control, but it has, by and large, accepted that the 'worker' is a masculine figure and failed to question the separation of (public) industry and economic production from private life. The women's movement has rescued and put into practice the long-submerged idea that movement for, and experiments in, social change must 'prefigure' the future form of social organization.[27]

If prefigurative forms of organization, such as the 'alternative' women's welfare services set up by the women's movement, are not to remain isolated examples, or if attempts to set them up on a wider scale are not to be defeated, as in the past, very many accepted conceptions and practices have to be questioned. [. . .] Debates [during the 1980s] over left alternatives to Thatcherite economic policies in Britain, and over the Accord between the state, capital and labour in Australia, suggest that the arguments and demands of the women's movement are still often unrecognized by labour's political spokesmen. For instance, one response to unemployment from male workers is to argue for a shorter working week and more leisure, or more time but the same money. However, in women's lives, time and money are not interchangeable in the same way.[28] Women, unlike men, do not have leisure after 'work', but do unpaid work. Many women are arguing, rather, for a shorter working day. The point of the argument is to challenge the separation of part- and full-time paid employment and paid and unpaid 'work'. But the conception of citizenship needs thorough questioning, too, if Wollstonecraft's dilemma is to be resolved; neither the labour movement nor the women's movement (nor democratic theorists) has paid much attention to this. The patriarchal opposition between the private and public, women and citizen, dependant and breadwinner is less firmly based than it once was, and feminists have named it as a political problem. The ideal of full employment so central to the welfare state is also crumbling, so that some of the main props of the patriarchal understanding of citizenship are being undermined. The ideal of full employment appeared to have been achieved in the 1960s only because half the citizen body (and black men?) was denied legitimate membership in the employment society. Now that millions of men are excluded from the ideal (and the exclusion seems permanent), one possibility is that the ideal of universal citizenship will be abandoned, too, and full citizenship will become the prerogative of capitalist, employed and armed men. Or can a genuine democracy be created?

The perception of democracy as a class problem and the influence of liberal feminism have combined to keep alive Engels's old solution to 'the woman question' – to 'bring the whole female sex back into public industry'.[29] But the economy has a patriarchal structure. The Marxist hope that capitalism would create a labour force where ascriptive characteristics were irrelevant, and the liberal-feminist hope that anti-discrimination legislation would create a 'gender-neutral' workforce, look Utopian even without the collapse of the ideal of full employment. Engels's solution is out of reach – and so, too, is the generalization of masculine citizenship to women. In turn, the argument that the equal worth of citizenship, and the self-respect and mutual respect of citizens, depend upon sale of labour power in the market and the provisions of the patriarchal welfare state is also undercut. The way is opening up for the formulation of conceptions of respect and equal worth adequate for democratic citizenship. Women could not 'earn' respect or gain the self-respect that men obtain as workers; but what kind of respect do men 'achieve' by selling their labour power and becoming wage-slaves? Here the movement for workplace democracy and the feminist movement could join hands, but only if the conventional understanding of 'work' is rethought. If women as well as men are to be full citizens, the separation of the welfare state and employment from the free welfare work contributed by women has to be broken down and new meanings and practices of 'independence', 'work' and 'welfare' created.

For example, consider the implications were a broad, popular political movement to press for welfare policy to include a guaranteed social income to all adults, which would provide adequately for subsistence and also participation in social life.[30] For such a demand to be made, the old dichotomies must already have started to break down – the opposition between paid and unpaid work (for the first time all individuals could have a genuine choice whether to engage in paid work), between full- and part-time work, between public and private work, between independence and dependence, between work and welfare – which is to say, between men and women. If implemented, such a policy would at last recognize women as equal members of the welfare state, although it would not in itself ensure women's full citizenship. If a genuine democracy is to be created, the problem of the content and value of women's contribution as citizens and the meaning of citizenship has to be confronted.

To analyse the welfare state through the lens of Hegel's dilemma is to rule out such problems. But the history of the past 150 years and the contemporary record show that the welfare of all members of society cannot be represented by men, whether workers or capitalists. Welfare is, after all, the welfare of all living generations of citizens and their children. If the welfare state is seen as a response to Hegel's dilemma, the appropriate question about women's citizenship is: how can women become workers and citizens like men, and so members of the welfare state like men? If, instead, the starting-point is Wollstonecraft's dilemma, then the question might run: what form must democratic citizenship take if a primary task of all citizens is to ensure that the welfare of each living generation of citizens is secured?

The welfare state has been fought for and supported by the labour movement and the women's movement because only public or collective provision can maintain a proper standard of living and the means for meaningful social participation for all citizens in a democracy. The implication of this claim is that democratic citizens are both autonomous and interdependent; they are autonomous in that each enjoys the means to be an active citizen, but they are interdependent in that the welfare of each is the collective responsibility of all citizens. Critics of the class structure of the welfare state have often counterposed the fraternal interdependence (solidarity) signified by the welfare state to the bleak independence of isolated individuals in the market, but they have rarely noticed that both have been predicated upon the dependence (subordination) of women. In the patriarchal welfare state, independence has been constructed as a masculine prerogative. Men's 'independence' as workers and citizens is their freedom from responsibility for welfare (except insofar as they 'contribute' to the welfare state). Women have been seen as responsible for (private) welfare work, for relationships of dependence and interdependence. The paradox that welfare relies so largely on women, on dependants and social exiles whose 'contribution' is not politically relevant to their citizenship in the welfare state, is heightened now that women's paid employment is also vital to the operation of the welfare state itself.

If women's knowledge of and expertise in welfare are to become part of their contribution as citizens, as women have demanded during the twentieth century, the opposition between men's independence and women's dependence has to be broken down, and a new understanding and practice of citizenship developed. The patriarchal dichotomy between women and independence-work-citizenship is under political challenge, and the social basis for the ideal of the full (male) employment society is crumbling. An opportunity has become visible to create a genuine democracy, to move from the welfare state to a welfare society without involuntary social exiles, in which women as well as men enjoy full social membership. Whether the opportunity can be realized is not easy to tell now that the warfare state is overshadowing the welfare state.

Notes

From C. Pateman, *The Disorder of Women*, Cambridge, Polity Press, 1989, pp. 185–9, 192–209, by permission of Polity Press Ltd.

1   The graphic phrase is Judith Stiehm's, in 'Myths Necessary to the Pursuit of War', unpublished paper, p. 11.
2   See especially F. Cobbe, 'Wife Torture in England', *The Contemporary Review*, 32, 1878, pp. 55–87. Also, for example, Mill's remarks when introducing the amendment to enfranchise women in the House of Commons in 1867, reprinted in *Women, the Family and Freedom: The Debate in Documents*, ed. S. Bell and K. Offen, vol. 1, Stanford, CA, Stanford University Press, 1983, p. 487.
3   D. Deacon, 'Political Arithmetic: The Nineteenth-Century Australian Census and the Construction of the Dependent Woman', *Signs*, 11(1), 1985, p. 31 (my discussion draws on Deacon); also H. Land, 'The Family Wage', *Feminist Review*, 6, 1980, p. 60.
4   T. Skocpol, 'The Limits of the New Deal System and the Roots of Contemporary Welfare Dilemmas', in *The Politics of Social Policy in the United States*, ed. M. Weir, A. Orloff and T. Skocpol, Princeton, NJ, Princeton University Press, 1988.
5   B. Nelson, 'Women's Poverty and Women's Citizenship: Some Political Consequences of Economic Marginality', *Signs*, 10(2), 1984, pp. 222–3.
6   M. Owen, 'Women – A Wastefully Exploited Resource', *Search*, 15, 1984, pp. 271–2.
7   L. J. Weitzman, *The Divorce Revolution*, New York, The Free Press, 1985, ch. 10, esp. pp. 337–40.
8   J. Dale and P. Foster, *Feminists and the Welfare State*, London, Routledge and Kegan Paul, 1986, p. 112.
9   H. Land, 'Who Cares for the Family?', *Journal of Social Policy*, 7(3), 1978, pp. 268–9. Land notes that even under the old Poor Law twice as many women as men received outdoor relief, and there were many more old men than women in the workhouse wards for the ill or infirm; the women were deemed fit for the wards for the able-bodied.
10   B. Campbell, *Wigan Pier Revisited: Poverty and Politics in the 80s*, London, Virago Press, 1984, p. 76.
11   Nelson, op. cit., pp. 229–30.
12   Both quotations are taken from Land, op. cit., p. 72.
13   Cited in Dale and Foster, op. cit., p. 17.
14   H. Land, 'Who Still Cares for the Family?', in *Women's Welfare, Women's Rights*, ed. J. Lewis, London and Canberra, Croom Helm, 1983, p. 70.
15   M. Davis, *Maternity: Letters from Working Women*, New York, Norton, 1978 (first published 1915).
16   Information taken from Land, op. cit. (n. 9), pp. 263–4.
17   Land, op. cit. (n. 14), p. 73.
18   Cited in Dale and Foster, op. cit., p. 3.
19   Cited in Land, op. cit. (n. 3), p. 63.

20 Cited in B. Cass, 'Redistribution to Children and to Mothers: A History of Child Endowment and Family Allowances', in *Women, Social Welfare and the State*, ed. J. Goodnow and C. Pateman, Sydney, Allen and Unwin, 1985, p. 57.

21 Cited in ibid., p. 59.

22 Ibid., pp. 60–1.

23 Campbell, op. cit., pp. 66, 78, 71.

24 F. Fox Piven, 'Women and the State: Ideology, Power, and the Welfare State', *Socialist Review*, 14(2), 1984, pp. 14, 17.

25 M. Sawer, 'The Long March through the Institutions: Women's Affairs under Fraser and Hawke', paper presented to the annual meeting of the Australasian Political Studies Association, Brisbane, 1986, p. 1.

26 J. S. Mill, 'The Subjection of Women', in *Essays on Sex Equality*, ed. A. Rossi, Chicago, University of Chicago Press, 1970, p. 137.

27 See S. Rowbotham, L. Segal and H. Wainright, *Beyond the Fragments: Feminism and the Making of Socialism*, London, Merlin Press, 1979, a book that was instrumental in opening debate on the left and in the labour movement in Britain on this question.

28 See H. Hernes, *Welfare State and Woman Power: Essays in State Feminism*, Oslo, Norwegian University Press, 1987, ch. 5, for a discussion of the political implications of the different time-frames of men's and women's lives.

29 F. Engels, *The Origin of the Family, Private Property and the State*, New York, International Publishers, 1942, p. 66.

30 See also the discussion in J. Keane and J. Owens, *After Full Employment*, London, Hutchinson, 1986, pp. 175–7.

The Welfare State and Women Power

Helga Maria Hernes

Introduction

Women's absence from central societal institutions and decision-making forums has until a short time ago been characteristic of all Western democracies. This has changed in some countries, notably the Nordic ones, where women have made significant advances in terms of political power. [. . .] Norway's prime minister and Iceland's president are women. Eight of Norway's eighteen ministers are women, and all the other Nordic governments have a high percentage of women ministers. One third of all members of Scandinavian parliaments are women. Their representation in public commissions on the national and local levels, the corporate system of decision-making, is also higher than elsewhere in the Western world.

This [essay] is not really an attempt at telling the story of 'how it all happened'. [. . .] It is a partial explanation and an analysis of the combined factors that have facilitated the massive entry of women into the public sphere, the participation of women in political processes, and the gradual inclusion of women's issues onto the political agendas of parties and governments. It is the story of 'reproduction going public' – the way in which advanced Nordic welfare states, through their policies, have 'pulled' women into the public sphere, and how women have then begun to 'push' developments in accordance with their own interests. There is considerable difference between being powerless and having little power, the difference between being outside the forums of decision-making and being a part of them. People with little power may lose most battles; yet they do at least participate and dictate some terms. And it is at this decisive stage in their political history that Nordic women are today.

[. . .]

Women were until recently of very little interest to political science. Their absence from the political decision-making process at almost all levels did not pose a serious normative problem in democratic theory. Women were treated as deviants in terms of their interest in politics and of political behaviour. Those women who despite all odds did manage to enter the ranks of the political elites were often active within the field regarded as the least interesting, namely social policy. Here one met other women: clients as unwed, divorced, widowed or 'working' mothers. This was not the kind of stuff interesting political science, or political scientists for that matter, was made of. Until recently the marginality of social policy as a field of inquiry was well established. In the wake of welfare state development, women's life patterns are becoming less and less deviant, more and more the source of new norms, policies, and ideology. Women have entered the public sphere from below, through the kitchen door so to speak, partly through the pull of economic development, partly through the push of the women's movement. Women's agitation, 'feminization from below', and official response in the form of 'state feminism' from above have had lasting effects on Nordic welfare state development. Once women had arrived they were integrated into the public sphere through a variety of public policies and organizational measures, designed partly to solve general social and economic problems, partly to respond to women's demands. [. . .] The fact that welfare states and especially social democratic regimes empower women to a greater extent than other political systems do is by now well established (Haavio-Mannila 1985, Piven 1985, Piven and Cloward 1985). [. . .]

Women and the Study of Power

[. . .]

The following [essay] should be read as an attempt to develop thoughts on the potential possibility for a philogynous or woman-friendly (*kvinnevennlig, frauenfreundlicher*) polity begun in my earlier analysis of woman's access to the corporate state. As I stated then, a woman-friendly state would enable women to have a natural relationship to their children, their work, and public life (Hernes 1982: 32–40). I wish to make the claim here that Nordic democracies embody a state form that makes it possible to transform them into woman-friendly societies. This claim rests on an analysis of these countries' history and potential for development, as well as assumptions about the needs of women that are not uncontroversial. Most feminists would deny that states can be non-repressive and non-violent, and thus be friendly to women (or children and men for that matter).

A woman-friendly state would not force harder choices on women than on men, or permit unjust treatment on the basis of sex. In a woman-friendly state women will continue to have children, yet there will also be other roads to self-realization open to them. In such a state women will not have to choose futures that demand greater sacrifices from them than are expected of men. It would be, in short, a state where injustice on the basis of gender would be largely eliminated without an increase in other forms of inequality, such as among groups of women. This is not to say that all forms of injustice or all hard choices or all forms of scarcity would be eliminated. Reducing gender injustice without increasing other forms of injustice and inequality is thus a limited policy goal. What makes it difficult to achieve is the fact that gender is a basic principle of social organization, and that the requirement of not increasing other forms of inequality will mean that most men will lose some of their present privi-leges, i.e. their unjust advantages. This process will in other words involve power struggles. This is not to say that a woman-friendly state is inimical to men. I hope to show in the following that this kind of state and society demand deep-going, even revolutionary transformations of present arrangements, yet that the inner logic of post-war Scandinavian develop-ment has created the potential for evolution towards woman-friendly states and societies. The questions that arise in regard to this development concern the boundaries between public and private responsibility for reproductive tasks, and the acceptance of legitimate gender differences in societies that have equality as an over-riding and long-standing policy aim. There is no normative agreement on these issues among feminists, among women in general, or among political decision-makers. Nor is there any theoretical agreement. While their relevance is perhaps especially evident in Scandinavia, [. . .] questions of the balance between private and public, and of reconceptualizations of equality are shared by colleagues in many countries.

Social Democracy: Blessings and Limitations

The transformation of socialist theory into social democratic practice in Norden was made possible by a culture characterized by a historically based 'passion for equality', to cite the title of a recent anthology (Graubard 1985). This passion for equality, a highly pragmatic attitude toward all human action, including political action, and common concepts of equity and justice, are the basis for political dialogue in all five countries. The content of this passion for equality is closely linked with egalitarian prin-ciples that have informed distribution policies and institution-building in all these countries. Others have described the historical background for the evolution of this political culture, its roots in rural radicalism, the tradition of non-violence which is of decisive importance from a feminist perspective and the special type of welfare state that is its political product (Esping-Andersen and Korpi 1984, 1987, H. F. Dahl 1984, Hentilae 1978, Korpi 1985). What is important in this context is the fact that egalitarian values and policies have had a positive effect on the welfare of women, and that they have their limitations when it comes to introducing pluralism in any form, including gender difference. Equality policies have by no means led to equality among men and women, but they have had two important consequences: they have reduced the distance between men and women more than in most parts of the world, and they have given women, regardless of social status and labour market tie, a standard of living above the poverty line. Yet, as Dahl and Eduards so penchantly argue, there remains an inescapably male bias in regard to the content of Nordic equality, which has consequences for a wide variety of issues (Eduards et al. 1985, Eduards 1986, Dahl 1984, 1987).

The present struggle for gender equality is thus a struggle for the redefinition of the content and concept of equality as much as it is a struggle for equal status between men and women, i.e. for women's inclusion into the world of men, and thus a struggle for power. 'We don't want equality at the behest of men and according to their rules' is a common expression among women of all political persuasions. Giving political content to this abstract claim is a difficult and conflict-filled process, particularly because the passion for equality is shared by men and women alike. [. . .]

What are the boundaries between the private and the public in the type of states analysed and where should they be drawn? The importance of this question should be obvious. The division of labour between family, market, and state is decisive for the welfare of women and for their social power. The boundaries between these three spheres have moved progressively in the wake of welfare state development [. . .]. In contrast to many other Western countries, where traditional 'family work' has been marketized, the Nordic solution has been its incorporation into the public sector administered by the state and municipalities (*Verstaatlichung*). One of the weaknesses of much of the feminist literature, especially from a Northern European point of view, is a persistent overemphasis on women's dependence on the kinship system despite the fact that this state of affairs changed several decades ago (Scott 1986: 1061). The normative (and thus also political) question has been where the new boundaries between 'private', or family, and 'public', or public sector, should lie. Some have even raised the possibility of a market solution or collective, non-state solutions as practised outside Norden. If one looks at the recent history of the articulation of women's interests, their demands have been as much for gaining control over their own destinies within private settings, as about institution building. Women's claims have for example been for longer maternity leaves and shorter working hours per day rather than institutional facilities in order to be able to take care of their own children and other social responsibilities. Public responsibility lies of course in the acknowledgement that this kind of work is deemed to be socially neces-sary labour, and should be rewarded (O'Brien 1979, Dahl 1985). In terms of policy this has meant that the strict division between social policy and labour market policy is not in the interests of women. The general trend towards the integration of these two policy spheres has been observed by many, notably in the work of Walter Korpi and Gøsta Esping-Andersen (1984, 1987). This integrative policy development, which is occurring in all Nordic countries, is not prompted by a concern for women's welfare, yet it is one of the major reasons for my optimistic claim. The new boundaries between private and public involve in other words both the acknowledgement that certain values, such as care for the young and the elderly, are a public concern, and their institutionalization in humane organizational forms. Social-democratic and feminist aims of 'going public' and of devolution and decentralization in terms of organization coincide.

Which gender differences do we want to legitimize within the confines of states that have had equality as a long-standing policy aim? The strength and fervour of the ideology of equality has become a two-edged sword for women. As a matter of fact, in the early days of the new women's movement the most frequent assertion by opponents was that gender equality would increase social inequality, and women spent a great deal of energy claiming that the two were connected. Scandinavian languages differentiate between the two. In Swedish *jämställdhet* refers to gender equality and is defined in terms of equality of status between women and men, while the richer concept of social equality that evokes solidarity is termed *jämliket*. In Norwegian and Danish *likestilling* (*ligestilling*) is the word for gender equality, while *likhet* (*lighed*) is the term for general equality. The ideological force of this verbal differentiation must not be underestimated. Women may gain equal status *within* the confines of dominant ideology and public policy, but the thrust of that tradition must not be threatened by 'special' interests. Women's interests are defined even in Scandinavia as 'special' interests, and Nordic women's movements' major ideological aim has been to define them as general interests, and to change the content of equality in all its forms and expressions in accord-ance with women's interests and preferences.

Yet much of the legislation that has finally been passed has been couched in gender-neutral terms (Eduards et al. 1985). In the name of social equal-ity, women have become the 'under-represented gender' in most public documents. Only Norway has been willing to pass some women-specific legislation, yet even its major clause in the Equal Status Act of 1977 is gender-neutral. Public documents refer to the 'under-represented gender' and women have felt threatened in 'their' labour market niches as a result. Most policies of gender equality have been or have started out as labour market policies. One can discern three phases: Phase one encourages women (in preference to male immigrant labour) to enter the labour market. Phase two addresses problems of unequal treatment once they get there in gender-neutral terms of equal access. Phase three encourages men to take over their share of family work by giving them parental leave. The goal is gender neutrality within the family and society at large (see also Jonung 1982). This is a departure from Gunnar and Alva Myrdal's recipe for the 1930s and Viola Klein or Alva Myrdal's for the 1950s. These books encouraged women to enter the labour market before motherhood in order to get a foothold, to leave the market during the years of intensive child-rearing, and then to return to the market on a full-time basis for the last phase (Myrdal and Myrdal 1935, Klein and Myrdal 1956, Bjøru and Sørensen 1983). The life courses of men and women, which is what these policies aim to regulate, were still deemed to be 'naturally' divergent in the 1930s and 1950s, while today's policy is to synchronize them in order to make men and women 'equal'.

It would be a considerable overstatement to claim that the great changes that have affected Scandinavian women's lives during the 1970s and 1980s came about as a result of public policy. Even in very active states, policy regulates rather than initiates changes that are already occurring for a variety of reasons. Policies can, however, affect the direction and speed of social changes. During the 1970s women entered the labour market, albeit on a part-time basis; they stayed longer in the educational system, although in traditionally feminine areas; Scandinavian men began to participate more in child care, although not in housework strictly speaking; women increased their political participation and representation rates to the highest in the world, although without achieving parity or a majority of seats. Very loosely, one might say that these changes were a result partly of economic development, partly of the activities of the women's movement, and partly a result of governmental policies.

There can be no doubt that it is the gradual political empowerment of women that will have the greatest and most far-reaching effect in the long run. As life patterns, mainly women's life patterns, have changed, the interrelationship between the above three forces of change has become clearer. Most of the growth in women's labour market participation has occurred in the form of part-time labour. This trend was severely criticized within the feminist movement and by trade unions as being inimical to the interests of women and labour power in general. Part-time women, the majority of working women, were thus denied labour union support. They are and were most active in movements, in issue-oriented politics, and in political parties. There is no doubt that political parties have increased their recruitment of women as a result of pressures by move-ment women and their own members. In the wake of the activities of a lively women's movement during the 1970s, women's under-representation in or complete absence from central power positions had come to be regarded as a public problem and an area for policy intervention. Representation and participation rights became a policy issue in them-selves. Political powerlessness, i.e. lack of representative office and access to decision-making and higher level positions, came to be regarded as unjust, against the interests of women, and ultimately as a disadvantage for society as a whole. This attitude was widespread among women of all political persuasions, and received lip service from male politicians, especially those on the left. The legitimacy of the issues increased very rapidly.

Policies of gender-neutral equality have not been equally well received in all quarters. The tone of the equality debate has changed character with the influx of a large number of women into political and professional life. For it must be remembered that the clustering effects of labour market segregation, and the fact that most women work within the semi-professions that dominate the public sector and tend to identify public sector interests with women's interests, have also influenced public debate. Many of the conflicts of interest within mature welfare states coincide today with gender conflicts. One of these conflicts centres on the question of which gender differences may be the legitimate basis of public policy. The question of gender difference and gender conflict has thus challenged the ideology and policy goal of gender equality in a variety of ways [. . .]. Gender differences and gender conflicts have clearly come to the fore as a consequence of the political empowerment of women. And this political empowerment is at least in part attributable to the activities of part-time working women, the 'deviants' of dominant labour market ideology, an ideology of full employment by which is meant full-time employment, and until recently the 'traitors' to class soli-darity (Hoel 1983). The untidy life patterns of women are thus slowly undermining the dominant life patterns on which public policies have been based until now.

Varieties of Gender Legitimacy

All public policies have until recently been formulated by political bodies dominated by men and implemented by bureaucracies dominated by men. This has changed drastically. Nordic parliaments (with the exception of Iceland) and governments now have a 'critical mass' (30–35 per cent) of women members (Dahlerup 1986).

[. . .]

In accordance with the Scandinavian mould, progress towards equality should now proceed in predictable fashion. However, in practice 'map and terrain do not coincide' to use a well-known Norwegian saying. Old concepts of equality and methods of arriving at it, which were developed within the context of class politics, cannot easily be transferred to gender politics. And the process of transformation affects a growing number of issues. On which issues and under which conditions should men and women be treated equally or differently? This question still awaits an answer both in the form of a theory of gender justice and in the form of policies.

[. . .]

In the Norden of today there is no arena that is so strategic that its 'conquest' alone could lead to a permanent change in the balance of power between women and men. The struggle for influence and power has only begun. It is fragmented and its outcomes are often unpredictable. Under what conditions can manifestations of collective interests lead to permanent changes in women's legal and political status? At present there is conflict and competition with men at several levels. A juster distribution of unpaid and paid time, and an increase in the rewards that accompany unpaid work will cost individual men more of their 'free' time and will cost the treasuries money. An increase in the political representation of women at all levels and in the number of high-level civil servants will reduce the number of men who can hold these posts. Feminist scientists who challenge male interpretations of reality are very slowly beginning to gain access to the universities. There are practically no women in the economic elites. The question is whether alliances and cooperation between women, both those in power and the majority, who are still without, will contribute to the evolution of woman-friendly societies, where men and women can be both autonomous individuals and parents.

Note

From H. M. Hernes, *Welfare State and Women Power: Essays in State Feminism*, Oslo, Norwegian University Press/Universitetsforlaget, 1987, pp. 9–11, 15–22, 28–9, by permission of Aschehoug & Co.

References

Bjøru, K. and Sørensen, A. M. 1983. Fragmenter av norske kvinners livsløp. In Skrede and Tornes (eds.) *Studier i kvinners livsløp*. Oslo: Universitetsforlaget.

Dahl, H. F. 1984. Those Equal Folk. In Graubard (ed.) *Norden – The Passion for Equality*. Oslo: Norwegian University Press.
Dahl, T. S. 1984. Women's Right to Money. In Holter (ed.) *Patriarchy in a Welfare Society*. Oslo: Universitetsforlaget.
Dahl, T. S. 1985. *Kvinnerett I*. Oslo: Universitetsforlaget.
Dahl, T. S. 1987. *Women's Law*. Oslo: Norwegian University Press.
Dahlerup, D. 1975. Korporatismebegrebet og studiet af samspillet mellem politiske institutioner. (The Concept of Corporatism and the Study of the Interaction between Political Institutions) *Økonomi og Politik*, 4.
Eduards, M. L. 1986. Kön, stat, och jämställdhetspolitik. *Kvinneovetenskapelig Tidsskrift*, 6, 4–15.
Eduards, M., Halsaa, B. and Skjeie, H. 1985. Equality: How Equal? In Haavio-Mannila (ed.) *Unfinished Democracy*. London: Pergamon.
Esping-Andersen, G. and Korpi, W. 1984. Social Policy and Class Politics in Post-War Capitalism: Scandinavia, Austria, Germany. In Goldthorpe (ed.) *Order and Conflict in Contemporary Capitalism*. Oxford: Clarendon Press.
Esping-Andersen, G. and Korpi, W. 1987. From Poor Relief to Institutional Welfare States: The Development of Scandinavian Social Policy. In Erikson et al. (eds.) *The Scandinavian Model: Welfare States and Welfare Research*. New York: M. E. Sharpe.
Graubard, S. (ed.) 1985. *Norden: The Passion for Equality*. Oslo: Norwegian University Press.
Haavio-Mannila, E. (ed.) 1985. *Unfinished Democracy*. London: Pergamon Press.
Hentilä, S. 1978. The Origins of the Folkhem Ideology in Swedish Social Democracy, *Scandinavian Journal of History*, 3, 323–345.
Hernes, H. M. 1982. *Staten – kvinner ingen adgang?* (The State – No Access for Women?) Oslo: Universitetsforlaget.
Jonung, C. 1982. Kvinnornav i Svensk Ekonomi. Særtrykk nr. 50. Lund: Nationalekonomiska Institutionen.
Klein, V. and Myrdal, A. 1956. *Women's Two Roles. Home and Work*. London: Kegan Paul.
Korpi, W. 1985. *Economic Growth and the Welfare State: Leaky Bucket or Irrigation System?* Paris: Paper presented at the World Congress of the International Political Science Association.
Myrdal, A. and Myrdal, G. 1935. *Kris i Befolkningsfrågan*. Stockholm: Liber.
O'Brien, M. 1979. Reproducing Marxist Man. In Clark and Lange (eds.) *The Sexism of Social and Political Theory*. Toronto: University of Toronto Press.
Piven, F. F. 1985. Women and The State: Ideology, Power and The Welfare State. In Rossi (ed.) *Gender and the Life Course*. New York: Aldine.
Piven, F. F. and Cloward, R. A. 1985. *The New Class War: Reagan's Attack on the Welfare State and its Consequences*. (rev. ed.) New York: Pantheon Books.
Scott, J. 1986. Gender: A Useful Category of Historical Analysis. *The American Historical Review*, 91, 1053–1075.

Part II

Welfare Regimes Under Threat

In Part II of the reader, we adopt a more empirical and comparative approach, focusing on the factors shaping the form and influencing the contemporary development of modern welfare states. The selections here are chosen with three goals in mind. The first is to locate the trajectories of development that have given rise to the varieties of welfare state activity manifested in the contemporary practice of advanced, industrial nations. The second is to identify the major constraints and challenges likely to face, and possibly threaten the continued viability of, the welfare state over coming decades. The third is to introduce some of the more important topics of debate and policy issues currently preoccupying scholars from the many disciplines – including sociology, political science, economics and social policy – which see the welfare state and the public sector more broadly as among their central concerns. Since social provision in its many forms is now the predominant activity of the state in all modern societies, these are topics and policy issues clearly pivotal to understanding the contemporary functioning of such societies and how they are changing.

Our preference for comparative studies has a double rationale. Partly, we want to avoid the parochialism that comes from identifying any particular welfare state as the template for welfare states in general. More importantly, comparison is a key to better understanding. By the standards of the classic contributors to the welfare state literature discussed in Part I, virtually all modern states are welfare states, but that does not mean that they are all the same. Different welfare states achieve different degrees of poverty alleviation, income inequality and risk reduction. Their welfare systems have different implications for welfare dependency and they structure gender inequalities in different ways. Such differences are relevant to both policy goals and normative concerns, because they help us to establish the conditions under which desired social policy objectives may be achieved in practice.

A comparative approach also helps us to locate sources of weakness in welfare state arrangements and institutions. As noted above, one of our major concerns is to identify constraints and challenges to the contemporary welfare state. But again there are important differences between countries. Some appear to have coped better with economic and demographic problems than others. In some, economic crisis has done little to disrupt existing patterns of provision; in others, retrenchment policies have threatened the very fabric of the caring society. In some countries, support for the welfare state project has remained rock solid, while in others there has been a strong political backlash against at least some forms of public intervention. Locating the reasons why such differences occur may tell us why some welfare states are more vulnerable to attack than others and may even provide us with the knowledge required to redesign welfare state institutions so that they are less vulnerable in future.

The first section of Part II focuses on Trajectories of contemporary welfare state development and, in particular, the factors that have shaped distinctive models of social provision. Here, the by now classic formulation comes from Gøsta Esping-Andersen's *Three Worlds of Welfare Capitalism* in which he identifies 'liberal', 'conservative/corporatist' and 'social democratic' regime types, each with its own distinctive pattern of social rights. In this account, the trajectory of welfare state development over the past century, and, in particular, during the 'golden age' of the post-Second World War decades, has been shaped by the power resources of social classes as expressed through the democratic political process. Where the economic liberalism of the middle classes was dominant in politics, as in the UK and USA, the role of the state remained limited and welfare has been seen as a minimalist anti-poverty strategy rather than a means of creating greater social and economic equality. Where centrist parties – often of a Christian Democratic persuasion, as in much of Western Europe – have been dominant, the emphasis has been on status preservation, ensuring that those without incomes from employment through no fault of their own (the sick, the invalid, the old, the unemployed) can enjoy lifestyles similar to those when they were employed. Finally, in the social democratic regime, substantially identified with the countries of the Nordic area, in which socialist parties backed by strong trade unions have been dominant, the social policy goal has been to create social solidarity by using the welfare state as a means of economic redistribution and of furthering social equality. Esping-Andersen's analysis moves beyond earlier comparative accounts of differences among welfare states by focusing less on how much countries spend on social policies and more on the goals of each regime and the social rights they confer.

There has been a huge literature debating how accurately Esping-Andersen's regimes typology describes the variety of contemporary Western welfare states, but his account has remained the starting point for virtually all subsequent analyses of patterns of welfare state development. This remains true of the two pieces making up the remainder of the Trajectories section. Both involve critiques of the factors that according to Esping-Andersen drive present and future trajectories of welfare state development. Philip Manow and Kees van Kersbergen have no disagreement with Esping-Andersen as to the kinds of welfare regimes that emerged in Western nations in the course of the twentieth century, but they do want to modify his account of a development of the welfare state based exclusively on a class-based power resources model. No less important, they argue, were religious ideas and religious cleavages in conjunction with electoral system dynamics. Reformed Protestantism (as particularly in the United States) was deeply antagonistic to the state; Lutheranism of the kind prevalent in Scandinavia, in contrast, viewed state action positively. Where Catholicism was strong, as in continental Europe, Church and State were opposed but contested social policy leadership. Where majoritarian electoral systems existed, as in the English-speaking countries, class cleavages were dominant and middle-class liberal ideas tended to prevail in politics. Where proportional electoral systems existed, the absence of a major religious cleavage, as in Scandinavia, allowed a class alliance of workers and agrarian parties to dominate twentieth-century politics, while the strong religious cleavage in continental Europe between the Church and anti-clerical liberals favoured the emergence of Christian Democratic parties.

Paul Pierson equally has no quarrel with Esping-Andersen's account of the three regime types or, indeed, of their emergence as a function of different patterns of partisan control of government. What he disputes is the relevance of this 'old politics of the welfare state' to the welfare state trends observed in recent decades. He suggests that the old class politics has been superseded by a 'new politics of the welfare state' in which the natural wish of politicians to avoid blame for unpopular policies has combined with the development of new constituencies of support for established welfare programmes to make welfare retrenchment in an era of economic austerity an issue of extreme political sensitivity. In Pierson's view, this is ultimately why both Thatcher and Reagan failed in their ideologically driven campaigns against public sector spending. His argument suggests that the factors driving the trajectory of future welfare state development in what looks increasingly likely to be a continuing era of fiscal austerity may well be quite different from those that faced politicians in the 'golden age' of economic and welfare state growth.

The remaining two sections of Part II deal with some of the more important factors that make fiscal austerity a probable permanent feature of the immediate future of the welfare state. On the one hand, there are constraints that are likely to limit the resources available for further social policy expansion or even exert pressures for welfare state retrenchment. On the other, there are economic and demographic challenges that suggest the desirability of enhanced spending and for the introduction of new programmes to cater for new sources of need. Even if financial resources are not as constrained as many suggest, the expansion of social policy into new areas more or less guarantees that social welfare budgets will always be subject to severe scrutiny and political controversy, whether such controversy takes 'old' or 'new' forms.

The section on Constraints starts out by focusing on debates over factors seen as limiting the room for manoeuvre of individual nations to expand the welfare state as they wish. One such factor is the increasing globalization of the international economy, which has been seen by many writers as forcing governments to cut back welfare entitlements in order for domestic firms to compete internationally. Another has been the emergence in Western Europe of a model of social provision, which, while not necessarily restrictive in financial terms, does potentially impose legal and political limits on the nature of the social programmes on offer. Both factors suggest that countries will become more alike in the nature of their social policies, either across the universe of modern welfare states as a whole or at least across the now twenty-seven member states of the European Community. Our first two readings – Duane Swank on globalization, and Jon Kvist and Juho Saari on Europeanization – suggest that these fears of welfare state convergence are exaggerated. However, the third reading, by Carina Schmitt and Peter Starke, argues strongly that, once we take into account a number of conditional factors, including globalization, EU membership and the diverse structure of social programmes, the tendency of recent development has been decisively convergent. Consolingly for welfare state advocates, however, the expenditure trends uncovered by these various studies are not downwards as predicted by the globalization hypothesis but mildly positive in aggregate and across most programmes.

The empirical data on which these three studies are based only goes up to midway through the first decade of the twenty-first century. Since then, arguably, prospects for welfare state development have darkened further as a consequence of the Global Financial Crisis of 2008 onwards. The Constraints section's concluding paper by Klaus Armingeon examines responses to the crisis and suggests that by 2010 'austerity was the only game in town', although providing evidence that austerity was substantially a function of prior levels of fiscal deficit and that where debt levels were low there remained some scope for Leftist governments to contain cuts in social spending.

The final section of Part II on Challenges contains papers identifying particular problem areas for modern welfare states where demographic, economic and social trends seem to imply a need either for expanding existing programmes, creating new ones or, perhaps, most controversially, shifting resources from older programmes to new ones. Two of these challenges are demographic. The piece by Volker Meier and Martin Werding discusses the social policy implications of the ageing of the population across most industrialized nations, with a consequent need for more spending on pensions and health and a strong incentive for the reform of existing pensions systems. The ageing problem is exacerbated by the associated demographic phenomenon of declining fertility highlighted here by Peter McDonald's discussion of the Japanese case. Declining fertility simultaneously increases the need for spending by undercutting the base for family support of the elderly and infirm while creating pressures on funding by radically reducing the size of the active working population which pays the taxes that support the welfare state. A further challenge is to use social policy to diminish the marginality of ethnic minorities, the increasing differentiation of which, according to Carl-Ulrik Shierup and Stephen Castles, has itself been used by neoliberal reformers to attack former principles of welfare universalism and social redistribution. Finally, to complete Part II, Giuliano Bonoli brings us back to the question of how we manage the politics of building a welfare state designed to cope with a whole range of 'new social risks', including not only the challenges highlighted above, but also the often quite radically changing employment, gender and preference patterns of recent decades. Many of these issues are further explored in Part III.

Trajectories

Three Worlds of Welfare Capitalism

Gøsta Esping-Andersen

What is the Welfare State?

Every theoretical paradigm must somehow define the welfare state. How do we know when and if a welfare state responds functionally to the needs of industrialism, or to capitalist reproduction and legitimacy? And how do we identify a welfare state that corresponds to the demands that a mobilized working class might have? We cannot test contending arguments unless we have a commonly shared conception of the phenomenon to be explained.

A remarkable attribute of the entire literature is its lack of much genuine interest in the welfare state as such. Welfare state studies have been motivated by theoretical concerns with other phenomena, such as power, industrialization or capitalist contradictions; the welfare state itself has generally received scant conceptual attention. If welfare states differ, how do they differ? And when, indeed, is a state a welfare state? This turns attention straight back to the original question: what is the welfare state?

A common textbook definition is that it involves state responsibility for securing some basic modicum of welfare for its citizens. Such a definition skirts the issue of whether social policies are emancipatory or not; whether they help system legitimation or not; whether they contradict or aid the market process; and what, indeed, is meant by 'basic'? Would it not be more appropriate to require of a welfare state that it satisfies more than our basic or minimal welfare needs?

The first generation of comparative studies started with this type of conceptualization. They assumed, without much reflection, that the level of social expenditure adequately reflects a state's commitment to welfare. The theoretical intent was not really to arrive at an understanding of the welfare state, but rather to test the validity of contending theoretical models in political economy. By scoring nations with respect to urbanization, level of economic growth, and the proportion of aged in the demographic structure, it was believed that the essential features of industrial modernization were properly considered. Alternatively, power-oriented theories compared nations on left-party strength or working-class power mobilization.

The findings of the first-generation comparativists are difficult to evaluate, since there is no convincing case for any particular theory. The shortage of nations for comparisons statistically restricts the number of variables that can be tested simultaneously. Thus, when Cutright (1965) or Wilensky (1975) find that economic level, with its demographic and bureaucratic correlates, explains most welfare-state variations in 'rich countries', relevant measures of working-class mobilization or economic openness are not included. Their conclusions in favour of a 'logic of industrialism' view are therefore in doubt. And, when Hewitt (1977), Stephens (1979), Korpi (1983), Myles (1984) and Esping-Andersen (1985) find strong evidence in favour of a working-class mobilization thesis, or when Schmidt (1982, 1983) finds support for a neo-corporatist, and Cameron (1978) for an economic openness argument, it is without fully testing against plausible alternative explanations.

Most of these studies claim to explain the welfare state. Yet their focus on spending may be misleading. Expenditures are epiphenomenal to the theoretical substance of welfare states. Moreover, the linear scoring approach (more or less power, democracy or spending) contradicts the sociological notion that power, democracy or welfare are relational and structured phenomena. By scoring welfare states on spending, we assume that all spending counts equally. But some welfare states, the Austrian one, for example, spend a large share on benefits to privileged civil servants. This is normally not what we would consider a commitment to social citizenship and solidarity. Others spend disproportionately on means-tested social assistance. Few contemporary analysts would agree that a reformed poor-relief tradition qualifies as a welfare-state commitment. Some nations spend enormous sums on fiscal welfare in the form of tax privileges to private insurance plans that mainly benefit the middle classes. But these tax expenditures do not show up on expenditure accounts. In Britain, total social expenditure [grew] during the Thatcher period, yet this is almost exclusively a function of very high unemployment. Low expenditure on some programmes may signify a welfare state more seriously committed to full employment.

Therborn (1983) is right when he holds that we must begin with a conception of state structure. What are the criteria with which we should judge whether, and when, a state is a welfare state? There are three approaches to this question. Therborn's proposal is to begin with the historical transformation of state activities. Minimally, in a genuine welfare state the majority of its daily routine activities must be devoted to servicing the welfare needs of households. This criterion has far-reaching consequences. If we simply measure routine activity in terms of spending and personnel, the result is that no state can be regarded as a real welfare state until the 1970s, and some that we normally label as welfare states will not qualify because the majority of their routine activities concern defence, law and order, administration and the like (Therborn, 1983). Social scientists have been too quick to accept nations' self-proclaimed welfare state status. They have also been too quick to conclude that if the standard social programmes have been introduced, the welfare state has been born.

The second conceptual approach derives from Richard Titmuss's (1958) classical distinction between residual and institutional welfare states. In the former, the state assumes responsibility only when the family or the market fails; it seeks to limit its commitments to marginal and deserving social groups. The latter model addresses the entire population, is universalistic, and embodies an institutionalized commitment to welfare. It will, in principle, extend welfare commitments to all areas of distribution vital for societal welfare.

The Titmuss approach has fertilized a variety of new developments in comparative welfare state research (Korpi, 1980; Myles, 1984; Esping-Andersen and Korpi, 1984, 1986; Esping-Andersen, 1985, 1987). It is an approach that forces researches to move from the black box of expenditures to the content of welfare states: targeted versus universalistic programmes, the conditions of eligibility, the quality of benefits and services, and, perhaps most importantly, the extent to which employment and working life are encompassed in the state's extension of citizen rights. The shift to welfare state typologies makes simple linear welfare state rankings difficult to sustain. Conceptually, we are comparing categorically different types of state.

The third approach is to theoretically select the criteria on which to judge types of welfare state. This can be done by measuring actual welfare states against some abstract model and then scoring programmes, or entire welfare states, accordingly (Myles, 1984). But this is ahistorical, and does not necessarily capture the ideals or designs that historical actors sought to realize in the struggles over the welfare state. If our aim is to test causal theories that involve actors, we should begin with the demands that were actually promoted by those actors that we deem critical in the history of welfare state development. It is difficult to imagine that anyone struggled for spending *per se*.

A Re-specification of the Welfare State

Few can disagree with T. H. Marshall's (1950) proposition that social citizenship constitutes the core idea of a welfare state. But the concept must be fleshed out. Above all, it must involve the granting of social rights. If social rights are given the legal and practical status of property rights, if they are inviolable, and if they are granted on the basis of citizenship rather than performance, they will entail a de-commodification of the status of individuals *vis-à-vis* the market. But the concept of social citizenship also involves social stratification: one's status as a citizen will compete with, or even replace, one's class position.

The welfare state cannot be understood just in terms of the rights it grants. We must also take into account how state activities are interlocked with the market's and the family's role in social provision. These are the three main principles that need to be fleshed out prior to any theoretical specification of the welfare state.

Rights and De-Commodification

In pre-capitalist societies, few workers were properly commodities in the sense that their survival was contingent upon the sale of their labour power. It is as markets become universal and hegemonic that the welfare of individuals comes to depend entirely on the cash nexus. Stripping society of the institutional layers that guaranteed social reproduction outside the labour contract meant that people were commodified. In turn, the introduction of modern social rights implies a loosening of the pure commodity status. De-commodification occurs when a service is rendered as a matter of right, and when a person can maintain a livelihood without reliance on the market.

The mere presence of social assistance or insurance may not necessarily bring about significant de-commodification if they do not substantially emancipate individuals from market dependence. Means-tested poor relief will possibly offer a safety net of last resort. But if benefits are low and associated with social stigma, the relief system will compel all but the most desperate to participate in the market. This was precisely the intent of the nineteenth-century Poor Laws in most countries. Similarly, most of the early social-insurance programmes were deliberately designed to maximize labour-market performance.

There is no doubt that de-commodification has been a hugely contested issue in welfare state development. For labour, it has always been a priority. When workers are completely market-dependent, they are difficult to mobilize for solidaristic action. Since their resources mirror market inequalities, divisions emerge between the 'ins' and the 'outs', making labour-movement formation difficult. De-commodification strengthens the workers and weakens the absolute authority of the employer. It is for exactly this reason that employers have always opposed de-commodification.

De-commodified rights are differentially developed in contemporary welfare states. In social-assistance dominated welfare states, rights are not so much attached to work performance as to demonstrable need. Needs-tests and typically meagre benefits, however, service to curtail the decom-modifying effect. Thus, in nations where this model is dominant (mainly in the Anglo-Saxon countries), the result is actually to strengthen the market since all but those who fail in the market will be encouraged to contract private-sector welfare.

A second dominant model espouses compulsory state social insurance with fairly strong entitlements. But again, this may not automatically secure substantial de-commodification, since this hinges very much on the fabric of eligibility and benefit rules. Germany was the pioneer of social insurance, but over most of the [twentieth century] can hardly be said to have brought about much in the way of de-commodification through its social programmes. Benefits have depended almost entirely on contribu-tions, and thus on work and employment. In other words, it is not the mere presence of a social right, but the corresponding rules and precondi-tions, which dictate the extent to which welfare programmes offer genuine alternatives to market dependence.

The third dominant model of welfare, namely the Beveridge-type citi-zens' benefit, may, at first glance, appear the most de-commodifying. It offers a basic, equal benefit to all, irrespective of prior earnings, contribu-tions or performance. It may indeed be a more solidaristic system, but not necessarily de-commodifying, since only rarely have such schemes been able to offer benefits of such a standard that they provide recipients with a genuine option to working.

De-commodifying welfare states are, in practice, fairly recent. A minimal definition must entail that citizens can freely, and without poten-tial loss of job, income or general welfare, opt out of work when they themselves consider it necessary. With this definition in mind, we would, for example, require of a sickness insurance that individuals be guaranteed benefits equal to normal earnings, and the right to absence with minimal proof of medical impairment and for the duration that the individual deems necessary. These conditions, it is worth noting, are those usually enjoyed by academics, civil servants and higher-echelon white-collar employees. Similar requirements would be made of pensions, maternity leave, parental leave, educational leave and unemployment insurance.

Some nations have moved towards this level of de-commodification, but only recently, and, in many cases, with significant exemptions. In almost all nations, benefits were upgraded to nearly equal normal wages in the late 1960s and early 1970s. But in some countries, for example, prompt medical certification in case of illness is still required; in others, entitlements depend on long waiting periods of up to two weeks; and in still others, the duration of entitlements is very short. [...] The Scandinavian welfare states tend to be the most de-commodifying; the Anglo-Saxon the least.

The Welfare State as a System of Stratification

Despite the emphasis given to it in both classical political economy and in T. H. Marshall's pioneering work, the relationship between citizenship and social class has been neglected both theoretically and empirically. Generally speaking, the issue has either been assumed away (it has been taken for granted that the welfare state creates a more egalitarian society), or it has been approached narrowly in terms of income distribution or in terms of whether education promotes upward social mobility. A more basic question, it seems, is what kind of stratification system is promoted by social policy. The welfare state is not just a mechanism that intervenes in, and possibly corrects, the structure of inequality; it is, in its own right, a system of stratification. It is an active force in the ordering of social relations.

Comparatively and historically, we can easily identify alternative systems of stratification embedded in welfare states. The poor-relief tradition, and its contemporary means-tested social-assistance offshoot, was conspicuously designed for purposes of stratification. By punishing and stigmatizing recipients, it promotes social dualisms and has therefore been a chief target of labour-movement attacks.

The social-insurance model promoted by conservative reformers such as Bismarck and von Taffe was also explicitly a form of class politics. It sought, in fact, to achieve two simultaneous results in terms of stratification. The first was to consolidate divisions among wage-earners by legislating distinct programmes for different class and status groups, each with its own conspicuously unique set of rights and privileges, which was designed to accentuate the individual's appropriate station in life. The second objective was to tie the loyalties of the individual directly to the monarchy or the central state authority. This was Bismarck's motive when he promoted a direct state supplement to the pension benefit. This state-corporatist model was pursued mainly in nations such as Germany, Austria, Italy and France, and often resulted in a labyrinth of status-specific insurance funds.

Of special importance in this corporatist tradition was the establishment of particularly privileged welfare provisions for the civil service (*Beamten*). In part, this was a means of rewarding loyalty to the state, and in part it was a way of demarcating this group's uniquely exalted social status. The corporatist status-differentiated model springs mainly from the old guild tradition. The neo-absolutist autocrats, such as Bismarck, saw in this tradition a means to combat the rising labour movements.

The labour movements were as hostile to the corporatist model as they were to poor relief – in both cases for obvious reasons. Yet the alternatives first espoused by labour were no less problematic from the point of view of uniting the workers as one solidaristic class. Almost invariably, the model that labour first pursued was that of self-organized friendly societies or equivalent union- or party-sponsored fraternal welfare plans. This is not surprising. Workers were obviously suspicious of reforms sponsored by a hostile state, and saw their own organizations not only as bases of class mobilization, but also as embryos of an alternative world of solidarity and justice; as a microcosm of the socialist haven to come. Nonetheless, these micro-socialist societies often became problematic class ghettos that divided rather than united workers. Membership was typically restricted to the strongest strata of the working class, and the weakest – who most needed protection – were most likely excluded. In brief, the fraternal society model frustrated the goal of working-class mobilization.

The socialist 'ghetto approach' was an additional obstacle when socialist parties found themselves forming governments and having to pass the social reforms they had so long demanded. For political reasons of coalition-building and broader solidarity, their welfare model had to be recast as welfare for 'the people'. Hence, the socialists came to espouse the principle of universalism; borrowing from the liberals, their programme was, typically, designed along the lines of the democratic flat-rate, general revenue-financed Beveridge model.

As an alternative to means-tested assistance and corporatist social insurance, the universalistic system promotes equality of status. All citizens are endowed with similar rights, irrespective of class or market position. In this sense, the system is meant to cultivate cross-class solidarity, a solidarity of the nation. But the solidarity of flat-rate universalism presumes a historically peculiar class structure, one in which the vast majority of the population are the 'little people' for whom a modest, albeit egalitarian, benefit may be considered adequate. Where this no longer obtains, as occurs with growing working-class prosperity and the rise of the new middle classes, flat-rate universalism inadvertently promotes dualism because the better-off turn to private insurance and to fringe-benefit bargaining to supplement modest equality with what they have decided are accustomed standards of welfare. Where this process unfolds (as in Canada or Great Britain), the result is that the wonderfully egalitarian spirit of universalism turns into a dualism similar to that of the social-assistance state: the poor rely on the state, and the remainder on the market.

It is not only the universalist but, in fact, all historical welfare state models which have faced the dilemma of changes in class structure. But the response to prosperity and middle-class growth has been varied, and so, therefore, has been the outcome in terms of stratification. The corporatist insurance tradition was, in a sense, best equipped to manage new and loftier welfare-state expectations since the existing system could technically be upgraded quite easily to distribute more adequate benefits. Adenauer's 1957 pension reform in Germany was a pioneer in this respect. Its avowed purpose was to restore status differences that had been eroded because of the old insurance system's incapacity to provide benefits tailored to expectations. This it did simply by moving from contribution- to earnings-graduated benefits without altering the framework of status-distinctiveness.

In nations with either a social-assistance or a universalistic Beveridge-type system, the option was whether to allow the market or the state to furnish adequacy and satisfy middle-class aspirations. Two alternative models emerged from this political choice. The one typical of Great Britain and most of the Anglo-Saxon world was to preserve an essentially modest universalism in the state, and allow the market to reign for the growing social strata demanding superior welfare. Due to the political power of such groups, the dualism that emerges is not merely one between state and market, but also between forms of welfare-state transfers: in these nations, one of the fastest growing components of public expenditure is tax subsidies for so-called 'private' welfare plans. And the typical political effect is the erosion of middle-class support for what is less and less a universalistic public-sector transfer system.

Yet another alternative has been to seek a synthesis of universalism and adequacy outside the market. This road has been followed in countries where, by mandating or legislation, the state incorporates the new middle classes within a luxurious second-tier, universally inclusive, earnings-related insurance scheme on top of the flat-rate egalitarian one. Notable examples are Sweden and Norway. By guaranteeing benefits tailored to expectations, this solution reintroduces benefit inequalities, but effectively blocks off the market. It thus succeeds in retaining universalism and also, therefore, the degree of political consensus required to preserve broad and solidaristic support for the high taxes that such a welfare state model demands.

Welfare State Regimes

As we survey international variations in social rights and welfare-state stratification, we will find qualitatively different arrangements between state, market and the family. The welfare state variations we find are therefore not linearly distributed, but clustered by regime-types.

In one cluster we find the 'liberal' welfare state, in which means-tested assistance, modest universal transfers or modest social-insurance plans predominate. Benefits cater mainly to a clientele of low-income, usually working-class, state dependants. In this model, the progress of social reform has been severely circumscribed by traditional, liberal work-ethic norms: it is one where the limits of welfare equal the marginal propensity to opt for welfare instead of work. Entitlement rules are therefore strict and often associated with stigma; benefits are typically modest. In turn, the state encourages the market, either passively – by guaranteeing only a minimum – or actively – by subsidizing private welfare schemes.

The consequence is that this type of regime minimizes de-commodification effects, effectively contains the realm of social rights, and erects an order of stratification that is a blend of a relative equality of poverty among state-welfare recipients, market-differentiated welfare among the majorities, and a class-political dualism between the two. The archetypical examples of this model are the United States, Canada and Australia.

A second regime-type clusters nations such as Austria, France, Germany and Italy. Here, the historical corporatist-statist legacy was upgraded to cater to the new 'post-industrial' class structure. In these conservative and strongly 'corporatist' welfare states, the liberal obsession with market efficiency and commodification was never pre-eminent and, as such, the granting of social rights was hardly ever a seriously contested issue. What predominated was the preservation of status differentials; rights, therefore, were attached to class and status. This corporatism was subsumed under a state edifice perfectly ready to displace the market as a provider of welfare; hence, private insurance and occupational fringe benefits play a truly marginal role. On the other hand, the state's emphasis on upholding status differences means that its redistributive impact is negligible.

But the corporatist regimes are also typically shaped by the Church, and hence strongly committed to the preservation of traditional family-hood. Social insurance typically excludes non-working wives, and family benefits encourage motherhood. Day care, and similar family services, are conspicuously underdeveloped; the principle of 'subsidiarity' serves to emphasize that the state will only interfere when the family's capacity to service its members is exhausted.

The third, and clearly smallest, regime-cluster is composed of those countries in which the principles of universalism and de-commodification of social rights were extended also to the new middle classes. We may call it the 'social democratic' regime-type since, in these nations, social democracy was clearly the dominant force behind social reform. Rather than tolerate a dualism between state and market, between working class and middle class, the social democrats pursued a welfare state that would promote an equality of the highest standards, not an equality of minimal needs as was pursued elsewhere. This implied, first, that services and benefits be upgraded to levels commensurate with even the most discriminating tastes of the new middle classes; and, second, that equality be furnished by guaranteeing workers full participation in the quality of rights enjoyed by the better-off.

This formula translates into a mix of highly de-commodifying and universalistic programmes that, nonetheless, are tailored to differentiated expectations. Thus, manual workers come to enjoy rights identical with those of salaried white-collar employees or civil servants; all strata are incorporated under one universal insurance system, yet benefits are graduated according to accustomed earnings. This model crowds out the market, and consequently constructs an essentially universal solidarity in favour of the welfare state. All benefit; all are dependent; and all will presumably feel obliged to pay.

The social democratic regime's policy of emancipation addresses both the market and the traditional family. In contrast to the corporatist-subsidiarity model, the principle is not to wait until the family's capacity to aid is exhausted, but to pre-emptively socialize the costs of familyhood. The ideal is not to maximize dependence on the family, but capacities for individual independence. In this sense, the model is a peculiar fusion of liberalism and socialism. The result is a welfare state that grants transfers directly to children, and takes direct responsibility of caring for children, the aged and the helpless. It is, accordingly, committed to a heavy social-service burden, not only to service family needs but also to allow women to choose work rather than the household.

Perhaps the most salient characteristic of the social democratic regime is its fusion of welfare and work. It is at once genuinely committed to a full-employment guarantee, and entirely dependent on its attainment. On the one side, the right to work has equal status to the right of income protection. On the other side, the enormous costs of maintaining a solidaristic, universalistic and de-commodifying welfare system means that it must minimize social problems and maximize revenue income. This is obviously best done with most people working, and the fewest possible living off social transfers.

Neither of the two alternative regime-types espouse full employment as an integral part of their welfare state commitment. In the conservative tradition, of course, women are discouraged from working; in the liberal ideal, concerns of gender matter less than the sanctity of the market.

[. . .] Welfare states cluster, but we must recognize that there is no single pure case. The Scandinavian countries may be predominantly social democratic, but they are not free of crucial liberal elements. Neither are the liberal regimes pure types. The American social-security system is redistributive, compulsory and far from actuarial. At least in its early formulation, the New Deal was as social democratic as was contemporary Scandinavian social democracy. And European conservative regimes have incorporated both liberal and social democratic impulses. Over the decades, they have become less corporativist and less authoritarian.

Notwithstanding the lack of purity, if our essential criteria for defining welfare states have to do with the quality of social rights, social stratification and the relationship between state, market and family, the world is obviously composed of distinct regime-clusters. Comparing welfare states on scales of more or less or, indeed, of better or worse, will yield highly misleading results.

The Causes of Welfare-State Regimes

If welfare states cluster into three distinct regime-types, we face a substantially more complex task of identifying the causes of welfare state differences. What is the explanatory power of industrialization, economic growth, capitalism or working-class political power in accounting for regime-types? A first superficial answer would be: very little. The nations we study are all more or less similar with regard to all but the variable of working-class mobilization. And we find very powerful labour movements and parties in each of the three clusters.

A theory of welfare state developments must clearly reconsider its causal assumptions if it wishes to explain clusters. The hope of finding one single powerful causal force must be abandoned; the task is to identify salient interaction effects. Based on the preceding arguments, three factors in particular should be of importance: the nature of class mobilization (especially of the working class); class-political coalition structures; and the historical legacy of regime institutionalization.

[. . .] There is absolutely no compelling reason to believe that workers will automatically and naturally forge a socialist class identity; nor is it plausible that their mobilization will look especially Swedish. The actual historical formation of working-class collectivities will diverge, and so also will their aims, ideology and political capacities. Fundamental differences appear both in trade unionism and party development. Unions may be sectional or in pursuit of more universal objectives; they may be denominational or secular; and they may be ideological or devoted to business unionism. Whichever they are, it will decisively affect the articulation of political demands, class cohesion and the scope for labour-party action. It is clear that a working-class mobilization thesis must pay attention to union structure.

The structure of trade unionism may or may not be reflected in labour-party formation. But under what conditions are we likely to expect certain welfare state outcomes from specific party configurations? There are many factors that conspire to make it virtually impossible to assume that any labour, or left-wing, party will ever be capable, single-handedly, of structuring a welfare state. Denominational or other divisions aside, it will be only under extraordinary historical circumstances that a labour party alone will command a parliamentary majority long enough to impose its will. [. . .] The traditional working class has hardly ever constituted an electoral majority. It follows that a theory of class mobilization must look beyond the major leftist parties. It is a historical fact that welfare state construction has depended on political coalition-building. The structure of class coalitions is much more decisive than are the power resources of any single class.

The emergence of alternative class coalitions is, in part, determined by class formation. In the earlier phases of industrialization, the rural classes usually constituted the largest single group in the electorate. If social democrats wanted political majorities, it was here that they were forced to look for allies. One of history's many paradoxes is that the rural classes were decisive for the future of socialism. Where the rural economy was dominated by small, capital-intensive family farmers, the potential for an alliance was greater than where it rested on large pools of cheap labour. And where farmers were politically articulate and well organized (as in Scandinavia), the capacity to negotiate political deals was vastly superior.

The role of the farmers in coalition formation and hence in welfare state development is clear. In the Nordic countries, the necessary conditions obtained for a broad red–green alliance for a full-employment welfare state in return for farm price subsidies. This was especially true in Norway and Sweden, where farming was highly precarious and dependent on state aid. In the United States, the New Deal was premised on a similar coalition (forged by the Democratic Party), but with the important difference that the labour-intensive South blocked a truly universalistic social security system and opposed further welfare-state developments. In contrast, the rural economy of continental Europe was very inhospitable to red–green coalitions. Often, as in Germany and Italy, much of agriculture was labour-intensive; hence the unions and left-wing parties were seen as a threat. In addition, the conservative forces on the continent had succeeded in incorporating farmers into 'reactionary' alliances, helping to consolidate the political isolation of labour.

Political dominance was, until after the Second World War, largely a question of rural class politics. The construction of welfare states in this period was, therefore, dictated by whichever force captured the farmers. The absence of a red–green alliance does not necessarily imply that no welfare-state reforms were possible. On the contrary, it implies which political force came to dominate their design. Great Britain is an exception to this general rule, because the political significance of the rural classes eroded before the turn of the century. In this way, Britain's coalition-logic showed at an early date the dilemma that faced most other nations later; namely, that the rising white-collar strata constitute the linchpin for political majorities. The consolidation of welfare states after the Second World War came to depend fundamentally on the political alliances of the new middle classes. For social democracy, the challenge was to synthesize working-class and white-collar demands without sacrificing the commitment to solidarity.

Since the new middle classes have, historically, enjoyed a relatively privileged position in the market, they have also been quite successful in meeting their welfare demands outside the state, or, as civil servants, by privileged state welfare. Their employment security has traditionally been such that full employment has been a peripheral concern. Finally, any programme for drastic income-equalization is likely to be met with great hostility among a middle-class clientele. On these grounds, it would appear that the rise of the new middle classes would abort the social democratic project and strengthen a liberal welfare state formula.

The political leanings of the new middle classes have, indeed, been decisive for welfare state consolidation. Their role in shaping the three welfare state regimes described earlier is clear. The Scandinavian model relied almost entirely on social democracy's capacity to incorporate them into a new kind of welfare state: one that provided benefits tailored to the tastes and expectations of the middle classes, but nonetheless retained universalism of rights. Indeed, by expanding social services and public employment, the welfare state participated directly in manufacturing a middle class instrumentally devoted to social democracy.

In contrast, the Anglo-Saxon nations retained the residual welfare state model precisely because the new middle classes were not wooed from the market to the state. In class terms, the consequence is dualism. The welfare state caters essentially to the working class and the poor. Private insurance and occupational fringe benefits cater to the middle classes. Given the electoral importance of the latter, it is quite logical that further extensions of welfare state activities are resisted.

The third, continental European, welfare state regime has also been patterned by the new middle classes, but in a different way. The cause is historical. Developed by conservative political forces, these regimes institutionalized a middle-class loyalty to the preservation of both occupationally segregated social-insurance programmes and, ultimately, to the political forces that brought them into being. Adenauer's great pension reform in 1957 was explicitly designed to resurrect middle-class loyalties.

Conclusion

We have here presented an alternative to a simple class-mobilization theory of welfare-state development. It is motivated by the analytical necessity of shifting from a linear to an interactive approach with regard to both welfare states and their causes. If we wish to study welfare states, we must begin with a set of criteria that define their role in society. This role is certainly not to spend or tax; nor is it necessarily that of creating equality. We have presented a framework for comparing welfare states that takes into consideration the principles for which the historical actors have willingly united and struggled. When we focus on the principles embedded in welfare states, we discover distinct regime-clusters, not merely variations of 'more' or 'less' around a common denominator.

The historical forces behind the regime differences are interactive. They involve, first, the pattern of working-class political formation and, second, political coalition-building in the transition from a rural economy to a middle-class society. The question of political coalition-formation is decisive. Third, past reforms have contributed decisively to the institutionalization of class preferences and political behaviour. In the corporatist regimes, hierarchical status-distinctive social insurance cemented middle-class loyalty to a peculiar type of welfare state. In liberal regimes, the middle classes became institutionally wedded to the market. And in Scandinavia, the fortunes of social democracy over the past decades were closely tied to the establishment of a middle-class welfare state that benefits both its traditional working-class clientele and the new white-collar strata. The Scandinavian social democrats were able to achieve this in part because the private welfare market was relatively undeveloped and in part because they were capable of building a welfare state with features of sufficient luxury to satisfy the wants of a more discriminating public. This also explains the extraordinarily high cost of Scandinavian welfare states.

But a theory that seeks to explain welfare state growth should also be able to understand its retrenchment or decline. It is generally believed that welfare state backlash movements, tax revolts and roll-backs are ignited when social expenditure burdens become too heavy. Paradoxically, the opposite is true. Anti-welfare-state sentiments [since the 1980s] have generally been weakest where welfare spending has been heaviest, and vice versa. Why?

The risks of welfare state backlash depend not on spending, but on the class character of welfare states. Middle-class welfare states, be they social democratic (as in Scandinavia) or corporatist (as in Germany), forge middle-class loyalties. In contrast, the liberal, residualist welfare states found in the United States, Canada and, increasingly, Britain depend on the loyalties of a numerically weak, and often politically residual, social stratum. In this sense, the class coalitions in which the three welfare-state regime-types were founded explain not only their past evolution but also their future prospects.

Note

References

Cameron, D. R. (1978) 'The Expansion of the Public Economy: A Comparative Analysis', *American Political Science Review*, 72, 4, pp. 1243–61.

Cutright, P. (1965) 'Political Structure, Economic Development, and National Social Security Programs', *American Journal of Sociology*, 70, pp. 537–50.

Esping-Andersen, G. (1985) 'Power and Distributional Regimes', *Politics and Society*, 14.

Esping-Andersen, G. (1987) 'Citizenship and Socialism', in M. Rein, G. Esping-Andersen and M. Rainwater, *Stagnation and Renewal in Social Policy: The Rise and Fall of Policy Regimes*, New York, Sharpe.

Esping-Andersen, G. and Korpi, W. (1984) 'Social Policy and Class Politics in Postwar Capitalism: Scandinavia, Austria and Germany', in *Order and Conflict in Contemporary Capitalism*, ed. J. Goldthorpe, Oxford, Oxford University Press, pp. 179–208.

Esping-Andersen, G. and Korpi, W. (1986) 'From Poor Relief to Institutional Welfare States: The Development of Scandinavian Social Policy', in R. Erikson et al., *The Scandinavian Model: Welfare States and Welfare Research*, New York, Sharpe.

Hewitt, C. (1977) 'The Effect of Political Democracy and Social Democracy on Equality in Industrial Societies: A Cross-National Comparison', *American Sociological Review*, 42, pp. 450–64.

Korpi, W. (1980) 'Social Policy and Distributional Conflict in the Capitalist Democracies', *West European Politics*, 3.

Korpi, W. (1983) *The Democratic Class Struggle*, London, Routledge and Kegan Paul.

Marshall, T. H. (1950) *Citizenship and Social Class*, Cambridge, Cambridge University Press.

Myles, J. (1984) *Old Age in the Welfare State*, Boston, Little, Brown.

Schmidt, M. G. (1982) 'The Role of Parties in Shaping Macro-Economic Policies', in *The Impact of Parties*, ed. F. Castles, London, Sage.

Schmidt, M. G. (1983) 'The Welfare State and the Economy in Periods of Economic Crisis: A Comparative Study of 23 OECD Nations', *European Journal of Political Research*, 11, 1983, pp. 1–26.

Stephens, J. (1979) *The Transition from Capitalism to Socialism*, London, Macmillan.

Therborn, G. (1983) 'When, How and Why does a Welfare State become a Welfare State?', Freiburg, ECPR Workshops.

Titmuss, R. M. (1958) *Essays on the Welfare State*, London, Allen and Unwin.

Wilensky, H. (1975) *The Welfare State and Equality: Structural and Ideological Roots of Public Expenditure*, Berkeley, University of California Press.

Religion and the Western Welfare State

Philip Manow and
Kees van Kersbergen

1.1 Introduction

Most comparativists who study welfare state development agree that religion has played a role in the development of modern social protection systems. The early protagonists of the power resources approach, however, had only stressed the causal impact of Socialist working-class mobilization on modern social policy (see Esping-Andersen and van Kersbergen 1992). In their view, it was the working class and its Socialist organizations that had been the driving force behind the 'social democratization' of capitalism via the welfare state. To them, it came as a surprise that both Social Democracy and (social) Catholicism promoted welfare state development. John D. Stephens (1979: 100), one of the leading spokesmen of this approach, put it in prudent terms when he argued that 'it seemed possible that anti-capitalist aspects of catholic ideology – such as notions of fair wage or prohibitions of usury – as well as the generally positive attitude of the catholic church towards welfare for the poor might encourage government welfare spending'. Similarly, Schmidt (1980, 1982) asserted that Social Democracy and Christian Democracy were functionally equivalent for welfare state expansion, at least during periods of economic prosperity. Wilensky (1981) argued that the two movements overlapped considerably in ideological terms and that Catholicism indeed constituted an even more important determinant of welfare statism than left power did. Catholic social doctrine called for a correction of the most abhorrent societal effects of the capitalist order. The Catholic principle of subsidiarity, moreover, posited that in the last instance the (nation-) state had a duty to intervene to correct for morally unacceptable market outcomes. At the centre of the doctrine was not the type of workers' social *rights* and *emancipation* argument that one finds in Social Democratic ideology, but rather the conviction that people have the Christian *obligation* to help the poor and that social policy can help protect a stable and fair social *order*.

However, it was not only the moral obligations defined in social doctrine and the preoccupation with the problem of social order that determined the pro-welfare stance of religious political parties. Stephens (1979) also suggested that there were more straightforward political reasons why Christian Democratic parties were supporters of the welfare state. These parties operated in the political centre, were seeking the working-class vote, and hoped to cooperate with the Catholic unions. Social policies promised to secure the support of the Catholic working class. Admitting the possibility that other political movements could be attractive to the working class, however, implied that one of the constitutional assumptions of the power resources model had to be relaxed, namely, that the political identity attached to wage labour in capitalism is inherently and of necessity Social Democratic. But, apparently, workers could also be mobilized and organized as Catholics. Of course, much of the apparent contempt for the continental European welfare state in the comparative literature stems from Marxian notions of a 'false consciousness' attached to all forms of political mobilization that do not follow class lines.

Through an elaboration of the power resources approach in Esping-Andersen's (1990) regime approach and a specification of the association between Christian Democracy and the welfare state (van Kersbergen 1995), the welfare state literature posited that it was the combination of Christian Democracy and Catholic social doctrine that explained why Christian Democratic welfare states were as generous in terms of social spending as the Scandinavian ones, but were not designed to counter market pressures (to decommodify labour) to the same extent as the Social Democratic welfare states. Christian Democracy–*cum*–Social Catholicism rather produced and preserved a traditional, patriarchic, status-oriented model of society.

It is this reading of the history of the western welfare state – which owes much to the power resources and regime approach – that is challenged in this book because it seems, at best, incomplete. First, an exclusive focus on the labour question and on worker mobilization ignores other highly contentious issues, particularly whether state or society should be responsible for protecting workers, as well as mothers and families, against the vagaries of life. Here, 'society' often had to be read as 'the church.' The church and the modern nation-state also waged bitter conflicts over which should be the central agent of socialization, as the Dutch '*schoolstrijd*' or the similar conflicts over education in France exemplify. These conflicts over education exerted a profound impact on early welfare state building as well [. . .].

Second, taking into account not only the capital–labour conflict due to the industrial revolution, but also the state–church conflict over education and social policy due to the 'national revolution' (in Stein Rokkan's terms, see Flora 1999), is key to our understanding of modern welfare state development because only in those countries where in the last quarter of the nineteenth century bitter state–church conflicts were waged did parties of religious defence emerge. These parties later became decisive as political actors that mobilized workers and the middle class *not* along class lines, but along cross-cutting lines of denominational belonging. To explain why parties of religious defence formed in continental Europe but not in Scandinavia or England, is a precondition for a thorough understanding of why the continental welfare state developed so differently from the Nordic or Anglo-Saxon welfare regimes.

Third, it is not easy to reconcile the historical facts with the power resources and regime narrative about European welfare state development. For instance, it was Liberalism and anticlericalism rather than Catholicism or Christian Democracy that prevailed in the formative period of the Italian and French welfare states. In fact, in these countries, much of the early social legislation had an obvious anticlerical momentum because the aim was to establish central national state responsibilities in a domain for which the church had always claimed exclusive competency. Yet, despite their obvious Liberal and anticlerical pedigree, countries such as Italy, Belgium, or France are regularly classified as belonging to the Conservative Catholic welfare state regime. Therefore, the dominant reading in the literature, which explains the specific features of the continental welfare regime as a manifestation of Catholic social doctrine, is historically inadequate and blurs the decisive causes for the institutional variance among Western European welfare states.

Fourth, an exclusive focus on Catholic social teaching and Christian Democracy also neglects the influence of Protestantism. For instance, a review of historically oriented studies of the social and political role of Protestantism and Protestant political parties led one of us (van Kersbergen 1995: 254, footnote 1) to reject the idea that Protestantism has had any positive contribution to either Christian Democracy or the welfare state. But this conclusion is only warranted in a limited context, that is, when one indeed focuses on the direct impact of political parties on the emergence and development of social policies and at the same time disregards the differentiation between Lutheran and reformed Protestantism. We have come to the conclusion that a universal statement on the irrelevance of Protestantism for welfare state development is not justified. Historical evidence suggests two things. First, reformed Protestantism substantially delayed and restricted the introduction of modern social policy and therefore had a *negative* impact on welfare state development. Second, the Lutheran state church in Germany or in Scandinavia held no major reservations against the state playing a dominant role in social protection or at least mounted no substantial resistance against the nation-state taking over this new responsibility. It even often supported and welcomed this development. Lutheran state churches therefore *positively* contributed to the early introduction of social protection programmes and to subsequent welfare state development.

In our view, the differences between Catholicism and Protestantism *and* between the major variants of Protestantism are very important for an accurate understanding of the different directions nations took in their social policy development. The Protestant free churches and other reformed currents (Dissenters, Calvinists, Baptists, etc.) held a strongly *antiétatist* position, whereas Lutheran state churches never questioned the prerogative of the central state in social policy and education. In contrast, when workers in Southern Europe fought for their political and social rights, and when Liberals in these countries tried to found modern nation-states, they always had to fight against the Catholic clergy as well, which had been closely attached to the ruling elite of the *ancien régime*. Bitter conflicts between the church and the Liberal elite in the new republican nation-states of Southern Europe were the consequence. It is for this reason that Liberal parties in these countries often introduced new social legislation with explicitly anticlerical motives. This clearly speaks against any unqualified statement that Catholic social doctrine was dominant in the development of the southern or continental welfare state. Christian Democratic parties, which to a large extent were the unintended offspring of the church's political fight against Liberalism, did play an important role, but only much later. Moreover, these parties did not always exactly play the pro-welfare state role that the literature imagines, as in the case of the Italian *Democrazia Cristiana* that used the welfare state primarily as a clientelist resource in its effort to mobilize voters and as a means of becoming more independent from the official church hierarchy.

In sum, according to the power resources and regime analysis, Protestantism has not played a significant role in modern welfare state development, and Catholicism did so only insofar as Christian Democracy possessed a Catholic social doctrine and was successful in organizing and mobilizing Catholic workers. We argue that the impact of political Catholicism and reformed Protestantism on welfare state development in the western world was quite different from what the literature so far has suggested. The role of religion in the development of the western welfare state is far more than just a variation of the dominant 'strength of the worker movement' theme or a question of doctrine influencing policies.

[. . .]

1.2 Protestantism, Secularization, and the Welfare State

[. . .]

Our argument runs as follows. We agree with Duverger and Iversen and Soskice that majoritarian electoral rules lead to a two-party system and that here the middle class more often votes for centre-right parties. In such a two-party system, mainly one societal cleavage is present, namely, the one dominant in all advanced industrial countries, the left–right or labour–capital cleavage. All other cleavages are absorbed, latent, or 'incorporated' in this basic cleavage. A good example would be the fierce conflict between the Anglican high church and the Protestant dissent in Britain in the last quarter of the nineteenth century. This was a virulent conflict line between the Tories and the Liberal Party (Parry 1986) that quickly receded into the background once the Labour Party crowded out the Liberal Party in the 1890s and the first two decades of the twentieth century. The religious dissent then lost its own strong political representation in the party system, the Liberal Party split, and, subsequently, Nonconformism became influential both within the Tories and within the Labour Party, where it strongly influenced the Labour Party's social policy programme (see Pelling 1965; Catterall 1993). It is here where the basic mechanism described by Iversen and Soskice (2006) applies: with only two parties, it is the economic cleavage that is predominantly represented in the party system, and within this setting, the middle class more often votes for Conservative parties. The welfare state remains residual.

   In Proportional Representation (PR) systems, in contrast, a larger (effective) number of parties allows for representation of more than the one dominant cleavage dimension in advanced industrialized countries, that is, more than the conventional labour–capital cleavage (Neto and Cox 1997; Clark and Golder 2006). Which kind of additional cleavages are represented in the party system depends on the cleavage structure of the country in question. Here, the distinction between the Nordic and the Continental countries and their welfare states achieves particular relevance. In the north of Europe, a religious cleavage did not become politicized and 'particized' (see Stoll 2008) because neither were these societies religiously heterogeneous nor did the 'national revolution' (Rokkan) lead to strong state–church conflicts. 'All the Nordic countries belong to (and, indeed, collectively constitute) Europe's sole mono-confessional Protestant region' (Madeley 2000: 29). The northern Protestant churches as Lutheran state churches, in contrast to the Catholic Church in southern Europe, did not feel fundamentally challenged when the new nation-state started to take over responsibilities that had previously fallen under the responsibility of the church. Anticlericalism never became a strong political current in the Scandinavian countries. A cleavage that did become politicized and particized was the cleavage between agrarian and industrial interests because the agrarian sector was still very strong at the moment of mass democratization in the late industrializing Scandinavian countries. It is in Europe's north where strong parties of agrarian defence emerged and where they received a substantial share of the votes over the entire postwar period.

[. . .]

In sum, the distinguishing feature of the Scandinavian party systems is the strong role that agrarian parties play in them. Over the entire postwar period from 1945 to 1999, agrarian parties in Finland, Norway, Sweden, and Denmark gained on average 20.6, 13.9, 8.9, and 7.3 per cent of the vote. No comparable figures can be found in any other European party system except in Switzerland, where the *Schweizerische Bauern-, Gewerbe-, und Bürgerpartei* (since 1971 *Schweizerische Volkspartei*) gained more than 10 per cent of the votes in each election in the postwar period (cf. Caramani 2004: 181). In all other European countries, 'the urban–rural cleavage was incorporated into other party alignments – state–church and left–right in particular – and did not give rise to specific political parties' (184). Given the strong position of the agrarian parties, it comes as no surprise that almost all accounts of the historical development of the Nordic welfare state stress the importance of red–green coalitions for the formation and the subsequent expansion of the welfare state (see Olson 1986: 5, 75; Esping-Andersen 1990: 30) or see agrarian parties even as *the* driving force of early welfare state development (Baldwin 1990: 55–94). The influence of the agrarian or centre parties was due to their pivotal position within the Scandinavian party systems. When not themselves a part of the government coalition, centre parties tolerated the minority governments often led by Social Democrats, especially in Norway and Sweden (see Bergman 2000; Narud and Strøm 2000). Social legislation depended on their consent and, therefore, was tailored to the agrarian needs and interests.

One could say that the place occupied by agrarian parties in the north is occupied by Christian Democratic parties on the continent. The German CDU, the Dutch CDA, the Austrian ÖVP, the Belgian CVP/PSC (*Parti Social-Chrétien* or *Christelijke Volkspartij*), the Italian *Democrazia Cristiana*, and the Swiss *Christlich-Demokratische Volkspartei* are parties with their roots in political Catholicism. They are the offspring of the fierce state–church conflicts in the last quarter of the nineteenth and the first quarter of the twentieth century – in the Belgian case, offspring of the national independence movement of the Catholic southern provinces against the Protestant northern provinces of the Low Countries (Kalyvas 1996). In these countries, which all introduced PR no later than 1919, the party system contains a relatively high (effective) number of parties and, subsequently, represents more than one cleavage (Neto and Cox 1997). However, instead of the urban–rural cleavage, which was prominent in the religiously homogeneous Protestant north, here in the religiously mixed or homogeneously Catholic countries (e.g., Belgium and Austria), it is the state–church conflict that is prominently represented in the party system in addition to the left–right cleavage.

Both with respect to vote shares and time in government, the Christian Democratic parties have been dominant (if not hegemonic like the Italian *Democrazia Cristiana*) in the continental countries. Because Christian Democratic parties combined the religious and large parts of the bourgeois vote, their electoral fate was better than that of the Nordic agrarian parties. Only counting the vote shares of the Catholic parties such as the *Österreichische Volkspartei*, the *Christlich-Demokratische* Union, the *Democrazia Cristiana*, the *Christen Demokratisch Appèl* (and its former member parties such as the *Katholieke Volkspartij*), and the *Parti Social-Chrétien* or *Christelijke Volkspartij* of Belgium (and ignoring the Protestant parties in these countries for a moment), it becomes evident that Christian Democracy was much more successful than the agrarian parties in Scandinavia. On average, the Belgian PSC or CVP received 34.9 per cent of the vote in all elections that took place between 1945 and 1999, the German *Christlich-Demokratische* Union gained an average of 44.2 per cent of the vote during this period, the *Katholieke Volkspartij* (and later the *Appèl*) gained on average 28.6 per cent of the vote in the same period, the Austrian *Volkspartei* received 41.5 per cent, and the Italian DC received 33.8 per cent of the vote. If we do not count the elections after the breakdown of the first Italian republic – that is, if we discard the elections after 1992 – then this share rises to 37.9 per cent. The Swiss *Christlich-Demokratische Volkspartei* won around 20.9 per cent of the vote. At the same time, parties of agrarian defence remained largely absent in continental Europe. The urban–rural cleavage dimension remained latent and was not politicized and particized in the continental welfare states.

Put pointedly, according to our history of political class coalitions, we find liberal welfare states in countries with a majoritarian electoral system in which only one political cleavage dimension is present (exemplary case: the UK). The Social Democratic generous welfare states, which we find in the Nordic countries, however, have been the result of a coalition between Social Democratic parties and parties of agrarian defence (red–green coalition). One important precondition for this coalition has been the absence of a strong religious cleavage in the Scandinavian countries. On Europe's continent, in turn, we find welfare states that are the product of a coalition between Social and Christian Democracy (red–black coalition). This is due to the fact that the second cleavage represented in the party systems of continental Europe, besides the dominant left–right or labour–capital cleavage, has been the religious cleavage, a cleavage inherited from the state–church conflicts in the wake of the national revolution, in which Liberal state elites challenged the church in its former domains such as education or poor relief. What we propose here, in other words, is a Rokkanian complement to the Iversen and Soskice (2006) model of welfare state class coalitions. In our view, Iversen and Soskice are perfectly right in stressing the importance of a class coalition between lower and middle class, but once we look at the party political coalitions behind the Nordic and continental welfare states, we are also able to identify *which type* of middle class party has entered into a coalition with Social Democracy. This insight also allows us to explain the type of welfare state to which these party political class coalitions have led. Similarly, the variation in Christian Democracy on the European continent – sometimes being hegemonic like in the case of the Italian DC, sometimes having vanished over the course of the postwar years like the French *Mouvement Républicain Populaire* (MRP) – allows us to address systematically the question of the within-type variation in the case of the Conservative, Christian Democratic welfare state predominant on the continent.

To be clear, there have been and still are religious parties in the Nordic countries, such as the most important and electorally successful Norwegian *Kristelig Folkeparti* founded in 1933, and there have been agrarian parties in continental Europe. But both remained marginal, without political influence and impact, especially when it comes to welfare state formation and growth. We also want to emphasize that we do *not* claim that the PR electoral systems can explain the *formation* of either agrarian parties or parties of religious defence. In numerous cases, these parties were founded before the introduction of PR, which in most countries occurred only after World War I. However, in contrast to the simple majority system in force in Britain, the two-ballot/two-round majority system in place before the Great War in almost all other European countries has the non-Duvergian tendency to sustain a higher effective number of parties, despite its 'Duvergian drive' toward the formation of two blocks or party camps (cf. Blais et al. 2005). This was a crucial difference between Britain and the rest of Western Europe in the period of suffrage extension.

[. . .]

If we explain the 'Christian Democratic welfare state' as the outcome of a cross-class coalition with which Christian Democratic parties fabricated electoral majorities bringing together Catholic workers and the Catholic middle class, how do we explain that Catholic workers were not wooed away by Social Democrats with more generous welfare promises? In other words, what explains the relative stability of the confessional vote in post-1945 continental Europe? We briefly address both points in the following paragraphs.

[. . .]

In response to the question of why the Catholic vote proved stable even when the conflicts between nation-state and Catholic Church had lost much of their fervour, we should start by pointing to the empirical evidence that clearly confirms the surprising stability of religion as a determinant for party choice in continental Europe. For instance, Lewis-Beck, in his analysis of postwar France covering elections up to the mid-1980s, finds that as a determinant of voting 'religious practice appears twice as important as social class' (1984: 438; see Lewis-Beck and Skalaban 1992), and in their analysis of the German elections over the same time period, Pappi and Mnich state that 'religion/church attendance is by far the most important single determinant of party choice' (1992: 193). Until the late 1960s, the party choice of Dutch voters could be accurately predicted by simply asking two questions: what is your income and to what church or denomination do you belong? (Thomassen et al. 2000). Similar findings for Italy (Mackie et al. 1992: 242) or Belgium (Mughan 1992: 89) could easily be added. Again, a large and controversial literature has tried to detect the causes for electoral stability in the immediate postwar decades and the (slowly) increasing electoral volatility since the 1970s (Dalton et al. 1984; Franklin et al. 1992). Party system theory in the tradition of Rokkan (Gallagher et al. 2005) suggests that cleavages and their party political translations tend to persist for four interconnected reasons. First, cleavages are based on real conflicts that do not disappear overnight. Secularization is a long-term process and involves at least one, and most likely two, generations. Second, since the introduction of universal suffrage, all voters are mobilized and politically aligned, and parties work hard to keep their voters, especially when the organic link between party and voter is diluted. Third, PR helps parties survive and compete, even if they face declining popularity, whereas in plurality systems such parties would disappear faster. Finally, parties employ various techniques, strategies, and activities to 'establish a presence in many different areas of their individual supporters' lives, organizing social clubs, welfare services, recreational facilities, and the like, thus offering adherents a range of services to sustain them "from the cradle to the grave"' (243). Even when the ideological ties weaken, the social bonds may survive for quite some time.

In the context of our study, however, we want to highlight that it was often not so much the lack of competition between Christian and Social Democrats for the workers' vote that explains why Catholic workers continued to vote for Christian Democracy. Often more important was the left's Marxian legacy of vehement anticlericalism because Catholic workers were often repelled by the left's articulate anti-church position. In Germany, it was only after the 1961 Godesberg programme of the SPD that the party toned down its aggressive position *vis-à-vis* the Catholic

Church, and in France, the highly contentious school question pitted left parties against the MRP and later the Gaullist party far into the 1960s. Also in Italy, a compromise between the anticlerical left and the *Democrazia Cristiana* was only becoming a realistic option in the early to mid-1970s. In this perspective, it seems noticeable that once, by the early 1970s, much of the former ideological heat had evaporated, sharper party competition via welfare promises set in. For instance, the late, but steep take-off of the Dutch welfare state has to be seen in connection with the postwar competition between Social Democrats and Catholics and later the depillarization of Dutch society, which increased competitive pressures. However, it is also to the desideratum of a systematic analysis of the nexus between electoral politics and social policies to which our study points. Although it might be true that social protection has increasingly substituted for the comfort and feeling of security that people had previously found in religion (Norris and Inglehart 2004), it might also be that parties increasingly have used social policies to tie those electoral groups to them that they could not tie any more on ideological, in particular, religious grounds only. This, however, would be a topic for future research.

In this chapter, we do not deal with the many institutional consequences that the different welfare state coalitions in Europe's north and on its continent had. We restrict ourselves to simply mentioning some of the more important ones [. . .]. One important difference, however, is evident from the outset: agrarian parties in the north voiced resistance against the income-differentiated social benefits that Social Democrats favoured (cf. Johansen 1986; Olson 1986). Instead, they preferred universalist, flat-rate benefits because many small landholders had no long history of steady income and therefore feared that they would actually be unable to benefit from welfare entitlements that were contribution financed with contribution-related benefit levels (cf. Baldwin 1990: 55–94). Christian Democratic parties, however, which mobilized workers as did their Social Democratic counterparts, had far less reasons to object to differentiated, wage-based contributions and entitlements. Social insurance contributions promised to ease the party-internal conflict over social policy between Catholic workers and the middle class because contributions 'naturally' seemed to limit the extent of welfare state redistribution. Moreover, during the severe economic crisis of the late 1920s and early 1930s, which had particularly affected Scandinavian agriculture, many farmers became less interested in unemployment payments, which would bridge the spells without work. Rather, they demanded active labour market policies to ease the transition to the second and third sector. The problem was perceived as one of sectoral change, in which the loss of employment in the first sector had to be compensated through employment growth in industry and services. Another important difference was the integration of the churches in the continental welfare states in the provision of social services (e.g., hospitals, old-age homes, kindergartens) as compared to state provision of these services in the Nordic countries. This had long-term consequences not only for female labour force participation but also for the relative ease with which child rearing and dependent employment could be combined. Agrarian parties were also strongly in favour of financing the welfare state through indirect taxes because this promised to shift 'the expense of meeting risk from the most progressively assessed levies of the day – the direct land taxes they (the agrarians) paid to underwrite the poor-relief system – to the consumption habits of their urban political opponents' (64).

It is therefore in the most crucial dimensions of the welfare state – the mode of financing, the benefit structure, the provision of social services – that we see the varying impact of the different party political coalitions in the North and on the continent.

Notes

From P. Manow and K. van Kersbergen, *Religion, Class Coalitions and Welfare States*, Cambridge, Cambridge University Press, 2009, pp. 1–5, 10–28, copyright © Cambridge University Press, by permission of Cambridge University Press and the authors.

We are grateful for extremely helpful comments by Thomas Ertman, Bo Kaspersen, David Leege, Kimberly Morgan, Kenneth Wald, and two anonymous referees from Cambridge University Press.

References

Alexander, Gerard (2004), France: Reform-Mongering between Majority Runoff and Proportionality, in Josep M. Colomer (ed.), *Handbook of Electoral System Choice*, Houndmills, Basingstoke: Palgrave Macmillan, pp. 209–21.
Baldwin, Peter (1990), *The Politics of Social Solidarity. Class Bases of the European Welfare State 1875–1975*, Cambridge: Cambridge University Press.
Bergman, Torbjörn (2000), Sweden: When Minority Governments Are the Rule and Majority Coalitions the Exception, in Wolfgang C. Müller and Kaare Strom (eds), *Coalition Governments in Western Europe*, Oxford: Oxford University Press, pp. 192–230.
Blais, André, Dobrzynska, Agnieszka, and Indridason, Indridi H. (2005), To Adopt or Not To Adopt Proportional Representation: The Politics of Institutional Choice, *British Journal of Political Science* 35 (1): 182–90.
Caramani, Daniele (2004), *The Nationalization of Politics: The Formation of National Electorates and Party Systems in Western Europe*, New York: Cambridge University Press.
Catterall, Peter (1993), Morality and Politics: The Free Churches and the Labour Party between the Wars, *The Historical Journal* 36 (3): 667–85.

Clark, William Roberts, and Golder, Matt (2006), Rehabilitating Duverger's Theory: Testing the Mechanical and Strategic Modifying Effects of Electoral Laws, *Comparative Political Studies* 39 (6): 679–708.

Dalton, Russell, Flanagan, Scott, and Beck, Paul (eds) (1984), *Electoral Change in Advanced Industrial Democracies: Realignment or Dealignment?* Princeton, NJ: Princeton University Press.

Elgie, Robert (2005), France: Stacking the Deck, in Michael Gallagher and Paul Mitchell (eds), *The Politics of Electoral Systems*, Oxford, New York: Oxford University Press, pp. 119–36.

Esping-Andersen, Gøsta (1990), *The Three Worlds of Welfare Capitalism*, Cambridge: Polity Press.

Esping-Andersen, Gøsta, and van Kersbergen, Kees (1992), Contemporary Research on Social Democracy, *Annual Review of Sociology* 18: 187–208.

Flora, Peter (with Stein Kuhnle and Derek Urwin) (1999), *State Formation, Nation-building, and Mass Politics in Europe: The Theory of Stein Rokkan Based on His Collected Works*, Oxford: Oxford University Press.

Franklin, Mark, Mackie, Tom, and Valen, Henry (eds) (1992), *Electoral Change: Responses to Evolving Social and Attitudinal Structures in Western Europe*, New York: Cambridge University Press.

Gallagher, Michael, Laver, Michael, and Mair, Peter (2005), *Representative Government in Modern Europe: Institutions, Parties, and Government*, 3rd edition. Boston: McGraw-Hill.

Iversen, Torben, and Soskice, David (2006), Electoral Institutions and the Politics of Coalitions: Why Some Democracies Redistribute More Than Others, *American Political Science Review* 100 (2): 165–81.

Johansen, Lars Norby (1986), Denmark, in Peter Flora (ed.), *Growth to Limits: The Western European Welfare States since World War II*, Berlin, New York: De Gruyter, pp. 293–381.

Kalyvas, Stathis (1996), *The Rise of Christian Democracy in Europe*, Ithaca, NY: Cornell University Press.

Lewis-Beck, Michael (1984), France: The Stalled Electorate, in Russell Dalton, Scott Flanagan, and Paul Beck (eds), *Electoral Change in Advanced Industrial Democracies: Realignment or Dealignment?* Princeton, NJ: Princeton University Press, pp. 425–48.

Lewis-Beck, Michael, and Skalaban, Andrew (1992), France, in Mark Franklin, Tom Mackie, and Henry Valen (eds), *Electoral Change: Responses to Evolving Social and Attitudinal Structures in Western Europe*, New York: Cambridge University Press, pp. 167–78.

Mackie, Tom, Mannheimer, Renato, and Sani, Giacomo (1992), Italy, in Mark Franklin, Tom Mackie, and Henry Valen (eds), *Electoral Change: Responses to Evolving Social and Attitudinal Structures in Western Europe*, New York: Cambridge University Press, pp. 238–54.

Madeley, John (2000), Reading the Runes: The Religious Factor in Scandinavian Electoral Politics, in David Broughton and Hans-Martien ten Napel (eds), *Religion and Mass Electoral Behaviour in Europe*, London: Routledge, pp. 28–43.

Manow, Philip (2009), Electoral Rules, Class Coalitions and Welfare State Regimes, or How to Explain Esping-Andersen with Stein Rokkan, *Socio-Economic Review* 7 (1): 101–21.

Mughan, Anthony (1992), Belgium, in Franklin, Mark, Mackie, Tom, and Valen, Henry (eds), *Electoral Change: Responses to Evolving Social and Attitudinal Structures in Western Europe*, New York: Cambridge University Press, pp. 83–100.

Narud, Hanne Marthe, and Strøm, Kaare (2000), Norway: A Fragile Coalitional Order, in Wolfgang C. Müller and Kaare Strøm (eds), *Coalition Governments in Western Europe*, Oxford: Oxford University Press, pp. 158–91.

Neto, Octavio Amorim, and Cox, Gary W. (1997), Electoral Institutions: Cleavage Structures and the Number of Parties, *American Political Science Review* 41 (1): 149–74.

Norris, Pippa, and Ronald Inglehart (2004), *Sacred and Secular: Religion and Politics Worldwide*, Cambridge: Cambridge University Press.

Olson, Sven (1986), Sweden, in Peter Flora (ed.), *Growth to Limits: The Western European Welfare States since World War II: Volume 1, Sweden, Norway, Finland, Denmark*, Berlin, New York: de Gruyter, pp. 1–116.

Pappi, Franz Urban, and Mnich, Peter (1992), Germany, in Mark Franklin, Tom Mackie, and Henry Valen (eds), *Electoral Change: Responses to Evolving Social and Attitudinal Structures in Western Europe*, New York: Cambridge University Press, pp. 179–204.

Parry, J. P. (1986), *Democracy and Religion: Gladstone and the Liberal Party, 1867–1875*, Cambridge: Cambridge University Press.

Pelling, Henry (1965), *Origins of the Labour Party*, Oxford: Clarendon Press.

Rodden, Jonathan (2005), *Red States, Blue States, and the Welfare State: Political Geography, Representation and Government Policy around the World*, Manuscript, Massachusetts Institute of Technology, Boston.

Rogowski, Ronald (1987), Trade and the Variety of Democratic Institutions, *International Organization* 41 (2): 203–23.

Rokkan, Stein (1970), *Citizens, Elections, Parties*, Oslo: Universitetsforlaget.

Schmidt, Manfred G. (1980), *CDU und SPD an der Regierung. Ein Vergleich ihrer Politik in den Länder*, Frankfurt and New York: Campus.

Schmidt, Manfred G. (1982), *Wohlfahrtsstaatliche Politik unter bürgerlichen und sozialdemokratischen Regierungen*, Frankfurt and New York: Campus.

Stephens, John D. (1979), *The Transition from Capitalism to Socialism*, London: Macmillan.

Stoll, Heather (2008), Social Cleavages and the Number of Parties: How the Measures You Choose Affect the Numbers You Get, *Comparative Political Studies* 41 (11), forthcoming.

Thomassen, Jacques, Aarts, Kees, and van der Kolk, Henk (2000), *Politiek veranderingen in Nederland 1971–1998: Kiezers en de smalle marges van de politiek*, The Hague: SDU.

van Kersbergen, Kees (1995), *Social Capitalism: A Study of Christian Democracy and the Welfare State*, London, New York: Routledge.

van Kersbergen, Kees (1999), Contemporary Christian Democracy and the Demise of the Politics of Mediation, in Herbert Kitschelt, Gary Marks, Peter Lange, and John D. Stephens (eds), *Continuity and Change in Contemporary Capitalism*, Cambridge: Cambridge University Press, pp. 346–70.

Wilensky, Harold L. (1981), Leftism, Catholicism, and Democratic Corporatism: The Role of Political Parties in Recent Welfare State Development, in Peter Flora and Arnold J. Heidenheimer (eds), *The Development of Welfare States in Europe and America*, New Brunswick and London: Transaction Books, pp. 345–82.

The New Politics of the Welfare State

Paul Pierson

Why the Politics of Retrenchment is Different

This essay's central claim is that because retrenchment is a distinctive process, it is unlikely to follow the same rules of development that operated during the long phase of welfare state expansion. There are two fundamental reasons for this. First, the political *goals* of policy makers are different; second, there have been dramatic changes in the political *context*. Each of these points requires elaboration.

There is a profound difference between extending benefits to large numbers of people and taking benefits away.[1] [After the Second World War] expanding social benefits was generally a process of political credit claiming. Reformers needed only to overcome diffuse concern about tax rates (often sidestepped through resort to social insurance 'contributions') and the frequently important pressures of entrenched interests. Not surprisingly, the expansion of social programmes had until recently been a favoured political activity, contributing greatly to both state-building projects and the popularity of reform-minded politicians.[2]

A combination of economic changes, political shifts to the right, and rising costs associated with maturing welfare states has provoked growing calls for retrenchment. At the heart of efforts to turn these demands into policy have been newly ascendant conservative politicians. Conservative governments have generally advocated major social policy reforms, often receiving significant external support in their effort, especially from the business community.[3] Yet the new policy agenda stands in sharp contrast to the credit-claiming initiatives pursued during the long period of welfare state expansion. The politics of retrenchment is typically treacherous, because it imposes tangible losses on concentrated groups of voters in return for diffuse and uncertain gains. Retrenchment entails a delicate effort either to transform programmatic change into an electorally attractive proposition or, at the least, to minimize the political costs involved. Advocates of retrenchment must persuade wavering supporters that the price of reform is manageable – a task that a substantial public outcry makes almost impossible.

Retrenchment is generally an exercise in blame avoidance rather than credit claiming, primarily because the costs of retrenchment are concentrated (and often immediate), while the benefits are not. That concentrated interests will be in a stronger political position than diffuse ones is a standard proposition in political science.[4] As interests become more concentrated, the prospect that individuals will find it worth their while to engage in collective action improves. Furthermore, concentrated interests are more likely to be linked to organizational networks that keep them informed about how policies affect their interests. These informational networks also facilitate political action.

An additional reason that politicians rarely get credit for programme cutbacks concerns the well-documented asymmetry in the way that voters react to losses and gains. Extensive experiments in social psychology have demonstrated that individuals respond differently to positive and negative risks. Individuals exhibit a *negativity bias*: they will take more chances – seeking conflict and accepting the possibility of even greater losses – to prevent any worsening of their current position.[5] Studies of electoral behaviour, at least in the United States, confirm these findings. Negative attitudes towards candidates are more strongly linked with a range of behaviours (for example, turnout, deserting the voter's normal party choice) than are positive attitudes.[6]

While the reasons for this negativity bias are unclear, the constraints that it imposes on elected officials are not. When added to the imbalance between concentrated and diffuse interests, the message for advocates of retrenchment is straightforward. A simple 'redistributive' transfer of resources from programme beneficiaries to taxpayers, engineered through cuts in social programmes, is generally a losing proposition. The concentrated beneficiary groups are more likely to be cognisant of the change, are easier to mobilize, and because they are experiencing losses rather than gains are more likely to incorporate the change in their voting calculations. Retrenchment advocates thus confront a clash between their policy preferences and their electoral ambitions.

If the shift in goals from expansion to cutbacks creates new political dynamics, so does the emergence of a new *context*: the development of the welfare state itself. Large public social programmes are now a central part of the political landscape. As Peter Flora has noted, 'Including the recipients of [pensions,] unemployment benefits and social assistance – and the persons employed in education, health and the social services – in many countries today almost 1/2 of the electorate receive transfer or work income from the welfare state.'[7] With these massive programmes have come dense interest-group networks and strong popular attachments to particular policies, which present considerable obstacles to reform. To take one prominent example, by the late 1980s the American Association of Retired People (AARP) had a membership of 28 million and a staff of 1,300 (including a legislative staff of more than 100).[8] The maturation of the welfare state fundamentally transforms the nature of interest-group politics. In short, the emergence of powerful groups surrounding social programmes may make the welfare state less dependent on the political parties, social movements, and labour organizations that expanded social programmes in the first place. Nor is the context altered simply because welfare states create their own constituencies. The structures of social programmes may also have implications for the decision rules governing policy change (for example, whether national officials need the acquiescence of local ones) and for how visible cutbacks will be. 'Policy feedback' from earlier rounds of welfare state development is likely to be a prominent feature of retrenchment politics.[9]

In short, the shift in goals and context creates a new politics. This new politics, marked by pressures to avoid blame for unpopular policies, dictates new political strategies.[10] Retrenchment advocates will try to play off one group of beneficiaries against another and develop reforms that compensate politically crucial groups for lost benefits. Those favouring cutbacks will attempt to lower the visibility of reforms, either by making the effects of policies more difficult to detect or by making it hard for voters to trace responsibility for these effects back to particular policy makers.[11] Wherever possible, policy makers will seek broad consensus on reform in order to spread the blame. Whether these efforts succeed may depend very much on the structure of policies already in place.

[. . .]

To what extent have welfare states undergone retrenchment? What countries and programmes have been most vulnerable to retrenchment initiatives and why? In this section I address these questions by reviewing the evolution of welfare states in four affluent democracies since the late 1970s. The evidence supports a number of claims. (1) There is little evidence for broad propositions about the centrality of strong states or left power resources to retrenchment outcomes. (2) The unpopularity of retrenchment makes major cutbacks unlikely except under conditions of budgetary crisis, and radical restructuring is unlikely even then. (3) For the same reason, governments generally seek to negotiate consensus packages rather than to impose reforms unilaterally, which further diminishes the potential for radical reform. And (4) far from creating a self-reinforcing dynamic, cutbacks tend to replenish support for the welfare state.

Measuring retrenchment is a difficult task. Quantitative indicators are likely to be inadequate for several reasons. First, pure spending levels are rarely the most politically important or theoretically interesting aspects of welfare states. As Esping-Andersen put it in his analysis of welfare state expansion, 'It is difficult to imagine that anyone struggled for spending *per se*'.[12] In particular, rising unemployment may sustain high spending even as social rights and benefits are significantly curtailed. Second, spending estimates will fail to capture the impact of reforms that are designed to introduce retrenchment only indirectly or over the long term. Analysis must focus on qualitative and quantitative changes in programmes and on prospective, long-term changes, as well as on immediate cutbacks. My investigation therefore relies on a combination of quantitative data on expenditures and qualitative analysis of welfare state reforms. Rather than emphasizing cuts in spending *per se*, the focus is on reforms that indicate structural shifts in the welfare state. These would include (1) significant increases in reliance on means-tested benefits; (2) major transfers of responsibility to the private sector; and (3) dramatic changes in benefit and eligibility rules that signal a qualitative reform of a particular programme.[13] The selection of countries to investigate was based on the desire to achieve significant variation on what the welfare state expansion literature suggests are the most plausible independent variables. The cases vary widely in the structure of political institutions, the extent of shifts in the distribution of power resources, the design of pre-existing welfare states, and the severity of budgetary crisis.

Beginning with the quantitative evidence, aggregate measures provide little evidence that any of the four welfare states have undergone dramatic cutbacks. From 1974 to 1990 the expenditure patterns across the four cases are quite similar, despite widely different starting-points. As tables 1 and 2 show, social security spending and total government outlays as a percentage of GDP are relatively flat over most of the relevant period. The exception is the recent surge in Swedish expenditures, which will be discussed below. There is a slight upward trend overall, with fluctuations related to the business cycle. Table 3, which tracks public employment, reveals a similar pattern (although the expansion of Swedish public employment from an already high base stands out). For none of the countries does the evidence reveal a sharp curtailment of the public sector.

Table 4 offers more disaggregated indicators of shifts in social welfare spending among the four countries; spending patterns are reported for what the OECD terms 'merit goods' (primarily housing, education and health care) as well as for various income transfers. The figures suggest a bit more divergence among the cases, with the United States and Germany emerging as somewhat more successful in curbing spending. A very few programme areas – notably British housing and German pensions

Table 1 Social security transfers as % of GDP, 1974–90

	Britain	Germany	Sweden	United States
1974	9.8	14.6	14.3	9.5
1980	11.7	16.6	17.6	10.9
1982	14.0	17.7	18.3	11.9
1984	14.0	16.5	17.6	11.0
1986	14.1	15.9	18.4	11.0
1988	12.3	16.1	19.5	10.6
1990	12.2	15.3	19.7	10.8[a]

[a] 1989.

Source: OECD, *Historical Statistics, 1960–1990* (1992), table 6.3.

Table 2 Government outlays as % of nominal GDP, 1978–94

	Britain	Germany	Sweden	United States
1978	41.4	47.3	58.6	30.0
1980	43.0	47.9	60.1	31.8
1982	44.6	48.9	64.8	33.9
1984	45.2	47.4	62.0	32.6
1986	42.5	46.4	61.6	33.7
1988	38.0	46.3	58.1	32.5
1990	39.9	45.1	59.1	33.3
1992	43.2	49.0	67.3	35.1
1994[a]	44.8	51.4	70.9	33.9

[a] Projection.

Source: OECD, *Economic Outlook* (December 1993), table A23.

Table 3 Government employment as % of total employment, 1974–90

	Britain	Germany	Sweden	United States
1974	19.6	13.0	24.8	16.1
1980	21.1	14.6	30.3	15.4
1982	22.0	15.1	31.7	15.4
1984	22.0	15.5	32.6	14.8
1986	21.8	15.6	32.2	14.8
1988	20.8	15.6	31.5	14.4
1990	19.2	15.1	31.7	14.4[a]

[a] 1989.

Source: OECD, *Historical Statistics, 1960–1990* (1992), table 2.13.

Table 4 Government outlays by function as % of trend GDP[a], 1979–90

	Britain			Germany			Sweden			United States		
	1979	1990	1979–90	1979	1990	1979–90	1979	1990	1979–90	1979	1989	1979–89
Total	44.9	43.2	-1.7	49.9	45.8	-4.1	63.2	61.4	-1.8	33.2	36.9	+3.6
Public goods[b]	9.5	9.7	+0.1	10.0	9.2	-0.8	10.5	8.8	-1.7	8.2	9.3	+1.1
Merit goods	13.6	12.2	-1.4	12.3	10.9	-1.4	15.9	13.4	-2.6	6.1	6.0	-0.1
Education	5.5	5.0	-0.5	5.2	4.2	-1.0	6.6	5.6	-1.0	4.7	4.7	-0.0
Health[c]	4.8	5.1	+0.3	6.3	6.0	-0.3	8.1	6.9	-1.1	0.9	0.9	-0.0
Housing and other	3.4	2.1	-1.2	0.8	0.7	-0.1	1.2	0.8	-0.4	0.5	0.4	-0.1
Income trans.	12.5	13.4	+0.9	20.2	18.5	-1.7	24.6	26.8	+2.2	11.2	11.9	+0.7
Pensions	6.7	6.5	-0.2	12.7	11.2	-1.5	11.0	11.5	+0.4	6.9	7.0	+0.1
Sickness	0.4	0.3	-0.1	0.8	0.7	-0.1	3.4	4.5	+1.2	0.1	0.2	+0.1
Family allowance	1.7	1.6	-0.0	1.2	0.8	-0.4	1.6	1.3	-0.3	0.4	0.4	-0.0
Unemployment	0.7	0.6	-0.1	0.9	1.3	+0.4	0.4	0.5	+0.1	0.4	0.3	-0.1
Other income supports	0.1	0.8	+0.7	1.3	1.6	+0.3	0.1	0.2	+0.1	0.0	0.0	0.0
Admin. and other spending	1.4	1.6	+0.3	2.6	2.4	-0.2	4.9	5.2	+0.3	0.6	0.6	-0.0
Add. transfer	1.4	1.8	+0.5	0.5	0.4	-0.1	3.2	3.7	+0.6	2.7	3.5	+0.8

[a] Numbers may not sum to total due to rounding.
[b] Defence and other public services.
[c] For the US, social security related to health spending is included under 'Additional transfers' below.
Source: OECD, *Economic Outlook* (December 1993), table 21.

– experienced significant reductions. Nonetheless, similarities across countries remain more striking than differences. None of the cases show major rises or declines in overall effort, and there are few indications of dramatic change in any of the subcategories of expenditure.

[. . .]

The New Politics of the Welfare State

Economic, political and social pressures have fostered an image of welfare states under siege. Yet if one turns from abstract discussions of social transformation to an examination of actual policy, it becomes difficult to sustain the proposition that these strains have generated fundamental shifts. This review of four cases does indeed suggest a distinctly new environment, but not one that has provoked anything like a dismantling of the welfare state. Nor is it possible to attribute this to case selection, since the choice of two prototypical cases of neo-conservatism (Britain and the United States) and two cases of severe budgetary shocks (Germany and Sweden) gave ample room for various scenarios of radical retrenchment. Even in Thatcher's Britain, where an ideologically committed Conservative Party [. . .] controlled one of Europe's most centralized political systems for over a decade, reform [was] incremental rather than revolutionary, leaving the British welfare state largely intact. In most other countries the evidence of continuity is even more apparent.

To be sure, there has been change. Many programmes have experienced a tightening of eligibility rules or reductions in benefits. On occasion, individual programmes (such as public housing in Britain) have undergone more radical reform. In countries where budgetary pressures have been greatest, cuts have been more severe. Over the span of two decades, however, *some* changes in social policy are inevitable; even in the boom years of the 1960s specific social programmes sometimes fared poorly. What is striking is how hard it is to find *radical* changes in advanced welfare states. Retrenchment has been pursued cautiously: whenever possible, governments have sought all-party consensus for significant reforms and have chosen to trim existing structures rather than experiment with new programmes or pursue privatization.

This finding is striking, given that so many observers have seen the post-1973 period as one of fundamental change in modern political economies. A harsher economic climate has certainly generated demands for spending restraint. Additional pressures have stemmed from the maturation of social programmes and adverse demographic trends. Yet compared with the aspirations of many reformers and with the extent of change in fields such as industrial relations policy, macroeconomic policy or the privatization of public industries, what stands out is the relative stability of the welfare state.

I have suggested that to understand what has been happening requires looking beyond the considerable pressures on the welfare state to consider enduring sources of support. There are powerful political forces that stabilize welfare states and channel change in the direction of incremental modifications of existing policies. The first major protection for social programmes stems from the generally conservative characteristics of democratic political institutions. The welfare state now represents the status quo, with all the political advantages that this status confers. Nondecisions generally favour the welfare state. Major policy change usually requires the acquiescence of numerous actors. Where power is shared among different institutions (for example, Germany, the United States), radical reform will be difficult.

As the British and Swedish cases show, radical change is not easy even in a situation of concentrated political power. A second and crucial source of the welfare state's political strength comes from the high electoral costs generally associated with retrenchment initiatives. Despite scholarly speculation about declining popular support for the welfare state, polls show little evidence of such a shift, and actual political struggles over social spending reveal even less. On the contrary, even halting efforts to dismantle the welfare state have usually exacted a high political price. Recipients of social benefits are relatively concentrated and are generally well organized. They are also more likely to punish politicians for cutbacks than taxpayers are to reward them for lower costs. Nowhere is there evidence to support the scenario of a self-reinforcing dynamic, with cutbacks leading to middle-class disenchantment and exit, laying the foundation for more retrenchment. Instead, the recurrent pattern in public-opinion polls has been a mild swing against the welfare state in the wake of poor economic performance and budgetary stress, followed by a resurgence of support at the first whiff of significant cuts.

Nor does the welfare state's political position seem to have been seriously eroded – at least in the medium term – by the decline of its key traditional constituency, organized labour. Only for those benefits where unions are the sole organized constituency, such as unemployment insurance, has labour's declining power presented immediate problems, and even here the impact can be exaggerated.[14] The growth of social spending has reconfigured the terrain of welfare state politics. Maturing social programmes produce new organized interests, the consumers and providers of social services, that are usually well placed to defend the welfare state.

The networks associated with mature welfare state programmes constitute a barrier to radical change in another sense as well. As recent research on path dependence has demonstrated, once initiated, certain courses of development are hard to reverse.[15] Organizations and individuals adapt to particular arrangements, making commitments that may render the costs of change (even to some potentially more efficient alternative) far higher than the costs of continuity. Existing commitments lock in policy makers. Old-age pension systems provide a good example. Most countries operate pensions on a pay-as-you-go basis: current workers pay 'contributions' that finance the previous generation's retirement. Once in place, such systems may face incremental cutbacks, but they are notoriously resistant to radical reform.[16] Shifting to private, occupationally based arrangements would place an untenable burden on current workers, requiring them to finance the previous generation's retirement while simultaneously saving for their own.

Over time, all institutions undergo change. This is especially so for very large ones, which cannot be isolated from broad social developments. The welfare state is no exception. But there is little sign that the last two decades have been a transformative period for systems of social provision. As I have argued, expectations for greater change have rested in part on the implicit application of models from the period of welfare state expansion, which can be read to suggest that economic change, the decline in union power, or the presence of a strong state creates the preconditions for radical retrenchment. I find little evidence for these claims.

Notes

From *World Politics*, 48, January 1996, pp. 143–79, copyright © Trustees of Princeton University, by permission of Cambridge University Press and the author.

I am grateful to the Russell Sage Foundation for financial and administrative support and to Miguel Glatzer for considerable research assistance, as well as helpful comments.

1   R. Kent Weaver, 'The Politics of Blame Avoidance', *Journal of Public Policy*, 6, October–December 1986.
2   Peter Flora and Arnold J. Heidenheimer, eds, *The Development of Welfare States in Europe and America*, New Brunswick, NJ, Transaction, 1982.
3   As recent research has suggested, it would be wrong to treat business as always and everywhere opposed to welfare state programmes. For illuminating studies of the United States, see, for example, Colin Gordon, *New Deals: Business, Labor, and Politics in America, 1920–1935*, Cambridge, Cambridge University Press, 1994; and Cathie Jo Martin, 'Nature or Nurture? Sources of Firm Preference for National Health Reform', *American Political Science Review*, 89, December 1995. Nonetheless, it is clear that *most* business organizations in all the advanced industrial democracies have favoured – often vehemently – cutbacks in the welfare state over the past fifteen years.
4   Mancur Olson, *The Logic of Collective Action: Public Goods and the Theory of Groups*, Cambridge, MA, Harvard University Press, 1965; James Q. Wilson, *Political Organizations*, New York, Basic Books, 1973, pp. 330–37.

5   Daniel Kahneman and Amos Tversky, 'Prospect Theory: An Analysis of Decision under Risk', *Econometrica*, 47, March 1979; idem, 'Choices, Values and Frames', *American Psychologist*, 39, April 1984.

6   Howard S. Bloom and H. Douglas Price, 'Voter Response to Short-Run Economic Conditions: The Asymmetric Effect of Prosperity and Recession', *American Political Science Review*, 69, December 1975; Samuel Kernell, 'Presidential Popularity and Negative Voting: An Alternative Explanation of the Midterm Congressional Decline of the President's Party', *American Political Science Review*, 71, March 1977; and Richard R. Lau, 'Explanations for Negativity Effects in Political Behavior', *American Journal of Political Science*, 29, February 1985.

7   Peter Flora, 'From Industrial to Postindustrial Welfare State?', *Annals of the Institute of Social Science* (University of Tokyo), special issue 1989, p. 154.

8   Christine L. Day, *What Older Americans Think: Interest Groups and Aging Policy*, Princeton, NJ, Princeton University Press, 1990, pp. 25–6.

9   Gøsta Esping-Andersen, *Politics against Markets: The Social Democratic Road to Power*, Princeton, NJ, Princeton University Press, 1985; Paul Pierson, 'When Effect Becomes Cause: Policy Feedback and Political Change', *World Politics*, 45, July 1993.

10 Weaver, op. cit.; Paul Pierson, *Dismantling the Welfare State? Reagan, Thatcher and the Politics of Retrenchment*, Cambridge, Cambridge University Press, 1994, ch. 1.

11 R. Douglas Arnold, *The Logic of Congressional Action*, New Haven, Yale University Press, 1990.

12 Gøsta Esping-Andersen, *The Three Worlds of Welfare Capitalism*, Cambridge, Polity Press, 1990, p. 21.

13 Establishing what constitutes 'radical' reform is no easy task. For instance, it is impossible to say definitively when a series of quantitative cutbacks amounts to a qualitative shift in the nature of programmes. Roughly though, that point is reached when because of policy reform a programme can no longer play its traditional role (e.g. when pension benefits designed to provide a rough continuation of the retiree's earlier standard of living are clearly unable to do so).

14 Indeed, a cross-national comparison of unemployment programmes provides further support for this analysis. The OECD has measured replacement rates for UI (benefits as a percentage of previous income) over time in twenty countries, with data to 1991. These data thus permit, for one programme, a [. . .] quantitative appraisal of programme *generosity* rather than simply spending levels. In the majority of cases (twelve out of twenty), replacement rates were *higher* in 1991 than the average rate for either the 1970s or the 1980s, while most of the other cases experienced very marginal declines. Organization for Economic Co-operation and Development, *The OECD Jobs Study: Facts, Analysis, Strategies*, Paris, OECD, 1994, chart 16, p. 24.

15 See Paul David, 'Clio and the Economics of QWERTY', *American Economic Review*, 75, May 1985; and W. Brian Arthur, 'Competing Technologies, Increasing Returns, and Lock-In by Historical Events', *Economic Journal*, 99, March 1989, pp. 116–31. For good extensions to political processes, see Stephen A. Krasner, 'Sovereignty: An Institutional Perspective', in James A. Caporaso, ed., *The Elusive State: International and Comparative Perspectives*, Newbury Park, CA, Sage Publications, 1989; and Douglas North, *Institutions, Institutional Change and Economic Reformance*, Cambridge, Cambridge University Press, 1990.

16 Thus in Germany, Sweden, and the United States the maturity of existing schemes limited policy makers to very gradual and incremental reforms of earnings-related pension systems. More dramatic reform was possible in Britain because the unfunded earnings-related scheme was far from maturity, having been passed only in 1975. Pierson, '"Policy Feedbacks" and Political Change Contrasting Reagan and Thatcher's Pension-Reform Initiatives', *Studies in American Political Development*, 6, Fall 1992.

Constraints

Globalization, the Welfare State and Inequality

Duane Swank

Neoliberal reforms in social welfare policy have been common across the developed capitalist democracies in the latter decades of the twentieth century (Castles, 2004; Huber and Stephens, 2001; Swank, 2002). Governments have periodically reduced income replacement rates, tightened eligibility rules and limited benefit indexation for core social insurance programmes. They have also employed greater targeting of benefits and encouraged the expansion of private insurance against labour market risks. Health and other social service programmes have been subject to budget caps, user co-payments, internal markets and other efficiency-oriented reforms. A central question for political economists has been whether or not economic globalization has played a significant role in fostering these reforms in public social welfare provision.

In the present paper, I review the best recent work on globalization and the democratic capitalist welfare state. I also provide a synopsis of recent arguments about the domestic political sources of contemporary trajectories of the welfare state. After brief surveys of welfare state retrenchment and this recent scholarship, I utilize newly available data to offer an analysis of the impacts of globalization and key features of domestic politics on 1981–2000 variations in social welfare entitlements and decommodification.

Welfare Retrenchment in Developed Capitalist Democracies

Substantial disagreement exists over the degree to which national systems of social protection have been retrenched (e.g., Castles, 2004; Clayton and Pontusson, 1998; Green-Pedersen, 2002; Pierson, 1994, 1996). Early expenditure-based studies of contemporary welfare policy change reveal little in the way of post-1970s retrenchment of social protection in the advanced democracies (e.g., Pierson, 1996). Other studies that use data on social service programmes and welfare state employment (e.g., Clayton and Pontusson, 1998) and detailed surveys of programmatic change across time in large numbers of developed democracies (e.g., Huber and Stephens, 2001; Swank, 2002) conclude rollbacks of the welfare state have been more widespread than aggregate spending patterns reveal.[1] Recent availability of the 'Comparative Welfare State Entitlements Data Set, 1960–2000' (Allen and Scruggs, 2004), as well as published research from the 'Social Citizenship Rights Project' (e.g., Korpi and Palme, 2003), make the systematic assessment of the scope and depth of social welfare retrenchment much more tractable today than before.

I offer a succinct snapshot of 1981–2000 welfare state trajectories in Table 1. I display changes in national net (after tax) income replacement rates for unemployment compensation and pensions by category of welfare state regime (Esping-Andersen, 1990). Unemployment compensation may serve as a proxy for social protection for current workers, while pension benefits form the core of social protection for dependent populations outside the labour market. I also display trends in public social service spending (i.e., for older people, disabled, families and workers); this area involves to a large extent social protection for those who face 'new social risks', attendant to post-industrial family and labour market structure (e.g., Armingeon, 2004). Finally, Table 1 displays changes in overall welfare state decommodification (e.g., Esping-Andersen, 1990; Allen and Scruggs, 2004) from the early 1980s to the turn of the century.

As most scholars of the welfare state readily agree, there is no evidence of systematic dismantling of national systems of social protection, nor is there evidence of significant convergence across welfare regimes. While unemployment compensation (and other social insurance areas such as sickness benefits) has been reduced modestly in a majority of nations (and on average in all welfare regime types), pension benefits have been remarkably stable. This is so despite moderate cuts in (standard) pension income replacement rates in some nations, such as the Netherlands, Sweden, France and New Zealand. Social services for frail older people, families with children, and the long-term unemployed, among other groups, have been increased on average in social democratic and corporatist conservative welfare states; interestingly, both passive unemployment and related support for workers and active labour market policies (a large component of social services) have been reduced in liberal welfare states. Overall, aggregate welfare state decommodification has on average modestly declined in both large social democratic welfare states and predominantly liberal welfare states; some more notable changes in decommodification have occurred in individual welfare states, such as the Netherlands,

Table 1 Trends in social welfare protection and decommodification, 1981–2000

Nation	Unemployment income replacement		Pension income replacement		Social services as a percent of GDP		Decommodification by the welfare state	
	1981–83	1998–2000	1981–83	1998–2000	1985–87	1998–2000	1981–83	1998–2000
Social democratic welfare states								
Denmark	0.824	0.617	0.480	0.523	5.37	6.82	36.58	36.38
Finland	0.327	0.581	0.598	0.629	3.08	4.20	29.70	31.04
Netherlands	0.881	0.733	0.551	0.496	1.97	2.69	37.68	34.56
Norway	0.671	0.657	0.563	0.594	3.18	5.22	41.20	42.11
Sweden	0.803	0.699	0.715	0.612	6.16	6.71	41.14	36.19
Average	**0.701**	**0.657**	**0.581**	**0.571**	**3.95**	**5.13**	**37.26**	**36.06**
Corporatist conservative systems								
Austria	0.580	0.563	0.815	0.883	1.83	2.56	30.71	34.60
Belgium	0.684	0.634	0.766	0.795	1.60	1.63	34.20	35.63
France	0.664	0.701	0.599	0.547	1.75	3.35	27.19	30.36
Germany	0.680	0.600	0.758	0.751	1.58	2.75	29.58	29.73
Italy	0.340	0.386	0.697	0.885	0.95	1.03	20.64	27.26
Switzerland	0.683	0.720	0.384	0.428	0.40	1.65	27.64	21.45
Average	**0.605**	**0.601**	**0.670**	**0.715**	**1.35**	**2.16**	**28.33**	**29.84**

Liberal welfare states

Australia	0.239	0.283	0.293	0.315	0.84	1.64	15.49	14.80
Canada	0.606	0.629	0.385	0.481	0.69	0.46	23.78	26.06
Ireland	0.545	0.293	0.432	0.374	2.09	1.49	24.75	22.07
Japan	0.693	0.613	0.675	0.688	0.40	0.99	21.42	23.12
New Zealand	0.327	0.267	0.427	0.390	0.90	0.80	24.07	20.40
United Kingdom	0.309	0.195	0.419	0.538	1.77	1.42	19.34	21.40
United States	0.712	0.578	0.568	0.555	0.51	0.49	19.65	18.90
Average	**0.490**	**0.408**	**0.457**	**0.477**	**1.03**	**1.04**	**21.21**	**20.96**

Note: Income and pension income replacement rates apply to standard net (after tax) benefits for the average (unmarried) production worker; the measure of decommodification follows Esping-Andersen (1990) and indexes the benefit levels and programme quality (e.g., wait times, duration of benefits, population coverage) for unemployment, sickness, and pension programmes. *Source:* The Comparative Welfare State Entitlements Data Set, 1960–2000. Social services include publicly provided services for older people, disabled, families and workers. *Source:* OECD (2004).

Sweden, Ireland, and New Zealand. Has globalization contributed to the changes in social welfare that we can observe?

Globalization and Contemporary Social Protection

Political economists have long argued that economic internationalization reduces the ability of governments to sustain or expand generous social welfare provisions.[2] In the contemporary literature, the impact of globalization on the welfare state is transmitted through three mechanisms (Swank, 2001, 2002). The most commonly recognized mechanism involves the 'economic logic' of globalization. The second and third mechanisms link globalization to welfare state retrenchment through politics. With respect to the notable post-1970s expansion of capital mobility, the economic logic suggests that the internationalization of capital markets constrains incumbent governments' social policy goals through the individual economic behaviour of firms. Specifically, with technology-driven reduction in transactions costs and the liberalization of national capital controls, mobile asset holders seek the highest rate of return on investment in global markets. In the absence of substantial international coordination of national policies, national policy makers face a prisoner's dilemma: even though some clear policy choices remain (e.g., public infrastructure and human capital policies), incumbent governments in each nation confront strong incentives to engage in competition to retain and attract mobile capital through reductions in 'non-productive' social spending and the large (often progressive) tax burdens that finance it. Trade openness, in the conventional view, also places significant pressures on social policy makers. Expansions of trade may force governments to retrench social protection in order to reduce labour costs, the disincentives to work and invest, public sector debt (and hence interest rates), and to otherwise foster efficiency and international competitiveness.

In terms of the 'political logic' of globalization, economic internationalization may foster welfare state retrenchment through conventional democratic politics. Indeed, the credible threat of capital flight certainly increases the electoral and organizational political resources of private enterprises. For instance, firms and their interest associations often lobby governments for rollbacks and efficiency-oriented reforms in national systems of social protection by arguing that social programmes negatively affect profits, investment, and job creation and by invoking the advantages of foreign investment environments. Furthermore, rises in capital mobility and trade bolster the appeal of neoliberal economic orthodoxy. That is, business economists and centre-right parties commonly use the 'economic logic' of globalization when appealing for market-oriented reforms of social welfare, tax and a variety of economic policies.

Embedded Liberalism and the Welfare State

A major challenge to the conventional globalization thesis comes from those who, like Polanyi (1944), see the welfare state as integral to embedded liberalism. Specifically, in seminal work on post-World War II public policies, David Cameron (1978), John Stephens (1979) and Peter Katzenstein (1985) argue that a large public sector and welfare state enables governments to lessen insecurities and risks attendant to internationalization, and otherwise pursue flexible adjustment to international openness.[3] John Ruggie (1982), echoing these themes, argues that, in fact, a multinational regime of embedded liberalism emerged in the post-war era in which the international liberal trading order was supported by varying albeit significant levels of government intervention and social insurance. More recently, Geoffrey Garrett (1998a, 1998b) and Dani Rodrik (1997, 1998), among others, stress that the welfare state continues to provide ample social insurance against international market risks to employment and income as well as compensation to those who lose from international competition. These scholars have, in fact, argued that it may be desirable to maintain systems of ample social insurance and compensation in order to minimize socio-political volatility that can emanate from public anxiety over economic vulnerability and from realized job and income losses.

The Evidence

Do rises in trade and capital mobility negatively impact the welfare state or do they reinforce the demands and purported structural imperatives for social insurance and compensation? After a near decade of systematic research on this question, political economists have generally concluded that there are few if any strong, direct and systematic impacts of economic internationalization on social welfare provision. In fact, some of the best recent research has argued that welfare policy change has been driven by deindustrialization (Iversen and Cusack, 2000) or both deindustrialization and the fiscal stresses that flow from ageing populations and sustained higher unemployment rates (Hicks and Zorn, forthcoming). In my own work (Swank, 2001, 2002, 2003), I find no systematic relationships between the multiple dimensions of international capital mobility and multiple dimensions of social welfare protection. The two partial exceptions to this conclusion, confirmed in extensive econometric and case study analysis, is that high capital mobility, on the one hand, and high public sector deficits and debt, on the other, interact to pressure moderate programmatic retrenchments (also see Mosley, 2003). Second, where national configurations of political institutions disfavour pro-welfare state coalitions (i.e., the Anglo liberal political economies), post-1970s rises in capital mobility are associated with rollbacks with social provision.

Other recent research largely supports these conclusions that the welfare impacts of internationalization are, at best, limited or conditional.[4] Using extensive expenditure-based measures of welfare state retrenchment, Castles (2004), Hicks and Zorn (forthcoming), Huber and Stephens (2001) and Kwon and Pontusson (2002) find virtually no robust associations between trade and capital openness, on the one hand, and various dimensions of the welfare state, on the other. Reflecting a recent spate of studies that use the Luxembourg Income Study data on income inequality, Bradley *et al.* (2003) report no robust trade or foreign direct investment impacts on measures of fiscal redistribution. Another set of rigorous, systematic studies effectively reports substantively very weak, mixed or inconclusive evidence on the effect of the dimensions of trade and capital openness on areas of social policy change or redistribution (Allen and Scruggs, 2004; Burgoon, 2001; Garrett and Mitchell, 2001; Kittel and Obinger, 2003; Korpi and Ralme, 2003). Burgoon (2001) offers one of the most interesting analyses (albeit built around simple expenditures data alone); he theorizes and reports supportive evidence for the argument that where concerns over compensation are low or diffuse, and political actor hostility over welfare policy is significant (e.g., investor concerns with pension or health costs), rises in economic internationalization engenders retrenchment. Where social policy is highly relevant to compensation or domestic adjustment to internationalization, and is minimally damaging to potential political opposition (e.g., active labour market policies), the systematic relationship between internationalization and social welfare is modestly positive. Again, the thrust of recent research has been to suggest that rises in trade and capital openness are not systematically related to notable retrenchment of the welfare state; the relationship between globalization and social protection is more complex.

Domestic Politics and Welfare State Retrenchment

The conclusion that globalization is not strongly and systematically linked to welfare retrenchment leads one back to domestic politics and institutions in search of theory and evidence to explain contemporary trajectories of welfare reform.[5] Recent theory on the 'new politics' of the welfare state, originating largely in the work of Raul Pierson (1994; 1996), has emphasized that welfare states are highly resistant to pressures attendant to international and domestic structural socio-economic change (e.g., internationalization, deindustrialization, and ageing). Incumbent governments find it very difficult to reduce concentrated benefits to well-defined, mobilized constituencies in return for future, diffuse benefits. Generally, welfare states are path dependent in that the cognitive and political consequences of past policy choices constrain and otherwise shape efforts at programmatic and systemic welfare retrenchment.

While the 'new politics' literature tends to focus on extant programme structures and the constituencies that they have formed, political economists have increasingly emphasized the welfare roles of 'varieties of democratic capitalism'. In this view, as in the traditional power resources school of welfare analysis (see below), the institutionally embedded interests of labour, capital and the state are brought centre stage. Specifically, the nature of the production regime should be important to the pace and depth of neoliberal welfare reforms. As Soskice (1990, 1999) has argued, countries may be classified by the extent of national level coordination through centralized collective bargaining among relatively well-organized union and employer associations. Second, nations will vary according to the extent of sector (or business group) organization of the economy, or the level of cooperation by enterprises in organizing product, financial and labour markets. With regard to national coordination, supply-side oriented economic policies emphasize growth and employment. Active labour market policies generously fund training, relocation and general employment services (and social transfer programmes contain strong work incentives). Macroeconomic and supply-side policies have sought full or near-full employment, and extensive public control of finance has allowed governments to channel credit. High marginal tax rates on uninvested profits, coupled with general investment reserves, investment tax credits and other incentives for saving, complement other supply-side policies in fostering growth and employment. Corporatist institutions, where labour has regularly exchanged wage restraint for full employment commitments and expansions in universal social protection, complement macroeconomic and supply-side policies.

Sector-coordinated market economies typically have moderately high centralization of collective bargaining; wage bargaining is supported by cooperative arrangements between business and labour at the firm level. In addition, as Soskice and collaborators have argued (Soskice, 1999; Hall and Soskice, 2001), the sector-coordinated economy is structured by significant organization of economic activity within industrial sectors oriented to the long-term development and production of high-quality, diversified consumer and industrial goods. Cooperative business groups typically organize research and development and technology transfer, export marketing strategy, vocational training, and some features of competition and pricing behaviour. Coordination of economic activity by business is supported by stable long-run labour–business relations and by state regulatory frameworks. Traditionally interventionist tax policy has generally facilitated state targeting of investment during periods of economic modernization, and restructuring and high marginal capital tax rates (and high employer social insurance contributions) have fostered social solidarity and long-term stability in labour and industrial relations (Swank, 2002: Ch. 5).

The corporatist conservative welfare state, integral to the sector-coordinated model, integrates labour and capital and promotes long-term stable if not cooperative employer–employee relations. Specifically, the welfare state provides generous employment-based social protection for labour without fundamentally altering class and status distinctions or challenging market incentives. The conservative welfare state provides generous social security for workers, social stability for capital, and generally facilitates the cooperative relations necessary for long-term economic development strategies; the occupational basis of a generous system of social insurance (coupled with employment protection laws) fosters the acquisition of firm-specific skills by workers and, in turn, enhances the long-term employment commitments valued by workers and employers (Ebbinghaus and Manow, 2003).[6]

The significance to welfare state retrenchment of the coordinated model should be clear. As Hall and Gingerich (2001) have argued, elements of national economic models are functionally interdependent. Fundamental reforms in one area have significant implications for other elements of the model. More concretely, business, labour, and the state have interests in the preservation of the basic components of the extant model. For instance, employers in sector-coordinated market economies may not embrace (or they may even oppose) significant neoliberal reforms when faced with the uncertainty those reforms generate (e.g., Thelen, 1999). In fact, German employer support for maintenance of basic features of the generous welfare state (and its funding arrangements) is arguably rooted in business' interests in promoting long-term stability in the labour and industrial relations system (Swank, 2002: Ch. 5). Generally, the greater the national or sector coordination of the economy, the higher the costs (e.g., economic uncertainty, political resistance) to policy makers from adoption of neoliberal welfare state reforms in the face of pressures from globalization, deindustrialization or other extant socio-economic structural changes.

A Note on Political Parties

Although the varieties-of-capitalism literature has fostered a widely accepted reconceptualization of the welfare interests and roles of labour, capital, and the state, more controversy exists with respect to the contemporary role played by alternations in social democratic, Christian democratic, and centre-right party control of government. Widely held to be the formative political influence on welfare state development (e.g., Hicks, 1999; Huber and Stephens, 2001: Chs 1–4), the 'new politics' thesis and mainstream globalization theory both predict minimal influence of partisan government on social policy change in an era of internationalization and austerity. In fact, some long-time proponents of power resources theory have argued that the once robust partisan effects on multiple dimensions of social policy disappear in the 1980s and 1990s (Huber and Stephens, 2001: Ch. 5). However, as Korpi and Palme (2003) argue, citizens' positions in employment and labour relations still determine the resources, opportunities, and constraints on their ability to realize economic interests and, in turn, shape their interests with regard to social citizenship rights. In fact, in their careful study of episodes of welfare retrenchment from 1975 to 1995, Korpi and Palme find strong evidence that rollbacks in social protection vary by the political strength of traditional class- and ideologically based parties. Retrenchments are less likely to occur under left governments than confessional and centre-right party governments; this finding holds at every level of international openness and socio-economic and institutional context.

Globalization, Domestic Forces, and Welfare State Protection

Using new cross-sectional and annual time-series data on welfare state entitlements and decommodification in OECD nations (see Table 1), I provide a succinct, synoptic analysis of the central questions raised above. Do rises in trade and capital mobility promote retrenchment or the maintenance of insurance and compensation? Do domestic forces – the institutions of national and sector coordination of markets and the power of left and Christian democratic parties – determine welfare state trajectories in the era of globalization and austerity? As such, these two questions reflect the tension between two fundamental and disparate views of democratic capitalism in the early twenty-first century.

I move to answer these questions by regressing the well-known index of welfare state decommodification as well as unemployment, sickness and standard pension income replacement rates on the degree of financial liberalization (a core indicator of formal and actual capital mobility), trade openness and measures of national and sectoral coordination of markets and of party control of government. The period of analysis covers the years 1981 to 2000 in 18 advanced capitalist democracies. Statistical and measurement details are given in the notes to Table 2. Based on theory and evidence reviewed above, our best general expectations are that international factors should be unrelated or positively related to unemployment, sickness, and other programmes that form the core of insurance and compensation for current workers; internationalization should be unrelated or negatively

Table 2 The impact of internationalization and domestic political factors on programmatic dimensions of the welfare state, 1981–2000

	Decommodification	Unemployment income replacement	Sickness income replacement	Pension income replacement
International factors				
Liberalization of	−0.0478	0.0059**	0.0024	−0.0031
capital controls	(0.1000)	(0.0039)	(0.0044)	(0.0030)
Trade openness	0.0258**	0.0005	0.0002	−0.0009**
	(0.0106)	(0.0004)	(0.0004)	(0.0002)
Domestic factors				
National	0.6236**	0.0185*	0.0327**	−0.0010
coordination	(0.2998)	(0.0126)	(0.0146)	(0.0094)
Sector coordination	0.6776*	0.0114	0.0629**	0.1149**
	(0.5022)	(0.0241)	(0.0280)	(0.0149)
Left party control	0.3108**	0.0027**	0.0099**	0.0015*
of govt	(0.0446)	(0.0015)	(0.0016)	(0.0010)
Christian Dem	0.0716*	−0.0007	0.0157**	0.0050**
control of govt	(0.0476)	(0.0019)	(0.0021)	(0.0010)
Constant	0.9489	0.4478	0.7264	0.5600
Observations	360	356	349	336
R-squared	0.7814	0.5950	0.7443	0.8129

Notes: Social welfare models are estimated with annual 1981–2000 data for 18 advanced democracies by OLS; models are first-order autoregressive. The table reports unstandardized regression coefficients and panel-correct standard errors. Models contain the following controls: decommodification model includes the percentage of population 65 years and older, unemployment rate, and per capita GDP in international prices. Unemployment and sickness replacement rate models include the unemployment rate and per capita GDP.
* significance at the 0.10 level.
** 0.05 level.
Financial liberalization: 14-point scale of removal of capital and exchange controls (Quinn, 1997). Trade openness: Exports and imports as a percentage of GDP.
National coordination: Standard score index of (1) level of bargaining, (2) union organization (standard score index of union density and centralization of union confederation power; and (3) employer organization: Index (standard score) of the presence of a national association of employers and powers of that association (see Swank, 2002, 2003 for details on the methodology and data sources).
Sector coordination: Standard score index of (1) labour management Cupertino; (2) investor-productive enterprise linkage; (3) purchaser-supplier relations; and (4) cooperative arrangements-competitive firms. (see Swank, 2002, 2003 for details on the methodology and data sources).
Left and Christian Democratic Government: Cumulative years of office since 1950 of left and Christian Democratic parties (see Swank, 2002).

related to pensions. That said, overall decommodification is likely to be influenced only modestly if at all by internationalization. As to domestic factors, the greater the national and sector coordination (i.e., the weaker the liberal, uncoordinated market institutions), and the greater the political power of social democratic and Christian democratic parties (i.e., the weaker the centre-right), the higher the decommodification and income replacement rates (i.e., the less welfare retrenchment).

The findings reported in the first two rows of Table 2 largely confirm our expectations about globalization and welfare state retrenchment. The majority of possible relationships are insignificant. Yet, the associations between international financial liberalization and trade openness, on the one hand, and decommodification as well as unemployment and sickness replacement rates, on the other, are – with one exception – either positive and statistically significant or in the positive direction (with some associations falling just below statistical significance). In addition, the effect of international factors on pensions is negative, and, in the case of trade, the relationship is highly significant and negative. This pattern of findings confirms the conclusions from the literature of no strong, systematic, and significant pro-retrenchment impacts of globalization. It also underscores arguments, such as Burgoon's (2001), that suggest capital mobility and trade may prompt continued or expanded insurance and compensation for contemporary workers, while at the same time fostering rollbacks in areas only diffusely related to compensation and directly related to business costs and efficiency issues.

As to domestic factors, the second portion of Table 2 reports strong evidence that, as we move from liberal, uncoordinated economies toward national and sectoral coordinated systems, the chances of general and programme-specific welfare retrenchment significantly declines. Both forms of market coordination are related to overall decommodification, while national organization principally supports programmes for contemporary workers, and sector coordination is associated most notably with maintenance of generous pension systems. In addition, party government still matters. In fact, left party government, net of other forces, is significantly related to every dimension of social protection; Christian democratic government control is most significantly associated with high sickness and pension income replacement rates (although it too fosters maintenance of overall decommodification of the welfare state). Additional tests and controls for socio-economic factors (beyond the controls that are in these models) and other domestic political factors (e.g., veto points) do not affect the pattern of findings. Moreover, all effects reported in Table 2 hold if analyses are shifted to the 1991–2000 period, alone.

Conclusions

The latest research on the direction and magnitude of the impacts of economic internationalization on the welfare state largely dispels what for a decade or more was conventional wisdom, namely that globalization means the inevitable retrenchment of generous systems of social protection and the diminution of democratic policy choice. At the same time, recent theory and research on the domestic political sources of contemporary social policy also suggest that democracy is alive and well. Mature welfare states deflect significant pressures for dismantlement or dramatic reductions in social protection; variations in domestic political economic institutions and, in turn, the interests and behaviours of labour, capital and the state still shape the course of welfare state policy. In addition, the alternation in power of class and ideological disparate political parties, now widely regarded as the most important force in welfare state development, still matters in an era of globalization and austerity. My own analysis reported above – work that draws on recent theory and evidence as well as the best new data on social protection in the advanced capitalist democracies – clearly supports these contentions.

Yet, some caution about these conclusions and the degree they may be extrapolated into the future is in order. Continuing international integration of markets – both through conscious regionalization and broader processes of economic globalization – continues to place pressures on governments to reduce the costs and inefficiencies associated with state intervention in domestic markets. Extension of the European Union to several Central European nations is just one example of potentially significant regionalization pressures on mature welfare states. These pressures are dramatically reinforced by the ageing of the advanced nations' populations. As Hicks and Zorn (forthcoming) have demonstrated, the increase in the size of elderly population and its fiscal implications is one of the strongest predictors of episodes of welfare retrenchment over the last couple of decades in the advanced democracies. In addition, further liberalization of domestic markets in heretofore sector coordinated economies, and continued pressures for decentralization and flexibility of labour and industrial relations systems in nationally coordinated economies, raises the prospect of a weakened institutional bedrock of the welfare state. As the first decade of the twenty-first century unfolds, it does seem clear, however, that domestic politics will have a lot to do with the future course of these developments and of the welfare state itself.

Notes

From *Social Policy & Society*, vol. 4, No. 2, pp. 183–95, copyright © Cambridge University Press, 2005, by permission of Cambridge University Press and the author.

The author would like to thank James Allen and Lyle Scruggs for unpublished data on income replacement rates and decommodification in contemporary social programmes and Dennis Quinn for unpublished data on financial and capital market liberalization.

1   Welfare state scholars have also produced volumes of studies on policy area and country-specific patterns of welfare retrenchment. See, for instance, recent contributions to *Journal of European Social Policy* and the literature cited therein.

2   The globalization thesis dates at least to Adam Smith (1976[1776]). For extensive surveys of the literature on the globalization thesis and its challengers, see Swank (2002) and Genschel (2004), among others.

3   These scholars also pointed out that trade openness is often associated structurally with highly concentrated industrial sectors and, in turn, strong trade union organizations, centralized wage bargaining, and electorally successful social democratic parties. These factors are strongly correlated with welfare state development.

4   Two additional indirect mechanisms that link globalization and welfare state retrenchment have been touted in the literature: Globalization induced unemployment (Huber and Stephens, 1998; 2001) and globalization induced declines in taxation. With regard to taxation, there appears to be no systematic downward impact of trade and capital mobility on capital (and other types of) taxation (e.g., Basinger and Hallerberg, 2004; Garrett and Mitchell, 2001; Hayes, 2003; Swank and Steinmo, 2002; but see Bretschger and Hettick, 2001).

5   Because of space limitations, I focus my attention primarily on welfare state impacts of models of national democratic capitalism and traditional power resources theory. I comment briefly on the relevance of domestic political institutions that serve as veto points. See Swank (2002: esp. Ch. 2) and Bonoli (2001) for extensive reviews of the literature as well as applications of veto points theory in analyses of welfare retrenchment.

6   The notion that the absence of general, portable skills, characteristic of liberal market economies, or more specifically, the presence of significant firm/industry-specific skills, has been causally associated with development and maintenance of generous systems of social protection (Iversen and Soskice, 2001).

References

Allen, J. and Scruggs, L. (2004), 'Political partisanship and welfare state reform in advanced industrial societies', *American Journal of Political Science*, 48, 3, 496–512.

Armingeon, K. (2004), 'Reconciling competing claims of the welfare state: the politics of old and new social risk coverage in comparative perspective', Paper presented at the Annual Meeting of the American Political Science Association, Chicago, IL, 2 September–5 September.

Bonoli, G. (2001), 'Political institutions, veto points, and the process of welfare state adaption', in Paul Pierson (ed.), *The New Politics of the Welfare State*, New York: Oxford University Press, pp. 238–64.

Basinger, S. and Hallerberg, M. (2004), 'Remodeling the competition for capital: how domestic politics erases the race to the bottom', *American Political Science Review*, 98, 2, 261–76.

Bradley, D., Huber, E., Moller, S., Nielsen, F. and Stephens, J. (2003), 'Distribution and redistribution in postindustrial democracies', *World Politics*, 55 (January), 193–228.

Bretschger, L. and Hettich, F. (2001), 'Globalization, capital mobility and tax competition: theory and evidence for OECD countries', *European Journal of Political Economy*, 18, 675–715.

Burgoon, B. (2001), 'Globalization and welfare compensation: disentangling the ties that bind', *International Organization*, 55, 3, 509–51.

Cameron, D. (1978), 'The expansion of the public economy: a comparative analysis', *American Political Science Review*, 72, 1243–61.

Castles, F. (2004), *The Future of the Welfare State: Crisis Myths and Crisis Realities*, New York: Oxford University Press.

Clayton, R. and Pontusson, J. (1998), 'Welfare state restructuring revisited: entitlement cuts, public sector restructuring, and inegalitarian trends in advanced capitalist democracies', *World Politics*, 51, 1, 67–98.

Ebbinghaus, B. and Manow, P. (eds.) (2003), *Varieties of Welfare Capitalism: Social Policy and Political Economy in Europe, Japan and the USA*, London: Routledge.

Esping-Andersen, G. (1990), *Three Worlds of Welfare Capitalism*, London: Polity Press.

Garrett, G. (1998a), *Partisan Politics in a Global Economy*, New York: Cambridge University Press.

Garrett, G. (1998b), 'Global markets and national policies: collision course or virtuous circle', *International Organization*, 52, 4, 787–824.

Garrett, G. and Mitchell, D. (2001), 'Globalization and the welfare state: income transfers in the advanced industrialized democracies, 1965–1990', *European Journal of Political Research*, 39, 145–77.

Genschel, P. (2004), 'Globalization and the welfare state: a retrospective', *Journal of European Public Policy*, 11, 4, 613–36.

Green-Pedersen, C. (2002), *The Politics of Justification: Party Competition and Welfare State Retrenchment in Denmark and the Netherlands from 1982 to 1998*, Amsterdam: University of Amsterdam Press.

Hall, P. and Gingerich, D. (2001), 'Varieties of Capitalism and Institutional Complementarities in the Macroeconomy.' Paper presented at the Annual Meeting of the American Political Science Association, 30 August–2 September, San Francisco, CA.

Hall, P. and Soskice, D. (eds.) (2001), *Varieties of Capitalism: The Institutional Foundations of Comparative Advantage*, New York: Oxford University Press.

Hayes, J. (2003), 'Globalization and capital taxation in consensus and majoritarian democracies', *World Politics*, 56 (October), 79–113.

Hicks, A. (1999), *Social Democracy and Welfare Capitalism*, Ithaca: Cornell University Press.

Hicks, A. and Zorn, C. (Forthcoming), 'Economic globalization, the macro economy, and reversals of welfare expansion in affluent democracies 1978–1994', *International Organization*.

Huber, E. and Stephens, J. D. (1998), 'Internationalization and the social democratic welfare model: crises and future prospects', *Comparative Political Studies*, 33, 3 (June), 353–97.

Huber, E. and Stephens, J. D. (2001), *Partisan Choice in Global Markets: Development and Crisis of Advanced Welfare States*, Chicago: University of Chicago Press.

Iversen, T. and Cusack, T. (2000), 'The causes of welfare state expansion', *World Politics*, 52 (April), 313–49.

Iversen, T. and Soskice, D. (2001), 'An asset theory of social preferences', *American Political Science Review*, 95, 4, 875–93.

Katzenstein, P. (1985), *Small States in World Markets*, Ithaca: Cornell University Press.

Kittel, B. and Obinger, H. (2003), 'Political parties, institutions, and the dynamics of social expenditure in times of austerity', *Journal of European Public Policy*, 10, 1, 20–45.

Korpi, W. and Palme, J. (2003), 'New politics and class politics in the context of austerity and globalization', *American Political Science Review*, 97, 3, 425–46.

Kwon, H. Y. and Pontusson, J. (2002), 'Welfare spending in OECD countries visited: has the salience of partisanship really declined?', Paper presented at the Annual Meeting of the American Political Science Association, Boston, MA, 29 August to 1 September.

Mosley, L. (2003), *Global Capital and National Governments*, New York: Cambridge University Press.

Pierson, P. (1994), *Dismantling the Welfare State. Reagan, Thatcher and the Politics of Retrenchment in Britain and the United States*, New York: Cambridge University Press.

Pierson, P. (1996), 'The new politics of the welfare state', *World Politics*, 48, 2, 143–79.

Polanyi, K. (1944), *The Great Transformation*, New York: Rinehart.

Quinn, D. (1997), 'The correlates of change in international financial regulation', *American Political Science Review*, 91, 531–52.

Rodrik, D. (1997), *Has Globalization Gone too Far?*, Washington, DC: Institute for International Economics.

Rodrik, D. (1998), 'Why do more open economies have bigger governments?' *Journal of Political Economy*, 106, 5, 997–1032.

Ruggie, J. G. (1982), 'International regimes, transactions, and change: embedded liberalism in the postwar economic order', *International Organization*, 36, 2, 379–415.

Smith, A. (1976), *An Inquiry into the Nature and Causes of the Wealth of Nations*, Oxford: Clarendon Press.

Soskice, D. (1990), 'Wage determination: the changing role of institutions in advanced industrial societies', *Oxford Review of Economic Policy*, 6, 36–61.

Soskice, D. (1999), 'Divergent production regimes: coordinated and uncoordinated market economies in the 1980s and 1990s', in Hebert Kitschelt, Peter Lange, Gary Marks, and John Stephens (eds.), *Continuity and Change in Contemporary Capitalism*, New York: Cambridge University Press, pp. 101–34.

Stephens, J. D. (1979), *The Transition from Capitalism to Socialism*, Atlantic Highlands, NJ: Humanities Press.

Swank, D. (2001), 'Political institutions and welfare state restructuring', in Paul Pierson (ed.), *The New Politics of the Welfare State*, New York: Oxford University Press.

Swank, D. (2002), *Global Capital, Political Institutions, and Policy Change in Developed Welfare States*, New York: Cambridge University Press.

Swank, D. (2003), 'Whither welfare? Globalization, political institutions, and contemporary welfare states', in Linda Weiss (ed.), *States in the Global Economy. Bringing Domestic Institutions Back In*, New York: Cambridge University Press.

Swank, D. and Steinmo, S. (2002), 'The new political economy of taxation in advanced capitalist democracies', *American Journal of Political Science*, 46, 3, 642–55.

Thelen, K. (1999), 'Why German employers cannot bring themselves to dismantle the German model', in Torben Iversen, Jonas Pontusson, and David Soskice (eds.), *Unions, Employers, and Central Banks*, New York: Cambridge University Press, pp. 138–72.

The Europeanization of Social Protection: Domestic Impacts and National Responses

Jon Kvist and Juho Saari

[. . .] Two waves of research have examined the relationship between the EU and social protection. First-wave scholars noted the weak foundation and mandate of EU institutions in social policy. Because the EU had no legal or monetary means of carrying out its own social policies, it resorted to regulatory social policy (Majone, 1993). Typical of many first-wave studies, a study on the impact of membership on British social policy found an impact in only two domains: gender equality and non-discrimination against EU nationals (Baldwin-Edwards and Gough, 1991). Scholars in this period generally shared the view that the EU had little impact on national social protection (for example, Lange, 1992) and that EU social policy was regulatory and symbolic (Majone, 1993).

[. . .]

Inspired by neofunctionalism arguments, second-wave scholars made an analytical distinction between positive and negative integration. Their starting point was the observation that European integration in social policy was characterized less by positive integration (that is, initiatives of political actors for developing either EU social policies or common social policies across Member States) than by negative integration (that is, spillover from economic markets to social policy). Their argument was that the ECJ [European Court of Justice] and markets drove the process of negative integration, leading to both adjustments of national welfare states to market requirements (see Leibfried and Pierson, 2000) and an erosion of national competence over social policy. At the same time, second-wave scholars – in agreement with first-wave scholars – found that the positive integration of social policy was limited, not making up for losses made nationally (Streeck, 1995; Scharpf, 1999). Thus they depict a development towards a multi-tiered social policy system in Europe, with fragmented EU social policy and semi-sovereign welfare states (Leibfried and Pierson, 1995).

These important observations are still valid today. However, what could not be known 10 years ago were the changes that have since unfolded, with implications for social protection. [We focus] on four such developments: new policy processes, the internal market, the European Economic and Monetary Union (EMU) and EU enlargement. [. . .] These developments are among the factors that have transformed the relationship between the national and EU levels since the mid-1990s. These developments also stimulate the emergence of a new third wave of studies on the relationship between the EU and social policy. [. . .] This relationship – transformed markedly over the last ten years – is best described as 'the Europeanization of social protection'.

What does the Europeanization of social protection mean? We find that EU social policy is indeed driven by negative integration, or by courts and markets, as elegantly phrased by second-wave scholars (Leibfried and Pierson, 2000). However, we also find significant developments at the EU level, including developments driven by politics (that is, not by courts or markets) that amount to more than 'fragmented EU social policy'. The point here is that positive integration in social protection is no longer geared towards a transfer of sovereignty from the national to the EU level, but rather to facilitate collaboration among sovereign Member States. Collaboration is primarily achieved by the establishment of an EU-level arena and procedures for exchanging knowledge, monitoring developments, collecting statistics and information, and much more. We also find that EU-level developments like the EMU, internal market extensions, and EU enlargement have significant potential influence on national social policy.

[. . .]

Europeanization Effects on the National Level

[. . .] Here we adopt a broad perspective on the possible impact of the EU on social protection by investigating the situation of eleven countries: Germany, France, Italy, the UK, Poland, Spain, Czech Republic, Denmark, Finland, Greece and the Netherlands). [. . .] We investigate the impact of four types of EU-level developments – new policy processes, internal markets, EMU and EU enlargements – on national social protection, that is welfare reform and governments' responses to the various EU-level developments, assuming that country size, welfare regime, membership record, political legacy and competitiveness act as intervening variables.

We examine the impact on welfare reform by looking at whether national welfare reform was inspired by the European Social Model (ESM) and if the reform agenda was influenced by the EU [. . .]. Has the ESM worked as a blueprint for welfare reform? Have EU developments facilitated or pressured MSs to specific reforms of social protection systems?

The European Social Model and National Welfare Reform

Member States do not share a common understanding of the ESM which means different things to different countries. [. . .] Not only is there general agreement that Europe has different social models, the dominating perception is that these models more or less reflect the welfare regimes described earlier [see above, pp. 136–50].

At a more abstract level, however, most countries acknowledge that there may be a common ESM in the sense of certain common values and a commitment to social objectives, thus making Europe stand apart from other regions of the world. One such shared understanding is that the ESM is a normative device for collaboration in the EU, as when the 2000 Nice European Council concluded that: 'the European social model can be characterised in particular by systems that offer a high level of social protection, by the importance of social dialogue and by services of general interest covering activities vital for social cohesion, is today based, beyond the diversity of the Member States' social systems, on a common core of values'. This definition is generally accepted by national governments.

In practice, however, many national politicians and social policy debates stick with stereotypes or even enemy images of the ESM [. . .]. Julia Le Grand, Elias Mossialos and Morgan Long note that many 'opinion formers in the UK have a perception that only one kind of ESM exists – one close to their understanding of the Continental model' and that 'many decision-makers in the rest of Europe have a perception of the UK model that is almost the mirror perception of the UK perception of the Continental model' and that in the UK 'key policy-makers are not impressed by what they interpret to be the ESM' (Le Grand et al., 2007). In Germany, Milena Büchs and Karl Hinrichs (2007) note the perception that the ESM is different from the German social model (Sozialstaat), although the latter has moved closer to the ESM in recent years. The French believe, according to Bruno Palier and Luana Petrescu (2007) that the ESM should be like the French social model, perceived as high quality jobs offering high minimum wage, high employment protection, and high social protection. When this is not the case, the ESM or a given EU policy initiative is by French definition not French and thereby not social, and therefore, following French logic, might be considered a possible threat to the French social model.

Post-authoritarian countries have a more favourable view of the ESM, one largely matching the Nice definition. For some of these countries the ESM works as a beacon, a signpost of an ideal, whereas others see it as a potential threat. In particular Greece, as Theodoros Sakellaropoulos (2007) notes, uses the ESM as a 'constant point of reference' in national debates over social protection. In sharp contrast, Poland is sceptical of attempts at harmonizing Member State social protection following the ESM, as Poles fear 'pressure from certain older MSs to increase social spending and labour costs' [Wóycicka and Grabowski, 2007]. In other words, two countries that presently share a dismal record on competitiveness have different ideas of how the ESM may work to improve their situation: Greece sees the ESM as carrying the promise of catch-up convergence, while Poland fears losing economic competitiveness.

In any case, given different national understandings of what constitutes the ESM and varying opinions on whether the ESM works or should work as a template for national reforms, the ESM has not been a common blueprint for recent European welfare reforms.

Have EU Developments Influenced National Welfare Reforms?

Although the ESM may not function as a template for reform, there may be other direct and indirect influences on national social protection. [. . .] The Lisbon Strategy, the extension of the internal market, the EMU and EU enlargements may all have had a considerable impact on national welfare reform.

[. . .]

The EU has contributed to a reorientation of national social protection towards more modern, universal and active policies in the Czech Republic, Greece, Italy, Poland, and Spain. The EU has also stimulated institution building and sometimes even the introduction of certain social protection schemes, especially of universal social assistance. Paradoxically, Greece, while perhaps the most pro-EU country, still has not introduced a universal social assistance scheme [Sakellaropoulos, 2007]. In addition, the EU, especially by facilitating a forum for discussion, has inspired certain policy developments in the other countries, for example, a tax credit in France.

The indirect impact of the EMU on national social protection is clear in some countries. In Italy the need to restructure public financing and cost-containment led to two health reforms and four pension reforms

[Sacchi, 2007]. In Spain, the EMU has helped national governments legitimize the rationalization of social protection [Guillén, 2007]. But other countries that faced difficulties in meeting the criteria of the SGP, [the Stability Growth Pact], for example France and Germany, do not report such effects.

Enlargement has so far had little impact on national welfare reform. The old Member States have introduced transitional measures for the free mobility of workers from the new Member States or restrictions on their access to social protection. Fears of the adverse affects of a larger and more heterogeneous EU resulting in regulatory dumping or a race-to-the-bottom in social protection are as yet unfounded. EU enlargements, however, are likely to stay on the national social protection agenda for some time, as transitional measures run out and as more enlargements are discussed.

The influence of the EU on national social protection increased after 2000. The Lisbon Strategy and the wider application of the OMC [Open Method of Coordination] in the field of social protection and (for Czech Republic and Poland) the start on accession talks all contributed to social protection getting more national focus.

[. . .]

The Europeanization of Social Protection – The Interweaving of National and EU Levels

Member States do not merely receive stimuli from above, that is, from the EU level, as is implicit in the previous section. Member States are actors that also interact at both the national and the EU levels. The Europeanization of social protection is a multi-dimensional process where Member States interact with other Member States at the national level, where Member States upload ideas to the EU level, where actors at the EU level are active, and where initiatives at the EU level download to or impact on the national level. [. . .]

First we examined the government responses to EU developments. Are governments embracing or being positive towards the new policy processes as exemplified by the Lisbon Strategy (later the revised Lisbon Strategy) and the OMC, attempts to extend the internal market to social services, the EMU and EU enlargements? Or are national governments either critical of or indifferent to these developments?

No Member State is against the Lisbon Strategy. The original strategy adopted at the 2000 Council Spring Meeting in Lisbon had varying impacts on national social protection debates. Two extremes are observable. In France the adoption of the Strategy was not observed due to internal politics [Palier and Petrescu, 2007]. In contrast, the Danish prime minister heralded the Lisbon Strategy as the coming of a new and more social Europe up to the euro referendum in 2001, albeit with little success [Kvist, 2007]. After a few years the Strategy became more complex and heavy, leading to a more streamlined version adopted in 2005. This version made growth and jobs the prime objectives, with social protection no longer officially part of the Strategy. Again, all Member States officially support the revised Strategy. Representative of many countries, Britain and Poland argue that pursuing economic objectives is the best way of ensuring social objectives [Le Grand et al., 2007; Wóycicka and Grabowski, 2007].

Most Member States also support the use of the OMC in social protection. In the 1990s the OMC had been applied in economic and employment policy; however, with the Lisbon Strategy in 2000, the OMC also became applicable to social protection. Traditionally considered foot-dragging in EU social policy matters, Denmark and the UK have become ardent supporters of the OMC. They believe that the OMC incorporates subsidiarity, autonomy, flexibility and transparency [Le Grand et al., 2007; Kvist, 2007]. But Denmark and the UK are not proponents of a stronger or more binding OMC. Meanwhile, Spain and the Netherlands want more country rankings and more naming and shaming, while Italy wants stronger procedures in pensions [Guillén, 2007; Hemerijck and Sleegers, 2007; Sacchi, 2007]. Germany directly opposes more naming and shaming, and fears a creeping expansion of EU competence (Le Grand et al., 2007).

However, the OMC also has its critics, especially Greece and Finland. Both were against the adoption of the OMC, which they think is too weak an instrument. For some years, these two countries preferred the old Community Method of social protection (Saari and Kangas, 2007; Sakellaropoulos, 2007). Over the years, however, they have become luke-warm proponents of the OMC. The two new MSs also politely support the OMC, although Poland is critical of the measure of relative poverty and the social exclusion strategy which it considers of little relevance, and the Czech Republic believes the OMC has little impact on national policies [Wóycicka and Grabowski, 2007; Potůček, 2007]. As we can see, the seemingly unanimous support for the OMC masks important national differences in the motivation behind the support, the strength of the support, and the perceptions on the use and effectiveness of the OMC. Similarly, ideas for how to reform the OMC differ, although all countries officially support the streamlined version after the integration of the social inclusion and social protection strategies.

The extension of the internal market to the field of services has become perhaps the most disputed area of social protection in the EU. This is most vividly illustrated through government responses to the recent Services Directive. Two camps are distinct: they differ on their views on the scope of the Services Directive, that is, whether or not to exclude health and social services in particular, and the legislation to be applied for the cross-border service provider, that is, the country-of-origin principle or some amended version, making more of the host country legislation or standards applicable. One camp argues that as many services as possible should be covered and that the country-of-origin principle should apply. Broadly speaking this was also the content of the first proposal of a service directive by the Commission in 2004. The other camp wanted social and health services to be exempt from the service directive. These countries also believed that the country-of-origin principle should not be applied, as they feared the adverse impact on service provision standards and guarantees as well as social dumping in the service sector.

[. . .] the first camp included the Czech Republic, Italy, the Netherlands, and Poland, while the second camp included Denmark, Finland, France, Germany, Greece and, to some extent, the UK. However, the European Parliament was instrumental in brokering a widely supported compromise, receiving so many parliamentary votes that changing the amended directive became immensely difficult for national governments. On 12 December 2006, the Council passed the Parliament's version of the service directive, meaning that social and health services were explicitly exempted and the country-of-origin principle was replaced with a demand that any MS requirements on service providers must be non-discriminatory, proportional and necessary for securing public order, health, or the environment. Indeed, when the market-making process of the EU seriously entered the core fields of social protection, it became high politics.

National government views on the EMU vary, especially on the usefulness of the SGP [Strategic Growth Pact] criteria. Most Member States have full participation as their goal. To enter the third phase of the EMU and adopt the euro, MSs must meet the criteria of the SGP. Originally, the SGP was proposed by German Minister of Finance Theo Waigel in the mid-1990s. In 2003 and 2004, however, Germany faced economic problems that meant she could not meet the criteria. The same was true for France. Normally, the result would be an 'excessive deficit' procedure, whereby the country in question could be fined. However, the Council decided in 2004 not to initiate the procedure against France and Germany, a decision that the ECJ deemed unlawful in 2004. Obviously, the EMU is a sensitive issue. Some countries within the Eurozone, e.g. Finland and the Netherlands, argued that France and Germany should be ready to take their own medicine. For the old EU 15 MSs currently outside the Eurozone – Denmark, Sweden and the UK – this lack of enforcement strengthened their opposition to entry. Even though all three countries meet the SGP criteria, they are unlikely to adopt the euro any day soon.

In any case, the Council decided in March 2005 to relax the rules to respond to the criticism. Although the thresholds of 3 per cent annual budget deficit to GDP and 60 per cent gross public debt to GDP were maintained, MSs were allowed greater flexibility in exceeding the annual deficit threshold adverse and a longer time for reversing their excessive deficits. These changes received broad support, even among critics, because [. . .] MSs hope that the SGP is now more enforceable.

[. . .]

Many current Eurozone countries still experience difficulties meeting the SGP criteria. Six of the 12 old EU 15 Member States within the Eurozone did not meet one or two of the criteria for the third year running, as of 2007. The EMU and the SGP criteria are thus likely to remain important means of legitimizing cost-containment measures in many national social protection systems in the coming years.

At the same time there is a risk of an EU backlash from the EMU if it is perceived nationally as the catalyst for unpopular social protection reform [Büchs and Hinrichs, 2007]. In France and Italy, the EMU is already associated broadly with a deterioration of purchasing power and thus relative wealth [Palier and Petrescu, 2007; Sacchi, 2007]. To avoid unpopular social protection reforms and EU backlashes, MSs will likely further reform or even cancel the SGP criteria.

Enlargement has figured high on the EU agenda in the 2000s. The Eastern enlargements in 2004 and 2007 have nearly doubled the number of Member States [. . .]. Enlargement was supported by all national governments, some more strongly than others. However, it is similarly evident that enlargement has caused national debates in the old EU 15 Member States over the potential adverse impact on national social protection and labour markets in the form of social tourism and social dumping that may stem from allowing less prosperous countries with smaller benefits and lower earnings to enter the EU. In response to public pressure or to pre-empt xenophobic fears, all old EU 15 Member States (except Sweden) restricted access for workers from the Central and Eastern European new Member States either to national labour markets or to national social protection. While these transitional measures may last only for seven years, many Member States used the first occasion in 2006 to ease or cancel them. Almost at the same time, many Member States decided to introduce transitional measures for Bulgaria and Romania (entering in 2007).

For historical and geopolitical reasons some MSs are stronger supporters of EU enlargements than others. Finland, for example, has not been a strong supporter of enlargement whereas Denmark has actively advocated a large Eastern enlargement so as to include the small Baltic countries [Saari and Kangas, 2007; Kvist, 2007]. Greece supported the last enlargement, not least to include Cyprus, just as Greece welcomes the inclusion of Balkan countries into the EU so as to obtain stability and growth for its region [Sakellaropoulos, 2007].

[. . .]

Concluding Remarks

The Europeanization of social protection has taken place over the last ten years, with a remarkable intensity in the ways in which the national and EU levels have become interwoven in social protection. Without a doubt the competence over social protection rests firmly and primarily at the national level. No strong direct influence from the EU to the national level dictates the form, scope or principles of social protection. Indeed, according to EU legislation, national social protection must not discriminate, and other EU nationals have increasing access to national systems, just as nationals can increasingly receive services in other EU countries at the expense of the national exchequer. But perhaps the most profound impact lies in the way Europe plays a much greater role in how policy-makers think about social protection than it did only ten years ago.

The new policy processes, represented by the Lisbon Strategy and the OMC, show how the Member States turn to the EU for a platform for discussing social protection solutions for the common problems of globalization, ageing populations, and technological change. We view this change as a new form of positive integration, as it does not entail a transfer of sovereignty from the national to the EU level (as was the case in the old Community method and as neofunctionalism described the old form of positive integration). Instead, this new form of positive integration enables a non-binding form of collaboration between MSs, a form that [. . .] enjoys wide support among national governments. Although the impact of the new policy processes in social protection is hard to discern, [. . .] social protection has moved up the political agenda and become oriented towards more universal, modern and active approaches.

Negative integration or market-making measures persist in having their say in social protection. They have been expanded by a series of spectacular ECJ rulings starting with the *Kohll* and *Decker* cases in 1998. However, market-making in social protection has moved from a low- to a high-politics area, as the debates on the service directive testify. Not only national governments but also the European Parliament has taken a much greater interest in social protection than was the case a decade earlier.

In recent years, the EMU and especially the SGP criteria have been seen as having potential negative effects on social protection. When governments have to cut costs they are likely to cut where expenses are large, that is, in social protection. Indeed, national governments [. . .] use the EMU to legitimize cost-containment measures in a blame-avoidance strategy. But perhaps this strategy, too, has its limits, and SGP criteria could be further loosened to avoid unpopular retrenchment of social protection and EU backlash.

The possible adverse effects of EU enlargement on national social protection have also been heavily discussed. Transitional measures regulating the free movement of workers and restricting access to social protection have been put in place and later lifted either in part or completely. Although evidence of social tourism and social dumping is limited and the contribution of workers from the new MSs is considerable, enlargements and social protection are likely to remain on the national and EU agendas for years to come.

The Europeanization of social protection has so far not led to a convergence of welfare models. [. . .] There is no sign of the formation of a common European social model in different countries. By the same token, there seems to be an influence on the timing and agenda of reforms. In other words, individual MSs appear occupied with the same range of welfare reforms, namely pensions and care for the elderly, social inclusion, and child family policies. However, significant differences remain in the reasons for reform and in the type of reforms made.

As expected different patterns of Europeanization of social protection manifest across countries. Those with the biggest adjustment pressures are also the ones that report an EU impact on national social protection. This goes for the countries with the lowest rankings on competitiveness and for countries with welfare regimes of either the Southern European or Central and Eastern European types. In these countries we have seen a certain downloading of ideas. By contrast, one group of countries is happy with the OMC in social protection, perceiving themselves as being perhaps particularly active in the process of uploading ideas – particularly Denmark, the Netherlands and the UK.

However, this last observation is not meant to dichotomize countries as either recipients of EU-level ideas or donors to the EU level of ideas. Indeed, the overall most striking feature of the Europeanization of social policy is that EU-level developments increasingly interact with social protection in all countries.

Note

References

Büchs, M. and Hinrichs, K., 'Germany Moving Towards Europe but Putting National Autonomy First', in Kvist and Saari, 2007, pp. 21–40.

Guillén, A., 'Spain: Starting from Periphery, Becoming Centre', in Kvist and Saari, 2007, pp. 117–36.

Hemerijck, A. and Sleegers, P., 'The Netherlands: Social and Economic Normalisation in an Era of European Union Controversy', in Kvist and Saari, 2007, pp. 175–94.

Kvist, J., 'Denmark: From Foot Dragging to Pace Setting in European Union Social Policy', in Kvist and Saari, 2007, pp. 195–210.

Kvist, J. and Saari, J. (eds.), *The Europeanisation of Social Protection*, Bristol, Policy Press, 2007.

Le Grand, J., Mossialos, E. and Long, M., 'The United Kingdom: More an Economic than a Social European', in Kvist and Saari, 2007, pp. 41–60.

Palier, B. and Petrescu, L., 'France: Defending our Model', in Kvist and Saari, 2007, pp. 61–76.

Potůček, M., 'The Czech Republic: Tradition, Compatible with Modernisation?', in Kvist and Saari, 2007, pp. 137–52.

Saari, J. and Kangas, O., 'Finland: Towards more Proactive Policies', in Kvist and Saari, 2007, pp. 153–74.

Sacchi, S., 'Italy: Between Indifference, Exploitation and the Construction of a National Interest', in Kvist and Saari, 2007, pp. 77–98.

Sakellaropoulos, T., 'Greece: The Quest for National Welfare Expansion through More Social Europe', in Kvist and Saari, 2007, pp. 211–28.

Wóycicka, I. and Grabowski, M., 'Poland: Redefining Social Policies', in Kvist and Saari, 2007, pp. 99–116.

Explaining Convergence of OECD Welfare States: A Conditional Approach

Carina Schmitt and Peter Starke

Convergence is the process in which countries or other kinds of entities become more similar. While it is certainly not a new theme, it surfaced in the context of the globalization debate in the 1990s. Convergence is not only an academic issue. The notion of a world growing ever closer together in which cultural and institutional differences have been levelled out is commonplace. Journalists and political commentators argue over whether the world has become 'flat' (Friedman, 2005) due to globalization or whether it remains 'spiky' (Florida, 2005).

In economics, convergence has been a central issue for some time, particularly in macroeconomic research on the determinants of economic growth (Barro and Sala-i-Martin, 1992). In other social scientific disciplines, there has been much less systematic research and it is only recently that interest has grown in empirically testing the convergence hypothesis. Often, the issue is discussed in the context of studies on policy transfer and policy diffusion – two closely related but analytically distinct concepts.

Convergence is a multifaceted concept. Different conceptualizations are used (see Holzinger and Knill, 2005 on concepts). The most straightforward version of the concept is *sigma-convergence*, which denotes a narrowing of differences between units – or a shrinking distribution of values – over time. An alternative conceptualization is *beta-convergence*. It has its origins in the economic growth literature and refers to the phenomenon that poor countries grow faster than rich countries (as predicted by neoclassical growth theory) or, put differently, that the growth rate is inversely related to the initial (or lagged) level of economic development (Barro and Sala-i-Martin, 1992). This catch-up movement implies that, in the long term, countries move towards a 'steady state' equilibrium rate.

The starting point of this paper is the question of whether a central policy area of the modern state, namely the welfare state, has converged

across OECD countries over the last three decades. Starting in the 1980s
(O'Connor, 1988), this question became subject to a growing body of
articles from political scientists, economists and sociologists (see the
extended version of this article for a comprehensive literature review,
Schmitt and Starke, 2011). What is clearly missing from the literature on
welfare state convergence, so far, is an analysis that combines four elements: first, simultaneous testing at both aggregate and disaggregate levels;
second, the systematic inclusion of conditional factors; third, a robust test
of several explanatory accounts of convergence; and, fourth, the use of
panel estimation techniques particularly suited for this task. This article
is a first attempt at such an analysis. We examine welfare state changes in
terms of social expenditure – both aggregate and disaggregate spending
– for 21 OECD countries in the period between 1980 and 2005.

The empirical analysis reveals several striking results. In contrast to the
existing literature which only finds convergence for some social spending
schemes, we show, by applying dynamic panel models, that convergence
is present *in all central types of social expenditure*. Moreover, we identify
conditional factors that highly influence the speed of convergence. Three
conditional factors turn out to be particularly important: globalization,
membership of the European Union and the structure of the social programmes in question.

The following section contains our central hypotheses about the influence of conditional factors on the rate of adjustment of welfare state
expenditure. We then present the empirical results as well as a discussion
of their relevance. Finally, the main findings are summarized in the
conclusion.

Hypotheses

What could explain the convergence of welfare states (or the lack thereof)?
Economic *globalization* has been cited as the prime source of convergence
pressure in the recent literature. According to what is commonly known
as the 'efficiency thesis' in the comparative welfare state literature, economic globalization of the trade in goods and services and the movement
of capital should lead to regulatory competition and a (downward) convergence of welfare states (Busemeyer, 2009; Garrett and Mitchell, 2001).
Hence, our first hypothesis is as follows:

> H_1: *The higher the degree of a country's global integration, the greater the
> extent of welfare state convergence.*

Many observers expect competition and transnational communication to
be of high relevance within clubs of regional integration, most notably

within the *European Union* (EU). Through processes of 'positive integration' (harmonization through regulations and directives) and 'negative integration' (abolition of impediments to the Common Market) national social policies have been shaped by EU-level developments (Ferrera, 2005; Leibfried and Pierson, 1995; Scharpf, 2002). Furthermore, EU social policy actively encourages learning processes through the Open Method of Co-ordination (OMC). The rate of convergence should therefore differ between members and non-members of the EU.

> H_2: *Welfare state convergence should be stronger among EU members than among non-members.*

Veto points, veto players and domestic constitutional hurdles have been discussed for some time in comparative welfare state research (Bonoli, 2001; Huber et al., 1993; Immergut, 1992; see also Tsebelis, 2002). At a very general level, a higher degree of fragmentation of decision-making should make convergence more difficult. That is because more actors are involved – many of them holding a formal veto over decisions – and because decision-making procedures become protracted and complex. Also, constitutional structures that disperse power offer more access points for interest groups, including opponents of reform. We assume that the rate of adjustment is slower in political systems which are characterized by a high number of constitutional barriers. The hypothesis is therefore as follows:

> H_3: *The greater the fragmentation of a political system and the greater the number of veto points, the lower the extent of welfare state convergence.*

Institutional effects that influence welfare state convergence may also be caused by *policy feedback*. We differentiate between five programme-specific feedback hypotheses ($H_{4.1}$ to $H_{4.5}$). Since, to our knowledge, there is no generally agreed typology of active labour market policy regimes, we cannot test the impact of policy-specific regime types on the rate of convergence.

With respect to the overall structure of a country's 'welfare regime', we expect the financing structures and the forms of governance that are dominant in a country to matter for the rate of convergence. 'Corporatist' welfare states in particular, such as Germany, France or Italy, are said to be less prone to reform, since they involve the social partners in the organization of social insurance funds and because financing is largely based on earmarked social contributions instead of general tax revenue. Hence, employers and trade unions, in particular, have a direct stake in the welfare state and are easier to mobilize in times of reform and restructuring (Korpi and Palme, 2003: 442; Palier and Martin, 2007). In other words, the welfare state creates its own constituency (Pierson, 1994). Our hypothesis can be formulated as follows:

$H_{4.1}$ *The rate of welfare state convergence should be lower in corporatist welfare states.*

In addition, some parts of the welfare state are generally thought of as prime examples of *path dependency* (on the concept, see Mahoney, 2000; Pierson, 2000; 2004). In terms of pension systems, the historical distinction is between Bismarckian social-insurance schemes, which provide earnings-related pensions mainly for workers, and Beveridge schemes which only provide universal, flat-rate benefits. In the course of the twentieth century, however, virtually all Beveridge countries added earnings-related supplements to their basic schemes. Some such as Sweden did this relatively early on ('early birds') while the so-called 'latecomers' (e.g. the Netherlands) set up supplementary provision only after the early 1970s (Hinrichs, 2006; Hinrichs and Lynch, 2010). Mature social-insurance-based pension systems, as found in 'Bismarckian' and 'early bird' countries, in particular, are said to be path dependent.

$H_{4.2}$ *Pension policy convergence should be slower among 'Bismarckian' and 'early bird' pension systems.*

In 'voluntary state-subsidized' unemployment insurance systems, trade unions run the administration of most of the schemes. In a similar manner, the 'corporatist' social-insurance schemes of continental Europe involve the social partners in the administration of the system. The politics around the reform of unemployment compensation schemes can be expected to differ in these countries compared to purely state-run and tax financed systems (Sjöberg et al., 2010). This leads to specific expectations regarding their convergence rate:

$H_{4.3}$ *The rate of convergence of unemployment compensation schemes should be lower in voluntary state-subsidized insurance systems and in corporatist insurance systems.*

Family policy can pursue various aims. With respect to the gender dimension, Korpi (2000) distinguishes welfare states that follow policies of 'general family support' (e.g. Italy) from those that provide 'dual-earner support' (the Nordic countries). Furthermore, some welfare states follow a relatively hands-off strategy of 'market-oriented policies' (e.g. the US and Australia). Since dual-earner countries rest on a large public childcare and elderly care sector and (relatively) less on cash transfers, we expect a policy feedback stemming from the vested interests of those who provide care as well as the receivers of subsidized or universally free care (see Pierson, 1994):

$H_{4.4}$ The rate of convergence in family policy should be lower in countries providing 'dual-earner support'.

In health care, the involvement of actors beyond the state (whether non-profit or for-profit actors) should make a difference regarding the rate of adjustment. The greater the number of actors involved, the lower the rate of adjustment, due to the more difficult politics of negotiation and coordination. In social health insurance countries (e.g. Germany), non-state actors are heavily involved, for example, in the administration of sickness funds. Private insurance countries (e.g. the US) involve non-state actors more indirectly. Here the state typically regulates private insurance and the provision of services through private actors. These vested interests, in turn, have an important stake in health policy and try to lobby the government.

$H_{4.5}$ The rate of convergence in health policy should be lower in social health insurance countries and in private insurance countries.

In the following section, we empirically test the conditional hypotheses about the impact of global integration, European integration, veto players and policy feedback on social policy convergence.

Empirical Findings

In order to test our theoretical hypotheses about welfare state convergence, we use as dependent variable the annual change in social expenditure as a percentage of GDP for 21 OECD countries for the period from 1980 to 2005 (OECD, 2008).[1] We use dynamic panel modelling, namely error correction models (ECMs), as the most suitable strategy for testing convergence (see extended version for a detailed discussion of modelling convergence processes). To draw a more differentiated picture we separately analyse total public social expenditure and disaggregated programme expenditure in several models (Castles, 2008). Following the OECD classification, we differentiate expenditure into spending on old age, unemployment, active labour market policies, family, and health.

The findings are summarized in Table 1. We run three sets of models highlighting different aspects of convergence, namely absolute convergence, conditional convergence and the speed of convergence. For reasons of space, we limit the discussion of the empirical results to the effects of the lagged expenditure level and to the effects of the abovementioned

Table 1 Hypotheses and empirical findings

Models	Hypotheses	Total	Old age	Unemployment	ALMP	Family	Health
1st set of models	*Absolute convergence* Lagged expenditure level	–	/	– – –	/	/	– –
2nd set of models	*Conditional convergence* Lagged expenditure level	– –	– – –	– – –	– –	– –	– –
3rd set of models	*Speed of convergence* Trade openness (H1)	–	–	+	–	–	–
	Foreign direct investment (H1)	/	– –	/	/	/	/
	EU membership (H2)	/	/	n.a.	–	–	/
	Veto points (H3)	/	/	– – –	/	/	/
	Welfare state institutions (H4.1 to H4.4)	+++ Corporatist	++ Bismarckian ++ Early birds	++ Voluntary state subsidized	n.a.	– Dual earner support	+ Private insurance

Note: Significance levels are indicated by the number of + or – (e.g. +++: p, z < .001; ++: p, z < .01; +: p, z < .05). / denotes no statistically significant effect.

factors on the speed of convergence. See the extended version for a more comprehensive discussion. In the first two sets of models, a negative sign indicates convergence. In the third set of models, the negative sign indicates an acceleration effect of the conditional factor (e.g. trade openness) on convergence and a positive sign a decelerating effect.

In line with existing studies (e.g. Starke et al., 2008), we find absolute beta-convergence in total social expenditure as well as in spending on unemployment and health. In contrast, expenditures on old age and family schemes as well as active labour market programmes seem not to have converged over time.

We then analyse conditional convergence by controlling for the main theoretically relevant explanatory factors of social expenditure dynamics. The operationalization of all variables is described in detail in the extended version of the article. We show that beta-convergence can be detected across the board when the theoretically relevant variables are taken into account. This is a striking result since previous research found welfare state convergence to be a much more limited phenomenon, especially when tests were restricted to absolute convergence.

Additionally, we estimated a third set of models to analyse whether the *rate of adjustment* or *speed of convergence* is conditioned by economic globalization, EU membership, veto points and welfare state institutions. In order to test whether the rate of adjustment is influenced by the conditional factors, interaction effects are estimated (Plümper and Schneider, 2009). With respect to the globalization hypothesis H_1, the results clearly show that an increase in trade openness tends to accelerate the convergence process (except for unemployment expenditure). Moreover, a higher level of FDI inflows advances convergence particularly in old age and family expenditure.

With regard to the influence of EU membership (H_2), EU members converge faster than non-member countries. In all models the interaction between the lagged expenditure level and EU membership shows a negative sign, even though the effects do not reach significance level in all models. However, given the low statistical power, effects close to conventional significance levels, such as the EU effect on total expenditure convergence, can be considered meaningful. The results for the effect of domestic constitutional arrangements (H_3) on unemployment expenditure convergence are counterintuitive: a higher number of veto points *increases* the rate of adjustment. Given the very strong theoretical expectations that veto points slow down welfare state convergence, this is a truly puzzling result that is in need of explanation. It can be argued that a high number of veto points restrict the scope for political action. Politicians have only a limited number of policy instruments available and expenditure development within a narrow institutional framework may be more likely to follow the driving forces of overall convergence. Conversely, a wider room for manoeuvre may lead to a variety of divergent policy solutions and therefore to a lower rate of convergence within countries with a low number of veto points.

A number of very interesting results concern the impact of the existing welfare state structure on the rate of adjustment or, in other words, policy feedback. For instance, we use the classification of the pension system – Bismarckian, 'early birds' etc. – when testing for the convergence of old age expenditure, and typologies of unemployment compensation schemes – 'voluntary state-subsidized', 'corporatist' etc. – when analysing expenditure on unemployment.

With regard to total expenditure, our central hypothesis ($H_{4.1}$) which stated that the rate of adjustment should be lower in corporatist welfare regimes is supported by the empirical results. Furthermore, the analysis of convergence clubs in old age expenditure clearly shows that Bismarckian systems converge differently in comparison to all other countries. The convergence process of Bismarckian systems is slower, which is in line with the hypothesis that these systems are very difficult to modify ($H_{4.2}$), perhaps due to their strong contribution-benefit nexus. More surprisingly, 'early bird' countries such as Sweden also show a lower rate of convergence. Yet, in contrast to the 'latecomers' (e.g. Australia), these are also countries where the second additional pension pillar is based on pay-as-you-go principles and public provision. They could be subject to rather similar pressures as Bismarckian countries. The voluntary state-subsidized system of unemployment compensation constitutes a convergence club (as hypothesized in $H_{4.3}$), but not the corporatist insurance type. Concerning family expenditure, dual-earner regimes tend to have a higher rate of convergence which contradicts the theoretical hypothesis formulated above. Last but not least, the private health care systems of Switzerland and the United States also constitute a convergence club. In sum, programme-specific welfare institutions have an impact on the speed of adjustment. This demonstrates that it is worth using programme-specific indicators when studying disaggregated expenditure dynamics.

Conclusion

In this article, we examined whether social policy has converged in 21 OECD countries from 1980 to 2005. We have shown that it has and explained why. The substantial contribution of this analysis to the research literature on welfare state convergence can be summarized as follows. The overall conclusion from this article is that welfare state convergence is a much more common phenomenon than suggested by the literature so far.

Earlier studies exclusively focused on absolute convergence when analysing disaggregated social expenditure. Therefore, they were not able to detect how widespread convergence in social expenditure rates really is. More specifically, previous research did not identify convergence in old age, family and active labour market schemes. Our analyses, by contrast, reveal that, when taking important conditional factors into account, convergence exists both at the aggregate level of the 'whole' welfare state and at the disaggregated levels of the main spending categories. This fills an important gap in the literature.

The speed of welfare state convergence is influenced by the degree of globalization, EU membership and welfare regime type. First, globalization clearly brings national policies closer together. The more open the economy to trade and investment, the stronger the tendency to become more alike. Second, there are indications that the EU constitutes a convergence club and accelerates the speed of convergence among its member states. Perhaps this result comes as no surprise given the EU's goal of creating an 'ever closer union', but the hypothesis has rarely been empirically tested so far. What is more, the speed of convergence depends, thirdly, on the welfare regime type. This holds not just for the overall welfare regime but also for the more policy-specific typologies. In particular, structures that emphasize the link between contributions and benefits (e.g. corporatist welfare regimes and Bismarckian pension systems) inhibit convergence.

There are several avenues for further research. The question of convergence mechanisms, for instance, could be further differentiated. This is most clearly the case for the globalization effect on welfare state convergence. While, in this study, we have established a globalization effect, it remains unclear if this is primarily an economic phenomenon or if it has to do with increased cross-national policy transfer and learning. To answer these questions, one would have to find more precise globalization indicators and use methods designed to explicitly deal with competition and diffusion. In addition, in this analysis we deliberately left the question of direction largely unexamined. It seems promising to look not just at convergence effects but at the long-term steady states that countries are moving towards.

Note

An elaborated version of this article has subsequently appeared in *Journal of European Social Policy*, 21, 2011, pp. 120–35. By permission of the authors.

1　The countries are: Australia, Austria, Belgium, Canada, Denmark, Finland, France, Germany, Greece, Ireland, Italy, Japan, the Netherlands, New Zealand, Norway, Portugal, Spain, Sweden, Switzerland, the United Kingdom, and the United States.

References

Barro, R. J. and Sala-i-Martin, X. (1992) 'Convergence', *Journal of Political Economy* 100 (2): 223–51.

Bonoli, G. (2001) 'Political Institutions, Veto Points, and the Process of Welfare State Adaptation', in P. Pierson (ed.), *The New Politics of the Welfare State*. Oxford: Oxford University Press.

Busemeyer, M. (2009) 'From Myth to Reality: Globalisation and Public Spending in OECD Countries Revisited', *European Journal of Political Research* 48 (4): 455–82.

Castles, F. G. (2008) 'What Welfare States Do: A Disaggregated Expenditure Approach', *Journal of Social Policy* 38 (1): 45–62.

Ferrera, M. (2005) *The Boundaries of Welfare: European Integration and the New Spatial Politics of Social Protection*. Oxford: Oxford University Press.

Florida, R. (2005) 'The World is Spiky', *Atlantic Monthly* (October): 48–51.

Friedman, T. L. (2005) *The World Is Flat. Brief History of the 21st Century*. New York: Farrar, Straus and Giroux.

Garrett, G. and Mitchell, D. (2001) 'Globalization, Government Spending and Taxation in the OECD', *European Journal of Political Research* 39 (2): 145–77.

Hinrichs, K. (2006) 'Pension Reforms in Europe: Convergence of Old-Age Security Systems?', in P. K. Mydske and I. Peters (eds), *The Transformation of the European Nation State*. Berlin: Berliner Wissenschafts-Verlag.

Hinrichs, K. and Lynch, J. (2010) 'Old-Age Pensions', in F. G. Castles, S. Leibfried, J. Lewis, H. Obinger and C. Pierson (eds), *The Oxford Handbook of the Welfare State*. Oxford: Oxford University Press.

Holzinger, K. and Knill, C. (2005) 'Causes and Conditions of Cross-National Policy Convergence', *Journal of European Public Policy* 12 (5): 775–96.

Huber, E., Ragin, C. C. and Stephens, J. D. (1993) 'Social Democracy, Christian Democracy, Constitutional Structure, and the Welfare State', *American Journal of Sociology* 99 (3): 711–49.

Immergut, E. M. (1992) *Health Politics: Interests and Institutions in Western Europe*. Cambridge: Cambridge University Press.

Korpi, W. (2000) 'Faces of Inequality: Gender, Class, and Patterns of Inequalities in Different Types of Welfare States', *Social Politics* 7 (2): 127–91.

Korpi, W. and Palme, J. (2003) 'New Politics and Class Politics in the Context of Austerity and Globalization: Welfare State Regress in 18 Countries, 1975–95', *American Political Science Review* 97 (3): 425–46.

Leibfried, S. and Pierson, P. (eds) (1995) *European Social Policy: Between Fragmentation and Integration*. Washington D.C.: The Brookings Institution.

Mahoney, J. (2000) 'Path Dependence in Historical Sociology', *Theory and Society* 29 (4): 507–48.

O'Connor, J. S. (1988) 'Convergence or Divergence?: Change in Welfare Effort in OECD Countries 1960–1980', *European Journal of Political Research* 16 (2): 277.

OECD (2008) *Social Expenditure Data*. Paris: OECD.

Palier, B. and Martin, C. (2007) 'Editorial introduction – From 'a frozen landscape' to structural reforms: The sequential transformation of Bismarckian welfare systems', *Social Policy & Administration* 41 (6): 535–54.

Pierson, P. (1994) *Dismantling the Welfare State? Reagan, Thatcher, and the Politics of Retrenchment*. Cambridge: Cambridge University Press.

Pierson, P. (2000) 'Increasing Returns, Path Dependence, and the Study of Politics', *American Political Science Review* 94 (2): 251–67.

Pierson, P. (2004) *Politics in Time: History, Institutions, and Political Analysis.* Princeton, NJ: Princeton University Press.

Plümper, T. and Schneider, C. J. (2009) 'The analysis of policy convergence, or: how to chase a black cat in a dark room', *Journal of European Public Policy* 16 (7): 990–1011.

Scharpf, F. W. (2002) 'The European social model: Coping with the challenges of diversity', *Journal of Common Market Studies* 40 (4): 645–70.

Schmitt, C. and Starke, P. (2011) 'Explaining Convergence of OECD Welfare States: A Conditional Approach', *Journal of European Social Policy* 21 (2): 120–35.

Sjöberg, O., Palme, J. and Carroll, E. (2010) 'Unemployment Insurance', in F. G. Castles, S. Leibfried, J. Lewis, H. Obinger and C. Pierson (eds), *The Oxford Handbook of the Welfare State*. Oxford: Oxford University Press.

Starke, P., Obinger, H. and Castles, F. G. (2008) 'Convergence towards where: in what ways, if any, are welfare states becoming more similar?', *Journal of European Public Policy* 15 (7): 975–1000.

Tsebelis, G. (2002) *Veto Players: How Political Institutions Work*. Princeton, NJ: Princeton University Press.

Breaking with the Past? Why the Global Financial Crisis led to Austerity Policies but not to Modernization of the Welfare State

Klaus Armingeon

Introduction

Ever since Peter Gourevitch's 'Politics in Hard Times' (Gourevitch 1986) social scientists have been fascinated by the political opportunities created by national emergencies and crisis situations. These emergencies are so-called 'black swans' (Castles 2010) that policy makers did not expect. They put previous practices into question, reshuffle political coalitions, and provide scope for new ideas and policies. Arguably, party competition will have a particularly strong impact on policies if politicians are free to choose amongst many under circumstances in which previous policy sets are no longer sustainable.

The initial phase of the Global Financial Crisis (GFC) resembled previous crises of the 1930s and mid-1970s in terms of decline of gross domestic product and increase in unemployment (Brunetti 2011; EU Commission 2009). Just as its predecessors, the current great recession may be one of the rare opportunities to modernize the welfare state. Barack Obama's chief of staff, Rahm Emanuel, said: 'You never want a serious crisis to go to waste . . . Things that we have postponed too long, that were long-term, are now immediate and must be dealt with. This crisis provides the opportunity for us to do things that you could not do before' (Wall Street Journal, 21 Nov. 2008, http://online.wsj.com/article/SB12272127805634 5271.html, accessed on 13 August 2012).

Indeed in the early years of the current crisis, economic policies varied hugely and one was entitled to wonder whether now a period of policy experimentation and innovation had commenced. Some countries, such as Spain and the US, seemed to return to Keynesian recipes. Others, such as Germany and Switzerland, opted for a middle way between massive counter-cyclical policy and austerity, while others, such as the Baltic states, implemented resolutely tough austerity policies. However, by 2010 the range of anti-cyclical policies had narrowed radically and nearly all democratic countries seemed to converge programmatically on the path of fiscal consolidation (Armingeon 2012; Cameron 2012; Lindvall 2012).

In this paper, I pose two simple questions: (1) Were there major reforms in the fields of economic and social policies during the current economic crisis notwithstanding the common context of fiscal consolidation? Was there a break with the past and did countries embark on different and innovative policy developments – such as may have been the case in the previous big crises? (2) Did political parties make a difference for the course of fiscal consolidation? Or was policy design mainly conditioned by the magnitude of fiscal and economic problems?

I will present empirical evidence for these answers: (1) In sharp contrast to the crises of the late nineteenth century, of the 1930s and the 1970s, the crisis that started in 2007 did not lead to any major qualitative policy innovation. (2) By 2010, austerity has become the only game in town. One of the best predictors of the extent of planned austerity is the interest rate that governments currently pay on debts. Only in countries with low interest rates does partisan composition make an – albeit minor – difference for budgetary policy.

These answers qualify two literatures. They take issue with the argument that crises punctuate an equilibrium, opening a window of opportunity for policy reform. This is only the case if there are different, competing and plausible policy ideas (Kingdon 1984) – such as the ideas about opening or closing the national economy to the world market in the late nineteenth century; the idea of an activist welfare state and social partnership as compared to a minimalist welfare state and conflictual industrial relations in the 1930s, or the idea of varieties of democracies and varieties of capitalism in a post-Keynesian welfare state in the mid-1970s. By 2010, there is little programmatic difference between left and right parties in mature democracies with regard to macro-economic and social policies and hence there is little opportunity for major policy innovation made possible by the opening of a window of opportunity during the crisis. These answers also take issue with a simple 'politics-does-matter' or 'power-resources' theory. A crucial precondition for a differential impact of political parties is the existence of policy space, i.e. that there is a chance to introduce new or reform existing policies. Policy space is less likely to exist if a policy field is fully regulated and policies are sticky or if resources are lacking. The latter, at least, applies in the current crisis.

My basic research design is comparative. I analyse the 27 democracies of the EU plus other mature democracies of the OECD world (Australasia, Canada, Japan, Norway, USA). Due to data limitation, some analyses will be undertaken for fewer than these 35 nation states.

The next section provides evidence for the lack of policy innovation and section 3 deals with policy options during the crisis.

The Lack of Policy Innovation

Could national political systems depart from previous trajectories in the field of economic and social policies once the crisis opened windows of opportunities? In particular, we would expect that welfare states would be modernized in order to cope with future challenges. Such reforms could create additional fiscal leeway for the future by modernizing social security schemes and other policies requiring large shares of public spending. The obvious problems of the present welfare state are health and pension schemes that increasingly impact on the budget and are likely to become unsustainable in the coming years. There are also new social risks, which need to be covered. Examples of 'new social policies' are active labour market policies that help workers to adapt to changing economic structures; education expenditure reducing the risk that young citizens will be unable to participate in a rapidly changing labour market; family policies helping female workers to reconcile work and family and to escape from poverty traps (Armingeon and Bonoli 2006). Was the crisis used to modernize the welfare state: to shift resources from traditional policy fields to areas of new social risk? Or are there any other signs of dramatic and far-reaching qualitative social policy changes?

We have strong empirical evidence that during the crisis pension systems were reformed in many countries. Between 2007 and 2010 in at least fifteen countries of our sample, pension reforms were enacted increasing the statutory retirement age.[1] However, it is far from clear that the crisis has been the outstanding reform trigger. The Fondazione Rodolfo DeBenedetti (http://www.frdb.org/) has collected data on cost-reducing pension reforms in fourteen countries. If we compare the number of such reforms between 2000 and 2006 and those between 2007 and 2011, there is no significant increase in the number of reforms during the crisis.[2]

Likewise, active labour market policies, designed to increase the employability of workers by improved public employment services, training measures, wage subsidies etc. were extensively used during the crisis in the highly developed democratic nations (see surveys by the ILO and World Bank, 2012). However, comparing the number of reforms in favour of active labour market policies before (2000–2006) and during the crisis we cannot find a major acceleration of introduction of active labour market policies during the crisis.[3]

A re-analysis of a list of socio-economic reforms in the OECD area supports that finding. The OECD suggests structural reform policies to its members. These are policies which should increase economic efficiency. For the OECD secretariat this means particularly market-friendly ('neoliberal') policies. Among these policies are strategies that are primarily concerned with economic efficiency (such as increases of competition in network industries) and those which could be classified as 'new social risk' policies since they attempt both to increase efficiency and reduce the employment risks inherent in modern society. In the 2012 edition of its 'Going for Growth' report, the OECD listed its reform suggestions since 2007 and whether countries responded to these ideas (OECD 2012: 51–133). In each year of its surveillance the OECD picked three policy priorities based on internationally comparable OECD indicators of policy settings and performance. The OECD secretariat added two priorities which 'are often supported by indicator-based evidence, but may draw principally on country-specific expertise. These priorities are meant to capture any potential policy imperatives in fields not covered by indicators' (OECD 2012: 49). I coded any set of policies responding to one of these suggestions whether it related to a new social risk policy or an exclusively liberalizing (market-enabling) policy and calculated the sum of enacted policies covering new social risks versus the sum of policies which only attempted to increase market efficiency. In the 29 countries for which we have data, reforms in five policy categories occurred on average. The mean number of purely liberalizing reforms (2.9) clearly outnumbered the reforms that were not only liberalizing but also covered new social risks (1.9).[4]

These data do not demonstrate that the crisis was used to modernize the welfare state in order to cope with new social risks. However, there may have been other major breaks with previous patterns of social and economic policies and major innovations, which are overlooked when using only the OECD data.

I therefore checked the Bertelsmann database on policy achievements and reforms of 2009 and 2011 (http://www.sgi-network.org/, last accessed on 13 August 2012). This database offers expert ratings of policy fields. The experts – about three per country – were asked to provide qualitative information on various policies and rate them with regard to goal achievement, such as whether labour market policy addresses unemployment or taxation policy realizes goals of equity, competitiveness and the generation of sufficient public revenues etc. Policies were rated from 1 (complete failure) to 10 (full success). I considered a large number of policies[5] and calculated whether a major change of ratings occurred. As major change, I considered any increase of policy rating of 2 or larger. The results are substantively identical with the findings from the OECD and FRDB database. In general there was no major qualitative break with the past. According to the country experts, only in a few countries and policy fields were there any substantial reforms.[6]

Finally I looked at a fourth source of data: the *Political Data Yearbook of the European Journal of Political Research*. In this yearbook, country experts report on the major political events in the countries of our sample. I re-analysed the reports for 2009, 2010 and 2011[7] and added further information from newspaper reports as far as available to me. I started from the assumption that country experts would report any major policy reform in economic and social policy, and hence if the crisis triggered policy innovation, we should find signs of that in most country reports. However, as in the previous data analyses, no major policy reforms in most or at least many countries could be found. There was, however, one frequent type of change in national politics: the crisis has been conducive to the rise of xenophobic or right-populist sentiments, parties and movements in many countries and led sometimes to a contagion of existing centre-right governments or even left parties from the populist right or an increasingly xenophobic electorate as for example in Australia, Denmark, Finland, France, Greece, Hungary, The Netherlands, and Sweden (see also Caramani 2011: 870).

Austerity: The Only Game in Town

While we find no qualitative reform of the welfare state in the sense that the configuration of policy schemes has been changed, there is quantitative change with regard to the size of welfare state. Governments tried to halt the increase in expenditure and, in many cases, tried to reverse it. For example during the sovereign debt crisis, the Southern European countries have been forced to accept tough austerity programmes; the Baltics, Ireland and the conservative-liberal government of the UK explicitly pledged to reduce public spending and hardly any government published plans to expand government. There is, however, some variation in the extent of austerity, with a common surmise that the left political parties that supported the growth of the welfare state may have been particularly reluctant to retrench expenditures (Schmidt 2010; Korpi and Palme 2003).

A second explanation of the austerity course is functional: the extent of contraction is merely a consequence of previous problems; and the role of democratic politics – such as party competition – is very limited when governments consolidate the public deficit. This explanation is supported by analyses by the IMF (IMF 2010a) and political scientists (see Wagschal and Wenzelburger 2008; Wagschal and Wenzelburger 2012).

In my analysis, I use data on planned consolidations, i.e. what governments intend to do compared to the status quo. These data are provided by the IMF. They are based on information by governments about their budget decisions and their fiscal implications. If partisan politics is of any relevance it should be visible from this type of data. They come from four editions of the Fiscal Monitor of the IMF (IMF 2010a; IMF 2011a; IMF 2011b; IMF 2012). Each of these publications lists the historical data on deficits and the planned deficit. I compare the intended change of structural deficits ('cyclically adjusted overall balance'), i.e. deficits which are already adjusted for cyclical influences. Hence, my measure indicates discretionary governmental decisions on budgets.[8] For each country, I have four measures of fiscal consolidation from each edition of the IMF's Fiscal Monitor. Each of these indicators is the difference between the average of planned deficits in the current and the two following years minus the average of actual deficits in the previous three years.[9] I replicate this procedure also for historical and planned expenditures as a percentage of GDP. These are targeted changes: the differences between the planned balance or level of expenditure for this and the coming two years and the average of the past three years. These change rates are then regressed on vectors of economic and political variables. The selected economic variables are standard variables of economic models explaining budget consolidation: the level of deficits (or expenditures) averaged for the previous three years, the trend of historical deficits (or expenditures), measured as the difference of the average of the most recent three years minus the average of the three preceding years, the average percentage of the public debt (source: IMF Fiscal Monitor) in the last three years, the average of nominal government bond yields (10 years) for the previous three years (source: OECD Economic Outlook, various years, http://www.oecd.org/eco/economicoutlook.htm, and Eurostat, http://epp.eurostat.ec.europa.eu/poital/page/portal/eurostat/home; missing data for Estonia, Lithuania (2008–11) and Romania), and the level and trend of unemployment (source: OECD Labour Force Statistics, http://stats.oecd.org/index.aspx?queryid=251 and Eurostat; calculated analogously to level and trend of deficits). The political variables of partisan composition of government are the share of left cabinet seats, averaged for the three preceding years or in an alternative operationalization the Schmidt index for the political complexion of government (1 = hegemony of right parties to 5 = hegemony of left parties. Operationalization and source: Armingeon, Careja, Weisstanner, Engler, Potolidis, Gerber, and Leimgruber 2011 and updates.).

The regression analysis is based on robust Driscoll and Kraay standard errors[10] and I included fixed time effects (i.e. dummies for issues of Fiscal Monitor). The results are substantively the same without these fixed effects. Note that deficits have a negative sign. In order to avoid confusion when interpreting the regression analysis, I labelled the dependent variable 'balance'; a positive sign of the balance indicates surplus, and a

Table 1 The lacking correlation between pension reform and new social risk policies

		No. of new social risk policies during crisis			
		0	1	2	3
Pension reform during crisis	yes	Greece	Czech R., Denmark, Hungary, Netherlands, USA	Australia, France, UK	Germany, Spain
	no	Slovak Republic, Switzerland	Iceland, Ireland, Italy, Luxembourg, Norway	Austria, Belgium, Sweden, Poland, Japan	New Zealand, Canada, Portugal, Finland

Sources: IMF 2010b: 73–74; OECD 2010a and additions from national sources. No. of new social risks policy: sum of did the anti-crisis packages lead to investment in education (0/1), did the country introduce/substantially expand 4 or more active labour market policy schemes (0/1), did the country lower tax wedge (0/1).

negative sign indicates deficits. Table 1 displays the results. I interpret regression coefficients if they are significant at least on the 0.1 level (two-tailed), i.e. on the 0.05 level for one-tailed tests.

Models no. 1 and no. 2 show that the interest rate on government bonds is by far the most consistent and significant predictor of targeted changes in balances and expenditure. The higher the interest rates which governments have to pay for their debts, the larger are the targeted reductions of deficits and expenditures. In these regressions, the partisan composition of government has no remarkable explanatory power. The first conclusion from this analysis is that, in general, politics does not matter for consolidation. In the great recession that started in 2007, governments were forced to consolidate and they attempted that the more, the greater, the extent of their fiscal problems.

This conclusion leads to another question: If the pressure on governments is greater, the greater are fiscal problems, then politics could matter if fiscal problems are comparatively small. Nations that have to pay low interest rates could manifest a stronger impact of the partisan composition of government on the development of balances and expenditures. Hence there could be an interactive effect. Therefore I calculated an interaction term of interest rates and partisan composition of government.

Models no. 3 and no. 5 show no empirical evidence for such an interactive effect with regard to the overall balance. However, models no. 4 and no. 6 indicate an interactive effect for expenditures: provided fiscal problems are relatively small, left governments do not plan to cut expenditures as much as do governments of the right. By implication – under favourable fiscal conditions – they rely much more strongly on increasing revenues (i.e. tax increases) to achieve an improved balance. Calculating the marginal effects we see that this works only if interest rates are low. The reluctance of left governments to cut expenditures becomes insignificant if interest rates are moderate to high. (In case of very high interest rates, there is actually a significant tendency for left governments to reduce expenditures more than right governments.) The substantive conclusions from this statistical analysis are as follows: over the course of the current crisis, the extent of governments' deficit cutting intentions has been a function of their existing fiscal problems: the more you are in a fiscal mess, the more you have to save – and your politics doesn't matter at all. But if governments do not have intractable fiscal problems, they can choose between different modes of consolidation. Left governments have a preference to consolidate by increasing tax revenues; right governments have a preference to consolidate by cutting expenditures. But these partisan differences in modes of consolidation dwindle as the fiscal problems increase.

A Final Question

These conclusions raise the question of why this crisis has been so different in terms of impacts of politics on policy trajectories compared to other big crises? Why are established theories about crises and policy change of little help in understanding the policy trajectories during the current great recession? I present five arguments. Their base line is that the political context of this crisis is vastly different from that of previous big crises.

(1) No new coalitions. In his major study Gourevitch explains policy change during crises by the rise of new coalitions. The crisis destabilizes previous coalitions between social groups and their political representatives and leads to new coalitions which pursue new policies (Gourevitch 1986). Although quite a number of government changes have occurred since 2007, it is hard to see any new coalition of social groups and political parties. Rather the electorate just replaced the coach – just as chairmen of failing soccer clubs often fire the coach even though it is the team that is the problem (Colomer and Magalhaes 2012). But given the circumstances, the new government cannot make much difference – as dramatically shown by the

governmental changes in 2011 and 2012 in Portugal, Spain, Ireland and Greece (Armingeon and Baccaro 2012).

(2)   No new ideas. During the previous big crises there was a competition of big ideas. In the period since 2007, we have observed no competition of policy ideas such as a choice between free trade or protectionism or a choice between anti-cyclical welfare state or liberal-regulatory state. The only broadly accepted idea is that public policy should be based on fiscal prudence. Without major new economic growth or waves of productivity in sight, by implication there is no other major idea but austerity.

(3)   No crisis of the existing political order. In the late nineteenth century and in the 1930s economic crises had direct implications for the stability of the political systems. In 2007 to the present, there are few signs of a major instability of the democratic order – notwithstanding the rise of anti-foreigner movements and right-populist parties in many nations. One of the basic lessons of the crisis of the 1930s was the insight that the welfare state might prevent a spill-over from economic instability to political instability. This consequence of previous crises explains why in the present crisis political instability did not occur.

(4)   No feasible option for a new welfare state. In a study on the introduction of 'new social politics', Bonoli (2007) used Pierson's idea of 'policies in time' and argued that these new social risks policies are difficult to introduce if the available policy space is already preempted by existing 'old social policies'. The present reforms of the welfare state are mainly attempts to reduce its general costs. I did not find any textual or quantitative evidence that policy makers reduced expenditures for the old schemes in order to shift resources to new policies. Rather they tried to save where they could save money – without any master-plan of welfare state innovation. As the Southern European example shows, governments have a hard time to please the IMF and the European Union while having a fair chance to be re-elected by those whose welfare state benefits are slashed. Under these circumstances of multiple constraints, a re-modelling and modernizing of the welfare state becomes a utopian challenge. The policy space is empty.

(5)   No fiscal room for manoeuvre because of previous political decisions. The fiscal room for manoeuvre is severely limited not only because of the present broad intergovernmental consensus about fiscal prudence. Moreover, political decisions to create independent central banks with an emphasis on price stability and the political decisions to create the Euro have eliminated many previous options of national governments. Policy options such as devaluation or a deliberate systematic anti-cyclical policy are institutionally pre-

cluded. In this case, politics clearly mattered; however, these political decisions were taken a long time ago and they have pre-empted the policy space of present democratic governments.

Does this mean that all democratic nations are likely to converge towards a regime of austerity and slashed welfare states? There are at least three counter-arguments: (1) In all likelihood, politicians will not be able to honour all of the terms of their austerity plans. Research on fiscal consolidation points to the role of strong presidents (Alesina 2010), strong finance ministers (Hallerberg and Hagen 1999; Hallerberg, Strauch, and Hagen 2009) and institutions and welfare state structures (Wagschal and Wenzelburger 2008; Wagschal and Wenzelburger 2012). Implementing the same austerity plan may lead to quite different outcomes. With good reasons we may assume that these institutional effects will also work in the coming years making some austerity plans more realistic than others. (2) Much policy change in the past occurred through slight changes that accumulated to large changes after some time (Streeck and Thelen 2005; Thelen 2003). In all likelihood, the present changes during the crisis and due to the austerity programmes can also make a major qualitative difference over the long run. The future welfare state of the age of austerity may have many different faces. However, it will be difficult to link these changes to a major political design; e.g. Social Democratic versus Christian Democratic versus liberal. (3) The interaction of institutional rules and economic capabilities tends to produce very different national fiscal capabilities and hence options for welfare state design in the future. For example the imposed austerity plans in Greece and the precluded option of devaluation due to Euro-zone membership will reduce economic growth and policy space in that country; while Euro-zone membership is an important precondition for Germany's export-led growth and its ensuing policy spaces in the future (Armingeon and Baccaro 2012; Flassbeck 2012; IMF 2012).

Notes

Based on a longer version entitled 'Austeritätspolitik: Was Parteien bewirken und Märkte mögen' in K. Armingeon (ed.), *Staatstätigkeiten, Parteien und Demokratie: Festschrift für Manfred G. Schmidt*, Wiesbaden, Verlag für Sozialwissenschaften, 2013, by permission of the author.

1 Compiled from IMF (2010b: 73–4) and additions from national sources.
2 I am grateful to Rafael Labanino from the University of Bern who updated the FRDB database until 2011 and made these updates available to me.
3 This finding is again based on qualitative evidence from the FRDB database and its updates.
4 I coded policy reforms for families, expanded education and research opportunities, raising the employment rate for older workers (mainly reduction of

early retirement opportunities) as new social risks policy reforms; policy reforms that increased market competition, reduced social security, reduced taxes, reduced collective and solidaristic regulation of wages and liberalized housing as liberalizing policies.

5 Economic, labour market, enterprise, health, social inclusion, family, pension, integration, research and innovation, and education policy.

6 Education policy in Australia; labour market policy in Germany; economic and pension policy in Hungary; economic enterprise, family and education policy in Poland; economic policy in Portugal; and enterprise policy in Switzerland.

7 I am grateful to the editor of the Data Yearbook, Daniele Caramani, for making these reports for 2011 available to me. A few of these country reports for 2011 were still missing; some of the manuscripts were drafts in summer 2012.

8 Since data on the cyclically adjusted primary deficits – i.e. adjusted deficits after deduction of interest payments – are not available in this source, I use cyclically adjusted deficits, which include interest payments. Due to missing data, Malta, Cyprus and Luxembourg have been dropped from the sample.

9 In the case of the Fiscal Monitor of November 2010, the historical data pertain to the years 2007, 2008 and 2009; in the case of the Fiscal Monitors of April 2011 and of September 2011 to 2008, 2009, and 2010 and in the case of the Fiscal Monitor of April 2012 to 2009, 2010, and 2011. The planned deficits pertain to 2010, 2011, and 2012 (Fiscal Monitor November 2010), 2011, 2012, and 2013 (Fiscal Monitor April and September 2011), and 2012, 2013, and 2014 (Fiscal Monitor 2012).

10 'The error structure is assumed to be heteroskedastic, autocorrelated up to some lag, and possibly correlated between the groups (panels). Driscoll-Kraay standard errors are robust to very general forms of cross-sectional (spatial) and temporal dependence when the time dimension becomes large.'

References

Alesina, A. 2010. *Fiscal Adjustments Lessons from Recent History*. Cambridge, Mass. (Harvard University): Unpublished paper, prepared for Ecofin meeting, Madrid, 15 April 2010.

Armingeon, K. 2012. 'The Politics of Fiscal Responses to the Crisis of 2008–2009.' *Governance* no-no.

Armingeon, K. and Baccaro, L. 2012. 'The Sorrows of Young Euro: Policy Responses to the Sovereign Debt Crisis.' In *Coping with Crisis: Government Reactions to the Great Recession*, ed. Bermeo, N. and Pontusson, J. New York: Russell Sage.

Armingeon, K. and Bonoli, G. 2006. *The Politics of Postindustrial Welfare States. Adapting Postwar Social Policies to New Social Risks*. London: Routledge.

Armingeon, K., Careja, R., Weisstanner, D., Engler, S., Potolidis, P., Gerber, M. and Leimgruber, P. 2011. *Comparative Political Data Set III 1990–2009*. Bern: Institute of Political Science, University of Bern.

Bonoli, G. 2007. 'Time Matters: Postindustrialization, New Social Risks, and Welfare State Adaptation in Advanced Industrial Democracies.' *Comparative Political Studies* 40 (5): 495–520.

Brunetti, A. 2011. *Wirtschaftskrise ohne Ende?* Bern: H.E.P.

Cameron, D. R. 2012. 'Fiscal Responses to the Economic Contraction of 2008–09.' In *Coping with Crisis: Government Reactions to the Great Recession*, ed. Bermeo, N. and Pontusson, J. New York: Russell Sage.

Caramani, D., Deegan-Krause, K. and Murray, R. 2011. 'Political Data in 2010.' *European Journal of Political Research* 50 (7–8): 869–87.

Castles, F. G. 2010. 'Black Swans and Elephants on the Move: The Impact of Emergencies on the Welfare State.' *Journal of European Social Policy* 20 (2): 91–101.

Colomer, J. M. and Magalhaes, P. 2012. *Firing the Coach: How Governments Are Losing Elections in Europe*. Washington, D.C.: Paper prepared for the conference 'Political Consequences of the Economic Crisis: Voting and Protesting in Europe', Georgetown University, April 2012.

EU Commission. 2009. *Economic Crisis in Europe: Cause, Consequences and Responses*. Luxembourg/Brussels: EU Commission, DG Economic and Financial Affairs, Series European Economy # 7.

Flassbeck, H. 2012. *Zehn Mythen der Krise*. Frankfurt am Main: Suhrkamp.

Gourevitch, P. 1986. *Politics in Hard Times. Comparative Responses to International Economic Crises*. Ithaca/London: Cornell University Press.

Hallerberg, M. and v. Hagen, J. 1999. 'Electoral Institutions, Cabinet Negotiations, and Budget Deficits within the European Union.' In *Fiscal Institutions and Fiscal Performance*, ed. Poterba, J. and v. Hagen, J. Chicago: Chicago University Press, pp. 209–32.

Hallerberg, M., Strauch, R. R. and v. Hagen, J. 2009. *Fiscal Governance in Europe*. Cambridge: Cambridge University Press.

ILO and World Bank, n.d. (2012). *Inventory of Policy Responses to the Financial and Economic Crisis*. Geneva and Washington, D.C.: ILO and World Bank.

IMF. 2010a. *Fiscal Monitor. Fiscal Exit. From Strategy to Implementation. November 2010*. Washington, D.C.: IMF.

IMF. 2010b. *From Stimulus to Consolidation: Revenue and Expenditure Policies in Advanced and Emerging Economies*. Washington, D.C.: 2010.

IMF. 2011a. *Fiscal Monitor. Addressing Fiscal Challenges to Reduce Economic Risks. September 2011*. Washington, D.C.: IMF.

IMF. 2011b. *Fiscal Monitor. Shifting Gears. Tackling Challenges on the Road to Fiscal Adjustment. April 2011*. Washington, D.C.: IMF.

IMF. 2012. *Fiscal Monitor. Balancing Fiscal Policy Risks. April 2012*. Washington, D.C.: IMF.

Kingdon, J. W. 1984. *Agendas, Alternatives, and Public Policies*. Boston/Toronto: HarperCollins.

Korpi, W. and Palme, J. 2003. 'New Politics and Class Politics in the Context of Austerity and Globalization: Welfare State Regress in 18 Countries, 1975–95.' *American Political Science Review* 97 (3): 425–46.

Lindvall, J. 2012. 'Policies and Politics in Two Economic Crises.' In *Coping with Crisis: Government Reaction to the Great Recession*, ed. Bermeo, N. and Pontusson, J. New York: Russell Sage.

OECD. 2012. *Economic Policy Reforms 2012: Going for Growth*. Paris: OECD.

Schmidt, M. G. 2010. 'Parties.' In *Oxford Handbook on Welfare States*, ed. Castles, F., Leibfried, S., Obinger, H. and Pierson, Chris. Oxford: Oxford University Press, pp. 211–26.

Streeck, W. and Thelen, K. 2005. 'Introduction: Institutional Change in Advanced Political Economies.' In *Beyond Continuity. Institutional Change in Advanced Political Economies*, ed. Streeck, W. and Thelen, K. Oxford: Oxford University Press, 1–39.

Thelen, K. 2003. 'How Institutions Evolve: Insights from Comparative-Historical Analysis.' In *Comparative Historical Analysis in the Social Sciences*, ed. Mahoney, J. and Rueschemeyer, D. New York: Cambridge University Press, pp. 208–40.

Wagschal, U. and Wenzelburger, G. 2008. 'Roads to Success: Budget Consolidations in OECD Countries.' *Journal of Public Policy* 28 (03): 309–39.

Wagschal, U. and Wenzelburger, G. 2012. 'When do Governments Consolidate? A Quantitative Comparative Analysis of 23 OECD Countries (1980–2005).' *Journal of Comparative Policy Analysis: Research and Practice* 14 (1): 45–71.

Challenges

Ageing and the Welfare State: Securing Sustainability

Volker Meier and
Martin Werding

I. Introduction

While the economic consequences of ageing are open to debate in many other areas, its impact on the welfare state is unambiguous – and all in all rather unfavourable. Patterns of demographic ageing differ substantially across countries. However, in all developed countries it is expected to lead to major shifts in the age composition of total population over the next three to four decades, with a decreasing share of individuals in their active life span and an increasing share of those of retirement age. Given that, the impact of ageing on the welfare state is basically a function of how deeply the state is involved in the areas of old-age provision, provision and/or financing of health services and long-term care, as well as in the fields of child-care, education and financial support for families. Of course, it is also a matter of how the relevant schemes are designed.

[. . .]

In many countries, the welfare state could definitely not be considered sustainable vis-à-vis the prospects of ageing if the legal framework for its main branches had been kept unchanged since the 1980s and 1990s. This prediction has received attention by politicians and the greater public, soliciting debates about reforms virtually everywhere and triggering steps to actually reforming existing welfare programmes in quite a number of cases.

[. . .]

The remainder of the paper is organized as follows. In Section II, we highlight demographic trends and their impact on public expenditure in all major branches of the welfare state under constant policies. In Section III, we review recent trends in policy reforms aiming to mitigate the consequences of ageing in several OECD countries. Finally, in Section IV we discuss whether the reforms already implemented appear to be sufficient for making the welfare state sustainable and point to further aspects that may be relevant in this regard.

II. Dependency Ratios and Welfare Expenditure

II.1 Demographic Dependency: Projected Changes

Probably the most important indicator of demographic ageing and its consequences for the welfare state is given by the old-age dependency ratio (OADR). It is conventionally defined as the number of individuals aged 65 and over per individuals aged 15 to 64 in the population of a given country. This ratio feeds through, though not necessarily on a one-for-one basis, to the systems' dependency ratios of many welfare programmes, e.g., the ratio of pensioners over contributors in the working-age population, or the ratio of older individuals with higher average health costs over prime-aged individuals making net contributions to actually funding these costs. The OADR of course neglects the fact that many individuals aged 15–64 are still enrolled in secondary or tertiary education, do not participate in the labour force for various reasons, are unemployed or have already entered early retirement. But it describes the demographic fundamentals for financing benefits that mainly accrue to the elderly.

[. . .]

Figure 1 shows expected changes in the OADR for a number of OECD countries over the next decades. In the US, with a relatively high fertility rate, the ratio was at a low level of 19 per cent in the year 2000. It is expected to increase to 29 per cent until 2025 and to 34 per cent until 2050. In Japan, the OADR was at 25 per cent in 2000, and it is projected to increase to 50 per cent until 2025 and to 76 per cent until 2050 (UN Population Division, 2009). Most other developed countries lie in between these two scenarios, implying that the number of older people per individuals of working age will increase by between 50 per cent and 200 per cent and will typically more than double over the time period considered here. If labour force participation remains as it is and if contribution rates are kept constant, this means that the quasi-replacement rates of pension benefits, measuring the ratio of average pensions over average wages, will drop by 33 per cent to 66 per cent. If replacement rates were kept constant – a wide-spread feature of pension policies in many countries until the 1990s – contribution rates would have to increase by the same rate as the OADR.

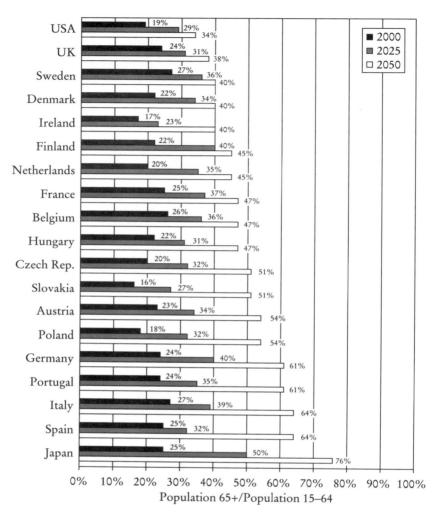

Figure 1 Old-age Dependency Ratios in OECD countries, 2000, 2025 and 2050
Source: UN Population Division (2009), constant-fertility variant.

Purely demographic effects for health costs are likely to be less dramatic. Age-specific per-capita expenditure on health is typically increasing around the retirement age, but an important fraction of total health costs is still falling on younger individuals. In some countries, the state actually concentrates on covering health costs of the elderly, implying that expenditure in these programmes could nevertheless grow in line with the OADR.

[. . .]

For long-term care, dependency ratios that would be similarly informative should probably consider individuals aged 85 and over compared to the number of individuals aged 15 to 64. These dependency ratios grow even much faster than the standard OADR because they are much more affected by increases in life expectancy. Unlike public pensions, however, long-term care has to be financed only for some of the elderly, so that the upward pressure on public expenditure in this area is less worrying on absolute terms.

[. . .]

Another indicator that is potentially important with respect to the consequences of ageing is the total dependency ratio (TDR), relating the number of children below age 15 plus the number of elderly people aged 65 and over to the number of individuals aged 15 to 64. To the extent that ageing is driven by a decline in fertility, the youth-dependency component of this measure decreases over time. This may compensate to some extent for the heavier burden involved in higher old-age dependency.

Indeed, the rise in total dependency is typically less pronounced than the increase in the OADR (see Figure 2). In the US, total dependency is projected to increase from 51 per cent in 2000 to 65 per cent in 2050; in the UK the respective figures are 53 per cent and 65 per cent. Countries that are facing a sharp increase in old-age dependency and, at the same time, have a low fertility rate already today should expect far stronger increases in the TDR. For example, in Germany the ratio increases from 47 per cent in 2000 to 80 per cent in 2050, and in Japan it rises from 47 per cent to 94 per cent (UN Population Division, 2009).

[. . .]

In public discussions it is sometimes asserted that benefits related to unemployment among the working-age generation should become less pressing in the ageing process as it is often associated with a shrinking workforce. By this naïve view, unemployment rates should decline as soon as the number of retiring workers exceeds the number of individuals entering the labour market. This conclusion ignores that there are institutional determinants of unemployment. For instance, wage setting may counteract the demographic processes if bargaining parties take into account both the shrinking labour supply and the expected increase in wage taxes which are needed to finance increasing old-age dependency. In fact, the financial burden for those in employment may well rise through higher benefits paid to members of their own generation, given that higher wage taxes could trigger higher unemployment through more aggressive wage setting.

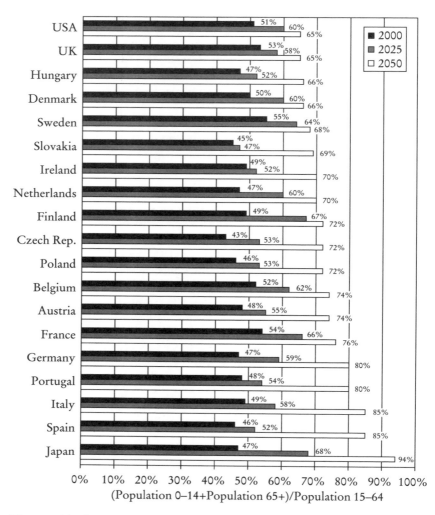

Figure 2 Total Dependency Ratios in OECD countries, 2000, 2025 and 2050
Source: UN Population Division (2009), constant-fertility variant.

II.2 The Impact on Welfare Expenditure if Policies Remain Unchanged

All in all, changes in the age structure of the population expected for the next three to four decades exert an enormous upward pressure on welfare expenditure in most industrialized countries. To illustrate this, let us consider some simple estimates regarding a 'constant-policy' scenario for changes in age-related public expenditure in the OECD countries looked at so far. Here, 'constant policy' is taken to indicate that eligibility rules, benefit levels and, most generally speaking, the extent of public involvement in any of the relevant branches of welfare expenditure remain as they were before ageing became really acute. Consequently, we also abstract from any behavioural changes on the side of future beneficiaries.

[. . .]

Table 1 reveals that the potential impact of ageing on welfare expenditure is very strong in many developed countries. From 2000 to 2050, the hypothetical increase in expenditure on old-age pensions, survivor benefits, health care and long-term care, corrected for potential reductions in expenditure on child benefits and public schooling, amounts to only 2.1 per cent of GDP in the UK. At the same time, it is 7.6 per cent in the US, no less than 11.5 per cent in France and over 20 per cent in Japan and Germany. By far the most important driver of these changes is pension expenditure under the assumption of constant eligibility rules, benefit levels and retirement behaviour. The impact of public health expenditure varies substantially. In spite of assumptions that are plausible, but relatively mild, its resulting increase is considerable in the US and definitely strong in Germany and Japan. Reductions in expenditure on children are small everywhere, exceeding 1 per cent of GDP only in Austria and in several transition countries which are otherwise rather strongly affected by the impact of ageing on their welfare expenditure.

Whatever the precise definition of 'sustainability', it appears that the welfare state could not be considered sustainable in the majority of countries considered here in a 'constant-policy' scenario based on year-2000 figures for benefit expenditure and current prospects for demographic ageing until 2050. Thus far, however, we have deliberately ignored the many steps to reform, some incremental in their nature and some very far-reaching, which have been taken in many developed countries in order to deal with this unfavourable outlook.

III. Trends in Policy Reforms

It is impossible to provide a full overview of policy measures aiming at improvements in the short-term and long-term fiscal stance of all branches of the welfare state which have been taken in OECD countries in recent years. As a stylized fact, many countries have embarked on serious approaches to reforming their pension systems, while little has been done about financing health care or long-term care that goes beyond some short-term cost containment.

[. . .]

Table 1 Age-related public expenditure in OECD countries, hypothetical increase under 'constant' policies

	Old-age & survivor pensions		Health care & LTC		Child benefits & education		Total	
	Level 2000	Change 2000 to 2050	Level 2000	Change 2000 to 2050	Level 2000	Change 2000 to 2050	Level 2000	Change 2000 to 2050
% of GDP								
UK	5.4	+3.0	6.2	−0.4	6.7	−0.6	18.3	+2.1
Sweden	9.2	+4.7	7.0	−0.5	7.6	−0.2	23.7	+4.0
Denmark	6.3	+4.9	6.8	+1.5	8.2	−0.3	21.2	+6.1
Ireland[a]	3.7	+5.2	5.6	+2.3	5.4	−0.4	14.7	+7.1
USA	5.9	+4.8	5.9	+3.1	4.9	−0.2	16.7	+7.6
Hungary	7.6	+8.5	5.2	+1.3	6.4	−1.4	19.2	+8.4
Belgium	7.6	+6.4	8.0	+2.4	6.6	±0.0	22.2	+8.7
Netherlands	4.5	+5.6	6.2	+3.5	5.2	−0.4	15.9	+8.8
Finland	7.7	+7.8	5.9	+2.2	6.8	−0.1	20.4	+9.9
France	11.0	+9.8	8.3	+1.7	7.8	±0.0	27.1	+11.5
Czech Rep.	7.7	+12.2	6.2	+3.3	5.1	−0.6	19.0	+14.9
Portugal	8.2	+12.7	6.5	+3.1	5.2	−0.9	19.9	+14.9
Spain	8.4	+13.4	5.6	+3.3	4.6	±0.0	18.7	+16.6
Slovakia	6.3	+13.5	5.1	+4.5	2.9	−1.1	14.4	+16.8
Austria	11.7	+15.9	7.5	+4.2	7.1	−1.4	26.3	+18.7
Italy	13.6	+18.4	5.9	+2.2	4.7	−0.1	24.2	+20.4
Germany	10.3	+15.9	8.6	+5.6	5.5	−1.0	24.4	+20.5
Japan	7.0	+14.0	7.1	+8.5	3.8	−0.6	17.9	+21.9
Portugal	10.3	+21.0	4.2	+3.7	5.1	−1.9	19.6	+22.8

[a] Figures for Ireland are expressed in % of Gross National Income.
Sources: OECD SOCX (2008); UN Population Division (2009), constant-fertility variant; own calculations.

III.1 Strengthening Actuarial Fairness

Where the earlier design of public pension schemes left room for that, authorities have often taken measures to strengthen actuarial fairness within these schemes. Even in many 'Bismarckian' pension schemes with a notable tax-benefit link, benefit assessment was traditionally based on a limited number of 'best years' with highest contributions, or on end-of-career levels of covered earnings. Actuarial adjustments then imply that benefits are now more and more assessed based on life-long earnings. Examples of relevant reforms are given by Italy (in a first round of reforms enacted in 1992), France (in 1993 and, again, in 2003) or Austria (in 2003).

In addition, many pension schemes used to provide non-contributory benefits tied to specific contingencies or periods typically not covered with contributions. Often, entitlements of this kind have been scaled back through series of incremental changes, e.g., in Germany (between 1992 and 2001). Exceptional and extreme steps to abolishing non-contributory benefits were made in Sweden, where survivor benefits were essentially wiped out (in 1990) and where the traditional pension system combining universal lump-sum benefits with earnings-related pensions for employees was transformed (in 2000) into a pension scheme which is now probably more Bismarckian than the German one. The main goal of such reforms is to reduce the tax-like character of contributions, thus promoting labour supply across the board.

On the other hand, countries that mainly rely on 'Beveridgean' pension schemes with lump-sum benefits in their public pillar of old-age provision have often tried to make sure that their systems really provide an adequate basic cover, effectively expanding the interpersonal redistribution of income involved in these schemes. Here, the most prominent example is given by the UK (from 2002 onwards), with a revitalization of the Basic State Pension and remarkable changes in the legal framework for supplementary, or second, public pensions, effectively making the latter less and less earnings-related.

Another field where actuarial principles have often been strengthened are the options to retire early drawing on public pensions (or other benefits that define an exit route from labour force participation to retirement). When unemployment was high in the 1980s and early 1990s, virtually all countries in continental Europe created incentives in favour of early retirement, implying that the average age of retirement often became rather low there (see Fenge and Pestieau, 2005). As this strategy which was also meant to promote employment among younger individuals did not work, it was later terminated and even reversed. As a rule, individuals who want to retire before they reach a certain age threshold are now faced with reductions in pension benefits through shorter periods with contributions as well as special deductions to compensate for their longer duration of benefits.

[. . .]

III.2 Switching from DB to NDC

[. . .]

Rules for indexing pension benefits over time are also important determinants of the long-term trends in pension expenditure. Traditionally, most public pension schemes employ indexation rules by which benefits are regularly up-rated in line with wages, prices, or some mixture between these two approaches. Within this range of options, it is thus possible to switch from a more generous to a less generous variant. For example, Germany switched from gross to net wage indexation (in 1992), and France switched from wage indexation to a US-style, mixed indexation regime (in 1993), that is, to an assessment of individual benefits based on wage indexation of previous earnings, followed by annual up-ratings based on price indexation. In contrast, the UK moved from price indexation of benefits and all relevant thresholds by which the Basic State Pension eroded substantially during the 1980s and 1990s to a mixed regime with wage up-ratings of benefits (in 2002).

Basically, indexation rules are elements of pension schemes which fall into the DB ('defined benefits') category: in these systems, benefits are determined and indexed so as to provide some defined amount or, rather, level of benefits. Contribution rates or taxes then have to be adjusted to meet the system's current financial obligations. As a new strategy for coping with the ageing problem, a few countries changed this logic, establishing what is now called NDC ('notionally defined contributions') schemes. In these schemes, contribution rates are essentially fixed at a level which, for various reasons, should not be exceeded. The level of benefits then becomes endogenous, corresponding to what can be financed for individual beneficiaries given this contribution rate and the current system's dependency ratio. Two countries that openly adopted NDC-type rules are Italy (in 1995) and Sweden (in 2000). Germany introduced a demographic factor into its indexation formula (in 2004) by which an increase in the dependency ratio feeds back on benefit up-ratings, implying that the German statutory pension scheme is now situated somewhere between a traditional DB and an NDC arrangement.

[. . .]

III.3 Is Funding a Way Out?

When ageing first appeared to become an issue, a widely-held view among economists was that unfunded public pension schemes are effective in securing some amount of old-age provision for all those covered, albeit at a low rate of return. The internal rate of return to contributions made to these systems is the rate of payroll growth, which must be expected to fall short of the market rate of interest over longer periods of time. Many economists concluded that converting unfunded systems into funded ones, while paying off all existing unfunded liabilities, should lead to welfare gains (see, e.g., Feldstein, 1995). However, Breyer (1989) and Fenge (1995) demonstrated that this view is flawed. The pay-as-you-go mechanism as such is 'intergenerationally efficient' in the sense that transforming unfunded pension schemes into funded schemes is impossible without harming at least some generation. The burden involved in ageing can thus be shared in various ways between future generations, the active generation and those in retirement, but it can never be removed (see also Fenge and Werding, 2004).

Yet, even if pre-funding is not unambiguously superior, there are still good reasons to expand the share in old-age income which is derived from funded pension plans when the return to unfunded schemes becomes even lower – for the young in a DB-type scheme, for the old under NDC rules – because of the demographic pressure. Additional considerations regarding risk diversification aside, the simple logic of such policies is to use financial and real capital as a substitute for human capital, by which pay-as-you-go schemes are effectively funded, now that the latter is increasingly lacking (for a pronounced exposition, see Sinn, 2000). Consequently, a number of countries have gone in this direction, either building up 'demographic buffer funds' inside their public pension schemes, as in the US (in 1983), Finland (in 1997), Ireland (in 1999), or Spain (in 2001); establishing new mandatory plans supplementing public pensions, as in Denmark (in 1999) or Sweden (in 2000); or subsidizing private, voluntary provisions, as in Germany (in 2001) or France (in 2003). Where complementary funding is meant to partially replace mandatory public old-age provision, making sure that individuals really participate may become important, at least in the sense that gaps in coverage through existing occupational or private pension plans could be filled through an automatic enrolment, as in the UK (starting from 2012).

[. . .]

III.4 Creating a Framework for Longer Working Lives

Many countries, especially in Europe, are still struggling to increase the effective age of retirement beyond age 60 and to increase the statutory retirement age to 65, which appears to be the current international standard for men and women alike. Meanwhile, a few countries have already started to increase the age threshold for claiming full benefits from 65 to 67. The first country to take this measure was the US, where a schedule was devised at a rather early stage (in 1983) by which the new age limit is phased in now from 2002 to 2027. More recently, Germany adopted a similar schedule (in 2007, phased in from 2012 to 2031). In Denmark, the statutory retirement age had been at 67 until a few years ago, while the effective retirement age was substantially lower through generous early retirement rules. Now, the statutory limit will be increased from age 65 to 67 again (enacted in 2009, taking effect from 2024 to 2027) and then linked to the conditional life expectancy at age 60.

Expanding the period of economic activity as longevity increases directly addresses a major cause of the impact of ageing on public pension schemes. Furthermore, it is a powerful instrument to slow down expected increases in systems' dependency ratios, affecting both the numerator and the denominator of this figure. As a consequence, it may allow for paying higher annual benefits to future pensioners than under any of the other approaches to reform discussed before – albeit for a shorter period of their lives (see Werding, 2007, for a demonstration of these effects taking the German reform as an example). All this is true, of course, only if individuals are really able to stay active for a longer period of their lives. Note that, in this regard, sickness and incapacity need not be limitations of growing importance as it can be expected that a major share of additional years of life expectancy is spent in good health.

In countries where structural unemployment is high, or where labour-force participation of particular groups – most notably among women and older workers – is relatively low, labour market reforms and other measures aiming to overcome these problems are useful for various reasons. Successful policies in both these areas are also important prerequisites for dealing with the ageing problem, if only for their positive impact on employment and GDP. Aspects which are particularly important for serious attempts at expanding the active life span of individuals relate to the supply of, and the demand for, older workers. For this strategy to work, several kinds of adjustments are required. First, individuals need to adapt their life-cycle plans, a major condition being that the changes in relevant rules are announced in good time. Second, firms may have to re-consider their current habits regarding additional training for older workers, and they may also have to think about working conditions and new jobs which are suitable for people working until age 65 and beyond. Last but not least, further adjustments in labour market institutions and welfare schemes are needed as they still tend to accommodate early exits from the labour market in many ways.

[. . .]

IV. Is Sustainability Secured?

[. . .]

IV.1 The Impact of Ageing on Welfare Expenditure Under Actual Policies

To illustrate the current stance of public finances as a whole, and of welfare expenditure in particular, in terms of their long-term sustainability, let us first return to projected increases in public age-related expenditure (as in Table 1) now referring to recent, more subtle projections conducted by the European Commission and the Economic Policy Committee (2006), respectively by the OECD (2001, ch. 4) for non-EU member countries. The results (see Table 2) are meant to show the consequences of current policies pursued in each country, including changes which have already been legislated, but will become effective only over time. The table also displays results for the EPC's sustainability gap which have been calculated building on these expenditure projections by the European Commission (2006) and by Hauner et al. (2007).

In Table 2, countries are ranked according to the strength of the impact of ageing on total age-related expenditure. A ranking according to the size of the sustainability gap would be similar, but not identical since the latter is also affected by the initial amount of (explicit) public (net) debt, also reflecting the extent of pre-funding for future benefit expenditure, and by the initial budgetary position. The table shows that, under actual policies which have been devised for the future, expected increases in welfare expenditure are substantially smaller in most cases than is suggested by purely demographic trends (cf. Table 1). In particular, where they have been made, pension reforms strongly contribute to improving the fiscal sustainability of the welfare state as this is where the reductions mainly come from. Another remarkable observation is that reforms appear to have been strongest where the pressure involved in ageing is most imminent.

A downside involved in far-reaching pension reforms which often came in several rounds is that expected reductions in replacement rates are now so strong that future old-age poverty becomes an issue of major concern in a number of developed countries. To reflect this in their records of recent pension reforms, the OECD (2009, ch. I.3) has now introduced a new category of potential reform goals, viz. the 'adequacy' of provisions. Ironically, many measures that are listed there would be mentioned again under other goals, such as 'economic efficiency' or 'financial sustainability', if they were soon rolled back or abandoned. This points to material conflicts which certainly cannot be solved when setting up a synopsis of pension policies pursued in different countries. Striking the right balance between these conflicting goals in ageing societies is clearly a challenge for policy making which needs to be addressed at the national level. We may add here that, if public pensions have to be cut back to become sustainable, making complementary savings mandatory and extending the period of employment are certainly among the few options that remain.

Table 2 also shows that expected increases in expenditure on health and long-term care are now often larger than those projected for public pension schemes. Furthermore, these increases can even be bigger than is explained by purely demographic trends (cf. Table 1). The reason is that

Ageing and the Welfare State

Table 2 Age-related public expenditure in OECD countries, projected increase under current policies

	Public pensions		Health care & LTC		Education		Total		Sustainability gap[c]
	Level 2004	Change 2004 to 2050	Level 2004	Change 2004 to 2050	Level 2004	Change 2004 to 2050	Level 2004	Change 2004 to 2050	
				% of GDP					
Poland	13.9	-5.9	4.2	+1.5	5.0	-1.9	23.1	-6.3	-2.5
Austria	13.4	-1.2	5.9	+2.5	5.1	-1.0	24.4	+0.3	-1.5
Italy	14.2	+0.4	7.3	+2.0	4.3	-0.6	25.8	+1.8	-0.8
Sweden	10.6	+0.6	10.5	+2.7	7.3	-0.9	28.4	+2.4	+1.2
Germany	11.4	+1.7	7.0	+2.2	4.0	-0.9	22.4	+3.0	+1.3
Slovakia	7.2	+1.8	5.1	+2.5	3.7	-1.3	16.0	+3.0	+2.8
Japan[a]	7.9	+0.6	5.8	+2.4	n.a.	n.a.	13.7	+3.0	+6.2
France[b]	12.8	+2.0	7.7	+1.8	5.0	-0.5	25.5	+3.3	+2.2
UK	6.6	+2.0	8.0	+2.7	4.6	-0.6	19.2	+4.1	+2.8

Denmark	9.5	+3.3	8.0	+2.1	7.8	-0.3	25.3	+5.1	-0.8
Netherlands	7.7	+3.5	6.6	+1.9	4.8	-0.2	19.1	+5.2	+4.2
USA[a]	4.6	+2.1	2.6	+4.4	3.9	-1.0	11.1	+5.5	+6.9
Finland	10.7	+3.1	7.3	+3.2	6.0	-0.7	24.0	+5.6	+2.2
Belgium	10.4	+5.1	7.1	+2.4	5.6	-0.7	23.1	+6.8	+1.5
Hungary[b]	10.4	+6.7	5.5	+1.0	4.5	-0.7	20.4	+7.0	+2.7
Czech Rep.	8.5	+5.6	6.7	+2.4	3.8	-0.7	19.0	+7.3	+6.8
Ireland	4.7	+6.4	5.9	+2.6	4.1	-1.0	14.7	+8.0	+6.0
Spain	8.6	+7.1	6.6	+2.4	3.7	-0.6	18.9	+8.9	+2.9
Portugal[b]	11.1	+9.7	6.7	+0.5	-0.4	-0.4	17.4	+9.8	+6.3

[a] Initial level: 2000.

[b] Expenditure on long-term care not included in the projections.

[c] Reduction in annual primary deficit ratios required to meet the government's intertemporal budget constraint in spite of the projected impact of ageing on age-related public expenditure ('T-3' variant of the 'sustainability gap' as defined in Economic Policy Committee, 2003).

Sources: for EU-25 countries: European Commission and Economic Policy Committee (2006) and European Commission (2006); for the US and Japan: OECD (2001, ch. 4) and Hauner et al. (2007).

the projections related to actual policies also include an impact of technical progress on health costs that is independent of demographic change, but has consistently been observed in many countries in the past. It is impossible to predict whether these cost increases will continue if health systems and public finances are more and more under demographic pressure, or whether medical progress might change its direction in the future. There are thus substantial uncertainties concerning the future evolution of public health expenditure.

[. . .]

In any case, cost containment in the health-care sector is a major issue that remains to be addressed in many countries. The same applies to long-term care, where current levels of expenditure are smaller, while relative increases related to ageing are much more pronounced than in other areas. Thus far, no country has started to really deal with these problems. At least, certainly no country has found a key to avoiding continuous cost surprises without reducing the availability and/or the quality of services. Ideally, dealing with the prospects of increasing health costs could mean three things, alternatively or in combination. One could make attempts to reduce any inefficiencies involved in current systems of delivery and financing. One could try to push medical progress in a new, cost-saving direction. Or one must think about ways of paying for costly, high-quality medical services and of making them available for as many people as possible – in spite of the financial pressures through ageing. Partial pre-funding may thus also become an issue in health care and long-term care, as it already is in old-age provision. The distributive side of such reforms is probably even more delicate than it is with respect to pensions. Given this complication as well as the diversity of current national arrangements, there is apparently no one-size-fits-all solution which the countries affected most severely could simply borrow from each other.

Note

References

Breyer, F. (1989), 'On the Intergenerational Pareto Efficiency of Pay-as-you-go Financed Pension Systems', *Journal of Institutional and Theoretical Economics*, 145(4): 643–58.

Economic Policy Committee (2003), *The Impact of Ageing Populations on Public Finances: Overview of Analysis Carried out at an EU Level and Proposals for a Future Work Programme*, Doc. No. EPC/ECFIN/435/03.

European Commission (DG ECFIN, 2006), 'Public Finances in EMU 2006', *European Economy*, No. 3/2006.

European Commission and Economic Policy Committee (2006), 'The Impact of Ageing on Public Expenditure: Projections for EU-25 Member States on Pensions, Health Care, Long-term Care, Education and Unemployment Transfers', *European Economy*, No. 1/2006.

Feldstein, M. S. (1995), 'Would Privatizing Social Security Raise Economic Welfare?', *NBER Working Paper*, No. 5281.

Fenge, R. (1995), 'Pareto-efficiency of the Pay-as-you-go Pension System with Intragenerational Fairness', *Finanzarchiv N.F.*, 52(3): 357–63.

Fenge, R., and Pestieau, P. (2005), *Social Security and Early Retirement*, Cambridge, MA, London, MIT Press.

Fenge, R., and Werding, M. (2004), 'Ageing and the Tax Implied in Public Pension Schemes: Simulations for Selected OECD Countries', *Fiscal Studies*, 25(2): 159–200.

Hagemann, R., and Nicoletti, G. (1989), 'Population Ageing: Economic Effects and Some Policy Implications for Financing Public Pensions', *OECD Economic Studies*, No. 12.

Hauner, D., Leigh, D., and Skaarup, M. (2007), 'Ensuring Fiscal Sustainability in G-7 Countries', *IMF Working Papers*, No. WP/07/187.

OECD (2001), *Economic Outlook* No. 69 (June 2001), Paris, Organisation for Economic Co-operation and Development.

OECD SOCX (2008), *OECD Social Expenditure Database, 2008 Release*, Paris, Organisation for Economic Co-operation and Development (download via http://www.oecd.org/els/social/expenditure).

OECD (2009), *Pensions at a Glance 2009: Retirement-Income Systems in OECD Countries*, Paris, Organisation for Economic Co-operation and Development.

Roseveare, D., Leibfritz, W., Fore, D., and Wurzel, E. (1996), 'Ageing Populations, Pension Systems and Government Budgets: Simulations for 20 OECD Countries', *OECD Economics Department Working Paper* No. 168.

Sinn, H.-W. (2000), 'Why a Funded Pension System is Needed and Why it is Not Needed', *International Tax and Public Finance*, 7(4/5): 389–410.

UN Population Division (2009), *World Population Prospects, 2008 Revision*, New York, United Nations, Dept. of Economic and Social Affairs (download via http://www.un.org/esa/population/unpop.html).

Werding, M. (2007), 'Social Insurance: How to Pay for Pensions and Health Care?', in I. Hamm, H. Seitz and M. Werding (eds.), *Demographic Change in Germany. The Economic and Fiscal Consequences*, Berlin, Heidelberg, New York, Springer, pp. 89–128.

Very Low Fertility: Consequences, Causes and Policy Approaches

Peter McDonald

Introduction

This paper addresses the issue of very low fertility in countries with advanced economies including its consequences and its causes. It ends with a discussion of policy approaches to reverse very low fertility. Very low fertility is defined as being fertility sustained for a long period below 1.5 births per woman. It is recognized that annual fertility rates are affected by changes in the timing of births (tempo effects) and may fall temporarily below 1.5 births per woman. It is important to recognize tempo effects but it is difficult to estimate their impact on lifetime fertility because, where births are delayed, many may never occur even though there was an intention to have these births. Even the strongest intentions can fade with changes in the life circumstances of the woman and her partner.

The Consequences of Very Low Fertility

How Generation Size Changes When Fertility Remains at 1.3 Births per Woman

In the simplest terms, sustained very low fertility has an impact upon the size of a nation's population. This impact is exceptionally rapid if considered against the full course of human history. This is illustrated in Figure 1. The figure shows the impact on the size of successive generations of fertility sustained at the level of 1.3 births per woman, the level prevailing in Japan in recent years. The second generation after the present generation would be 40 per cent the size of the present generation and the fourth generation after the present generation would be only 15 per cent the size

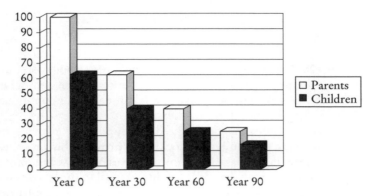

Figure 1 The comparative size of successive generations across time when fertility is constant at 1.3 births per woman

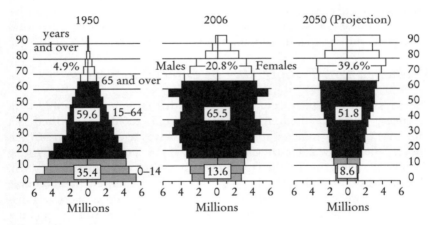

Figure 2 Changes in the population pyramid
Source: Statistics Bureau, MIC; Ministry of Health, Labour and Welfare.

of the present generation. These impacts are so devastating that it is difficult to believe that they would actually happen. Any nation facing this situation is very likely to take action to stop the trend at some time. However, delay of action has important consequences. First, very low fertility substantially reduces the size of the labour force within one generation just as the population is ageing rapidly (see Figure 2). Second, very low fertility almost certainly becomes more difficult to reverse the longer that it has been in place.

The Impact of Very Low Fertility on the Future Labour Force

Ogawa et al. (2005) refer to the sharp fall in the future labour force at the same time as the population is ageing as the onset of the demographic onus. Can the Japanese economy sustain a fall in its labour supply in the next 30 years of some 20 million workers?

Increased tax revenue may be required to support the growing older population but there will be fewer workers to provide this revenue. As the labour supply falls, wage inflation can throw the economy into turmoil. Furthermore, with very low fertility, the fall in the labour supply is most severe at the young ages. Young workers are the assimilators of new technology. They dominate a vital group in modern economies referred to as 'complex problem solvers' (McDonald and Temple 2006) In an increasingly competitive global economy, countries that have a shortage of young skilled workers will be vulnerable to competition. Their economies will lack the dynamism that will be essential in the competitive world economy. Investment may flow to those countries that are well-endowed with young, technologically skilled workers.

Sustained Low Fertility May Be Difficult to Reverse

Surveys in low fertility countries indicate that most young people want to marry and have children. For Japan, Suzuki (2006) has reported that the average ideal number of children (for wives aged less than 50) has never fallen below 2.5 in the past 25 years. If the natural desires of young people are frustrated by the ways in which society is organized, they will become disillusioned. As more people do not have children, the economic costs to those who do have children increase producing an increased disincentive to have children. This is known as the low fertility trap (Lutz et al. 2006). Japan may be falling into such a trap. A society like Japan that is organized around the importance of family will disintegrate unless it is able to reverse these conditions.

The Causes of Very Low Fertility

Drivers of Low Fertility

Low fertility in advanced societies today has been an unintended outcome of two major waves of social and economic change, social liberalism and economic restructuring (McDonald 2006a). Both these waves have enhanced individual aspirations in relation to the quality of personal and economic lives. However, in differing cultural and welfare environments, both have brought pressure to bear upon the capacity to form and maintain families. Social liberalism and economic restructuring have given rise to two important changes for individuals:

- the provision of gender equity through an opening up of opportunities for women beyond the household, and
- increasing levels of risk aversion among young people of both sexes in an increasingly competitive labour market.

Gender Equity and Fertility

Advanced societies today provide considerable freedom and gender equality to women as individuals. However, women are keenly aware that these gains will be distinctly compromised once they have a baby (McDonald 2000). This is especially the case in labour markets where little or no provision is made for the combination of work and family.

The central problem is that family formation involves greater risks for women than for men. Accordingly, women are wary about embarking upon marriage and childbearing if they do not feel confident about their ability to combine family with the other opportunities that have opened up for them, especially through paid employment.

Economic Restructuring, Risk Aversion and Fertility

Globalization and sharply rising education levels have created high economic aspirations among young people. At the same time, the competitive nature of labour market deregulation has led to a wider variation in their earnings, career stability and progression. Engagement in the deregulated labour market is now seen as involving greatly increased risk. In these circumstances, most young people become risk-averse, that is, they follow pathways that have lower risk.

Investment in one's own human capital (education and labour market experience) is seen by young people as being the optimal path of risk aversion. This investment involves considerable commitment to self and to one's employer, especially through long work hours, in opposition to a commitment to more altruistic endeavours such as service to family members and family formation. As a consequence, family formation is put on hold while human capital is accumulated.

Are These Causes More Acute in East Asia?

There is an argument that these conditions are more acute in the advanced countries of East Asia. First, gender inequity for women as family members is greater in East Asia than elsewhere. Second, today's potential parents in East Asia come from large cohorts with high levels of competition in education and employment. Further, they envisage that the same level of competition will apply to their own children. Third, the transition in labour market conditions has been more extensive in East Asia (often from jobs for life to jobs for three months). Fourth, East Asian economies have had recent economic shocks (the burst of the bubble economy, the 1997 financial crisis) and are based to a large extent on manufacturing where global competition is acute.

The Fertility Divide Among Advanced Economies

The social forces of gender equity and labour market deregulation have been common to all advanced economies. However, many of these advanced economies do not have very low fertility. Why is this so? Table 1 shows the variation in fertility rates across countries with advanced economies. They can be divided into two distinct groups. Group 1 countries with fertility rates above 1.5 births per woman include all of the Nordic countries, all of the French- and Dutch-speaking Western European countries and all of the English-speaking countries. Group 2 includes all of the Southern European countries, all of the German-speaking Western European countries and all of the advanced East Asian countries. Indeed, except for very brief periods when the fertility rates in Denmark and Canada nosed below 1.5, none of the Group 1 countries have ever had fertility rates below 1.5 and, once fallen below 1.5, none of the Group 2 countries have had fertility rates above 1.5. The cultural conformity of the groups suggests there may be a cultural explanation for the divide between Group 1 and Group 2 countries.

In general, Group 2 countries are countries in which there is a strong, traditional value that family and state are separate entities and that families should support their own members without intervention from the state. Accordingly, states in these regions have been slow to implement broad-based, family assistance measures. The opposite tends to be the case in the Group 1 countries; in general, they are notable for the family-friendly institutional arrangements that they have implemented in the past 20 years. Thus, the argument is that there are universal social and economic trends that draw young people away from family formation but that in Group 1 countries the effect of these trends is less severe because of the family support policies that they have introduced.

Policy Matters

Reasonable fertility rates are compatible with advanced economies so long as social institutions are supportive of families with children. It is the

Table 1 Total Fertility Rates, 2005

Group 1 Countries	TFR	Group 2 Countries	TFR
United States	2.05	Switzerland	1.42
Iceland	2.05	Austria	1.41
New Zealand	2.00	Portugal	1.40
France	1.94	Malta	1.37
Ireland	1.88	Germany	1.34
Norway	1.84	Italy	1.34
Australia	1.82	Spain	1.34
Finland	1.80	Greece	1.28
Denmark	1.80	Japan	1.26
United Kingdom	1.80	Singapore	1.24
Sweden	1.77	Taiwan	1.12
Netherlands	1.73	Republic of Korea	1.08
Belgium	1.72	Hong Kong SAR	0.97
Luxembourg	1.70	Shanghai City	0.60
Canada	1.60		

Source: Eurostat and national statistical offices.

business of government, with the cooperation of leaders of other social institutions, especially employers, to create this environment for families. An unenlightened business sector in fear of short-term competitive pressures is the largest obstacle to the required reforms. Businesses need to be made aware that they are surely killing themselves in the longer term by not cooperating with governments to reform the institutions of society that support family life. Governments need to reassess their commitment to the traditional family model in which families (essentially the women in families) are expected to support their own members with little or no assistance from the State. East Asian economies have been very quick to adopt new economic models but slow to adopt new social models. Fertility sustained at very low levels is evidence in itself that the old social models are failing. Group 2 countries in Europe are starting to move in this direction and my prediction is that they will be successful in raising their fertility rates to reasonable levels. I am less optimistic about such social reform being successful in East Asia because resistance to the social and economic reforms that are required is more entrenched in East Asia than it is in Europe. The European Union provides Group 2 European countries with a frame of reference beyond the purely national. East Asian countries have no similar frame of reference.

Inappropriate Policy Approaches

Low fertility has been recognized as a problem in some East Asian countries for some time. Singapore commenced its policy activities in the 1980s. Singapore's first efforts were directed at raising the fertility levels of educated Chinese women. Women in this group were provided with large tax incentives to have children and later were encouraged to marry through the provision of government dating agencies. From time to time, young women have been criticized for not fulfilling their national duty. Today, the fertility rate of Chinese women in Singapore is close to one child per woman and the rate for educated Chinese women would certainly be below one child per woman. Policy has clearly been a failure in Singapore. Japan also has been attempting to raise its fertility rate and, like Singapore, attention has been focused primarily upon increasing the rate of marriage. There has also been some level of vilification of young people in Japan through terms such as 'parasite singles'. Japan's fertility rate also remains low. I would argue that the thrusts of policy in Singapore and Japan have been wrong for the following reasons.

Low Marriage Rates are a Symptom rather than a Cause

It is not simply a matter of increasing the marriage rate. In East Asia, there is considerable pressure upon those who marry to have children. Decisions about marriage and childbearing are concurrently determined: the decision to marry is equivalent to a decision to have a child (Shirahase 2000). Incorrectly, policy makers in Singapore and Japan seem often to consider marriage and fertility within marriage as in some way independent of each other. Most women in Singapore and Japan are married by around age 30. This enables adequate opportunity for them to have two children, even three. They don't. That marriage alone is not the issue is also evidenced by the fact that there is a high marriage rate in South Korea but the fertility rate in that country is lower than it is in Japan and Singapore. I argue that low marriage rates are a symptom of the same social and economic circumstances that lead to low fertility. Policy needs to address the cause not the symptom.

The Causes of Low Fertility are Institutional Not Individual

The assumption of policy makers in East Asia has been that low fertility can be overcome by dealing with young people as individuals, not through broad social reform. Singapore first attempted to 'buy off' educated young Chinese women, both Japan and Singapore have tried to find ways to encourage individuals to marry. Both countries also have often been critical of the behaviour of young people essentially blaming young people for the problem. Counter to this individual approach, surveys of young people in all East Asian countries continue to show that they would prefer to have more children than they are actually having. This strongly suggests that the problem does not lie with the values or motivations of young people themselves but with the nature of the societies in which they live. Low fertility derives from social and economic institutions that are unfriendly to families with children. Older people control the nature of these institutions.

Appropriate Policy Directions

Young people need to be confident that, if they have children, they will not be unduly penalized in financial or employment terms. Because of entrenched gender inequities, this applies especially to young women. This means that young people need to have a sense of security about their future employment and income-earning capacity. In particular, young women need to be able to believe that they will be able to pursue their employment goals while still having the number of children they want to have.

Appropriate policy then is work and family policy. This includes income support for families with children, affordable/quality child care and early childhood education, flexible working hours, parental leave, family leave, part-time work in one's own job with pro-rata entitlements and reasonable working hours. The exact arrangements will be country-specific as countries need to build upon existing institutional arrangements and to make reforms that are broadly acceptable within the particular culture.

There is no 'silver bullet', no single policy that is affordable, politically acceptable and effective. What is required is no less than a comprehensive review and reform of all policies affecting the living standards of families with children. For more detail on the nature of such reviews, see McDonald (2003) and McDonald (2006b).

The review must have leadership at the highest level. It must be a national approach to a national priority. Reform must have the support of the main powerbases in the country including business groups, politicians and women's groups. Reform should be expected to be expensive in fiscal terms. East Asian economies are very ready to invest heavily in advanced economic infrastructure. What is implied here is heavy investment in social infrastructure. Reform can also be expected to involve major reform of work practices. Employers are a vital element of the solution. They must be convinced that it is in their long-term interest to take action now to avert future labour shortages that may destroy their businesses.

Symbolic Meaning is Important

Policy is not only about real benefits; it is also about the symbolic meaning of benefits.

> These policies also exert an effect through their symbolic meaning. The lack of childcare services, low benefit levels, long parental or care leaves, and gender-segregating policies signal to women that it might be difficult, if not impossible, to combine employment and motherhood. (Neyer 2006: p. 16)

The Final Word

Policy reform is likely

> to be confronting to existing social norms and values and to have potentially major implications for economic relations especially the conditions and costs of employment. These are major obstacles and so it is not surprising that governments have been slow to act. While there is no change, children become scarcer and the society becomes less child-oriented. Young people then become more convinced in their perception that they will be severely penalised (relative to others) if they have children, and that the government has little or no interest in their predicament. (McDonald 2007: p. 27)

The longer reform is delayed, the more intractable the problem becomes.

Note

From *The Japanese Journal of Population*, Vol. 6, No. 1, pp. 19–23, 2008, http://www.ipss.go.jp/webj-ad/webjournal.files/population/ps08_04.html, by permission of the National Institute of Population and Social Security Research and the author.

References

Lutz, W., Skirbekk, V. and Testa, M. 2006. 'The low fertility trap hypothesis; forces that may lead to further postponement and fewer births in Europe', *Vienna Yearbook of Population Research 2006*: 167–92.

McDonald, P. 2000. 'Gender equity, social institutions and the future of fertility', *Journal of Population Research* 17(1): 1–16.

McDonald, P. 2003. 'Reforming family support policy in Australia', *People and Place* 11(2): 1–15.

McDonald, P. 2006a. 'Low fertility and the state; the efficacy of policy', *Population and Development Review* 32(3).

McDonald, P. 2006b. 'An assessment of policies that support having children from the perspectives of equity, efficiency and efficacy', *Vienna Demographic Yearbook 2006*: 213–34.

McDonald, P. 2007. 'Low fertility and policy', *Ageing Horizons* 7: 23–8.

McDonald, P. and Temple, J. 2006. *Immigration and the Supply of Complex Problem Solvers in the Australian Economy*, Canberra: Australian Government, Department of Immigration and Multicultural Affairs.

Neyer, G. 2006. Family policies and fertility in Europe: Fertility policies at the intersection of gender policies, employment policies and care policies, MPIDR Working Paper WP 2006-010, Rostock: Max Planck Institute for Demographic Research.

Ogawa, N., Kondo, M. and Matsukura, R. 2005. 'Japan's transition from the demographic bonus to the demographic onus', *Asian Population Studies* 1(2): 207–26.

Shirahase, S. 2000. 'Women's increased higher education and the declining fertility rate in Japan', *Review of Population and Social Policy* 9: 47–64.

Suzuki, T. 2006. 'Lowest-low fertility and governmental actions in Japan', National Institute of Population and Social Security Research, Tokyo.

Migration, Minorities and Welfare States

Carl-Ulrik Schierup and Stephen Castles

Our central theme in this chapter is the ways in which immigration and the formation of new minorities have been linked with changes in welfare states. Our focus is on western Europe, although we also pay attention to strong influences from the United States. We argue that European welfare states helped set the conditions under which migration and minority formation took place from the 1950s to the 1970s. From the 1980s, the ascendancy of neoliberalism brought about major changes in welfare states, and migrants and minorities often bore the brunt of such changes. But our argument goes further: the existence of sizable, often marginalized minorities arising from recent immigration was a crucial factor in neoliberal reforms. The differentiation of populations on the basis of ethnicity, origins, and legal status – which we call 'racialized ethnicity' – has been crucial in the shift away from welfare universalism and social redistribution. Racialized ethnicity has complemented hierarchies based on gender, class, and location in the neoliberalization (or neo-Americanization) of European societies.

Within Europe, national situations and political approaches vary considerably. In each country, differing historical experiences of class struggle, territorial expansion, and colonialism have shaped welfare ideologies and policies. These differences have been important factors in shaping the ways in which migrants and minorities have become incorporated into societies. Yet all of these approaches are exposed to change through neoliberal practices such as trade liberalization, as well as through trends toward the Europeanization of economic and social policies. The transformation has been accompanied by Islamophobia, populist political movements centred on the 'problem of immigration', a growing preoccupation with 'terrorism', and the accelerated securitization of migration and asylum policies (Bigo, 2002).

These trends are matched by the increasing radicalism of social and political movements among immigrants and their descendants. Grievances over social exclusion and stigmatization in terms of race, culture, ethnicity, and religion merge in violent urban uprisings, such as those that occurred in northern British towns in 2001, in Paris and across France in 2005 and 2007, and in Copenhagen and elsewhere in Denmark in 2008. These urban rebellions were no less dramatic than the Los Angeles uprising in 1992, which gave momentum to the neoliberal turn in US politics and paved the way for increasingly brutalized approaches to the governance of welfare and race (see Schierup et al., 2006).

[. . .]

Migration and European Labour Force Dynamics Since 1945: An Overview

During western Europe's postwar economic boom, migrant workers played a vital part in economic growth, but most were not expected to stay permanently or make welfare claims. After the 1973 oil crisis, however, many so-called guest workers in fact stayed on, and were joined by spouses and children. They began to access social infrastructure (like schools, health services, and housing) and to claim benefits for unemployment, illness, and disability. Then, in the 1990s, Europe experienced new inflows of refugees, asylum seekers, highly skilled personnel, manual workers, and family members. Populations grew more diverse and welfare needs became more differentiated – and more pressing. The relationship between migration and welfare can be understood through an analysis of these phases in the development of European political economy (Schierup et al., 2006: 140–146).

The first phase of the post-1945 accumulation strategy of capital was to concéntrate capital investment in the existing core industrial areas and recruit additional labour in order to keep production costs from rising sharply. New labour resources included rural-urban migration, the increasing employment of women, and the recruitment of migrant workers from peripheral areas (including southern Europe, North Africa, and Mexico). This phase was also marked by Keynesian approaches to welfare capitalism. Typical of this model was mass production in large factories where manual workers were concentrated, facilitating strong unions. Trade unions were able to negotiate better wages and conditions, while social-democratic parties could introduce welfare state provisions to protect workers and their families. Many migrant workers were employed in unionized factories and enjoyed the benefits of good wages and strong welfare provisions.

In the 1970s, economic recession and growing competition from new industrial economies led to a second phase in which labour-intensive production was moved to low-wage economies, while migrant-labour recruitment was stopped. The new accumulation strategy was based on the creation of a global labour market, through which specific production stages could be sited wherever they could be carried out at the lowest possible cost. Neoliberal approaches in the old industrial countries included the squeezing out of skilled blue-collar workers, economic deregulation, and reduction of the public sector. The new strategy led to the closure of many rust-belt factories with their strong unions. Domestic economic restructuring was pushed forward by the rightist governments of the Reagan/Thatcher era of the 1980s, leading to a rollback in workers' rights. Many migrant workers were pushed out of regular employment; some got insecure, casualized jobs, while others set up marginal small businesses or became dependent on welfare benefits.

The very success of neoliberal globalization led to a third phase beginning in 1995, in which demand for labour in Europe grew due to a combination of demographic, economic, and social factors (Castles, 2006; CEC, 2004; Münz et al., 2007). At the same time, globalization encouraged the migration of both highly skilled and less skilled workers from less developed areas of Africa, Asia, and Latin America. Migrant workers entered European labour markets at all levels: as highly paid and privileged specialists; as regular workers in manufacturing, building, and services; and as irregular workers in exploitative jobs.

By 2005, foreign-born workers made up 25 per cent of the labour force in Switzerland, 20 per cent in Austria and Germany, and around 12 per cent in other western European countries (OECD, 2007a: 63–66). In Belgium, Luxembourg, Sweden, and Denmark, more than 40 per cent of the employed migrants who arrived from 1995 to 2005 had tertiary education. In many cases, migrant workers had higher qualification profiles than local-born workers. Only in southern European countries did low-skilled labour migration predominate (OECD, 2007a: 67–68). Nevertheless, migrants remained important to employers for low-skilled jobs, even in western Europe. Segmentation based on race, ethnicity, gender, and national origin has been a feature of European labour markets ever since the post-1945 reconstruction boom. For workers in general, formal employment within large-scale enterprises has in many cases been replaced by work arrangements that differentiate and separate them. Those who comprise the disadvantaged groups – migrant women, irregular workers, ethnic and racial minorities – end up in the most precarious positions. A labour market based on deprivation of human and workers' rights for vulnerable groups is obviously incompatible with a strong, redistributive welfare state. The new economy is contingent on a new welfare state that disciplines the workforce while legitimating inequality and impoverishment. This has been achieved through the racialization and social stigmatization of difference.

Welfare, Citizenship, and the Challenge of Social Exclusion

Until the early 1970s, labour migrants in the industrial metropolitan countries of western Europe were expected to work and pay taxes but not to make long-term claims on educational systems, welfare institutions and services. However, as already noted, many of these early migrants did stay on to form new minority communities, and they were soon joined by many more migrants from all over the world. Such groups followed similar trajectories of family reunion, settlement, and simultaneous marginalization and minority formation. Welfare planners had to face up to emergent new forms of impoverishment and exclusion as well as their disruptive consequences, such as marginalization, urban polarization, racism, and social conflict.

Colonial migrants in the United Kingdom, France, and the Netherlands were automatically incorporated into national welfare systems, while full social rights were also extended to migrant workers in Scandinavian countries. By contrast, the guest worker-recruiting countries (which included not only Germany, Switzerland, and Austria but also Belgium and the Netherlands for many workers) did not expect migrants to become social citizens. Germany, for instance, set up a special welfare regime based on the subsidization of charities in order to limit migrant use of mainstream benefits and services.

After the recruitment stop of 1973–1974, the ineffectiveness of special welfare approaches became clear. Migrant workers had been concentrated in those parts of the labour market most severely hit by restructuring and unemployment. Now many were unemployed or were forced out of the workforce, often following work-related accidents or illness. Yet the very universalism of most western European welfare regimes meant that immigrants could not, in the long run, be excluded from substantial rights of social citizenship (Guiraudon, 2000; Ryner, 2000). They were gradually incorporated as 'denizens' – long-term residents who obtained many of the formal rights associated with citizenship (Hammar, 1985) – or as full citizens. This trend was reinforced by employers' demands for the stabilization of large sections of the migrant labour force who were indispensable in filling the low-grade positions that local workers found unattractive.

Some liberal scholars have suggested that the long-term convergence of citizenship rights for immigrants and natives in Western societies is likely to continue (see Bauböck et al., 1996; Joppke, 1999). This positive expectation appears to be confirmed by the granting of citizenship rights to long-standing immigrants in northwestern Europe. The revised German Citizenship Law, which came into force in 2000, is an important example. However, in the United Kingdom, minorities are political citizens, but this does not necessarily confer social equality. In southern Europe, migrants remain non-citizens; even when they do obtain legal residence status, strong welfare rights are not guaranteed.

Trends toward the inclusion of migrants in the context of formal rights contrast with real economic and social exclusion. Throughout Europe, there are new categories of working poor – that is, people in employment but with wages too low to lift them out of poverty – among immigrants and new ethnic minorities. Multiple modes of racialized exclusion cluster together. Chronic social disadvantage and so-called welfare dependency are potential 'incubators' of a workforce whose jobs are 'precarious and underpaid and systematically performed by women, immigrants, and disadvantaged minorities' (Mingione, 1996: 382). The growth of low-paid, casual, and precarious jobs, in turn, puts pressure on welfare institutions. This situation can readily be exploited to support political programmes for dismantling the function of social citizenship as a sanctuary for the vulnerable from market forces.

Governments strive to meet employers' demands for cheap and flexible labour even as they seek to appease the anti-immigrant populism of some politicians and sections of the media. The resolution of this ambivalence is found in new discriminatory employment practices, ostensibly designed to avoid the errors of earlier labour migration policies that allowed migrants to settle and eventually achieve denizenship or citizenship. Such practices include short-term contract worker systems, 'circular' migration, international subcontracting relationships, and irregular labour migration. Highly restrictive refugee and asylum policies are part of the effort to placate anti-immigrant populism. Such measures have forced many refugees to join the most submerged segments of the clandestine labour force in the informal economy. Thus the boundaries between asylum seekers and illegal migrants are becoming increasingly blurred.

This new labour force segmentation further jeopardizes the already fragile relationship between ethnic minorities and the welfare state (Ryner, 2000). Given their particularly vulnerable position in the labour market, stabilized sections of the migrant and ethnic minority populations have had strong reasons to look toward the welfare state as a safety net. But as social citizenship deteriorates, ethnic minorities find themselves in a situation increasingly similar to that of temporary contract workers, clandestine migrants, or new and marginalized refugee groups. Ethnic minorities can no longer rely on the relatively newly acquired rights of social citizenship and are thus forced to watch as their access to the labour market, affected by deregulation and informalization, decreases (Slavnic, 2010).

They become part of the new working poor, as, at one and the same time, victims of the welfare state crisis and agents for the informalization of the labour market and the economy.

North Atlantic Perspectives

In the United States, race, ethnicity, and immigration have played a prominent role in ideological and political battles that have brought about a recommodification of labour and the dismantling of welfare programmes. We therefore start our comparison by looking at the case of the United States. This is followed by an examination of three western European cases with contrasting welfare regimes and modes of incorporation for migrants and ethnic minorities: the United Kingdom (the liberal welfare model), Italy (the conservative-corporatist model), and Sweden (the social-democratic model).

[. . .]

The United States

The flexibility of less regulated liberal welfare states has facilitated their fast adaptation to a service-dominated economy (Ellison, 2006). A propensity for market solutions and a low degree of commitment to social citizenship, combined with weak unions and a racially and ethnically fragmented working class, have made the United States particularly disposed toward choosing a 'low road' into post-Fordism (ibid.). A cocktail of neoliberalism, 'welfare chauvinism' (Banting, 2000: 21ff.), restriction of migrants' access to social citizenship, and racial discourses have cemented the function of migrants as a flexible reserve army of labour. This trend has been part and parcel of a wider 'war against labor' (Fox Piven and Cloward, 1993) integral to the strategies of US capital in the 1980s and 1990s (Pinder, 2007).

In the late twentieth century, a shift to globalized services and infor mation technology produced an 'hourglass economy' with two polarized but mutually dependent labour markets (see, e.g., Sassen, 2001): a high-wage sector dominated by financial and information services, corporate management, differentiated product design, and research and development; and a low-wage, precarious, and often informal sector, reliant on outsourced corporate activities and private service providers, as well as on sweatshop manufacturing. The disadvantaged pole of the labour market is mainly staffed by immigrants from Latin America, the Caribbean, Africa, Asia, and Eastern Europe. While experiencing social exclusion along ethnic lines, this disadvantaged group has also undergone 'feminization', with increasing employment of women migrant workers in part-time, low-salaried, insecure, and informal jobs, including domestic services.

During the 1990s alone, more than 12 million immigrants settled in the United States. Immigration has continued in the new millennium with a million or more new settlers per year (Martin et al., 2006: 28ff.). Between 1995 and 2005, more than half the net job creation of 16 million involved persons born abroad (OECD, 2007b: 66). A majority of those who arrive legally are the relatives of US citizens or highly educated professionals for whom employers have expressed special needs. Many immigrants hold temporary visas for study or through temporary-worker programmes; relatively few arrive as refugees. Since 2000, unskilled non-farm workers have become the largest category of temporary contract workers, with almost half a million recruited each year. Approximately a further half million undocumented migrant workers are estimated to settle in the United States per year as well; the total undocumented migrant population is about 12 million (Passel, 2006; Hoefer, 2006; Martin et al., 2006; Martin, 2011).

The North American Free Trade Agreement (NAFTA), established in 1994, has become a mechanism for the provision of cheap labour vital to the economic restructuring process in the United States (Delgado Wise and Márquez Covarrubias, 2007). While most immigrant professionals are recruited from Asian countries, the recruitment of unskilled labour is predominantly targeted at Latin America, especially Mexico. Mexicans make up 60 per cent of all undocumented migrants in the United States. They are concentrated in precarious jobs in agriculture, domestic work, menial services, and industrial production. Mexicans work under conditions of outsourcing, informality, and authoritarian management, beyond the protective cover of trade unions and legislation (Gonzales, 2006; Delgado Wise and Márquez Covarrubias, 2007a; Phillips, 2009). Working conditions have deteriorated since the mid-1980s in terms of hours worked, wage levels, and labour standards (Donato and Massey, 1993).

US migration legislation has contributed to this process of downward development (Donato et al., 2005). The politics of migration became increasingly authoritarian in the 1990s, enhancing the power of clandestine employers and causing a downward trend in wages and working conditions. Negotiations with Mexico since 2001 and prolonged debates in the US Congress on the legalization of undocumented migrants have not succeeded in shifting the status quo (Saucedo and Chretien, 2007). On the contrary, sharpened border controls, deportation measures, and the criminalization of migrants have all acted to increase the insecurity and vulnerability of the undocumented. The situation is worsened by the mushrooming of anti-immigrant organizations and private border guard services, violence perpetrated by far-right groups, and lax policies toward employers regarding the enforcement of labour standards (Smith, 2006).

This situation has led to pessimistic predictions regarding the future of children of migrant working-class parents in a still racist society with a segmented labour market. Such children, argue Alejandro Portes and Rubén Rumbaut (2001), risk 'downward assimilation' from their parents' working-class position into a new, ethnically diverse 'rainbow underclass' that exists outside the labour market altogether. Others (such as Waldinger et al., 2007) contest this prediction, arguing that, unlike the so-called underclass among African Americans (Wilson, 1987), youths in Mexican and other Latin American immigrant groups can rely on the social capital of ethnic and kinship networks to ensure their integration into the US labour market (albeit at fairly low levels).

There are additional reasons for not expecting a replication of a so-called underclass pattern among working-class immigrant groups and their children. Immigrants have always been excluded from central parts of means-tested welfare, and the Clinton administration's Personal Responsibility and Work Opportunity Reconciliation Act of 1996 meant further restrictions on the few benefits available to immigrants (Banting, 2000). This powerful welfare-to-workfare act meant a determined move toward making the welfare-dependent underclass an anachronism altogether, and moved the United States in the direction of an authoritarian workfare state (Fox Piven, 1998: 72). It led, among other things, toward the replacement of unionized workers with cheaper workfare labour (Cooper, 1997) and acted to push the African American unemployed and welfare-dependent 'ghetto poor' into 'a virtually indentured labour force' (Pinder, 2007), bound to compete with poor working-class immigrants.

The United Kingdom

The United Kingdom can be seen as the European society that has most closely followed a neoliberal or 'neo-American' path into post-Fordism and globalization. Under Prime Minister Margaret Thatcher, from 1979 to 1996 the United Kingdom pursued radical policies of economic deregulation, privatization, and restructuring of the welfare system. Such practices were continued after 1997 by the Labour governments of Tony Blair and then Gordon Brown. Deregulation was supposed to support two dynamic factors of a 'new economy': the growth of small and medium-sized businesses, and the motivation for individuals to become active and responsible stakeholders in their own futures. Until the financial crisis of 2008, British leaders promoted the so-called Anglo-Saxon model of neoliberal growth as an example for the rest of Europe. However, the essence of the neoliberal model was growing inequality, as vast rewards were bestowed on bankers, investors, and property speculators while the gap between the wealthy and the bulk of the population increased.

In a comparative study of what he calls the 'illiberal social policy' of liberal regimes in the United States and Britain, Desmond King (1999) demonstrates how an increasing emphasis on the obligations as opposed to the rights of citizenship during the 1980s led to the exclusion of poor population groups from the compact of citizenship in the 1990s. Under New Labour, social exclusion came to be seen as a problem of the underclass, defined, in line with US neoconservative discourse, as a behavioural and moral issue. Workfare-type policies were merged into a general system after 1997 by the Labour government under the labels Jobseeker's Allowance and then the New Deal. The decommodification embodied in the old unemployment benefit system was replaced by individual jobseeker's contracts, which obliged the unemployed, the disabled, and single parents to seek and accept work of any type. If the most vulnerable and exposed were to avoid a future of impoverishment and join the winners, it was their duty to become more flexible, to 'get on their bikes' in search of new opportunities, and not to be bothered about wages or health and safety; employment would ensure that the job escalator would take them upward (Jones and Novak, 1999: 71).

Immigration and ethnic minorities have played a crucial role in legitimating the restructuring of the welfare state. In the 1950s and 1960s, immigration from the New Commonwealth (especially the Caribbean and the Indian subcontinent) provided a crucial labour source for manufacturing industries. With Britain's industrial decline in the 1970s and 1980s, many immigrants and their descendants became unemployed and welfare recipients, while others set up often marginal firms. Problems of social exclusion and impoverishment could be largely redefined as issues of race. Thus immigrants were relabelled as ethnic minorities, and welfare measures were linked to their lifestyles and cultures. The race relations approach that emerged in the late 1960s and the 1970s was based on the management of intergroup relations by the state. It meant recognizing the existence of distinct groups, defined primarily on the basis of race. The acceptance of cultural and religious diversity was officially labelled as multiculturalism. The Race Relations Acts of 1965, 1968, and 1976 outlawed discrimination in public places, employment, and housing. A Commission for Racial Equality (CRE) was set up in 1976. However, there was general agreement among political leaders that integration and 'good race relations' in Britain were possible only on the basis of a restrictive immigration policy. Thus race relations and antidiscrimination acts have been 'inextricably linked' with a series of increasingly restrictive immigration acts (Solomos, 2003: 78).

But the facade of harmonious multiculturalism in the United Kingdom could not hide the reality of racism and social exclusion. Discontent among black youth led to repeated riots in inner-city areas. The government responded with measures to combat youth unemployment, improve education, rehabilitate urban areas, and change police practices. But the Stephen Lawrence Inquiry of 1999, which was set up to analyse the poor police response to the murder of a young black man by a white gang, revealed the continued strength of institutional racism. The situation was further complicated by immigration from new origin areas. Since the mid-1990s, inflows of both asylum seekers and economic migrants have been important both for sustaining economic growth and for developing the perceptions of an external threat that have legitimated the erosion of human rights and the creation of manipulative models of social cohesion.

The general picture in the early twenty-first century is that of a labour force stratified by ethnicity and gender, with a high degree of youth unemployment. On average, people of Indian, Chinese, and Irish background tend to have employment situations as good as or better than those of white British people. By contrast, other groups are worse off, with a descending hierarchy on most indicators of black African, black Caribbean, Pakistani, and, at the very bottom, Bangladeshi groups (Office for National Statistics, 2004). The strong trend toward the casualization of labour has been exacerbated by the deregulation and privatization of public services. Casualization has also extended into producers' services like architecture, banking, and engineering, leading to income polarization within the advanced service sector. Here part-time jobs have proliferated, facilitating the exploitation of a growing pool of female labour in a society with a shortage of public child-care facilities.

Most immigrants in the United Kingdom are British citizens and enjoy full voting rights. Most Commonwealth immigrants already had citizenship when they arrived. It is relatively easy for foreign immigrants to obtain citizenship after five years of legal residence. In the early years of the twenty-first century, the main immigration issue was asylum, while after 2004 concerns about large inflows from new Eastern European member states of the European Union (EU) became prominent. Successive governments introduced five new asylum and immigration laws between 1993 and 2006 that tightened up entry rules and introduced deterrent measures such as detention and restrictions on welfare. Asylum applications declined from 103,000 in 2002 to just 28,000 in 2006. However, by then public attention had shifted to a new issue: the growth of Islam. The London bombings of 7 July 2005, precipitated concern about the loyalty of young Muslims. Government policies shifted to emphasize social cohesion. Citizenship tests for immigrants were introduced, based on ideas of Britishness and core values. A strong contrast remains between the formal equality granted to ethnic minorities and their everyday experience of unemployment, inequality, and social exclusion. The UK experience shows that citizenship and antidiscrimination laws are not necessarily a protection against social disadvantage and racism (Castles and Miller, 2009; Schierup et al., 2006).

Italy

Until the mid-1970s, Italy had a history of large-scale emigration. The combination of rapid economic growth and demographic contraction led to a reversal, as most migrants from non-Organization for Economic Cooperation and Development (OECD) countries entering Italy in the 1980s were undocumented. Since then, several mass legalizations and the tightening of immigration controls related to the Schengen Agreement have modified the situation. Entries of asylum seekers are negligible (reflecting a high rejection rate), while the avenue of family unification, although limited, is on the increase. From 300,000 at the beginning of the 1980s, Italy's legally resident migrant population had increased to more than three million by the mid- to late 2000s. Migrants' residence status is mostly based on temporary labour contracts, so the danger of a (re-)lapse into illegality is constant. The great majority of foreign residents are from Africa, Asia, Latin America, and Central and Eastern Europe. Many have a high educational profile, yet are overwhelmingly employed in 'heavy, precarious, dangerous, poorly paid, and demanding' jobs (Triandafyhllidou and Gropas, 2007: 190). Patterns of employment vary between regions: agricultural labour and domestic services predominate in the south, while industrial employment prevails in the north; in addition, many domestic workers are to be found in cities like Rome and Milan.

Most migrants are *extracommunitari* (extracommunitarians), a term that denotes their origin outside the EU. But it also intimates their non-belonging (Petrillo, 1999) and reflects the nation's prevailing, exclusionary and ethnocultural self-definition (Sciortino, 2004). Immigration continues to be regarded as temporary and there is no explicit policy of integration. Before filing an application for citizenship, non-EU citizens must reside in Italy for as long as ten years. Legally resident foreigners have extended social rights. However, the prevailing practices of local authorities continue to obstruct access to welfare provisions and to ensure a discriminatory application of regulations concerning access to permanent residence and citizenship. The political rights of extracommunitarians are limited to involvement in voluntary associations and trade unions. Italy has not ratified EU clauses on immigrants' political rights (Triandafyhllidou and Gropas, 2007: 193). At the same time, by turning merely 'unauthorized' status at the beginning of the 1980s into a truly criminalized, 'illegal' status, Schengen membership and EU demands have contributed to the increasingly vulnerable social situation of irregular migrants or *clandestini* (see Schierup et al., 2006). A precarious situation in Italian society for regular as well as irregular migrants has been exacerbated by the rise of populist parties within ruling centre-right governments and the proliferation of media stereotypes of migrants as criminal outsiders.

Yet immigration has been essential to the development of the Italian economy and society for almost three decades (Ginsborg, 2001; Schierup et al., 2006). With the increasing exhaustion of the reserves of low-skilled labour in the Italian countryside, labour-intensive strategies for overcoming the Fordist crisis after 1980 have constantly been at loggerheads with the conservative welfare system and an industrial relations compact geared toward strict regulation of the formal sector, leaving no room for flexibility in employment contracts. In this context, immigrants have functioned as a cheap and flexible reserve army of labour. The 'second (post-Fordist) economic miracle' is a catchword for Italy's successful reorientation toward flexible industrial specialization of small and medium-sized enterprises, producing high-quality specialized goods for the world market. The exploitation of cheap, most often informal, immigrant labour functioned as a source of 'primitive accumulation', important for the takeoff of such enterprises. Today immigrants are an indispensable part of their regular industrial labour force.

Another important area for immigrant labour is domestic service. The educational achievements of a growing number of Italian women and their employment in professional jobs in public and private services has exposed the structural shortcomings of a conservative (male) 'breadwinner' welfare model. The virtual absence of publicly organized care has meant that the chief coping strategy for two-career professional households has become the employment of immigrant women as live-in maids and caretakers for elderly family members. Yet, because Italy has the lowest birth rate in Europe, it faces a looming demographic crisis. The industrial relations compact – which until recently outlawed part-time employment and other modes of labour market flexibilization, together with a lack of publicly organized care and an inflexible gender division of labour – has placed professional women in a quandary between career and having children (Andall, 2003; Trifiletti, 1999).

Both labour shortages and the demographic crisis are, however, relative. The female employment rate remains comparatively low and youth unemployment high. Barriers to the formal labour market are high, although young Italians can still afford to be selective in terms of the kind of jobs they will accept. Transfers of high wages or pensions to households and persistent norms of redistribution to family and wider kin still allow Italian youth to reject 'immigrant jobs'. However, as a response to EU directives and an accord between employers and unions, greater openings for part-time and temporary employment have been created. This has entailed a certain transfer of immigrant employment from informal work to formal, so-called atypical, jobs. Although the conservative welfare system continues to offer Italians alternative sources of sustenance and although Italy is still a far cry from adopting anything like the 'work first' imperative in the United States, the current configuration of differential access to decent work may exacerbate the competition between immigrants and Italians in parts of the labour market and fuel an already virulent anti-immigrant populism.

Sweden

The so-called Swedish model has been portrayed as the quintessence of the social-democratic welfare regime (Esping-Andersen, 1990) and its trajectory into post-Fordism. For decades, Sweden has enjoyed a reputation for devising an inclusive migrant-incorporation policy, recognizing the ethnically diverse character of its society, and granting voting rights to foreign citizens. Residence is, alongside birth, an unconditional criterion for access to citizenship, social rights, and the welfare system, as well as equity concerning employment (Sainsbury, 2006) – a criterion devoid of 'ethnic' conditions.

By 1972, the labour unions had largely succeeded in blocking Sweden's extensive post-World War II recruitment of migrant labour. They were able to sustain their veto on any attempt to reintroduce import of labour until 2008. Along with family reunion, refugees have long been the main source of immigration. However, a formerly solidaristic refugee policy has become increasingly restrictive following Sweden's participation in the Schengen Agreement in 2001. Yet substantial numbers of applicants (especially Iraqis) still receive asylum for humanitarian reasons at the time of this writing in 2011. Foreign-born residents and their children make up more than a fifth of a Swedish population of 9 million. Given that Sweden offers easy access to citizenship and has one of Europe's highest naturalization rates, most immigrants hold Swedish or dual citizenship. Only a quarter of the foreign-born remain foreign citizens. Until the late 1970s, immigrants from the other Nordic countries (in particular Finland) were still most numerous, but today immigrants from Asia, Africa, and Eastern Europe are the great majority.

The extensive Swedish welfare system, which reached its peak in the late 1970s, remains effective and is supported widely beyond the Social Democratic Party's core constituency. The welfare state's social basis and public legitimacy were strengthened by the incorporation of women into the labour market during the 1960s and 1970s. Women's equitable inclusion in the welfare system and the comprehensive public social service system, which substitutes for domestic care work, are distinctive elements of the Swedish model. During the same period, immigrant workers were incorporated on formally equal terms, but in fact exploited as a reserve army of expendable labour used to manage the peaks and troughs of the economic cycle. Immigrants were to be found in jobs rejected by an upwardly mobile, native working class, and often exposed to discrimination, as an unequal ethnic division of labour emerged (Persson, 1972; Ålund, 1985; Schierup and Paulson, 1994).

Yet immigrants also enjoyed a relatively high degree of social security and material welfare in a society where union power, the equalizing institutions of a large welfare state, and an active labour market policy continued to mitigate the effects of the ethnic division of labour on income differentials, at least until the early 1990s. It was then that the situation changed due to a deep economic recession, during which the ruling Social Democrats sacrificed the full employment regime upon which the postwar Swedish model had rested. Immigrants became the prime victims in terms of their overwhelming overrepresentation among the echelons of the new long-term unemployed. Politically, 'welfare dependency' among immigrants and their children became a central concern.

The racialized poverty associated with neoliberal flexibility regimes and the casualization of low-salaried jobs is still much more limited in Sweden than it is in the United Kingdom. Yet substantial groups find themselves not only outside the ordinary labour market but also excluded from unemployment insurance. Given its traditional priorities – the implementation of an active labour market policy and the upgrading of skills – Sweden's welfare regime was simply not geared to cope with large-scale and long-term unemployment. The active labour market policy of the post-World War II Swedish model was the baseline for a decommodification of labour, aimed at eliminating low-wage occupational ghettos. Its increasingly neoliberal character since 1990 has come to underpin a disciplinary adaptation toward a marginalized reserve army exposed to the market discipline of precarious low-wage niches, and increasingly reminiscent of a US-style workfare regime (Junestav, 2004). A growing number of migrants and ethnic-minority Swedes have been pushed from the centre to the periphery of the welfare system, into the casualized labour market and a degraded informal sector.

However, in contrast to the experiences of the United States, Italy, and Britain, the exploitation of irregular migrants has, so far, not had a key role in the restructuring of the Swedish labour market. Until 2000, irregular migration to Sweden and undocumented migrant workers were almost unknown. This was due to a still extraordinarily high level of labour unionization, even in small workplaces, which limited employment opportunities for undocumented workers (Hjarnø, 2003). At the end of the 2000s, the number of undocumented workers was estimated at around 50,000 – still negligible compared to most other European countries. Strong union insistence on adherence to Swedish collective agreements also continues to limit the potential impact of posted workers from the new low-wage member states of the EU, in terms of wage depression and the deterioration of labour standards.

However, in the late 2000s, the European Court of Justice ruled against established modes of trade union action, thus presenting a serious threat to Swedish labour unions. Moreover, since 2006, the centre-right government has dismantled cornerstones of the welfare edifice and squeezed growing numbers of low-wage workers out of the unions. Higher unemployment and health insurance charges are likely to exacerbate these trends. In short, organized labour saw its protective capacities significantly reduced in the 2000s, and migrants as well as other groups outside the core protected labour market are feeling the consequences in the forms of greater insecurity and the deterioration of employment conditions.

Certainly a countertrend to labour depreciation is considerable social mobility among Sweden's ethnic minorities, marked by the ascent of some to leading positions in business, public administration, politics, academia, and the media. Another important trend since the mid-1990s is the defeat of traditional, concerted opposition on the part of employers and unions to antidiscrimination legislation, forms of which have since been adopted following EU directives. Yet these are being implemented alongside the gradual demise of both the protective framework of social citizenship and the unique, active labour market policy that constituted the very linchpin of the universalist Swedish model and its powerful decommodification of labour.

[. . .]

Since the late 1990s, Sweden has introduced new discourses, legislation, and practices of diversity and antidiscrimination that closely match the US matrix on which they are modelled. However, given a parallel neoliberal twist to economics, welfare and labour market regulation, antidiscrimination legislation, and diversity management have come to operate under social circumstances that, step by step, are becoming more similar to structurally grounded forms of poverty and racialized exclusion in liberal welfare states like the United States or the United Kingdom (Schierup et al., 2006).

Our account is not to be read as implying that the road now lies open for the smooth liquidation of the Swedish welfare state or any of the other welfare states in the EU, or, for that matter, that the wholesale importation of the US model is just around the corner. Although there are strong currents of convergence toward overall neoliberal hegemony, the European cases discussed indicate how, compared with the United States, development in the EU's major immigration countries is still highly path-dependent. Europe's historical plurality of policies and regimes of citizenship has not come to an end. Nor has there been an EU-European common voice on the increasingly complex and controversial contemporary issues of social welfare and migration.

Yet an emergent EU regime, which is in many aspects modelled on neo-US policies, represents a common conditionality to which the member states are bound to adapt, and migration is becoming one of the EU's most pertinent policy areas. Following the Amsterdam Treaty of 1997, an impressive EU reform agenda was developed, as shown by a plethora of new initiatives that were often patterned on US models. A manifest anti-discrimination orientation was turned into mandatory directives and pro-grammes, which require member states to combat discrimination and social exclusion. Overall, EU policies also seem to be becoming increasingly parallel to those of the United States in terms of propagation of temporary worker schemes, the criminalization of undocumented immigration, the securitization of migration, and the dismantling of formerly humanistic norms and practices concerning asylum (Schierup et al., 2006).

But the US case shows clearly that antidiscrimination, equal opportunities, affirmative action, and diversity management policies are limited in scope, as long as the wider political economy continues to be oriented toward the recommodification of labour. An increasingly unequal ethnic division of labour, discriminatory migration management, and unequal access to civil, political, and social rights are not compatible with measures for the social inclusion of migrants and minorities. This ambiguity also applies to a European Union that continues to pivot uneasily around a central contradiction between economic and political goals (Chamberlayne, 1997; Williams, 1991), and between adjustment to the economic imperatives of global capitalism and the task of generating a new European identity based on a powerful notion of citizenship.

Note

References

Ålund, A. (1985), *Skyddsmurar: Etnicitet och klass in invandranammanhang* (Stockholm: Liber).
Andall, J. (2003), 'Hierarchy and Interdependence: The Emergence of a Service Caste in Europe', in Andall, J. (ed.), *Gender and Ethnicity in Contemporary Europe* (Oxford and New York: Berg), pp. 39–60.
Banting, K. G. (2000), 'Looking in Three Directions: Migration and the European Welfare State in Comparative Perspective', in Bommes, M. and Geddes, A. (eds.), *Immigration and Welfare: Challenging the Borders of the Welfare State* (London and New York: Routledge), 13–33.
Bauböck, R., Heller, A. and Zolberg, A. R. (eds.) (1996), *The Challenge of Diversity: Integration and Pluralism in Societies of Immigration* (Aldershot, UK: Avebury).

Bigo, D. (2002), 'Security and Immigration: Toward a Critique of the Governmentality of Unease', *Alternatives* 27 (11): 63–92.

Castles, S. (2006), 'Guestworkers in Europe: A Resurrection?' *International Migration Review* 40 (4): 741–66.

Castles, S. and Miller, M. J. (2009), *The Age of Migration: International Population Movements in the Modern World*, 4th ed. (Basingstoke, UK: Palgrave).

CEC (Commission of the European Communities) (2004), *Green Paper: A Common Approach to Managing Economic Migration*, COM(2004)811 final, Brussels.

Chamberlayne, P. (1997), 'Social Exclusion: Sociological Traditions and National Contexts', Sostris Working Paper 1, Centre for Biography in Social Policy, University of East London.

Cooper, M. (1997), 'When Push Comes to Shove: Who Is Welfare Reform Really Helping?,' *The Nation*, 2 June.

Delgado Wise, R. and Márquez Covarrubias, H. (2007), 'The Reshaping of Mexican Labor Exports Under NAFTA: Paradoxes and Challenges', *International Migration Review* 41 (3): 656–79.

Donato, K. M. and Massey, D. S. (1993), 'Effect of the Immigration Reform and Control Act on the Wages of Mexican Migrants', *Social Science Quarterly* 74 (3): 523–41.

Donato, K. M., Aguilera, M. and Wakabayashi, C. (2005), 'Immigration Policy and Employment Conditions of US Immigrants from Mexico, Nicaragua, and the Dominican Republic', *International Migration* 43 (5): 5–29.

Esping-Andersen, G. (1990), *The Three Worlds of Welfare Capitalism* (Cambridge: Polity Press).

Fox Piven, F. (1998), 'Welfare and Work', *Social Justice* 25 (1): 67–81.

Fox Piven, F. and Cloward, R. A. (1993), *Regulating the Poor: The Functions of Public Welfare* (New York: Vintage Books).

Ginsborg, P. (2001), *Italy and Its Discontents 1980–2001* (Allen Lane: Penguin Books).

Gonzales, G. G. (2006), *Guest Workers or Colonized Labor? Mexican Labor Migration to the United States* (Boulder, CO: Paradigm Publishers).

Guiraudon, V. (2000), 'The Marshallian Triptych Reordered: The Role of Courts and Bureaucracies in Furthering Migrants' Social Rights', in Bommes, M. and Geddes, A. (eds.), *Immigration and Welfare. Challenging the Borders of the Welfare State* (London: Routledge), pp. 72–89.

Hammar, T. (ed.) (1985), *European Immigration Policy: A Comparative Study* (Cambridge: Cambridge University Press).

Hjarnø, J. (2003), *Illegal Immigrants and Developments in Employment in the Labour Markets of the EU* (Aldershot, UK: Ashgate).

Hoefer, M., Rytina, N. and Campbell, C. (2006), 'Estimates of the Unauthorized Immigrant Population Residing in the United States: January 2005', Department of Homeland Security, Office of Immigration Statistics.

Jones, C. and Novak, T. (1999), *Poverty, Welfare, and the Disciplinary State* (London: Routledge).

Joppke, C. (1999), 'How Immigration Is Changing Citizenship: A Comparative View', *Ethnic and Racial Studies* 22 (4): 629–52.

Junestav, M. (2004), 'Arbetslinjer i svensk socialpolitisk debatt och lagstiftning 1930–2001', mimeo, Department of Economic History, Uppsala University, Sweden.

King, D. (1999), *In the Name of Liberalism: Illiberal Social Policy in the United States and Britain* (Oxford: Oxford University Press).

Martin, P. L., Abella, M. and Kuptsch, C. (2006), *Managing Labor Migration in the Twenty-first Century* (New Haven, CT: Yale University Press).

Martin, P. L., Martin, S. F. and Weil, P. (2006), *Managing Migration: The Promise of Cooperation* (Lanham, MD: Lexington Books).

Martin, S. (2011), 'Immigration Reform in the United States', in Phillips, N. (ed.), *Migration in the Global Political Economy* (Boulder, CO: Lynne Rienner Publishers), pp. 209–30.

Mingione, E. (1996), 'Conclusion', in Mingione, E. (ed.), *Urban Poverty and the Underclass: A Reader* (Oxford: Blackwell), pp. 372–83.

Münz, R., Straubhaar, T., Vadean, F. and Vadean, N. (2007), 'What Are the Migrants' Contributions to Employment and Growth? A European Approach', HWWI Policy Papers 3-3, Hamburg Institute of International Economics.

OECD (Organization for Economic Cooperation and Development) (2007a), *Policy Coherence for Development: Migration and Developing Countries* (Paris: OECD).

OECD (Organization for Economic Cooperation and Development) (2007b), *International Migration Outlook: Annual Report 2007* (Paris: OECD).

Office for National Statistics (2004), 'Focus on Ethnicity and Identity', http://www.statistics.gov.uk.

Passel, J. S. (2006), *The Size and Characteristics of the Unauthorized Migrant Population in the U.S.: Estimates Based on the March 2005 Current Population Survey*, Pew Hispanic Center, Washington, DC, http://pewhispanic.org.

Persson, G. (1972), 'Invandrarna och arbetarklassen i Sverige', *Zenit* 27.

Petrillo, A. (1999), 'Italy: Farewell to the "Bel Paese"', in Cote, M. and Dale, G. (eds.), *The European Union and Migrant Labour* (Oxford: Berg), pp. 231–64.

Phillips, N. (2009), 'Migration as Development Strategy? The New Political Economy of Dispossession and Inequality in the Americas', *Review of International Political Economy* 16 (2): 231–59.

Pinder, S. O. (2007), *From Welfare to Workfare: How Capitalist States Create a Pool of Unskilled Cheap Labour (A Marxist-Feminist Social Analysis)* (Lewiston, Queenston, Lampeter: Edwin Mellen Press).

Portes, A. and Rumbaut, R. E. (2001), *Legacies: The Story of the Immigrant Second Generation* (Berkeley: University of California Press).

Ryner, M. (2000), 'European Welfare State Transformation and Migration', in Bommes, M. and Geddes, A. (eds.), *Immigration and Welfare: Challenging the Borders of the Welfare State* (London: Routledge), pp. 51–70.

Sainsbury, D. (2006), 'Immigrants' Social Rights in Comparative Perspective: Welfare Regimes, Forms in Immigration, and Immigration Policy Regimes', *Journal of European Social Policy* 16 (229): 229–43.

Sassen, S. (2001), *The Global City: New York, London, Tokyo*, 2nd ed. (Princeton: Princeton University Press).

Saucedo, R. and Chretien, T. (2007), 'Legalization, Not Guest Worker Programs, Is the Solution: The New Challenges Facing the Immigrant Rights Movement', *Counterpunch*, 6 July.

Schierup, C.-U., Hansen, P. and Castles, S. (2006), *Migration, Citizenship, and the European Welfare State: A European Dilemma* (Oxford: Oxford University Press).

Schierup, C.-U. and Paulson, S. (1994), *Arbetets etniska delning: Studier från en svensk bilfabrik* (Stockholm: Carlssons).

Sciortino, G. (2004), 'Immigration in a Mediterranean Welfare State: The Italian Experience in Comparative Perspective', *Journal of Comparative Policy Analysis* 6 (2): 111–29.

Slavnic, Z. (2010), 'The Political Economy of Informalization', *European Societies* 12 (1): 3–23.

Smith, J. (2006), 'Guatemala: Economic Migrants Replace Political Refugees', Migration Information Source, April.

Solomos, J. (2003), *Race and Racism in Britain* (Basingstoke, UK: Palgrave).

Triandafyhllidou, A. and Gropas, R. (2007), *European Immigration: A Sourcebook* (Aldershot, UK: Ashgate).

Trifiletti, R. (1999), 'Women's Labour Market Participation and the Reconciliation of Work and Family Life in Italy', in den Dulk, L., van Doorne-Huiskes, A. and Schippers, J. (eds.), *Work-Family Arrangements in Europe* (Amsterdam: Thela-Thesis).

Waldinger, R., Lim, N. and Cort, D. (2007), 'Bad Jobs, Good Jobs, No Jobs? The Employment Experience of the Mexican-American Second Generation', *Journal of Ethnic and Migration Studies* 33 (1): 1–35.

Williams, A. (1991), *The European Community* (Oxford: Blackwell).

Wilson, W. J. (1987), *The Truly Disadvantaged: The Inner City, the Underclass, and Public Policy* (Chicago: University of Chicago Press).

The Politics of the New Social Policies: Providing Coverage against New Social Risks in Mature Welfare States

Giuliano Bonoli

[. . .]

What are New Social Risks?

The concept of new social risks (NSRs) is being used with increasing frequency in the literature on the welfare state (Esping-Andersen, 1999a; Hemerijck, 2002; Jenson, 2002; Taylor-Gooby, 2004). However, a precise definition of what is considered under this label is generally missing. Generally speaking, NSRs are related to the socioeconomic transformations that have brought post-industrial societies into existence: the tertiarization of employment and the massive entry of women into the labour force. New social risks, as they are understood here, include the following.

Reconciling Work and Family Life

The massive entry of women into the labour market has meant that the standard division of labour within families that was typical of the *trente glorieuses* or the golden age of welfare capitalism (1945–75) has collapsed. The domestic and childcare work that used to be performed on an unpaid basis by housewives now needs to be externalized. It can be either obtained from the state or bought on the market. The difficulties faced by families in this respect (but most significantly by women) are a major source of frustration and can result in important losses of welfare, for example if a parent reduces working hours because of the unavailability of adequate childcare facilities. As a result, the problem of reconciling work and family life can be labelled as a social risk.

Single Parenthood

Changes in family structures and behaviour have resulted in increased rates of single parenthood across Organization for Economic Cooperation and Development (OECD) countries, which presents a distinctive set of social policy problems (access to an adequate income, child care, relationship between parenthood and work). More generally, it is obvious that difficulties in reconciling work and family life are more serious for single parents than they are for two-parent households.

Having a Frail Relative

As in the case of children, during the *trente glorieuses* care for frail elderly or disabled people was mostly provided by non-employed women on an unpaid, informal basis. Again, with the change in women's patterns of labour market participation, this task needs to be externalized too. The inability to do so (because of lack of services) may also result in important welfare losses.

Possessing Low or Obsolete Skills

Low-skilled individuals have obviously always existed. However, during the postwar years, low-skilled workers were predominantly employed in manufacturing industry. They were able to benefit from productivity increases due to technological advances, so that their wages rose together with those of the rest of the population. The strong mobilizing capacity of the trade unions among industrial workers further sustained their wages, which came to constitute the guarantee of a poverty-free existence. Today, low-skilled individuals are mostly employed in the low value-added service sector or unemployed. Low value-added services such as retail sales, cleaning, catering and so forth are known for providing very little scope for productivity increases (Pierson, 1998). In countries where wage determination is essentially based on market mechanisms, this means that low-skilled individuals are seriously exposed to the risk of being paid a poverty wage (US, UK, Switzerland). The situation is different in countries where wage determination, especially at the lower end of the distribution, is controlled by governments (through generous minimum wage legislation) or by the social partners (through encompassing collective agreements). Under these circumstances, the wages of low-skilled workers are protected, but job creation in these sectors is limited, so that many low-skilled individuals are in fact unemployed (Iversen and Wren, 1998). Overall, the fact of possessing low or obsolete skills today entails a major risk of welfare loss, considerably higher than in the postwar years.

Insufficient Social Security Coverage

The shift to a post-industrial employment structure has resulted in the presence in modern labour markets of career profiles that are very different from that of the standard male workers of the *trente glorieuses*, characterized by full-time continuous employment from an early age and with a steadily rising salary. Yet the social security schemes (most notably pensions) that we have inherited from the postwar years are still clearly based on these traditional assumptions regarding labour market participation. Pension coverage, in most Western European countries, is optimal for workers who spend their entire working life in full-time employment. Part-time work usually results in reduced pension entitlements, as do career interruptions due to childbearing (Bonoli, 2003). The result of the presence of these new career profiles in the labour market may be, if pension systems are not adapted, the translation of the labour market and working poor problems of today into a poverty problem for older people in thirty or forty years' time. From an individual point of view, following an 'atypical' career pattern represents a risk of insufficient social security coverage, and hence a loss of welfare.

These situations are caused by different factors, but have a number of things in common. First they are all 'new', in the sense that they are typical of the post-industrial societies in which we live today. During the *trente glorieuses*, the period of male full employment and sustained economic growth that characterized the postwar years, these risks were extremely marginal, if they existed at all. In addition to newness, new social risks share another feature. They tend to be concentrated on the same groups of people, usually younger people, families with small children, or working women. While it is difficult to set clear borders around the section of the population that bears most NSRs, it is clear that the categories mentioned here are largely overlapping, and that it is possible to identify in every post-industrial society a fairly large minority of the population that struggles daily against the consequences of NSRs.

From Risk Exposure to Political Mobilization

It is tempting to see parallels between the groups that today are exposed to NSR and industrial workers whose lives were also shattered by social and economic change centuries ago. In so far as industrial workers are concerned, increased exposure to market risks resulted in what has probably been one of the most sustained and successful instances of political mobilization in modern Western history: the creation of labour movements and social democratic parties. These were able to bring workers' concerns to the centre of the political arena and to force through the adoption of labour market regulations, social insurance schemes and universal services, which tremendously improved their living conditions (Stephens, 1979; Castles, 1982; Korpi, 1983; Esping-Andersen, 1985).

To what extent can we draw a parallel between industrial workers in the early days of capitalism and NSR groups today? And in particular, is there any evidence that the political mechanisms that brought traditional welfare states into existence may be in some way replicated in relation to post-industrial social policies? This section looks at empirical evidence on the potential of political mobilization of NSR groups. It focuses on three key dimensions of mobilization: political participation, representation in key democratic institutions, and the policy preferences of members of NSR-exposed groups.

Participation

The key socio-demographic characteristics of NSR groups outlined above are the fact of being young, of possessing low skills and of being a woman. Two of these factors are also the main predictors of voting turnout across Western democracies, and are associated with lower participation. Age is a particularly strong predictor of political participation. Using survey data for seventeen countries, Norris finds that age is by far the best predictor of voting turnout at the micro-level. On average, turnout for the under-25s is just 55 per cent whereas it reaches 88 per cent for the late middle-aged voters (Norris, 2002). It is not entirely clear if the impact of age on turnout reflects a cohort or a life-cycle effect, however. With regard to the US, Putnam provides evidence that political participation of younger generations does not increase as they become older, suggesting that the link between age and turnout reflects a cohort effect (Putnam, 2000). However, other studies reviewed by Norris support the view that in Western Europe the age gap in voting turnout has remained more or less constant over the last thirty years, suggesting instead a life-cycle effect. From the point of view of this article, however, it is not essential to establish whether it is cohort or position in the life-cycle that determines participation. What matters is that those who today have to confront NSRs are less likely to participate in elections.

After age (and together with income), education is the second best predictor of voting turnout, though its impact varies across countries. Education does not successfully predict political participation in most Western European countries, but does so in the US and in Eastern Europe. Finally, gender used to be a powerful predictor of voting turnout, men being more likely to participate in elections than women, but in recent years this is no longer the case (Norris, 2002).

With the exception of women, NSR groups clearly suffer from a participation gap with regard to the rest of society. It is true that education is a strong predictor of turnout only in countries with big educational inequalities (such as the US) or in former communist countries, and not so in Western European countries, on which our analysis concentrates. However, the pre-eminence of age as a determinant of turnout and the fact that it is a key feature of NSR groups suggests that the capacity of this group to influence policy-making via standard democratic channels is likely to be limited.

Representation

When examining the problem of representation of NSR groups in key democratic institutions, two issues need to be addressed: presence and effective interest representation. Presence refers to whether or not individuals who belong to the social groups that are more exposed to NSRs belong to those institutions. In concrete terms, one needs to find out the extent to which governments, parliaments and labour market-based institutions of representation such as trade unions include among their members women, younger people, low-skilled people and so forth. But presence is arguably not a sufficient condition for effective interest representation. Given the fact that there are no political parties or trade unions that have the explicit function of defending the interests of NSR groups, those who get elected or appointed are unlikely to be under any form of constraint in so far as the interests they represent are concerned. There are reasons to believe the groups exposed to NSR, once elected, will be more sensitive to the demands of other NSR groups, because of empathy or because of the fact that socio-demographically similar people constitute some kind of 'natural' electoral constituency, but, given the absence of clear constraints and accountability relationships between the representatives and the represented, it is difficult to answer this question on a theoretical level, and it probably needs to be settled empirically.

[According to data from Inglehart and Norris (2003), women] are a minority in [most parliaments], although in some Nordic countries they approach 50 per cent of members. In the rest of Western Europe and in the US, however, the proportion of women in Parliament is between a tenth and a third. Women are seldom represented in government cabinets, again with the exception of some Scandinavian countries (Sweden) where they often represent 50 per cent of cabinet seats (Siaroff, 2000, p. 200). Young people do not have a strong presence in Western parliaments either. The average age of parliamentarians is around 50, with some variation (younger parliaments are found in the Nordic countries, older ones in continental Europe).

Turning to trade unions, a crucial institution in the fields of welfare and employment regulation, these are characterized in most countries by the predominance of older men among their members and leadership. There are, however, important country variations. In the Nordic countries and in the UK women are more likely to be union members than male workers. In addition, in these countries the age gap in union membership is virtually non-existent, with similar density rates for younger and older employees. In continental European countries, by contrast, there is a clear gender and age gap in unionization rates. It is here that the bias towards higher density among older male workers is stronger. The picture emerging from these data is one that can be described in terms of underrepresentation of NSR groups in key democratic institutions. Governments, parliaments and trade unions are mostly composed of late-middle-aged men. There are some clear country variations, which, interestingly, go in the same direction. The presence of NSR groups in key representative outfits is stronger in the Nordic countries, and to a lesser extent in the UK. Their parliaments are younger and more feminized, and their labour movements are more feminized and younger than those found in other Western European countries.

But presence is not a sufficient condition for effective interest representation. What matters is how elected NSR groups vote in their parliaments and the positions they defend. The question of whether members of a given social group tend to represent their fellow members when elected to a position of power is one that, in relation to women, has intrigued feminist political science for several decades.

There is a large corpus of literature on the voting behaviour of women MPs, on their political attitudes, and on their political activities in general. Overall, the message that one gets from this literature is that the presence of women in Parliament matters for decisions on issues that are of particular concern to women, such as childcare policy or equal opportunities (Norris and Lovenduski, 1989, 2003; Tramblay, 1998; Sawer, 2000). If we can rely on several studies on the behaviour of women acting as elected officials, we know much less about other social groups likely to be more strongly exposed to NSR, such as the young or the low-skilled. One study of British parliamentary candidates' attitudes found that support for gender equality measures was stronger among younger women (Norris and Lovenduski, 2003), suggesting that age might have an impact on issues that are of relevance to the lives of NSR groups. But we certainly need more empirical research on this issue if it is to be settled satisfactorily.

The available evidence suggests that, when elected, individuals belonging to NSR-exposed groups are likely to be more sensitive to the needs and demands of this social group than other elected officials, and that this trend may be on the increase. This finding goes in the direction of more political influence for NSR groups, as in spite of the lack of dedicated representative outfits, they seem capable of making themselves heard through the existing channels. However, the evidence reviewed is sketchy, and should be weighed against the presence gap outlined above before concluding that NSR groups have real opportunities to influence policy-making in parliaments and in labour market institutions.

Preferences

The third condition that needs to be fulfilled for NSR groups to be able to influence policy to their advantage is some degree of distinctiveness and homogeneity of their political preferences. Do NSR groups tend to express political preferences that are different from those of other voters? Are these shared by all NSR-exposed individuals? The last two decades have seen an interesting and rather puzzling development in the voting behaviour of women. Throughout the 1950s and the 1960s women's voting patterns were consistently slightly more right-wing than men's. More recently, first in the US and then in a majority of advanced democracies, women voters tend to prefer left-wing parties to a larger extent than their male counterparts. This shift has been explained with reference to a mix of structural and cultural factors: labour market participation, secularization, social support for gender equality and so forth (Inglehart and Norris, 2003).

The shift to the left of female electorates fits in well with the NSR perspective put forward in this article. Women, especially younger ones, who have become exposed to NSR only in the last few decades, are more likely to turn to left-wing parties in so far as they tend to promote the kind of policies that can improve their quality of life (child care, parental leave, etc.). As a matter of fact, the gender gap in voting behaviour is stronger in countries which have a higher female employment rate: the more women are exposed to NSR the more they tend to mobilize for left-wing parties.[1] Perhaps the clearer cases of gender-based cleavages in voting behaviour are the Scandinavian countries, where women are considerably more likely than men to support the Social Democrats (Esping-Andersen, 1999b).

Distinctive patterns of voting among those who are exposed to NSR emerge also from voting behaviour in referendums on age-related social policies in Switzerland. In a study of nineteen referendums on decisions with a different impact according to age group, age turned out to be a significant predictor of voting behaviour in fourteen. Policies for the younger groups, such as paid maternity leave, more funds for universities, better employment protection or unemployment compensation, were generally opposed by older voters. Improvements in the pension system, by contrast, were supported more strongly by older voters (Bonoli, 2004a).

Similar cleavages on age-related social policy issues can be observed also in opinion polls in virtually all countries (Esping-Andersen, 1999b, p. 312; Armingeon, 2004), but voting behaviour in referendums is certainly a more reliable indicator of political opinions. Note that public opinion data suggest the cleavage to be one-sided: older respondents do not support policies for the young, but there is no clear age-related distinction in support for retirement pensions and other policies for older people. This is also confirmed by surveys on referendum voting on old-age issues in Switzerland.

The overall impression is that there is some distinctiveness in the political preferences expressed by NSR groups but the correlations are usually rather weak. In addition, the defining socio-demographic features of NSR groups (age, gender, skill level, family configuration) tend to be less strong a predictor of policy and political preferences than the traditional determinants of class and religion: two factors that intersect the cleavage between traditional welfare state clienteles and welfare groups investigated in this study.

Limited Power Resources

This overview of patterns of political participation, representation and preferences of NSR groups paints a mixed picture in so far as their ability to influence policy is concerned. Low participation, internal divisions and the lack of dedicated representative outfits can be formidable obstacles to successful political mobilization. On the other hand, distinctiveness in political preferences and effective interest representation of elected officials are political assets for NSR groups. On balance, and especially if we compare the situation of NSR groups to that of industrial workers during the twentieth century, the evidence reviewed here suggests that, at least for the time being, the 'power resources' of NSR groups remain largely insufficient to impose the kind of policies that would serve their interests through the democratic game. The Nordic countries, and to a lesser extent the UK, however, may represent an exception here. It is there that, according to the data presented in this article, NSR groups have a stronger presence in democratic and labour market institutions and, as far as the Nordic countries are concerned, it is also where one finds the most developed policies for them. In other countries, especially in continental European nations, if policies providing coverage against NSR are being developed, this must be as a result of some different mechanism than through imposition in the political arena.

The political weight of new social risks groups is not insignificant. It is probably insufficient to bend the political system to their advantage, but it can still influence adaptation. New social risks groups, if unable to change the world on their own, may nonetheless represent an interesting constituency for vote-seeking politicians. At the same time, if capable of striking the right alliances with other groups in society, NSR groups may obtain at least some policies that protect their interests.

New Patterns of Social Policy-Making for New Social Risks

The particular nature of NSRs and of the policies aimed at addressing them generates a distinctive set of opportunities for policy-making that did not exist, or did not exist to such an extent, during the construction phase of postwar welfare states. Traditional social policies had among their key objectives the decommodification of wage earners and, in this respect, they were bound to develop in the context of an opposition between wage earners and employers, the latter trying to resist high levels of decommodification that could be detrimental to business profitability. Policies that cover NSRs do not decommodify workers; they just make their condition more attractive. If anything, they represent an additional incentive to work for those groups of the population who have traditionally been excluded from paid employment, especially women. One of the consequences of better NSR coverage is to increase labour supply. In the current context of population ageing and, in some countries, population decline combined with difficulties in integrating immigrant populations, an increase in domestic labour supply is likely to be welcomed by business.

The new social policies discussed here distinguish themselves from the traditional ones also in terms of cost. Generally speaking, to provide a service to a section of the population only, say working parents, is less costly than to set up a universal pension scheme. A quick comparison of expenditure figures in social programmes covering old and new risks shows very clearly that the latter come much cheaper. The biggest spenders on family services and on active labour market policies have outlays on these programmes not exceeding 2 per cent of GDP, whereas typical figures for programmes like health care and pensions are in the region of 10 per cent of GDP. The comparatively low cost of providing coverage of NSRs may reduce the opposition against it from those who have to foot the bill.

These key features of NSR coverage policies open up a set of new opportunities for policy-making that have been exploited, especially in continental European countries. By understanding the mechanisms that are behind policy decisions in this broad field, we may be better able to account for developments in countries where the political mobilization and representation of NSR groups are particularly weak, and which lack a tradition of social intervention in this area of policy, or where political institutions do not allow the unilateral imposition of government policy.

Turning Vice into Virtue

This mechanism for the modernization of conservative welfare states has been identified by Jonah Levy. It is an approach that 'targets inequities within the welfare system that are simultaneously a source of either economic inefficiency or substantial public spending', and generates savings that can be used to 'pursue a variety of virtuous objectives: redistributing income toward the poor . . . facilitating the negotiation of far-reaching, tripartite social pacts' (Levy, 1999, p. 240). Levy provides a few examples: in the Netherlands, reductions in public spending on disability pensions, a scheme that was widely abused in the 1980s, made it possible for the government to introduce tax breaks targeted on low-income households. In Italy, pension privileges for some workers (civil servants) were abolished but at the same time the reform introduced flexible retirement age, and inequities between occupational groups have been done away with.

These (and other) instances of policy-making based on 'turning vice into virtue' have in common the fact that they originate in the context of budget austerity that makes intolerable expenditure that is widely regarded as inefficient. The funds generated by reducing this kind of expenditure can be used to finance new initiatives. In fact, the prime objective of reform being cost containment, it is only a small part of the funds freed by the austerity measures that are assigned to the new programmes.

Modernizing Compromises

A similar mechanism, but with a stronger political dimension, has been observed especially in countries characterized by fragmented political institutions or by countries temporarily ruled by weak governments. Typically the compromise takes the shape of the inclusion, within a single reform, of measures of cost containment or retrenchment, and of improvements in provision. The cost containment measures generally concern policies that provide coverage for 'old risks', while the improvements and expansion concern NSR coverage. That is why these reforms can be qualified as 'modernizing compromises'.

Switzerland is probably the clearest case of such compromises. In the 1995 pension reform, an increase in women's retirement age was traded against contribution credits for carers and contribution sharing between spouses. The two measures were supported and opposed by important sections of the population. The inclusion of both in a single piece of legislation made the reform stronger in parliament and with voters. It survived the referendum obstacle and is now law. Similarly, the 1995 unemployment insurance reform combined a two-year time limit on passive benefits with increased spending on active labour market policies. Again, it was a compromise that contained measures strongly supported by the right (the time limit on benefits) and by the left (active labour market policies) and that was as a result able to attract the support of a large section of the political spectrum. It too is now law (Bonoli, 2001).

A modernizing compromise took place also in the Swedish pension reform of the 1990s. On the one hand, the reform reduced pension entitlements for some occupational groups. The main losers were white collar employees and managers, or those who start working relatively late after a long period spent in education, but overall about 80 per cent of the population is likely to lose between 7 and 8 per cent of their pension as a result of changes introduced (Anderson, 2001).[2] On the other hand, in order not to penalize women but also as a compensation for white collar workers who had lost out because of the change in the pension formula, the reform introduced generous contribution credits for several categories of non-employed people. These are granted for career interruptions due to childrearing, periods of unemployment, study, military service and sickness. With regard to childrearing, if a parent reduces working hours in the four years following the birth of a child, contributions are credited to his or her pension account on the basis of previous earnings. If he or she stops working completely, then the contribution credit will be based on 75 per cent of the average wage. The Swedish reform combined overall retrenchment in pensions with the introduction of one of the most generous systems of contribution credits for carers. Swedish contribution credits, unlike those in most other countries, apply not only to the state pension, but also to private individual retirement accounts. In this way, the reform package was able to attract the support of a sufficient number of political actors to guarantee its adoption.

Modernizing compromises seem a promising avenue to achieve advances in the coverage of NSRs. Supporters of welfare retrenchment and of increased coverage for NSRs usually belong to different political camps,

and if they do join forces on a single reform initiative, they are likely to
form an extremely strong coalition in the political arena. This mechanism
is more likely to exist in countries where political institutions, because of
their fragmentation, encourage the formation of large coalitions around
given policy proposals. Here the incentive for political actors to compromise is strongest (the alternative being stalemate). Paradoxically, one may
thus expect countries with fragmented political institutions to move faster
in the development of policies that cover NSRs.

Convergence of Interests with Employers

Some of the key features of NSR coverage policies make them particularly
attractive to employers. As seen above, these policies do not provide
decommodification, they are generally not as costly as the more traditional forms of social intervention, and they have a clearly favourable
impact on labour supply. This is the case especially of child care and other
policies aimed at making it easier for families to reconcile work and family
life. As a result of their introduction, one can expect the labour supply of
women to increase significantly (Daly, 2000). Active labour market policies (ALMPs) can have a similar impact, by encouraging the transition
from non-employment to employment of individuals belonging to various
groups of non-working people, most notably youth and long-term unemployed people, older working-age persons, and some disabled people.
ALMPs have a positive impact on labour supply not only in quantitative
but also in qualitative terms, and can contribute to matching labour supply
and demand.

These sorts of policies would obviously present a clear interest for
employers under any set of circumstances, but the ongoing process of
population ageing makes them essential measures. In virtually all industrial countries, all other things being equal, population ageing will lead to
a reduction of the working-age population and, as a result, of labour
supply. This could translate into labour shortage in some economic
sectors, a development already observed in the late 1990s and early 2000s,
and as a result lead to wage increases that could be detrimental to business
profitability. Many countries are turning to immigration as a solution to
the labour market problems that may be generated by population ageing
and decline. However, especially in the conservative welfare states of
continental Europe, this strategy is met with scepticism by large sections
of the population who, on many occasions, have contributed to the success
of extreme right-wing populist political parties.

This situation is resulting in an increasing tendency among employers
to look for solutions to the ageing-induced labour market problems
domestically, and particularly among the groups whose employment rates

are lower: above all women, but also older working-age people and some disabled people. This may be needed in order to strike the necessary alliances with the rest of the political right, which, under pressure from anti-foreigner extreme right parties, seems to be clearly turning away from immigration as the solution to the contraction of labour supply. In policy terms, this translates into support for childcare subsidies and ALMPs.

An example of this mechanism is provided by a recent bill, voted by the Swiss parliament, which makes provision for a substantial increase in subsidies for day care centres. The bill was supported by a coalition that included the left (Social Democrats), the Christian Democrats and a section of the Free Democrats, a Liberal party that closely represents employers' interests. The director of the Swiss employers' association publicly supported the bill. Swiss employers' attitude towards childcare policy contrasts sharply with their open opposition to any form of additional social expenditure, and with the position they took a few years ago on a paid maternity leave scheme, which they successfully fought (Ballestri and Bonoli, 2003).

Convergence of interests between working women and employers arguably played a big role in the expansion of publicly subsidized child care in other countries as well. In France, [while] an extensive pre-school system was organized as early as the late nineteenth century, the expansion of provision for the 0–3 year old group goes back to the early 1970s amid concerns for labour shortage (Morgan, 2001, pp. 26–9). In Sweden, employers' support for publicly subsidized child care goes back to the late 1950s and 1960s, a period also characterized by labour shortage (Naumann, 2001). The economic consequences of NSR coverage are such that they favour the formation of cross-class alliances between NSR groups, mostly represented by left-of-centre parties, and employers. The resulting coalition can be politically very influential and succeed in pushing through reform.

Affordable Credit Claiming for Post-Socialist Left-Wing Parties

The late 1990s saw the return to power of left-of-centre parties in twelve out of fifteen European Union member states. Often, this happened after long periods of time spent in the opposition (UK, Germany, Italy). As a result, the accession to government was met with strong expectations by the traditional and new constituencies of these progressive parties. Left-of-centre governments, however, were moving under tight constraints. Economic internationalization meant that it was extremely difficult to levy the funds needed to (re-)expand the traditional elements of the welfare state, such as pensions, health care and unemployment insurance.

This problem was compounded by the fact that population ageing, welfare state maturation and the transformation of labour market and family structure were imposing increasing costs on the welfare state. The fact that several of these left-ruled countries were also candidates for the European Monetary Union further reduced their room for manoeuvre in designing new policies or expanding existing ones.

The combination of electoral pressures to adopt policies that would be noticeably different from those of their predecessors, and the economic constraints that were externally and internally imposed upon them, pushed several governments towards the adoption of policies providing coverage against NSRs. If the social democratic parties that ruled most of Europe in the late 1990s were unable to respond to the expectations of their traditional electorates (who, in several cases, turned to more left-wing parties), they still could do something different from their predecessors that would 'speak' to a new potential constituency – NSR groups. Because of their lower cost, these policies were not incompatible with the economic constraints outlined above. Their attractiveness for employers meant that this group, whose support or at least acquiescence was essential for the social democratic governments of the 1990s, would probably refrain from openly fighting their policies.

Often under the label of 'third way', a move towards a new orientation in social policy has happened in virtually all European Union member countries. Active labour market policies and measures designed to help parents reconcile work and family life were introduced across Western Europe in the 1990s. The UK has been at the forefront in this development, but other countries like Germany, Italy or the Netherlands have taken significant steps towards improving the protection against the new social risks discussed in this article. Often this has been the result of brand new policies, but on many occasions reform has consisted of improvement or adaptation of existing provision (Bonoli, 2004b).

It is interesting to note, however, that this move did not generally pay off in electoral terms, as by 2002 most of these governments had suffered substantial electoral losses. In many cases, the strategy of focusing social policy on NSR groups has failed to gain the social democrats new votes. This may be explained with reference to the overall low levels of political participation of NSR groups. The fact that in the 1970s, contrary to the 1990s, political parties found child care to be a vote winner (for instance in France and Sweden) may reflect changes in political attitudes but also in the age composition of electorates. The proportion of the population aged 65 or more in France and Sweden in the 1970s was between 13 and 14 per cent. In contrast, in the late 1990s, in Italy and Germany, two countries where third way social democratic parties have suffered major electoral losses, the same figure is between 16 and 19 per cent. While the difference (between three and six percentage points) may not look dramatic, one needs to take into account that because of the participation gap between different age groups, it underestimates the increase in the political influence of older voters.

Conclusion

In a majority of OECD countries social programmes providing protection against new social risks are still at an embryonic stage, but virtually everywhere these issues are being discussed in public debates. There are big country variations in the extent to which NSR coverage has been developed, with the Nordic countries being at the forefront. However, even in those countries lagging behind in the adaptation of their social protection systems, essentially the conservative welfare state of continental and southern Europe, some steps in this direction have been taken.

This article has tried to put forward hypotheses capable of accounting for the observed patterns of policy-making. Political explanations developed for the postwar years, in fact, cannot be transposed to the post-industrial age. The low levels of participation, the weak representation and the existence of internal cleavages among those exposed to NSRs means that strong mobilization capable of obtaining protective legislation is unlikely. The power resources available to NSR groups are simply not comparable to those of industrial workers during the heyday of the industrial society. However, there is evidence that, on occasion, issues that are of interest to NSR groups are picked up by politicians and are, rightly or wrongly, believed to be vote winners. Under such circumstances the social groups exposed to NSRs can still exert political influence via democratic institutions, albeit of a different kind from the one deployed by labour movements during the twentieth century. Nonetheless, given the low level of participation among younger voters and the ageing of Western electorates, it is unlikely that political competition to attract the votes of NSR groups will be a sufficient force to restructure welfare states. The analysis of instances of policy-making that have resulted in improved coverage against NSRs suggests that this part of the process of welfare state adaptation will be characterized by mechanisms of political exchange, compromise and cross-class alliances. As the political weakness of NSR groups makes unilateral imposition of policy impossible, the only path to effective reform is to strike compromises and form alliances with other political forces. Ironically, these deals are most likely with those political actors that have been most inimical to the welfare state: retrenchers and employers. Alliances between NSR groups and the former can be made on the basis of what has been referred to above as a modernizing compromise, or the combination within a single piece of legislation of cuts in provision with improvements in the coverage of NSRs. Employers may also be interested in joining forces with NSR groups, especially when protection against NSRs means easier labour market participation. From the employers' point of view this means increased labour supply and a more efficient labour market, a goal for which it may be worth investing some public money.

Notes

From *Policy and Politics*, 33, 3, 2005, pp. 431–49, copyright © Policy Press, first published 2005, by permission of The Policy Press. Earlier versions of this article have been presented at the Nordic Social Policy Research Meeting, Helsinki, 22–24 Aug. 2002; at the American Political Science Association annual meeting, Boston, 29 Aug.–1 Sept. 2002; at the annual meeting of the Swiss Political Science Association, Fribourg, 9 Nov. 2003; and at the conference on The Politics of New Social Risks, Lugano, 25–27 Sept. 2003. It is based on research financed by the Swiss Office for Education and Science (grant 00.0438) in the context of the EU Framework 5 project WRAMSOC.

The author would like to thank Karen Anderson, Klaus Armingeon, Maurizio Ferrera, Silja Hausermann, Peter Taylor-Gooby and Martin Rein for their comments.

1   As a matter of fact there is a fairly strong and statistically significant correlation among OECD countries between the size of the gender gap in voting and the female employment rate ($r = 0,534$, sig. 0.049, two-tailed).
2   This loss should, however, be compensated by the income stream resulting from newly introduced individual private pensions, although this will depend to a significant extent on the returns on the invested capital, and is as a result unpredictable.

References

Anderson, K. M. (2001) 'The Politics of Retrenchment in a Social Democratic Welfare State: Reform of Swedish Pensions and Unemployment Insurance', *Comparative Political Studies*, 34, 9, pp. 1063–91.
Armingeon, K. (2004) 'Reconciling Competing Claims of the Welfare State Clientele', paper presented at the American Political Science Association annual meeting, Chicago, 2–4 Sept.
Ballestri, Y. and Bonoli, G. (2003) 'L'état social suisse face au nouveaux risques Sociaux', *Swiss Political Science Review*, 9, pp. 3, 35–58.
Bonoli, G. (2001) 'Political Institutions, Veto Points, and the Process of Welfare State Adaptation', in P. Pierson (ed.), *The New Politics of the Welfare State*, Oxford, Oxford University Press, pp. 238–64.
Bonoli, G. (2003) 'Two Worlds of Pension Reform in Western Europe', *Comparative Politics*, 35, 4, pp. 399–416.
Bonoli, G. (2004a) 'Generational Conflicts over Resource Allocation: Evidence from Referendum Voting on Social Policy Issues in Switzerland', paper presented at the conference on Erosion or Transformation of the Welfare State?, University of Fribourg, Switzerland, 15–16 Oct.

Bonoli, G. (2004b) 'Social Democratic Party Policies in Europe: Towards A Third Way?', in G. Powell (ed.), *Social Democratic Party Policies in Contemporary Europe*, London, Routledge, pp. 197–213.

Castles, F. G. (1982) *The Impact of Parties: Politics and Policies in Democratic Capitalist States*, London/Beverly Hills, CA: Sage Publications.

Daly, M. (2000) 'A Fine Balance: Women's Labor Market Participation in International Comparison', in F. V. Schmidt (ed.), *Welfare and Work in the Open Economy*, Oxford, Oxford University Press, vol. 2, pp. 467–510.

Ebbinghaus, B. (2003) 'Trade Union Movements in Post-industrial Welfare States', paper presented at the conference on The Political Regulation of New Social Risks', Lugano, 23–25 Sept.

Esping-Andersen, G. (1985) *Politics against Markets: The Social Democratic Road to Power*, Princeton, Princeton University Press.

Esping-Andersen, G. (1999a) *Social Foundations of Post-industrial Economies*, Oxford, Oxford University Press.

Esping-Andersen, G. (1999b) 'Politics without Class? Post-industrial Cleavages in Europe and America', in H. Kitschelt, P. Lange, G. Marks and J. D. Stephens (eds), *Continuity and Change in Contemporary Capitalism*, Cambridge, Cambridge University Press, pp. 293–316.

Hemerijck, A. (2002) 'The Self-Transformation of the European Social Model(s)', in G. Esping-Andersen (ed.), *Why we Need a New Welfare State*, Oxford, Oxford University Press, pp. 173–214.

Inglehart, R. and Norris, P. (2003) *Rising Tide: Gender Equality and Cultural Change*, Cambridge, Cambridge University Press.

Iversen, T. and Wren, A. (1998) 'Equality, Employment, and Budgetary Restraint: The Trilemma of the Service Economy', *World Politics*, 50, pp. 507–46.

Jenson, J. (2002) 'From Ford to Lego: Redesigning Welfare Regimes', paper presented at the American Political Science Association annual meeting, Boston, 31 Aug.–3 Sept.

Korpi, W. (1983) *The Democratic Class Struggle*, London, Routledge and Kegan Paul.

Levy, J. (1999) 'Vice into Virtue? Progressive Politics and Welfare Reform in Continental Europe', *Politics and Society*, 27, 2, pp. 239–73.

Morgan, K. (2001) 'Conservative Parties and Working Women in France', paper presented at the American Political Science Association annual meeting, San Francisco, 30 Aug.–2 Sept.

Naumann, I. (2001) 'The Politics of Child Care: Swedish Women's Mobilization for Public Child Care in the 1960s and 1970s', ECSR Summer School on Family, Gender and Social Stratification, Stockholm, 23–25 Aug.

Norris, P. (2002) *Democratic Phoenix: Reinventing Political Activism*, Cambridge, Cambridge University Press.

Norris, P. and Lovenduski, J. (1989) 'Women Candidates for Parliament: Transforming the Agenda?', *British Journal of Political Science*, 19, 1, pp. 106–15.

Norris, P. and Lovenduski, J. (2003) 'Westminster Women: The Politics of Presence', *Political Studies*, 51, 1, pp. 84–102.

Pierson, P. (1998) 'Irresistible Forces, Immovable Objects: Post-industrial Welfare States Confront Permanent Austerity', *Journal of European Public Policy*, 5, 4, pp. 539–60.

Putnam, R. D. (2000) *Bowling Alone: The Collapse and Revival of American Community*, New York, Simon and Schuster.

Sawer, M. (2000) 'Parliamentary Representation of Women: From Discourses of Justice to Strategies of Accountability', *International Political Science Review*, 21, 4, pp. 361–80.

Siaroff, A. (2000) 'Women's Representation in Legislatures and Cabinets in Industrial Democracies', *International Political Science Review*, 21, 4, pp. 197–215.

Stephens, J. (1979) *The Transition from Capitalism to Socialism*, Urbana, Illinois University Press.

Taylor-Gooby, P. (2004) 'New Risks and Social Change', in P. Taylor-Gooby (ed.), *New Risks, New Welfare?* Oxford, Oxford University Press, pp. 1–27.

Tramblay, M. (1998) 'Do Women MPs Substantively Represent Women? A Study of Legislative Behaviour in Canada's 35th Parliament', *Canadian Journal of Political Science*, 31, 3, pp. 435–65.

Part III

Emerging Ideas, Emergent Forms

In Part II we looked at the constraints and challenges facing advanced welfare states today. These themes are developed further in Part III of the reader with contributions that explore ways in which welfare states are responding to new challenges, in terms of changing understandings of the welfare state's role and changing patterns in the organization and delivery of welfare. Many contributions in this last part go beyond the analysis of the status quo, critically scrutinizing established concepts and frames of reference in welfare state research, many of which were introduced in Parts I and II, and suggesting new directions and visions for securing welfare and well-being.

Despite criticism from left and right (see Part I), welfare states developed largely on the basis of a broad societal consensus in the postwar period of the last century. Today, welfare states are under attack from many sides: on one hand, social protection is increasingly unstable and insufficient for a growing number of people – often the same groups for whom welfare state arrangements during the 'golden era' of the welfare state were not always so 'gold-plated': women, children, the frail and immigrants. On the other hand, welfare states in their current forms are increasingly deemed unsustainable. New ideas are more important than ever if the welfare state, this bold modern project, is to survive the twenty-first century. What should be the key priorities and aims of social policy today? What role and scope should the welfare state play therein? What other actors and institutions are or should be involved in developing new welfare arrangements?

In the section Emerging Ideas we bring together a series of approaches that introduce new perspectives on the changing role of welfare states. The first contribution by Peter Alcock discusses how the UK coalition government has recently begun to craft new policy programmes on the basis of a 'big society' vision, in many ways opposed to the classical welfare state concept (see Part I), shifting the focus of welfare provision away from the state and onto voluntary and community actors.

While some ideas such as the 'big society' are born out of political agendas, others develop and thrive in an environment where the boundaries between political and academic discourse are blurred. The social investment paradigm is such an example that has had great traction among academics, national governments and international agencies alike. Jane Jenson's chapter traces the diffusion of this idea on a global scale, highlighting that, contrary to political rhetoric in some countries, it would be wrong to assume that states are simply retreating from the field of welfare. Instead, they are changing their role from passive welfare providers to activating 'social investment states' with a new emphasis on lifelong learning, investment in children and enabling citizens to look out for themselves. Much of this reorientation in welfare states is triggered by the challenges of 'new social risks' – another concept that has been influential in framing welfare state debate (see Part II).

However, as Colin Crouch and Maarten Keune point out, the new social risk perspective starts from the premise that welfare states and people have to adapt to current socio-economic circumstances, particularly the dominant market model – and the same could be said for the social investment perspective – and neglects the possibility that these circumstances themselves could be changed. Shifting the focus from 'risks' in working people's lives to economic 'uncertainties', Crouch and Keune develop a new approach that outlines the broad range of areas beyond conventional social policy through which state policy, collective bargaining, corporatist practices and transnational regulations shape and regulate welfare and uncertainty.

Zahir Sadeque also argues for a broadening of perspective on social policy, one that takes into account the inadvertent effects climate change will have on social policy in this century and beyond. He urges the need for a conceptual reorientation of social policy lest we risk sacrificing human well-being on a global scale. Such a new framework would include global social policy objectives that address such issues as rising food prices, loss of livelihoods, employment and safe shelter, displacement, involuntary migration and an increase in climate-induced diseases. In other words, considerable adaptation of existing welfare states will be necessary that incorporate international and multi-sectoral coordination and cooperation, and the inclusion of the voice of affected people. This sobering perspective continues through to the last reading of this section, in which Philippe van Parijs highlights the dramatic rise of social inequalities in the Western world since the 1980s, also pointing to the global dimension of poverty and the way welfare states are inextricably linked. National welfare states today are faced with a dilemma, he argues: increasing national social provision to combat social inequality becomes economically unsustainable in light of global economic competition; rolling out welfare provision transnationally is politically unsustainable. Van Parijs suggests a solution to this dilemma that constitutes a radical alternative to the range of labour market policies European welfare states devise to incentivize, activate or protect workers in today's volatile labour markets: a guaranteed basic income.

In the second section Emergent Forms we present a series of analyses of current welfare state trends which, by directing their lens at often neglected themes and issues, pose a critical counterpoint to established perceptions of the welfare state. These readings also continue a key theme of the first section: the need to broaden the frame of analysis in order to fully understand current welfare state developments, thereby pointing to future directions for welfare state research.

The increasingly widespread notion that European welfare states are moving towards an 'adult worker model' in which women and men are treated as individual workers is critically put to the test by Mary Daly. Her analysis shows that, far from the supposed unidirectional trend towards greater individualization, contemporary reforms in European welfare states are conflicting and ambivalent, displaying also counter tendencies of the familization of individual entitlements that serve to support the family as an institution. The individualization theme is further taken up by Janet Newman and collaborators who ask what implications the current focus on personalization, independence and choice – all part of the wider modernization agenda of public services – has on social care, a social policy area generally marked by dependencies and interdependencies. By focusing on social care and tensions surrounding user involvement, they contribute to critical understanding of the emerging new roles and definitions of welfare providers and welfare recipients that are part of the wider restructuring of welfare states. They also concur with Crouch and Keune's point that governments are not the only actors in the regulation and production of welfare, suggesting a broadened focus on welfare governance.

Alexander Pacek and Benjamin Radcliff return to a well-developed theme in welfare state analysis, the politics of welfare states, but do so from a different angle. They consider whether the welfare state, in practical terms, contributes to people's happiness, or in other words, people's life satisfaction. The study of happiness is an emerging international research area emphasizing that subjective well-being extends beyond material aspects into emotional and social dimensions. It is arguably because of these non-financial aspects of well-being that policy makers with chronically tight budgets are increasingly becoming interested in this field of study (for example, the UK government recently set up its own programme to measure national well-being). However, while taking a new route of analysis, Pacek and Radcliff's conclusions echo statements of the classical social democratic approach developed in earlier parts of this reader: by limiting the market's potential for converting human beings into commodities, welfare states increase human well-being.

The short concluding piece of this reader by Jürgen Habermas brings us back to the beginning and the core questions of the welfare state: what was the modern welfare state? A commitment of social solidarity among citizens steeped in the national project of European democracies. But where do we go from here as national boundaries have become porous and social problems global? Habermas gives a radical answer: the national welfare state is a construct of the past – a Europe-wide community of civic solidarity is the future. As the European Union is rent by deep conflict, Habermas firmly maintains that more, not less, European integration is needed: economic integration that gives the EU the powers to increase social redistribution across nation states, and political integration that boosts political participation of European citizens. Only then, he argues, will Europe be able to protect its national diversity and cultural wealth against levelling in the midst of globalization.

Emerging Ideas

The Big Society: A New Policy Environment for the Third Sector?

Peter Alcock

A New UK Policy Discourse

Most countries around the world now recognize the importance of third sector, non-government or voluntary organizations to the development and delivery of welfare provision. Indeed in many countries, especially in the global South, this remains the major form through which much welfare is delivered. In Europe, and in particular, in the UK, the role of this third sector has recently become the focus of more direct policy engagement, focused in part on the involvement of the sector in welfare provision and how this relates to the role of the state. This has led to debate across Europe about what should be the relationship between the state and the third sector, and how this should be managed and supported by government (see Evers and Laville, 2004; Kendall, 2009a).

In the UK under the Labour governments of the early twenty-first century this relationship developed significantly, as mentioned below. Since 2010, however, there has been a new Coalition government in control of the country, and they have already begun to seek changes in this. In particular this has taken the form of a new policy discourse centred on the desirability of promoting the 'Big Society' within the country to bring about changes in the relations between government and citizens, in particular by shifting the balance of government support for voluntary and community action. This chapter explores the extent to which this new policy discourse has in practice produced a new policy environment for the third sector in the UK.

The Policy Legacy and the 2010 Election

The UK Coalition government elected in May 2010 inherited a significant and a challenging policy legacy on the third sector from the Labour governments of the previous decade therefore. Analysis of the third sector policy developed by New Labour is still being developed, but already it has been heralded as introducing a new spirit of partnership with government (Lewis, 2005), founded on an extensive range of policy levers described by Kendall (2009b) as resulting in 'hyperactive mainstreaming', and leading to a new found 'strategic unity' across the third sector based on a closer commitment to policy engagement (Alcock, 2010).

There was a significant expansion of government support for the sector, which had grown to £12.8 billion by 2008, around 36 per cent of total income for charities in England and Wales (Clark et al., 2010, p. 43). This included in particular major new programmes of 'horizontal' funding, such as the Futurebuilders and Change-Up programmes, which aimed to provide government funding for organizations and agencies across the sector (see Alcock, 2011), contrasting with previous government support which had often been focused in 'vertical' streams linked to particular service areas (see Kendall, 2003, Ch. 4).

This funding saw a step change in government support for the sector and it led to a political and economic profile for the sector which was unprecedented in the country (Alcock and Kendall, 2011). It was also largely welcomed by leading sector actors. For instance, Stuart Etherington, Chief Executive of the National Council for Voluntary Organizations (NCVO), opened a speech in 2002 with the words:

> This is an exciting and challenging time for people working in the voluntary sector. Over the past five years we have seen a growing understanding of, and emphasis on working with, the voluntary sector across government. Partnership working has become the norm . . . (Etherington, 2002)

However, it was not without its critics, who argued that with this new support came new problems for the sector, not least the shift in this support towards greater use of contracts for services with all their attendant regulatory and accountability frameworks, leading some to fear that independence could be challenged by incorporation and isomorphism (Smerdon, 2008).

The legacy of the New Labour years was therefore a higher profile for the third sector in political debate and policy practice. This might have been expected to lead to a high profile for the sector too in the campaigning for the 2010 general election. This was true for many of the leading sector agencies, who produced their own 'manifestos' for the election and sought to talk up the role that the sector could play in meeting various policy priorities. The Third Sector Research Centre (TSRC) followed these campaigning strategies and also the commitments made by the major parties to the sector. In the case of the latter, the evidence suggests that the third sector was not as big, or as controversial, an election issue as some might have hoped, or feared (Parry et al., 2011).

All the major parties stressed the important role of the sector in delivering public services and the need to improve the contractual basis for this with longer term funding and an independent Compact[1] to oversee relations. They also all supported encouragement of volunteering and donating, both individually and through work-place volunteering and corporate giving. And all emphasized too the importance of smaller, community-based organizations, alongside the larger more service-focused charities, recognizing that the former had a vital role to play in promoting and supporting community empowerment. Both Labour and the Conservatives supported the long campaigned for Social Investment Bank for the sector, utilizing the balances in dormant bank accounts – although the Conservatives promised to give this a new name, the Big Society Bank. This was linked to a major election theme from the Conservatives on the *Big Society*.

The Big Society was intended to be contrasted with the 'Big State' that Labour had supposedly advanced, and amongst other things was intended as an endorsement of the positive and proactive role that voluntary action and social enterprise could play in promoting improved social inclusion and 'fixing Britain's broken society'. By 'returning' power from the state to the citizen, social change could be put back in the hands of people and communities. According to the pollsters, however, the Big Society idea was not really understood on the doorstep, and its profile within the party's electioneering was reduced over the course of the campaign.

Building Coalition Policy

At the end of the day neither Labour nor the Conservatives won the 2010 UK election, and in May 2010 the Conservatives formed a Coalition government with the Liberal Democrats. In fact, the Liberal Democrats had not said much in the run-up to the election about third sector policy. In contrast, Conservative Party policy on the sector had been developed some time before the 2010 general election, with an influential *Policy Green Paper* published in 2008 (Conservative Party) in which they talked about establishing a new Office for Civil Society and outlined twenty policy pledges, including simplification of tax relief for charities, support for volunteering, more competitive markets for public contracts, and an improved version of the Compact. These and other policy initiatives were also outlined in a Big Society paper published just before the election (Conservative Party, 2010).

Thus Conservative policies now dominate the policy portfolio of the new Coalition government, which resurrected the Big Society idea and adopted in large measure the policy plans that the Conservatives had been developing. Shortly after taking office the new government moved to outline their policy plans for the third sector, with speeches from the Prime

Minister and Deputy Prime Minister which put 'the Big Society at the heart of public sector reform'. The Conservative Shadow Spokesman, Nick Hurd, was appointed as Minister for Civil Society, and a place in the House of Lords was found for Nat Wei, a prominent Big Society supporter, who became a government advisor. This was followed by a retitling of the Cabinet Office policy base, the Office of the Third Sector (OTS) established under Labour, which became the Office for Civil Society (OCS).

Devolution

Although these are UK government developments it is important to note that within the UK they are operating in what is now an English policy environment. Since the creation of the independent administrations in Scotland, Wales and Northern Ireland under Labour at the turn of the century, third sector policy across the country has been devolved to the separate administrations in these three nations. The Office for Civil Society therefore promotes and supports only the English third sector. Different offices have been established within the devolved administrations, with different structures and different policy programmes in each – for instance, in Northern Ireland, there is still a split between voluntary and community sector policy and support for social enterprise.

There is relatively little analysis of the impact of this devolution of policy on the third sector and government support for it across the UK. However, Alcock (2012) has argued that it has had the effect of opening up 'new policy spaces' for third sector actors to engage more directly with government in the three devolved administrations, assisted by the smaller scale of government here and the fact that the major umbrella agencies representing the sector were already organized along national lines. For most of the first decade of the new century, however, Labour was in practice in power in all three administrations, and third sector policy followed a largely similar trajectory to that led by the OTS in England. In 2011, however, elections in the devolved administrations which followed the UK national election in 2010 led to different political configurations in all three – and none led by the Conservatives. Politics and policy has begun to diverge in the devolved administrations now therefore. In particular, the Big Society agenda was not a feature of the election campaigns in 2011, and has largely been rejected by the administrations elected as a result of them (Alcock, 2012).

New Policy Programmes

Within England, however, progress in policy development has been rapid. The Coalition government moved quickly to publish more detail about their policies for 'Building the Big Society' (Cabinet Office, 2010), and a policy programme was incorporated into the work programme for the Cabinet Office. The Prime Minister, David Cameron, also made a series of high profile speeches to re-affirm his personal commitment to the Big Society idea and to launch key elements of the programme. Despite its poor reception in the election campaign, therefore, the Big Society remained Cameron's 'great passion'.

Three fundamental issues were identified in the Cabinet Office paper: making it easier to run organizations; getting more resources into the sector; and making it easier for organizations to work with the state. These are hardly revolutionary or indeed controversial commitments of course. They could also have been articulated by the previous Labour administration; and though many may have welcomed the warm words, the practical questions focused on what the new government would do to implement these. Within this rather windy rhetoric, however, there were some specific policy initiatives, and some progress has been made in seeking to implement them.

A 'red tape' task force was established to look at the practical barriers to voluntary and community action, and a report (*Unshackling Good Neighbours*) was published in 2011 (Cabinet Office, 2011). Public sector workers were given a new 'right to provide', to form employee-owned co-operatives to deliver what are currently public services, and a further task force on the potential role of 'mutualization' in the reform of public services was set up. In July 2010 Cameron announced the establishment of four 'vanguard communities' to provide sites for the exploration of more citizen power. These were Liverpool, Windsor and Maidenhead, Sutton, and Eden Valley in Cumbria. However, Liverpool withdrew following concerns over the impact of local authority funding cuts on local voluntary and community organizations, and quite what the others achieved is far from clear beyond isolated examples of new local transport schemes, taking over of local pubs and delivering improved broadband coverage.

Commitments to encourage charitable giving and philanthropy were explored in a White Paper on *Giving* (White Paper, 2011a), although there were few concrete proposals and no specific legislation followed. Early in 2012 a new source of investment funding for third sector organizations was established with the creation of Big Society Capital, the planned wholesale bank with initial capital of £200 million from the major retail banks, and the facility in time to draw on up to £400 million of unclaimed assets in dormant accounts. As mentioned, the creation of the bank had also been a Labour commitment, although support for this from the retail banks had taken some time to secure.

New volunteering opportunities were created for 16-year-old school leavers in the National Citizen Service, providing seven to eight week placements over the summer period. This was piloted in 2011 with 10,000 placements offered (though not all were taken up) and the pilot was being extended to 30,000 places in 2012. There were also plans for a new genera- tion of 5,000 community organizers to be recruited, with the first 500 to be trained by an independent organization (Locality) and the rest expected to be part-time volunteers. Community organizing was also to be sup- ported more generally by small grants and endowments for local organi- zations from a Community First budget of £80 million.

This rather limited financial support for communities was linked to a more general drive to transfer power from government, and in particular local government, to local citizens. It was orchestrated through a Localism Act which, amongst other things, provided a 'right to challenge' current arrangements for the delivery of local services, a 'right to buy' local authority assets such as unused buildings, and a 'right to provide' for public sector employees to establish alternative employee-owned delivery agencies.

Finally, and perhaps most importantly there was the commitment to reform the delivery of public services by extending the role of private and third sector organizations as provider agencies, commissioned by govern- ment. Plans for this were outlined in a White Paper (2011b) called *Open Public Services*, which promoted the value of diversity of provision, but did not contain any specific concrete legislative proposals. Following this, one of the largest and most high profile exercises in out-sourcing of serv- ices, the Work Programme to provide support and work experience to get the long-term unemployed back into employment, was rolled out through a commissioning process. Virtually all of the major contracting agencies were large private companies, with smaller third sector providers expected to become involved only at the level of sub-contractors.

Politics and Economics

There are a number of new policy commitments here, therefore, and they certainly give a lie to any suggestion that third sector policy is not a prior- ity for government or that the Big Society ideas were dropped or diluted by the Coalition government once in office. Despite the rhetoric of inno- vation, however, not all of these ideas are new. Indeed many build on previous government policy planning, such as the Big Society Bank, trans- fer of public services to new worker-led organizations, and the commis- sioning of third sector organizations to deliver public services. Some also require public support, both through direct funding and officer time, in order to facilitate the creation of new organizations (including the task forces), to support the vanguard communities, and to roll out the citizen service.

However, the public resources to support these developments have been drastically reduced, in particular following the autumn 2010 Spending Review and the commitment to remove the public expenditure deficit over four years through cuts in spending programmes of around 25 per cent. In the case of the OCS and the Cabinet Office, this cut was closer to 60 per cent, and it resulted in the closure of the provisions for horizontal support such as Futurebuilders and Change-Up, and the phasing out of financial support for the major third sector infrastructure agencies through the Strategic Partners scheme established under Labour. But the most far-reaching cuts were those that followed the reductions in the budgets for local government, who had always been the major providers of public support for voluntary and community activity. Local authorities are facing budget reductions of between 10 per cent and 25 per cent over four years and in many cases these have led to reductions in the support that they provide to local third sector organizations. Anticipating the immediate impact of these changes the Coalition government established a £107 million Transition Fund in England in late 2010 to help organizations losing large amounts of public funding to plan for an alternative future; but despite calls from sector agencies there were no plans to repeat it in later years.

The dramatic reduction in public expenditure was not directly a part of the Big Society agenda, and was led and managed by the Treasury. But critics pointed out that the Big Society discourse could provide a convenient cover for these spending cuts, by promoting the virtues of voluntary and community action, and social enterprise, as positive alternatives to undesirable, as well as unaffordable, state provision (Coote, 2010). The Prime Minister himself has often claimed that the Big Society is not just a cover for cuts, however, and that the government would be pursuing it whatever the economic climate. He was reported as claiming, during election campaigning, that he hoped that the Big Society would be the kind of legacy that could be compared with the twentieth-century welfare state.

The Big Society

The Big Society is also much bigger than just third sector policy reform. Some of the key policies outlined above are led by the newly retitled OCS within the Cabinet Office; but significant involvement is also expected from the Department of Communities and Local Government and, through this, local authorities. Moreover, all Departments will be expected to take on greater responsibility for planning and commissioning services from non-state providers, and changing procurement and contracting to facilitate this, although a National Audit Office (2012) report on coordination across government of third sector policy suggested that this was experiencing resistance in practice.

What is more, promotion of the Big Society idea does not just come from government. Websites and blogs have been springing up to explore the concept and suggest how it might be translated into action. Nat Wei, a social enterprise activist, was appointed to the House of Lords as a government advisor on the Big Society, and initially promoted it as a new way of thinking about all relations between citizens and government, although in 2011 he resigned from this (unpaid) position citing pressure of such voluntary activity on his ability to support his family. An even broader vision was outlined by Conservative Member of Parliament, Jesse Norman (2010), who argued that Big Society thinking could be traced back through political philosophy to the work of Oakeshott and even Hobbes.

More detailed discussion has come from the 'red Tory' think tank ResPublica. Its creator Philip Blond (2009) talked about an *Ownership State*, in which 'civic associations' would replace public bodies in a transfer of ownership of welfare services to a extended third sector, and has argued that it is the role of policy makers to facilitate and support this re-mixing of welfare provision. This was elaborated further in later papers from Singh (2010), which explored how public service commissioning could be reformed to support social enterprise, and Wilson and Leach (2011), which questioned how to increase levels of voluntary activity.

More evidence is provided by others, somewhat more independent of Conservative Party policy making. Chanan and Miller (2010) drew on long experience of community development practice to argue that well trained and publicly supported community development workers would be needed to make the community engagement aspirations of the Big Society work. Demos published research, funded by the Barrow Cadbury Trust, on two community neighbourhoods in Birmingham which, with a long-term commitment to local self-improvement, have been able to regenerate the local area and increase citizen engagement (Wind-Cowie, 2010). New Philanthropy Capital published a paper outlining the kind of evidence that policy makers would need in order to decide how to support 'scaling up' of third sector organizations to meet the increased expectations of the developing policy environment (Brookes et al., 2010). And the major third sector infrastructure agencies took up the challenge, with the NCVO (2010) establishing an online site to collect and disseminate evidence on Big Society issues and the Association of Chief Executives of Voluntary Organizations (ACEVO) setting up a Commission to provide an independent perspective on the Big Society (ACEVO, 2011).

These wider ranging debates reveal that the Big Society appeal has extended beyond senior government figures and Cabinet Office policy programmes. Indeed it has provided a space within which a range of actors and discourses can compete to articulate their visions and concerns. However, achieving some of the social and political changes hoped for is likely to be a long-term and, in practice, a potentially expensive investment. This may prove to be a critical contradiction within the Big

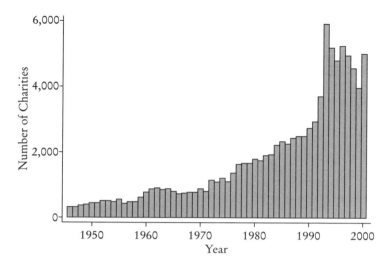

Figure 1 Growth in charity foundation from 1945–2000

Society agenda. The hope that charities, social enterprises and voluntary organizations can step in to replace a reduced public welfare provision, hard hit by the austerity needed to rebalance the public finances, is based in large part on the belief that public welfare provision has 'crowded out' voluntary action. But there is no evidence to support this claim, and much to refute it. For instance, Figure 1, constructed from long-term analysis of charity registrations in the TSRC, reveals that the post-war welfare state heralded a growth not a decline in charitable formation, although changes in regulatory criteria led to turbulence in the data after 1990.

Taking this longer view, it is clear that third sector activity has in practice prospered alongside the growth of public welfare support in the UK. What is more, much of this growth has been based upon support from government. In particular as mentioned above, in the first decade of the new century, funding from statutory sources for third sector organizations grew from £8 billion to £12.8 billion to comprise 36 per cent of total income (Clark et al., 2010, p. 43). The reductions in public expenditure planned for the coming decade may challenge this trajectory, and, rather than promoting further growth of the third sector, could lead to division and decline.

Civil Society and the State

The future of the third sector is formally challenged in any case by the new government's apparent refusal to embrace the term itself, and which it was suggested the Prime Minister himself said should be banned. There may be some in the sector who welcome the dropping of references to being in 'third place'; and supporters of the Big Society may believe that removing reference to the sector as such can create a space for the Big Society to flourish. But in practice the impact of a new discourse for the sector is likely to be more complex than this. The government now some-times refers to this as 'charities, social enterprises and voluntary organiza-tions'. However, the problem with a list-based approach to definition is that there is always somebody missed off the list – where are the mutuals or community groups? If this leads to some being missed off the policy agenda too, then one of the consequences of the new terminology could be the heralding of more divisive third sector politics, in particular if reduced public support is seen to flow to particular sub-sectors such as service delivery or community organizing.

The new term for the government office leading on policy – *Office for Civil Society* – deliberately replaced reference to a sector by embracing the potentially wider notion of an arena of social relations. It therefore appeals to a concept which has a longer and wider pedigree than the Big Society. The Big Society may be Cameron's great passion, but it is a politi-cal slogan (some have compared it to New Labour's 'Third Way') rather than an analytical concept. Perhaps civil society can provide a more enduring focus for the new government's developing policy agenda.

The NCVO now publish their annual statistical overview under the title *The UK Civil Society Almanac* (Clark et al., 2010), and many scholars have written about civil society as a space for independent social action (see Deakin, 2001). But for most of these commentators civil society is a distinct theoretical concept focusing on analysis of how we conceive of social relations rather than how we classify organizations. Evers and Laville (2004, Introduction p. 6) once argued that there can be no 'civil society sector'; and more recently Evers (2010) has repeated the argument that associational forms and social relations are quite different subjects.

Civil society is not just a synonym for third sector, therefore; and an active policy commitment to promote civil society would arguably require government intervention seeking to shape social relations and promote civic participation across the public and private sectors, as well as within voluntary and community action. However, this is not what the current Big Society agenda is seeking to embrace, and most of the policy pro-grammes within it remain focused narrowly on promoting voluntary and community activity. Indeed seen in this broader context, the Big Society has largely remained a political slogan, rather than a theoretical departure from existing forms of public action. As discussed earlier, it was based in large part on attempts by Conservative Party strategists to distance the new Party (and later the new government) from the previous Labour administration, who, they wanted to argue, had become too dependent on the promotion of a 'Big State'. In this sense the Big Society was intended to appeal to anti-state sentiments, rather than the positive creation of a new 'civil' society.

However, the failure of this strategy to secure political traction in the devolved administrations in Scotland, Wales and Northern Ireland, in the elections there in 2011 suggests that it has remained in practice closely tied to Cameron and the Conservative vision of supposedly popular anti-state politics. In Scotland, Wales and Northern Ireland, however, the Conservatives were not successful in securing power in the parliamentary and assembly elections there in 2011. Since these elections, although similar policies towards third sector development and public service reform have been pursued there, the Big Society rhetoric has been rejected and civil society promotion and state support are not seen as mutually exclusive. The new policy environment for the third sector which the Big Society offered, or threatened, to provide was therefore in fact very much an English one. Even here, however, the government's ability to translate the political rhetoric into significant social and economic reform remains open to question.

Note

This chapter includes some material from a journal article with much the same title, which appeared in *Voluntary Sector Review*, 1:3, pp. 379–90, by permission of the author. The support of the Economic and Social Research Council (ESRC), the Office for Civil Society (OCS) and the Barrow Cadbury UK Trust is gratefully acknowledged. The work was part of the programme of the joint ESRC, OCS, Barrow Cadbury Third Sector Research Centre. Thanks to Peter Backus for preparing Figure 1.

1   The Compact is a formal agreement outlining in general terms the relations between the state and the third sector in England, introduced in 1998 (Home Office, 1998) and taken up in a number of other countries (see Casey et al., 2010).

References

Alcock, P. (2010) 'A Strategic Unity: Defining the Third Sector in the UK', *Voluntary Sector Review*, 1:1, pp. 5–24.

Alcock, P. (2011) 'Voluntary action, New Labour and the "third sector"', in Hilton, M. and McKay, J. (eds.), *The Ages of Voluntarism: How we got to the Big Society*, Oxford, Oxford University Press/British Academy.

Alcock, P. (2012) 'New Policy Spaces: the Impact of Devolution on Third Sector Policy in the UK', *Social Policy and Administration*, 46:2, pp. 219–38.

Alcock, P. and Kendal, J. (2011) 'Constituting the Third Sector: Processes of Decontestation and Contention under the UK Labour Governments in England', *Voluntas: International Journal of Voluntary and Nonprofit Organizations*, 22:3, pp. 450–69.

Association of Chief Executives of Voluntary Organisations (ACEVO) (2011) *Powerful People, Responsible Society. The Report of the Commission on Big Society*, ACEVO, 2011.

Blond, P. (2009) *The Ownership State: Restoring excellence, innovation and ethos to the public services*, London, ResPublica/NESTA.

Brookes, M., Lumley, T. and Paterson, E. (2010) *Scaling up for the Big Society*, New Philanthropy Capital.

Cabinet Office (2010) *Building the Big Society*, London, Cabinet Office.

Cabinet Office (2011) *Unshackling Good Neighbours. Report of the Task Force established to consider how to cut red tape for small charities, voluntary organisations and social enterprises*, London, Cabinet Office.

Casey, J., Dalton, B., Melville, R. and Onyx, J. (2010) 'Strengthening Government-Nonprofit Relations: International Experiences with Compacts', *Voluntary Sector Review*, 1:1, pp. 59–76.

Chanan, G. and Miller, C. (2010) *The Big Society: How it Could Work*, London, PACES/Empowerment.

Clark, J., Kane, D., Wilding, K. and Wilton, J. (2010) *The UK Civil Society Almanac 2010*, London, NCVO.

Conservative Party (2008) *A Stronger Society: Voluntary Action in the 21st Century*, Policy Green Paper No. 5, London, Conservative Party.

Conservative Party (2010) *Building a Big Society*, London, Conservative Party.

Coote, A. (2010) *Cutting it: The 'Big Society' and the new austerity*, London, New Economics Foundation.

Deakin, N. (2001) *In Search of Civil Society*, Basingstoke, Palgrave Macmillan.

Etherington, S. (2002) 'Delivery: The Role of the Voluntary Sector', Public Management and Policy Association Lecture, 22 October 2002.

Evers, A. and Laville, J.-L. (eds.) (2004) *The Third Sector in Europe*, Cheltenham, Edward Elgar.

Evers, A. (2010) 'Observations on incivility: blind spots in third sector research and policy', *Voluntary Sector Review*, 1:1, pp. 113–19.

Home Office (1998) *Compact on Relations between Government and the Voluntary and Community Sector in England*, Cm. 4100, London, Stationery Office.

Kendall, J. (2003) *The Voluntary Sector: Comparative perspectives in the UK*, London, Routledge.

Kendall, J. (ed.) (2009a) *Handbook of Third Sector Policy in Europe: Multi-level Processes and Organised Civil Society*, Cheltenham, Edward Elgar.

Kendall, J. (2009b) 'The third sector and the policy process in the UK: ingredients in a hyperactive horizontal policy environment', in Kendall, J. (ed.) *Handbook of Third Sector Policy in Europe: Multi-level Processes and Organised Civil Society*, Cheltenham, Edward Elgar.

Lewis, J. (2005) 'New Labour's Approach to the Voluntary Sector: Independence and the Meaning of Partnership', *Social Policy and Society*, 4:2, pp. 121–33.

National Audit Office (NAO) (2012) *Central government's implementation of the Compact*, London, NAO.

National Council for Voluntary Organisations (2010) *Briefing on the 'Big Society'*, London, NCVO.

Norman, J. (2010) *The Big Society*, Buckingham, University of Buckingham Press.

Parry, J., Alcock, P. and Kendall, J. (2011) *Opportunity and influence: the third sector and the 2010 general election*, Third Sector Research Centre, Working Paper 44.

Singh, A. (2010) *The Venture Society: Fuelling aspiration, independence and growth through grass-roots social entrepreneurship*, London, ResPublica.

Smerdon, M. (ed.) (2009) *The First Principle of Voluntary Action: essays on the independence of the voluntary sector in Canada, England, Germany, Northern Ireland, Scotland, United States of America and Wales*, London, The Baring Foundation.

White Paper (2011a) *Giving*, Cm 8084, London, the Stationery Office.

White Paper (2011b) *Open Public Services*, Cm 8145, London, the Stationery Office.

Wind-Cowie, M. (2010) *Civic Streets: the Big Society in Action*, London, Demos.

Wilson, R. and Leach, M. (2011) *Civic Limits: How much more involved can people get?*, London, ResPublica.

Diffusing Ideas for After Neoliberalism: The Social Investment Perspective in Europe and Latin America

Jane Jenson

Beginning in the 1980s, neoliberalism's ideas and practices profoundly challenged and destabilized post-1945 political projects, policy arrangements and practices of governing. Both in Latin America, where the Washington Consensus reshaped economies and political institutions, and in the member countries of the Organisation for Economic Co-operation and Development (OECD) world there was a move away from the perspectives on social policy developed in the three decades after 1945. In particular, there were concerted efforts to roll back existing guarantees to social protection in the name of a larger role for the market, families and communities.

Neoliberalism had, however, limits and by the mid-1990s political space for new perspectives widened. In particular, the discourse of international as well as national and sub-national social policymakers began to cohere around new ideas about 'developmental welfare states'. [. . .]

The notion of 'investment' and particularly 'social investment' underpins this policy perspective. Starting from this observation, this article addresses two questions: (1) when and where did the social investment perspective emerge as an answer to classic neoliberalism; and (2) what were the social mechanisms of its diffusion? Each of the two main sections of the article addresses one of these questions. The first section documents convergence around the key objectives of a social investment perspective. [. . .] The second, and significantly larger, section [. . .] identifies three social mechanisms that contributed to the turn towards a social investment perspective.

Converging Around a Social Investment Perspective

[. . .]

The social investment perspective rests on three principles. First is the notion of learning as the pillar of the economies and societies of the future. This principle leads to significant policy attention to human capital, beginning with pre-school children. Second is an orientation to assuring the future more than to ameliorating conditions in the here and now; this leads to promotion of social spending designed to break the intergenerational cycle of poverty and a focus on children. Finally, there is the idea that successful individuals enrich our common future and investing in their success is beneficial for the community as a whole, now and into the future, a vision that easily leads to child-centred policy interventions (Jenson and Saint-Martin, 2006: 435).

No claim is made in this article that all countries have adopted the social investment perspective. In Western Europe, liberal and social democratic welfare regimes moved more quickly to take up the discourse and policy practices of social investment than did either Bismarckian regimes or the European Union itself. In Latin America only some countries have moved in this direction. Others have selected to return to state-centric development strategies, privileging redistribution of resource rents to the poor. And yet others are still mired in their classic neoliberalism. There are, however, increasing signs that a number of countries in Latin America as well as in Western Europe and in a number of international organizations are replacing their neoliberal ideas with the three principles of the social investment perspective.

The social investment perspective represents an approach to social policy different from the social protection logic of post-1945 welfare regimes as well as the safety-net stance of neoliberals. During their consolidation in the 1950s and 1960s, systems of social protection in Europe and the Americas were grounded in the shared objective of providing a measure of social security via health, pensions, unemployment insurance and other programmes to the worker and his family. The developmentalist state in Latin America 'was born out of the same process that generated Keynesianism and welfare states' in Europe (Draibe, 2007: 241). However, whereas a variety of welfare regimes were present in Europe after 1945, in Latin America the corporatist form dominated (Esping-Andersen, 1990; Yashar, 1999: 80).

The neoliberal perspective of the 1980s assaulted this social protection model. Neoliberals popularized the diagnosis that social spending and state intervention were in conflict with economic prosperity, and thus the state was labelled the source of the problems of many countries. Internationally as well as domestically neoliberals downplayed the role of the state and promoted 'structural adjustments' that would make markets distributors of well-being, families responsible for their own opportunities, and the community sector the final safety net. [. . .]

In the 1980s policy redesign was the norm. Some existing social citizenship rights were privatized, with the most draconian assaults being on public pension systems in Latin America (Madrid, 2002). Generous public pensions were one of the targets of neoliberals in Europe as well (Bonoli, 2000). Ideas about social solidarity also shifted as poverty and social exclusion were foregrounded and attention to the rights of the so-called mainstream faded. In Chile under the dictatorship for example, '. . . social spending was to reach the truly needy and not "special interest groups" such as organized labour and organized middle-class professionals and public servants' (Schild, 2000: 282). Similar notions of a divided society, with social policy attention focused on the margins and on those 'at risk' of social exclusion were increasingly popular not only in neoliberal Britain but also in France, the European Commission, the Council of Europe, the International Labour Organization and some agencies of the UN (Deacon, 2000: 7; Jenson, 1998).

In contrast, the social investment perspective recognizes a legitimate role for state action, but only of a certain kind. As the 2007 Peruvian anti-poverty law put it: 'we have to move from a vision based on social spending to one based on social investment'.[1] The final communiqué of the OECD social ministers in 2005 was just as blunt: 'social policies must be pro-active, stressing investment in people's capabilities and the realization of their potential, not merely insuring against misfortune'.[2] The perspective by no means rejects the premise of both post-1945 welfare regimes and neoliberalism that the market ought to be the primary source of well-being for most people; it too emphasizes the importance of paid employment and other forms of market income. But, whereas neoliberals assumed that market participation was the solution, the social investment perspective includes a suspicion that the market may not be producing sufficient income for everyone, that poverty and social exclusion are real problems requiring more than simply 'a job'. There is a basic recognition that opportunities – and increasingly capabilities – are neither equally nor equitably distributed. Some public spending, such as conditional cash transfers or childcare services, may be needed to ensure that children can be sent to school, to pre-school, or to the doctor, for example. Parents may not have enough resources, and therefore they will not be able to 'choose' to invest in their children. Nor will all adults be able to enter the labour force, if basic services and supports are unavailable.

[. . .]

A common social investment prescription is the need to 'make work pay', not simply by making it compulsory and competitive with social benefit rates but also by supplementing wages, providing low-cost services, or both. For example, in-work benefit programmes provide supplements to earned income when market earnings are judged to be insufficient. Examples are Britain's Working Tax Credit (instituted by New Labour in 1999), and France's *prime pour l'emploi* (since 2001). A survey in 2003 found that 8 of the EU 15 countries had instituted an in-work benefit (Immervoll et al., 2007: 35). Affordable childcare services are also frequently identified as necessary if women's employment rates are to rise.

Latin American countries have followed another strategy for dealing with the failure of labour markets to provide sufficient income. Faced with high levels of poverty as well as informal employment and 'truncated' social protection regimes that provide little coverage to much of the population, they have been experimenting with cash-transfer programmes (Fiszbein, 2005; Standing, 2008). In particular, conditional cash transfers (CCT) that are income-tested and conditional on certain behaviours with respect to schooling and health care for children have become widespread. By 2007 they were being used in 14 Latin American countries (Bastagli, 2007). Presented in the words of their promoters, CCT '. . . hold promise for addressing the inter-generational transmission of poverty and fostering social inclusion by explicitly targeting the poor, focusing on children, delivering transfers to women, and changing social accountability relationships between beneficiaries, service providers and governments' (De la Brière and Rawlings, 2006: 4).

This emphasis on breaking the intergenerational transfer of poverty is a key idea of the social investment perspective, making it 'child-centred' (Jenson, 2001; Lister, 2003; Sen cited in Morán, 2004). One expression of the idea comes in the form of an emphasis on investments in human capital as the route to future success. For example, the Mexican government, describing its national social development programme, *Oportunidades*, called for 'investing in human capital': 'Quality education means that educational achievements translate into real access to better opportunities to make use of the benefits of that education. There will be payoffs from the investment in the form of increases in the basic skills of poor Mexican girls, boys and youth' (Secretaría de Desarrollo Social, 2003: 65). Tony Blair and Gerhard Schröder (1999) said in their manifesto for a 'third way': 'The most important task of modernization is to invest in human capital: to make the individual and businesses fit for the knowledge-based economy of the future'. The focus orients social policy at the European level, having gained the status of one of the Guidelines for Growth and Jobs for 2005–8, and being a key theme in the 2008 *Renewed Social Agenda*. [. . .]

Another and very clear expression of the social investment perspective is the emphasis on early childhood education and care (ECEC). Whereas 'childcare' is part of a strategy for mobilizing female labour force participation, ECEC focuses on the long-term advantages of providing public support for early childhood education. In the last decade, and across all regime types, putting public money into ECEC has become the norm, justified as an investment in children's futures, with collective as well as individual payoffs. As the OECD's important publication *Starting Strong II* put it [. . .]:

> The move towards seeing early childhood services as a public good has received much support in recent years from economists as well as from education researchers [who] suggest that the early childhood period provides an unequalled opportunity for investment in human capital . . . A basic principle is that learning in one life stage begets learning in the next. . . . 'The rate of return to a dollar of investment made while a person is young is higher than the rate of return for the same dollar made at a later age'. (OECD, 2006: 37)

The Economic Commission on Latin America and the Caribbean (ECLAC) makes virtually the same claim [. . .] (ECLAC, 2007: 117).

So too does the Inter-American Development Bank (IDB), which has been promoting early childhood care and development (ECCD) since the mid-1990s (Morán, 2004: 1–4). Since the mid-1990s in Latin America there has been a flurry of new early childhood programmes, sponsored by national governments and international agencies providing preschool childcare; the OECD's (2006) overview of ECEC in its member states describes the increase in public involvement in ensuring better service provision.

[. . .] The social investment perspective informs the action programmes of a number of governments and international agencies. How did this position take hold? Was neoliberalism displaced simply by the weight of its failures? Its promises had been grandiose: freeing markets and reducing the role of the state would generate well-being for all. By the mid-1990s, however, straightforward neoliberalism had hit an ideational, political and economic wall. The promised cutbacks in state activity and massive savings in state expenditures failed to materialize (Castles, 2005), despite the insistence by neoliberals that their main goal was slashing state expenditures. Social problems deepened in the North as well as the global South and poverty rates mounted, notwithstanding neoliberals' promise that structural adjustments would reduce poverty. A fifth of Britain's children lived in poverty in the mid-1990s and the child poverty rate had tripled since the 1970s (UNICEF, 2000: 21). In 1997, the Asian crisis destabilized the international economy in a frightening way. As Moisés Naím, editor-in-chief of *Foreign Policy*, said about the 'global brand' invented in the mid-1980s and labelled the Washington Consensus: 'What was implemented was usually an incomplete version of the model and its results were quite different from what politicians promised, the people expected,

and the IMF and the World Bank's econometric models had predicted'
(Naím, 1999). There was a rethinking of what 'development' in a broad
sense should involve, and a search for a 'post-Washington Consensus' that
would pay more attention to social problems (Margheritis and Pereira,
2007: 38).

  As these results and patterns were revealed and recognized, the alternative we have labelled the social investment perspective began to coalesce.
This process was not an automatic one. Interpretations of neoliberalism's
weaknesses had to be constructed and alliances assembled to spread the
critique and alternative proposals. The next section documents the processes by which convergence around a social investment perspective
occurred, identifying three social mechanisms that underpin its diffusion.

[. . .]

Delegitimizing TINA: Creating Space for Alternatives

The first mechanism that supported the emergence of a social investment
perspective is an environmental one. Political space is an essential ingredient in policy learning (Murphy, 2006: 210). Even while neoliberalism still
held sway, this mechanism worked to expand the political space for discussions of alternatives to standard neoliberalism whose proponents had
made TINA – there is no alternative – their mantra. Initially the two
regions remained quite separate, one space being created within the world
of the agencies of development and a second in Europe. In the world of
development agencies, criticism targeted the structural adjustment paradigm, promoted by the Bretton Woods institutions and by 'institutions
and networks of opinion leaders . . . including "think tanks, politically
sophisticated investment bankers, and world finance ministers, all those
who meet each other in Washington and collectively define the conventional wisdom of the moment"' (Murphy, 2006: 221, citing Paul Krugman).
Opposition to the TINA mantra appeared in organizations less committed to this Washington Consensus. [. . .]

  UNICEF took the lead by promoting the concept of 'adjustment with
a human face' and refocusing attention on the negative consequences of
structural adjustment for the most vulnerable. The starting point for the
critique was the failure of neoliberalism's promises, and the mounting
evidence of worsening conditions on the ground (Jolly, 1999: 1809). These
observations generated a decision in the first half of the 1980s to undertake
research to gather (and in some cases foster the creation of) appropriate
data, and these led eventually to a series of UNICEF reports and studies
about the need to pay attention to the situation of the poor during structural adjustment (for an account see Jolly, 1999). These studies provided

UNICEF, a 'social' agency, with the tools to engage the battle of ideas and to help generate the 'New York dissent' to the economists purveying the Washington Consensus (Murphy, 2006: 220–31; Jolly [1999] recounts the meetings in which this 'battle' occurred). [. . .]

The fact that UNICEF was leading the charge had a secondary but important consequence for the political space within which the social investment perspective emerged. Critics of the macro-economic focus and lack of concern about distribution and social justice of the Bretton Woods agencies found themselves drawn to the political space created by UNICEF as well as the Economic Commission on Africa (much of this battle of ideas dealt with the African case) (see Murphy, 2006: 220ff.). As they entered this space they were obliged to speak from UNICEF's mandate. This meant focusing on the consequences of macro-economic adjustment for children. This obligation led, for example, a long-standing left-wing political economist and expert on Africa like G. K. Helleiner to write a position paper in 1984 that would allow UNICEF to stand up to the IMF entitled: 'IMF Adjustment Policies and Approaches and the Needs of Children' (Helleiner et al., 1999: 1823). With UNICEF in the lead, increased attention to the needs of children as the beneficiaries of a rejigged Washington Consensus was foreordained.

Implementation of 'adjustment with a human face' also depended upon neoliberalism's claims about governance that were embedded in its critiques of post-1945 social policies and used to justify not only the privatization of state services but also their decentralization. Under neoliberalism 'the role of the state shifts from that of "governing" through direct forms of control (hierarchical governance), to that of "governance", in which the state must collaborate with a wide range of actors in networks that cut across the public, private and voluntary sectors, and operate across different levels of decision making' (Newman et al., 2004: 204). Neoliberalism brought, therefore, increasing enthusiasm for decentralization to local governments and for community involvement in governance, via non-governmental organizations. This is as true in Latin America as in Europe.

This position on governance informed neoliberals' action around the concept of social safety nets (SSN) (Reddy, 1998). These were meant to plug the holes and alleviate the worst effects of structural adjustment. [. . .] One of these safety nets was the *social investment fund*, used by several international organizations as their preferred policy instrument for addressing poverty in Latin America. Very much a part of neoliberalism's arsenal, the first social investment fund was set up in Bolivia in 1986 (Van Domelen, 2003: 1–2). They quickly gained popularity with institutions like the World Bank and IDB because of the relative ease of creation and light bureaucracy (despite the weak evidence that they achieved their goals) (Lustig, 1997). The governance advantages of the social investment funds were vaunted as part of the arsenal to overcome the supposed limits of a too centralized state (IDB, 1998: i). Also to be avoided were too powerful 'interests', such as unions of traditional corporatism.

Despite emerging in neoliberalism, the design of social investment funds and the other forms of SSN helped enlarge the political space for considering alternatives to it. While demand was structured by the priorities of the granting agencies, reliance on local agencies and NGOs created space within which experiments with alternatives to macro-economic focused development could be undertaken in a bottom-up way (Van Domelen, 2003: 4).

In Europe as well discussions of alternatives to TINA also became more legitimate in the mid-1990s and ideas and practices of governance supported the working of this mechanism of enlarging space. In Western Europe, there had always been plenty of partisan space for critics of neoliberalism, on the political right and the left. However, the criticisms often lacked traction, making little headway against the claims of political neoliberalism. Several partisan Lefts in European countries struggled to maintain their traditional arguments, and virtually disappeared in the process. Others reworked their principles in significant ways, in effect remaking themselves in this process, as the British Labour Party had done by the mid-1990s, under the influence of several leaders (Lister, 2003). Similarly, around the institutions of the European Union, a grouping of policy entrepreneurs, experts, politicians, NGOs and unions all were working to legitimate the idea that it was necessary to correct the pro-business bias and neoliberalism of monetary union, a project being promoted as the one-best-way to create a common economic space (Hemerijck, 2007; Jenson and Pochet, 2006).

Commitment to decentralized governance also was part of the neoliberal agenda for Europe as well. In ways similar to Latin America, NGOs and local authorities gained purchase within the system via the notion of partnerships. Coupled with neoliberals' definition of the problem as one of social exclusion, there was a strong link between 'the "new geography" of deprivation' and the 'new orthodoxy of local partnerships' identified by Mike Geddes, with the instruments of governance promoted in this case by the European Union arising directly from within the space being opened via criticisms of standard neoliberalism (Geddes, 2000: 783–4).

With respect to Europe, the OECD played in some ways a role similar to UNICEF for the development community. Rather than focusing on correcting the stance of other agencies (as UNICEF did) the OECD undertook an *autocritique*, however. The OECD had been the leader of the 'welfare as a burden' position. At its 1980 conference on the welfare state in crisis, the organization had begun diffusing the idea among its membership and within policy communities that 'social policy in many countries creates obstacles to growth' (cited in Deacon et al., 1997: 71). By the mid-1990s, however, concerns about stability and the limits of structural adjustment, in the OECD and elsewhere, bubbled up in the idea sets of OECD experts and officials. Social cohesion became a key word in policy discussion, and warnings appeared of the need to balance attention to economic restructuring with caution about societal cohesion, in order to sustain that very restructuring (Jenson, 1998: 3, 5).

The discursive focus on social exclusion and inclusion mushroomed, and was often expressed as a problem of child poverty as UNICEF weighed into the debate. The agency contributed to social learning via its detailed and comparative analyses of countries' situations, both in the global South and increasingly in the rich nations. UNICEF's Innocenti Centre published its first report on causes and consequences of child poverty in the USA in 1990, and its research programme generated important publications (with large cross-national comparative data sets) by the end of the decade focused on rich countries (see for example UNICEF, 2000).

This first mechanism of enlarging the political space led to questioning straightforward macro-economic prescriptions and practices for both Latin America and Europe. But the space opened up was filled by a cacophony of voices. Neoliberals by no means simply gave up, and the diagnosis of 'lack of sufficient markets' kept many adherents. This enlarged space, moreover, was not a simple dualistic one. There was no simple stand-off either between two sets of ideas or two sets of international organizations: 'the intellectual map of the global discourse on social welfare is more complicated than is suggested by the simple European social market (ILO) versus US liberalism (World Bank, IMF) dichotomy' (Deacon, 2000: 8). Nonetheless, while opening political space delegitimized TINA, the mechanism cannot by itself account for the emergence of a social investment perspective. A second and relational mechanism comes into play to answer the question: why settle on social investment?

Polysemic Discourse: A Cognitive Mechanism

Policy conflict about the way forward for social policy characterized the crucial middle years of the 1990s in and across national and institutional institutions (Porter and Craig, 2004; for useful overviews see Deacon, 2000; Murphy, 2006). A cognitive mechanism was at work, as perceptions of policy challenges shifted and possible solutions were reinterpreted. But, as we will describe, there was no consensus on a single meaning of social investment. It is this polysemic character that increased its diffusion.

[. . .] ·

As described earlier, the term 'social investment' appeared in the development discourse in the 1980s, first as a minor instrument – the social investment fund – invented to respond to unanticipated shocks and then to correct certain effects of structural adjustment. The choice of the term reflects the supply-side orientation of the Banks and other bodies that promoted the instrument. Among economists and those familiar with markets, 'investments' will always appear in a more positive light than will other instruments, such as 'emergency transfers'. The social investment perspective retains a supply-side focus, but adds the notion that lack of access to services (including education) can hinder adequate supply.

As the OECD moved away from its classic neoliberalism it became one of the first institutional promoters of the notion of social investment for Europe and elsewhere. [. . .] Orientations adopted in a 1992 ministerial conference included the premise that 'non-inflationary growth of output and jobs, and political and social stability are enhanced by the role of social expenditures as investments in society' (cited in Deacon et al., 1997: 71). This position led to the argument that there was a need to spend rather than simply cut back in the social realm. The 1996 high-level conference, *Beyond 2000: The New Social Policy Agenda*, concluded with a call for a 'social investment approach for a future welfare state'. OECD experts immediately began diffusing a social investment argument structured in now familiar terms: 'Today's labour-market, social, macro-economic and demographic realities look starkly different from those prevailing when the welfare state was constructed . . . Social expenditure must move towards underwriting social investment, helping recipients to get re-established in the labour market and society, instead of merely ensuring that failure to do so does not result in destitution' (Pearson and Scherer, 1997: 6, 9).

This version of the social investment perspective is, of course, very different from the notion of emergency relief that had generated the first social investment funds in Bolivia and then around Latin America. Yet, despite this difference, they share the vision of the need for long-term investments and spending for the future. Neither is this perspective simply an anti-poverty measure; social investments are for the middle-class too. It is an understanding of public interventions, in other words, that rallies those who want social policy to focus on education, including early childhood education, on training, and on making work pay as well as those who are concerned about child poverty. Following the OECD's key notion that social spending is not a burden but an investment in economic growth, the European Union could quickly move towards its own version, describing *social policy as a productive factor* under the Dutch Presidency of 1997 (Hemerijck, 2007: 2).

Intellectuals from a variety of milieus became the promoters of the social investment perspective, including its child-centred focus. Their contribution was often to expand the ambiguity of the concept further. Perhaps the best-known intellectual promoting social investment in the

European context and in terms very similar to those already developed by the OECD in the mid-1990s is Gøsta Esping-Andersen. For him, a real 'child-centred social investment strategy' is what the Nordic welfare states have been doing, and is done best there (Esping-Andersen et al., 2002: 51). This strategy is essentially one to ensure 'social inclusion and a competitive knowledge economy' via activation, making work pay and reducing workless households, the need for all of which are included in the chapter on child-centred social investment (Esping-Andersen et al., 2002: 26–67).

His notions of social investment are quite different from those of another well-known European intellectual, Anthony Giddens (1998), who called in the mid-1990s for a 'social investment state' that would invest in human and social capital. His formulations were close to those of Tony Blair's New Labour, which frequently described its actions as being social investments (Lister, 2003). In other words, Giddens' use of the idea of social investment was more supply-side oriented and more limited in its proposed interventions than were Esping-Andersen's proposals. It is not surprising, therefore, that the latter is critical of New Labour and calls instead for his own 'truly effective and sustainable social investment strategy . . . biased towards preventive policy' (Esping-Andersen et al., 2002: 5). We see, in other words, not only a battle between two well-known intellectuals struggling for policy influence but also the range and ambiguity of the notion. Policy communities could appeal to one version or the other or even combine the two, as the European Union did in its preparations for the renewal of the Lisbon strategy between 2006 and 2008 (Jenson, 2008).

At the same time as social investment was making headway in Europe and Europe-centric organizations like the OECD, it was also being extended in Latin America. It was applied to slightly different economic ends but contained the familiar future orientation and focus on children and human capital. In addition to the examples given in the first section of this article, we can use that of the IDB. This agency focused on child-centred social investment to achieve its development goals in Latin America. It sought to nudge its social development communities towards investing in children by promoting the need for Early Childhood Care and Development (ECCD) programming. For the IDB, ECCD was part of a development strategy (hence the adjustment of the name), although the 1996 materials justifying 'why invest in early childhood care and development' deployed exactly the same arguments and cited the same social facts and the same experts that their counterparts in Europe were using at the time: invest now for future pay-offs; prevent failure rather than compensating for it, and so on. Then in 2004 its social development section also published *Escaping the Poverty Trap: Investing in Children in Latin America* with a chapter by Amartya Sen entitled 'Investing in

Childhood'. Sen used his capabilities approach in this analysis and asserts that '. . . the ultimate and common goal is to improve young children's capacity to develop and learn', while the first instrument he identifies is 'empowering parents' (Morán, 2004: 63, 64).

As these examples, and they are only examples, of intellectuals within policy communities working and reworking the notion of social investment show, the concept is polysemic and can be used in a variety of policy directions. A wide range of epistemic communities have been able to deploy the notion because it has the flexible qualities of a quasi-concept. It has scientific credentials but also a common-sense meaning. Moreover, both the scientific and common-sense versions are open to multiple meanings. Sometimes the focus has been on children, and their parents' needs have been quite secondary. Other times, investing in children was proposed as a way to help parents; getting them into the labour force or empowering parents were the key objectives. Sometimes the best investments were human capital expenditures and other times health and social justice or even gender equity came to the fore. This cognitive mechanism of polysemic discourse helped rally a range of actors and networks in the process of diffusion. But more was still needed. [. . .]

Boundary Crossing: A Relational Mechanism

Convergence around ideas such as social investment has involved crossing worlds of knowledge. The third mechanism that underpins the process of diffusion is a relational one; boundary crossing sustains links and alliances across disparate networks and policy communities. This concept has been developed by those who study science policy and '. . . it aims to explain linkages between different social worlds and the negotiations that are part of what appears objective and value-free codified knowledge' (St Clair, 2006: 64). [. . .] The concept of boundary work can be adopted and adapted here, in order to highlight three types of boundary crossings that have occurred as the notion of social investment has been diffused.

First, there has been the classic movement across the border of universities and political organizations. International organizations as well as national policy communities rely on university-based analysts to help develop their arguments and provide extra legitimacy to them. As the constructivist and other literature has documented, economists and their theoretical and methodological tools frequently predominate (Dobbin et al., 2007: 452). As the Washington Consensus began to unravel, so too did the acceptance of the scientific credentials of certain economists. Moisés Naím (1999) recounts the disputes among economists in Washington and elite American universities about what should be done in light of the financial crises of the mid-1990s. As we have seen, in the 'battle of ideas' about structural adjustment and its effects, UNICEF both mobilized university-based development experts like G. K. Helleiner and moved to arm itself with the quantitative data that would permit it to make claims in the economistic world of the IMF (Jolly, 1999: 1809). The United Nations Research Institute for Social Development (UNRISD) set up a research programme on *Social Policy in a Development Context* with the stated objective to 'move [thinking] away from social policy as a safety net . . . towards a conception of active social policy as a powerful instrument for development working in tandem with economic policy' (cited in Deacon, 2005: 22), and to do so it has utilized the services of large numbers of social scientists, sociologists and political scientists as well as economists. The OECD and European Union have also called upon a relatively limited set of academics to comment on welfare state reform, and therefore there are appearances and reappearances across the institutions by the same experts. The experts mobilized by national – and increasingly local – governments are too numerous to mention. As these academically-based experts intervene – usually at the behest of the institutions – they capture and systematize as much as they invent conceptualizations that can then be deployed more broadly within the institutions.

A second form of boundary crossing that allowed ideas to diffuse in unfamiliar circuits was the breakdown of the uniqueness of 'development economics'. 'One of the undoubted historical contributions of the Washington Consensus is that it marked the end of the de-coupling between development economics and mainstream economics that had gathered steam since the 1970s' (Naím, 1999). Neoliberals rejected the post-1945 stance that there was an economics for the 'developed world' – most often defined as Keynesian – and one for the 'developing world' – most often focused on import substitution industrialization. This breakdown of a boundary allowed the two worlds, each with its 'economic-technocratic nexus' (McNeill, 2006: 346), to begin to merge, and the separate literatures that drove 'development studies' and 'policy analysis' began to overlap.

It was not only hardcore neoliberals who drove this boundary crossing, however. Within organizations as well as across them, boundaries blurred. As already noted, UNICEF focused its exposés of 'child poverty' on Europe and North America as well as on poor children in the global South. The 1995 Copenhagen Summit on Social Development, a key step toward the Millennium Development Goals, presented its declaration as a response to 'profound social problems, especially poverty, unemployment and social exclusion, that affect every country', in this way promoting a social development and social investment perspective that applied to the North as well as the global South. Within the OECD, learning across units was [also] taking place. [. . .] (Deacon et al., 1997: 71).

An additional factor that encouraged this cognitive mechanism of boundary crossing between the 'first' and 'third' worlds was the collapse of the 'second' world. After 1989 numerous agencies turned their attention to the situation of the former Soviet bloc, seeking prescriptions for its integration into global capitalism and liberal democracy. The hybrid character of that region challenged the standard distinction between development and mainstream economics as well as the paradigms of the other social sciences.

Finally, the third form of boundary crossing was the creation of new and larger coalitions of institutions and NGOs and other actors in their orbit. This blurring of boundaries is most familiar in the European Union, which, as an institutional complex of 27 member states, has the explicit mission of, if not harmonizing social policy practices, certainly fostering coordination by exchanging best practices. While member state governments maintain their room for manoeuvre, ideas about social problems and solutions, including elements of the social investment perspective, are moving rapidly from place to place, and from level to level. [T]here was also the creation of a coalition around an anti-poverty paradigm that included actors from several UN agencies, the World Bank, national governments and the OECD (Deacon, 2005; Noël, 2006). A third example comes from NGOs, which maintain broad-based contacts across regions. These are too numerous to describe but one that is particularly relevant for the spread of the social investment perspective is the Progressive Governance Summits, in existence since 1999. Membership includes Chile and Uruguay, with Brazil partially integrated. It has an ongoing focus on social policy, social cohesion, and investing in children.

Concluding Remarks

[. . .]. Sometimes termed a time of post-Washington Consensus and sometimes 'after neoliberalism', the years since the mid-1990s have seen national governments and international organizations as well as the European Union moving towards what has been termed here the social investment perspective. This approach to social policy is oriented towards the medium- and long-term future, making it child-focused and committed to using human capital investments by states as well as families to prepare for the future knowledge-based economy. Within the logic of this perspective, social policy has other objectives than social protection; it should avoid 'spending to insure against misfortune' but be willing to make 'investments' that will increase capabilities. The vision of employment that informs it recognizes that 'informalization' of the labour market will characterize the future rather than the stable and often industrial employment that was the expectation in the years after 1945. While other analyses have followed the story within regions, this article shows that there was convergence across Latin America and Europe. Moreover, the direction of movement was by no means only from the second to the first.

The second contribution is to identify three social mechanisms that allowed the diffusion of this social policy perspective across two very different regions of the globe. One mechanism – creation of space for alternatives – operated primarily in the heyday of neoliberalism. The second was particular to the social investment perspective itself. The polysemic discourse of social investment, like Keynesianism before it, allowed it to penetrate numerous networks, carried by the many intellectuals working within and alongside national governments and international agencies. Third, the social investment perspective could spread across two quite different regions of the world and speak to their needs because borders of difference had been broken down. Boundary crossing as a relational mechanism depended on the shifts in the contours of scientific disciplines (the breakdown of distinctions within the economics profession) as well as the expansion of cross-regional networks of political exchange among NGOs and governments.

Notes

From *Global Social Policy*, vol. 10, No. 1, pp. 59–77, April 2010, copyright © 2010 Sage Publications, by permission of Sage Publications Ltd.

1 Decreto Supremo No. 029-2007-PCM, 30 March 2007.
2 www.oecd.org/.../0,3746,en_2649_34115_35405014_1_1_1_1,00.html; accessed 10 April 2009.

References

Bastagli, F. (2007) 'From Social Safety Net to Social Policy?: The Role of Conditional Cash Transfers in Welfare State Development in Latin America', paper presented at the annual meeting of RC 19, Florence, September.
Blair, T. and Schroeder, G. (1999) *Europe: The Third Way*, accessed 14 August 2007, http://www.socialdemocrats.org/blairandschroeder6-8-99.html.
Bonoli, G. (2000) *The Politics of Pension Reform. Institutions and Policy Change in Western Europe*. Cambridge: Cambridge University Press.
Castles, F. (2005) 'Social Expenditures in the 1990s: Data and Determinants', *Policy & Politics* 33(3): 411–30.
Deacon, B. (2000) 'Globalization and Social Policy: The Threat to Equitable Welfare', Occasional Paper No. 5. Geneva: UNRISD.
Deacon, B. (2005) 'From "Safety Nets" Back to "Universal Social Provision": Is the Global Tide Turning?', *Global Social Policy* 5(1): 19–28.
Deacon, B., Hulse, M. and Stubbs, P. (1997) *Global Social Policy. International Organizations and the Future of Welfare*. London: Sage.
De la Brière, B. and Rawlings, L. B. (2006) *Examining Conditional Cash Transfer Programs: A Role for Increased Social Inclusion?*, Social Safety Net Primer Series, SP Discussion Paper No. 0603. Washington, DC: World Bank.
Dobbin, F., Simmons, B. and Garrett, G. (2007) 'The Global Diffusion of Public Policies: Social Construction, Coercion, Competition, or Learning?', *Annual Review of Sociology* 33: 449–72.

Draibe, S. M. (2007) 'The Brazilian Developmental Welfare State. Rise, Decline and Perspectives', in M. Riesco (ed.) *Latin America: A New Developmental Welfare State Model in the Making* (pp. 239–81). Basingstoke: Palgrave.

Economic Commission for Latin America and the Caribbean (ECLAC) (2007) *Social Cohesion. Inclusion and a Sense of Belonging in Latin America and the Caribbean.* New York: United Nations.

Esping-Andersen, G. (1990) *The Three Worlds of Welfare Capitalism.* Princeton, NJ: Princeton University Press.

Esping-Andersen, G., Gallie, D., Hemerijck, A. and Myles, J. (2002) *Why We Need a New Welfare State.* Oxford: Oxford University Press.

Fiszbein, A. (2005) *Beyond Truncated Welfare States: Quo vadis Latin America?*, accessed 1 February 2008, http://geocities.com/rofman/fiszbein.pdf.

Geddes, M. (2000) 'Tackling Social Exclusion in the European Union?: The Limits to the New Orthodoxy of Local Partnerships', *International Journal of Urban and Regional Research* 24(4): 782–800.

Giddens, A. (1998) *The Third Way: The Renewal of Social Democracy.* Cambridge: Polity Press.

Helleiner, G. K., Cornia, G. A. and Jolly, R. (1999) 'IMF Adjustment Policies and Approaches and the Needs of Children', *World Development* 19(12): 1823–34.

Hemerijck, A. (2007) 'Joining Forces for Social Europe. Reasserting the Lisbon Imperative of "Double Engagement" and More', Lecture to the Conference Joining Forces for a Social Europe, organized under the German Presidency of the European Union, Nuremburg, 8–9 February.

Inter-American Development Bank (IDB) (1998) *The Use of Social Investment Funds as an Instrument for Combating Poverty: A Strategy Paper.* Washington, DC: IDB, No. POV–104.

Immervoll, H., Jacobsen Kleven, H., Thustrup Kreiner, C. and Saez, E. (2007) 'Welfare Reform in European Countries: A Microsimulation Analysis', *The Economic Journal* 117(January): 1–44.

Jenson, J. (1998) *Mapping Social Cohesion: The State of Canadian Research.* Ottawa: CPRN, http://www.cprn.org.

Jenson, J. (2001) 'Re-Thinking Equality and Equity: Canadian Children and the Social Union', in E. Broadbent (ed.) *Democratic Equality: What Went Wrong?* (pp. 111–29). Toronto: University of Toronto Press.

Jenson, J. (2008) 'Writing Women Out, Folding Gender In: The European Union "Modernises" Social Policy', *Social Politics. International Studies in Gender, State and Society* 15(2): 1–23.

Jenson, J. and Pochet, P. (2006) 'Employment and Social Policy since Maastricht: Standing up to European Monetary Union', in R. M. Fishman and A. M. Messina (eds.) *The Year of the Euro: The Cultural, Social and Political Import of Europe's Common Currency.* Notre Dame, IN: University of Notre-Dame Press.

Jenson, J. and Saint-Martin, D. (2006) 'Building Blocks for a New Social Architecture: The LEGO™ Paradigm of an Active Society', *Policy & Politics* 34(3): 429–51.

Jolly, R. (1999) 'Adjustment with a Human Face: A UNICEF Record and Perspective on the 1980s', *World Development* 19(12): 1807–21.

Lister, R. (2003) 'Investing in the Citizen-workers of the Future: Transformations in Citizenship and the State under New Labour', *Social Policy and Administration* 37(5): 427–43.

Lustig, N. (1997) 'The Safety Nets which are Safety Nets: Social Investment Funds in Latin America', prepared for Conference on Governance, Poverty Eradication, and Social Policy, organized by HIID and UNDP, Harvard University, 12–13 November.

McNeill, D. (2006) 'The Diffusion of Ideas in Development Theory and Policy', *Global Social Policy* 6(3): 334–54.

Madrid, R. (2002) 'The Politics and Economics of Pension Privatization in Latin America', *Latin American Research Review* 37(2): 159–82.

Margheritis, A. and Pereira, A. W. (2007) 'The Neoliberal Turn in Latin America. The Cycle of Ideas and the Search for an Alternative', *Latin American Perspectives* No. 154, 34(3): 25–48.

Morán, R. (ed.) (2004) *Escaping the Poverty Trap: Investing in Children in Latin America*. Washington, DC: Inter-American Development Bank.

Murphy, C. (2006) *The United Nations Development Programme: A Better Way?* Cambridge: Cambridge University Press.

Naím, M. (1999) 'Fads and Fashions in Economic Reforms; Washington Consensus or Washington Confusion?', paper prepared for the IMF Conference on Second Generation Reforms, Washington, DC, 26 October, accessed 14 August 2007, http://www.imf.org/external/pubs/ft/seminar/1999/reforms/Naim.HTM.

Newman, J., Barnes, M., Sullivan, H. and Knops, A. (2004) 'Public Participation and Collaborative Governance', *Journal of Social Policy* 33(2): 203–23.

Noël, A. (2006) 'The New Global Politics of Poverty', *Global Social Policy* 6(3): 304–33.

Organisation for Economic Co-operation and Development (OECD) (2006) *Starting Strong II*. Paris: OECD.

Pearson, M. and Scherer, P. (1997) 'Balancing Security and Sustainability in Social Policy', *The OECD Observer* 205(April–May): 6–9.

Porter, D. and Craig, D. (2004) 'The Third Way and the Third World: Poverty Reduction and Social Inclusion in the Rise of "Inclusive" Liberalism', *Review of International Political Economy* 11(2): 387–423.

Reddy, S. (1998) *Social Funds in Developing Countries: Recent Experiences and Lessons*, UNICEF Staff Working Papers, Evaluation, Policy and Planning Series, no. EPP-SVL-98-002. New York: UNICEF.

Riesco, M. (ed.) (2007) *Latin America. A New Developmental Welfare State Model in the Making*. Basingstoke: Palgrave.

St Clair, A. L. (2006) 'Global Poverty. The Co-Production of Knowledge and Politics', *Global Social Policy* 6(1): 57–77.

Schild, V. (2000) 'Neo-liberalism's New Gendered Market Citizens: The "Civilizing" Dimension of Social Programmes in Chile', *Citizenship Studies* 4(3): 275–305.

Secretaría de Desarrollo Social (2003) *Programa Institucional Oportunidades 2002–2006*. Mexico: Programa de Desarrollo Humano Oportunidades, accessed 1 February 2008, http://www.oportunidades.gob.mx/pdfs/prog_oportunidades.pdf.

Standing, G. (2008) 'How Cash Transfers Promote the Case for Basic Income', *Basic Income Studies: An International Journal of Basic Income Research* 3(1): 1–29. http://www.bepress.com/bis/vol3/iss1/art5.

UNICEF (2000) *The League Tables of Child Poverty in Rich Nations*. Florence: UNICEF Innocenti Research Centre.

Van Domelen, J. (2003) *Social Capital in the Operations and Impacts of Social Investment Funds*. Washington, DC: World Bank.

Yashar, D. (1999) 'Democracy, Indigenous Movements, and the Postliberal Challenge in Latin America', *World Politics* 52(1): 76–104.

The Governance of Economic Uncertainty: Beyond the 'New Social Risks' Analysis

Colin Crouch and Maarten Keune

Introduction

The New Social Risks (NSR) school of social policy analysis has enabled scholars and policymakers alike to reshape their approach to take account of the main relevant changes that have affected advanced societies since the major reformulation of welfare state arrangements that took place, in most cases, after World War II (Bonoli 2007; Taylor-Gooby 2004). Major examples of these changes are deindustrialization, female labour-force participation, ageing, flexibilization and an increased variety in employment relationships. It shows how these changes have created new vulnerable groups; and it also shows that welfare policies have changed, bringing increasing diversity rather than convergence across Europe. Perhaps its most important contribution has been to identify the intricate set of relationships that link care policies (for children, the elderly and other vulnerable groups) to women's labour-force participation, and to family structures, breaking down the divisions that led to these being viewed as separate areas during the heyday of male-breadwinner, industrial economies.

However, now that approaches to social policy have been reoriented in response to the NSR agenda, it is time to point to certain deficiencies in it, or to problems that it has either overlooked or discounted as unimportant. These can be grouped under the headings of scope, market dominance, interests, and governance.

Scope. The NSR school argues that welfare states have to be reoriented in a way that *reflects* changed socio-economic circumstances that are themselves taken for granted. There is no consideration for the possibility of changing these circumstances through state policy, conflict, collective bargaining, corporatist practices, transnational regulations or other means.

Hence, certain socio-economic circumstances remain outside the political sphere; their definitions are not questioned, and no inquiry is made into the sources of those definitions. Politics and policy are restricted to social and educational policy that merely reacts to changes. [. . .] This is problematic, since it may well be possible that certain welfare problems are best addressed through, for example, a different regulation of international finance, changes in dismissal protection systems and the range of possible employment contracts, or alternative minimum wage policies. This is particularly relevant today, when policymakers in several countries are insisting that social spending must bear the brunt of the consequences of the crisis that has been caused by the malfunctioning of the Anglo-American neo-liberal financial model.

Market dominance. Further, the NSR perspective concentrates on adapting people to the market rather than reducing their dependency on it. The welfare state needs to prepare the labour supply in demand (both qualitatively and quantitatively), stimulate female participation and reduce welfare dependency. There is a risk that this leads to a situation in which people in low wage employment or working poverty become defined as social problems, and issues relating to them are removed from the labour relations and labour standards agenda. Also, the individual is seen as responsible for ensuring her own employment and can choose from the jobs offered, become self-employed, or seek forms of education that will improve her employability. Unemployment is thus an individual problem to be addressed through active labour market policies and education. The most obvious weak point in this reasoning is that it assumes that ordinary individuals have the capacity to predict and identify the kinds of jobs for which they should prepare themselves in the future, while even specialist job-research institutions have difficulty making such predictions.

Interests. The NSR approach also fails to take account of the fact that it is to an important extent employers, managers and financial capital that drive and manage the uncertainties that emerge in the new circumstances, which are rarely 'natural' phenomena (Crouch 2009a; Keune and Schmidt 2009). Their strategies have important effects on welfare and uncertainty, but the NSR approach tends to take these for granted as facts of life. The questions whether these strategies are acceptable, or whether there are alternatives to them, are not on the table. A conflict of interests between classes is therefore obscured by the NSR approach.

Governance. Although NSR pays attention to governance, and has clear links to research on 'new modes of governance', [. . .] it does not do so systematically. In particular, while claiming a new diversity of governance following a perceived decline in the role of government, it in reality concentrates only on the resurgence of the market and questionable claims for the importance of networks. In its concern to describe a shift from vertical (state) to horizontal (market and network) governance, it tends not to notice the growing role of the vertical governance of individual large corporations, for example in setting the terms of new forms of labour contracts and supply chains, or in replacing defined benefits pension schemes (for employees) with less advantageous defined contribution schemes. It also fails to notice the reduction in governance diversity involved in the decline in associational governance. The NSR approach risks to reduce this to macro-level participation in public policy through such devices as social pacts. It misses out on the role of collective bargaining, which has important direct and indirect welfare effects, and which is giving way in several industries and countries to autonomous governance by corporate managements. [. . .]

Towards a New Approach

The NSR school is rooted in certain premises about the mainly benign character of the forces at work in post-industrial economies. In trying to go beyond the achievements of the school, we need to rebalance that assumption of benignity. Rapid change and globalization, as well as the move away from Keynesian demand management, have together brought new vulnerabilities to working people's lives, uncertainties which are in the first instance defined and managed by employers and the owners of finance capital. They have considerable scope to decide how uncertainties, experienced initially as exogenous shocks, will impact on different parts of the population, both within and beyond the labour force. Social policy, in the expanded sense of all interventions (positive and negative) that come between economic shocks and the lives of working people, has to be studied primarily in terms of this process. It should not be assumed that the crude old risks associated with labour's helplessness in the face of major market forces have disappeared. This is clearly demonstrated by the global crisis that emerged in the late 2000s, which resulted in rapidly growing unemployment and the decline of the real value of pensions in many countries. Indeed, distinctions such as that between old and new risks are of secondary importance in this respect. This then leads us to examine various phenomena that go beyond the scope of the new social risks agenda.

The economic uncertainty of people with limited personal wealth and dependent on their place in the labour market for their security, the heart of the 'old' social risks, has in fact re-emerged as the central theme of labour policy through the dialectic over flexibility and security emerging from international, and particularly European, policy debates over the past two decades, with the European Commission's White Paper *Growth, Competitiveness and Employment* (1993) and the OECD's *Jobs Study* (1994) standing as crucial documents. [. . .] Globalization and associated sectoral changes in employment, as well as rising costs of social policy, have been presented as challenging an earlier approach to work and welfare based on guaranteeing security to the working population, as well as to those remaining outside the labour force on grounds of age, disability, inability to find work, or motherhood. The new approach, of which the NSR school is a part, is based on maximizing labour force participation in order to reduce dependency rates and increase the tax base, and on increasing work flexibility both among those within the existing work force and those considered to be outside it.

While these new priorities bring some distinct gains to many parts of the work force, they have had the unfortunate indirect consequence of turning attention away from the guarantee of protection from uncertainty. The one word that embodied the new priority was, and remains, 'flexibility'. This has brought a total reorientation of perspectives on all policies associated with labour. Davies and Freedland (1993), who in 1993 were able to remark that employment law is primarily about protecting workers from insecurity, have more recently (2007) declared that, at least in the UK, this has changed: employment law is now about fitting workers to the exigencies of the market and maximizing labour force participation. They point out, in particular, how legislation that seems to be giving workers new rights (such as law for the promotion of employment among women or elderly people) is actually about increasing the supply of labour. Policy for skills is about improving potential employees' quality and therefore their employability. One might summarize by saying that, if earlier labour law was concerned with human rights, today's law is concerned with human resources.

But flexibility clearly stands in a relationship of some tension, not only with the demand of working people for stability in their lives, but also with the dependence on consumer confidence of an economy based on mass consumption. Some forms of labour flexibility are unwelcome to employers themselves, if it becomes difficult to sustain continuity of employment among skilled and well-trained staff, or where firms are trying to develop strong corporate cultures. Policymakers, including senior managements of large corporations, have not been presented with the simple possibility of tearing down protections that they had come to see as inhibiting economic performance, but have been required simultaneously to provide alternative forms of assurance to at least sections of the working population that, barring natural disasters and the unforeseen, should be able to plan their lives with reasonable confidence. This includes consideration of the different forms of labour flexibility, which can have very different implications for security. There has been particular interest in policies and practices that claim to combine flexibility and security, leading policymakers to develop such hybrids as the primarily Danish and Dutch concept of 'flexicurity' (Madsen 2006; Wilthagen and Tros 2004), but the overall range of policies and practices involved in the reformulation of the balance between flexibility and security is considerably more extensive than this (Burroni and Keune 2011).

It is clear that new approaches are needed for bringing together analysis of the full ensemble of issues affecting labour market policies, related social policies, and industrial relations regimes in this changed situation, in terms of collective action games around the distribution of uncertainty. This can be tackled as a collective problem, in various ways, or it can be one of 'dumping' the uncertainty burden on different sections of the population. This is not because economic life today is more uncertain than in the past; the very reverse is likely to be true. Rather, people in modern democratic societies have high expectations that they will find protection from economic uncertainty; but after the collapse of the post-war model, they experience greater difficulty in meeting those expectations; and there is some diversity in the possible answers to their problems.

[. . .]

Policies and Practices Concerning the Governance of Uncertainty

There can be no exhaustive list of policies and practices, as they are empirical, and capable of considerable multiplication as human beings tackle issues in new ways and find creative and innovative solutions, sometimes not even aware that they are doing so. The following discussion will embrace what appear to be the major examples of these that are relevant to the task of moving beyond the NSR agenda and developing an extended concept of the social policy environment. [. . .]

Employment law: First, employment law provides frameworks of employment rights and limits to them. As noted above, during at least democratic periods, the main purpose of labour law has been to protect the rights of employees against employers who are regarded as being *prima facie* more powerful than they are (Davies and Freedland 2007; Knegt 2008). Labour law has therefore reinforced security, in some cases at the expense of flexibility. As such, it has come under sustained criticism from economists and others during recent years when employment sustainability has been seen to depend on increasing flexibility. The aim of much of this criticism has been to encourage labour law to accept a role in achieving a balance between security and flexibility. This is sometimes expressed in terms of degrees of deregulation, but deregulation nearly always requires some re-regulation, as maintenance of the market order itself requires a framework of rules (Majone 1990). [. . .]

Social policies: Prominent within the realm of formal public policy is the delivery of various services. These have a wide variety of implications for security, not all of them obvious. In the first instance, directly provided services remove certain important areas of activity from the market, providing security of continuing access to them during times of economic difficulty. Especially among lower-paid workers, this can relieve the strain of labour-market insecurity, possibly enabling them to accept more uncertainty in that market than counterparts in societies where social service provision is much lower.

[. . .] Public services offered in kind include a range of care services: child care, sickness care, elderly care. Where these services are provided by the market, they tend to be too expensive for people on modest incomes, so there is under-provision. They are often provided within the family, primarily by women. In that case the provision exists, but not as part of the labour market. Where government provides or subsidizes services, they are still primarily provided by women, but within the labour force, generating jobs, incomes, and therefore purchasing power. Further, other women, relieved of family caring roles by the availability of the public services, enter other parts of the labour force. This leads to a kind of femino-multiplier of job creation. At least within Europe, those economies that provide high levels of publicly funded direct services have higher levels of female and aggregate employment (Esping-Andersen 1999). To the extent that populations live in male/female partnerships, the increase in female participation has brought the stability of two separate employment incomes to households. In such cases, given the differences in the sectors in which men and women are likely to work (with women less likely to work in the exposed sectors), the dependence of individual households on individual industries and on the private market will often be reduced. Most important, the femino-multiplier has both created employment and, as a consequence, taxation revenues, which make possible further public-service provision.

Improving skill levels and employability: A form of security provision that is fully compatible with the free market is when individuals insure against future labour-market risk by investing in their own educational opportunities, including when they engage in mid-career education and training in order to anticipate future adverse labour-market change affecting their current employment. While wealthy individuals might do this unaided, this is a field with considerable government involvement; there is considered to be a collective interest in workforce upskilling, which extends beyond individuals' perceptions of their own interests; it is very difficult for individuals to anticipate future labour-market skill changes. Given that most education involves young people, it is also a form of future investment that requires a major contribution from the family. An exception may be training provided to employees by the employer. Here the issues are the amount of training employers provide and the type of training, i.e. if it equips employees only with firm-specific skills or also with skills that increase their employability and mobility beyond the firm. [. . .] In many countries many transfer payments are increasingly being linked to active labour market policy (ALMP) measures which are in turn often linked to official encouragement of training and education. These are responses to fears about the sustainability of social transfer regimes alone. There is an important triangle linking social insurance and social security, ALMP and personal investment in education. To the extent that ALMP policies are linked to transfers, they take the form of 'workfare', threatening loss of benefit if advantage is not taken of activation opportunities. If they are more linked to improved access to investment in personal futures, we may speak of Danish and Dutch 'flexicurity' measures (Muffels et al. 2008; Rogowski 2008; Wilthagen 2002; Wilthagen and Tros 2004), though the distinction is far from clear. [. . .]

Demand management: In Keynesian demand management government acts alongside the market. It uses its own spending to boost the economy to avert recession and to cool the economy during inflation. By damping the impact of the trade cycle it seeks to reduce the degree of insecurity in the labour market. This was the main macro-economic strategy pursued in the USA, the UK and the Nordic countries for the first three decades after World War II. The approach fell into relative disuse after it was considered to have worsened the inflationary crises of the 1970s. This change precipitated the chain of developments that led eventually to the questioning of employment security regimes that emerged during that same post-war period, but it remains among the policy devices that governments still use. It operates over time, using government's own spending to smooth trade cycles, and its impact within a society tends to be egalitarian. But these characteristics depend on governments being willing to act counter-cyclically during both parts of the trade cycle, and not only to encourage demand during potential recessions.

Insurance: [. . .] In a pure market economy, workers and others would insure themselves against risks that might affect their security. But, important though the insurance model is for many purposes, it is not common for the mass of a workforce to insure privately against labour market risk. Such behaviour is vulnerable to three market failures. First, the costs of such insurance are likely to take the poor to very low levels of subsistence, leading them to place a small improvement in comforts today over provision for the future. Second, [. . .] individuals are myopic in relation to likely major economic developments and would find it hard to make rational calculations concerning their insurance needs. Third, [. . .] – adverse selection and moral hazard – are likely to be a severe problem, particularly for insurance against sickness and unemployment. Finally, given that the collective interest in achieving sustainable security is greater than that of any individual, individuals must be expected to take precautions below the level needed for this collective purpose.

This is therefore an area where governments have intervened. [. . .] The most direct form of government intervention to seek to reduce economic uncertainty is the provision of social insurance systems, usually reinforced by social security measures. In the former, management of schemes is often shared with associational governance. These systems are limited to distribution within the risk community identified, though they also operate across the time dimension as does all insurance. In principle they are relatively egalitarian, but systems comprising schemes for different occupational groups have certain inegalitarian effects. For example, workers on flexible contracts often build up fewer entitlements than their colleagues on open-ended contracts. Also, many workers may be left outside the scope of all insurance schemes, in particular workers in the informal sector or workers active as dependent self-employed. The market has been more active in the pensions part of social insurance. [. . .]

Credit-based economies: A market-driven practice that has developed in some countries in recent years has been to separate individuals' consumption behaviour from their labour market income through extensive unsecured credit, usually mortgage debt but also credit cards. Although these practices developed solely for reasons associated with the financial sector's search for profits, it had the unanticipated effect of reducing the stress placed on individuals' concern for labour-market security as such. It required three conditions to grow. The first was a general rise in home ownership funded by mortgages, giving individuals on moderate and even low incomes forms of collateral partly independent of labour market position. The second was the growth of secondary financial markets that enabled the risks associated with housing and other forms of debt (such as credit cards, which were growing during the same period) to be shared among an increasing number of players in the financial markets. The third was the global deregulation of financial markets, which enabled more and more players and holders of different kinds of funds to enter these markets. Eventually, risks were being shared so widely that collateral requirements on mortgages, credit cards and other forms of debt became nugatory. The sums that people could borrow both rose strongly and became detached from their labour market positions.

The system can be seen as a market-generated functional equivalent of government demand management – a form of 'house price Keynesianism' (Hay et al. 2008), or 'privatized Keynesianism' (Bellofiore and Halevi 2009; Crouch 2009b). Whereas under straight Keynesianism government, mass demand is sustained through its own borrowing, here the borrowing is undertaken by individuals themselves, incurring mass individual debt. Financial irresponsibility curiously became a collective good. This element – the maintenance of consumer confidence – has meant that public policy eventually became involved in sustaining it. The model depends on continued housing market buoyancy, and governments may intervene to ensure this situation. This regime is vulnerable to eventual questioning of the value of the risks being traded, as was demonstrated in 2007–08 in the Global Financial Crisis.

Managerial organization of activities: The corporate hierarchies of major companies, acting alongside the market, have an impact on the spatial distribution of security when they devise a strategy for locating jobs with different levels of security in different parts of the world, or perhaps regions of a large nation state. Individual corporate practice, alongside other governance forms, is also important in structuring different security outcomes for different parts of the work force within a society through the way in which it defines different work categories and their attendant privileges. [. . .]

Management strategy is concerned to maximize the interests of the firm; the geographical distribution of degrees of security and insecurity within different societies that flow from its actions is just a by-product, but the social implications and resulting inequalities of this can be extensive. Complications are introduced if firms use their geographical flexibility to create labour insecurity in all countries in which they operate, in the stereotypical 'race to the bottom' in labour standards. [. . .]

Within internal markets explicit or implicit guarantees of employment and/or stable incomes are offered to parts of the work force, often combined with having other parts within the firms on flexible contracts or in the external market through sub-contracting and supply-chains. The protection offered to privileged groups or, more generally, to insiders is partly dependent on outsiders bearing the brunt of any difficulty encountered in maintaining the stability guarantee given major market fluctuations. In explicit cases, employers distinguish between categories of workers who enjoy guarantees and those who are regarded as temporary or casual. [. . .]

More implicit policies take the form of widespread understandings that certain principles will be followed in cases of redundancy or short-time working, such as tacit understandings that women, or immigrants, or very old workers will have the weakest claims to tenure. Anti-discrimination and equal opportunities legislation has often restricted the scope for such explicit practices. Nevertheless, demographic distinctions might produce implicit distinctions. For example, workers of different ages, ethnicities, genders might be typically found working for sub-contractors rather than in leading firms themselves. Use can also be made of illegal workers (usually illegal immigrants) in order to concentrate insecurity in particular groups and provide reassurance to others. All such cases of distinction between secure and insecure workers enable core workers to remain confident consumers while labour markets become flexible, but at the expense of potentially low confidence among the outsiders.

Collective bargaining: Associational governance, here collective bargaining between trade unions and either individual firms or groups of employers, is normally associated with reinforcing labour-market security, and is often criticized for doing so at the expense of flexibility and therefore in unsustainable ways. Alternatively, it may achieve a balance between security and flexibility by enforcing distinctions between insiders and outsiders. However, because collective bargaining involves negotiation and is capable of operating at a strategic level, it is possible for the participants in bargaining to trade flexibility and security. This can happen under a variety of contexts, but not all. For example, when bargaining takes place at the level of the individual firm, workers' representatives may have to trade the short-term protection of their members' security against possible needs for flexibility if the firm is to survive and thrive. This is generally known as concession bargaining. Alternatively, unions may protect the positions of current insiders at the expense of outsiders, through such formulae as 'first in, last out' (which tends to discriminate against young workers, as discussed above), or discriminating between a permanent core work force and one on temporary contracts [. . .].

Above individual firm level, collective bargaining may be involved in explicit flexibility/security trade-offs, but only where bargaining takes a co-ordinated form, with unions and employers associations being so structured that they cannot easily avoid taking responsibility for macro-economic consequences of their actions, including a significant role for unions and associations representing the exposed sector of the economy (Traxler 2003; Traxler, Blaschke and Kittel 2001; Traxler, Brandl, and Glassner 2008). [. . .]

Inter-generational transfers and support: Family also appears prominently as an institution for managing security balances among individuals and over time, outside the scope of the market. It is an important channel for inter-generational financial transfers, for example in housing finance. While elements of its role can be seen in most societies, there is considerable diversity. There is also a considerable difference in mean ages for young people leaving the parental home – ranging from the early 20s in north-west Europe to over 30 in the south-west. This is relevant to different ways in which young people are helped through difficult labour-market situations in different societies. Social norms about family obligations play a part in determining these differences, but they are sometimes supported by social and fiscal policy (Jurado Guerrero 1999). [. . .]

Family has particular implications for the labour market position of women. They often occupy insecure places in the labour market, but may be deemed to have a primary identity as working within the family, with security provided by a husband or other male 'bread-winner'. Studies of social policy and redistribution usually concentrate on relations between markets and state provision, leaving out these activities of the family. While its welfare role was historically considerably reduced by the rise of the welfare state, it remains fundamental for the living standards and security of persons not participating in the labour market, whether because of age, disability, household responsibilities or unemployment. There is also considerable diversity in the relationship between families, welfare states and commercial activities and the provision of care services. Family members both provide and receive care, in both cases affecting the labour market. This kind of role for the family perpetuates inequalities across generations, and there may be doubts about its sustainability. It depends today on certain incentives from social policy and transfer payments (mainly pensions), and certain forms of gender relations. In some countries the family's capacity to support its members through insecurity depends on the house price phenomenon discussed above, with older generations being able to stand by younger ones because of the security of their property assets.

Note

From G. Bonoli and D. Natali (eds.), *The Politics of the New Welfare State*, Oxford, Oxford University Press, 2012, pp. 45–9, 52–3, 56–62, by permission of Oxford University Press.

References

Bellofiore, R. and Halevi, J. (2009) Deconstructing Labor. A Marxian-Kaleckian perspective on what is 'new' in contemporary capitalism and economic policies. In Gnos, C. and Rochon, L.-P. (eds.) *Employment, Growth and Development. A Post-Keynesian Approach*. Cheltenham, Elgar.

Bonoli, G. (2007) Time Matters: Postindustrialization, New Social Risks, and Welfare State Adaptation in Advanced Industrial Democracies. *Comparative Political Studies*, 40, 495–520.

Burroni, L. and Keune, M. (2011) Flexicurity: a conceptual critique. *European Journal of Industrial Relations*, 17, 75–91.

Crouch, C. (2009a) Collective bargaining and transnational corporations in the global economy: Some theoretical considerations. *International Journal for Labour Research*, 1, 43–60.

Crouch, C. (2009b) Privatized Keynesianism: an unacknowledged policy regime. *British Journal of Politics and International Relations*, 11, 382–99.

Davies, P. and Freedland, M. (1993) *Labour Legislation and Public Policy*. Oxford, Clarendon Press.

Davies, P. and Freedland, M. (2007) *Towards a Flexible Labour Market: Labour Legislation and Regulation since the 1990s*. Oxford, Oxford University Press.

Esping-Andersen, G. (1999) *The Social Foundations of Post-Industrial Economies*. Oxford, Oxford University Press.

European Commission (1993) *Growth, Competitiveness and Employment*. Luxembourg, Office for Official Publication of the European Communities.

Hay, C., Riiheläinen, J. M., Smith, N. J. & Watson, M. (2008) Ireland: the outside inside. In Dyson, K. (ed.) *The Euro at 10*. Oxford, Oxford University Press.

Jurado Guerrero, T. (1999) *Why Do Spanish Young People Stay Longer at Home than the French? The Role of Employment, Housing and Social Policies*. Florence, European University Institute, unpublished PhD thesis.

Keune, M. and Schmidt, V. (2009) Global Capital Strategies and Trade Union Responses: Towards Transnational Collective Bargaining? *International Journal for Labour Research*, 1, 9–26.

Knegt, R. (ed.) (2008) *The Employment Contract as an Exclusionary Device. An Analysis on the Basis of 25 Years of Developments in The Netherlands*. Antwerp, Intersentia.

Madsen, P. K. (2006) How can it possibly fly? The paradox of a dynamic labour market in a Scandinavian welfare state. In Campbell, J., Hall, J. and Pedersen, O. (eds.) *National Identity and the Varieties of Capitalism: The Danish Experience*. Montreal, McGill-Queen's University Press, pp. 321–55.

Majone, G. (1990) *Deregulation or Re-regulation? Regulatory Reform in Europe and the United States*. London, Pinter.

Muffels, R., Chung, H., Fouarge, D., Klammer, U., Luijkx, R., Manzoni, A., Thiel, A. and Wilthagen, T. (2008) *Flexibility and security over the life course*. Dublin, European Foundation for the Improvement of Working and Living Conditions.

OECD (1994) *The Jobs Study*. Paris, OECD.

Rogowski, R. (ed.) (2008) *The European Social Model and Transitional Labour Markets: Law and Policy*. Aldershot, Ashgate.

Taylor-Gooby, P. (ed.) (2004) *New Risks, New Welfare: The Transformation of the European Welfare State*. Oxford, Oxford University Press.

Traxler, F. (2003) Bargaining, (de)centralization, macroeconomic performance and control over the employment relationship. *British Journal of Industrial Relations*, 41, 1–27.

Traxler, F., Blaschke, S. and Kittel, B. (2001) *National Labour Relations in Internationalized Markets*. Oxford, Oxford University Press.

Traxler, F., Brandl, B. and Glassner, V. (2008) Pattern Bargaining: an Investigation into its Agency, Context and Evidence. *British Journal of Industrial Relations*, 46, 33–58.

Wilthagen, T. (2002) Managing Social Risks with Transitional Labour Markets. In Mosley, H., O'Reilly, J. and Schömann, K. (eds.) *Labour Markets, Gender and Institutional Change: Essays in Honour of Günther Schmid*. Cheltenham, UK, and Northampton, Edward Elgar, pp. 264–89.

Wilthagen, T. and Tros, F. (2004) The Concept of 'Flexicurity': a new approach to regulating employment and labour markets. *Transfer – European Review of Labour and Research*, 10, 166–87.

How Climate Change Will Shape the Social Policy Framework

Zahir Sadeque

Social policy as an applied field of study is always facing new challenges as national, regional and global changes and events are shaping human life everywhere. This is particularly important because as an academic discipline its boundaries are neither very tightly defined nor jealously guarded, and rightly so because of the interconnected nature of the issues it studies. The Global Financial Crisis and climate change are two major events and processes that will surely change the way we articulate the boundaries of social policy. Here I raise a few issues on how climate change will affect social policy in this century and beyond.

The earth's climate is changing and is projected to continue to change under a variety of emissions scenarios. Average temperatures will continue to increase, rainfall patterns will change, polar ice will melt at a faster rate and sea levels will rise. Extreme weather events (hurricanes, storms, flooding, drought, heat waves) are likely to become more common and more widespread, causing frequent and greater damage. Melting glaciers will increase flood risk during the wet season and reduce dry season water supply. These changes will affect food production, increase human mortality and morbidity and cause numerous other negative impacts for habitats. Such profound changes mean that the vulnerability of people globally will increase. A third of the world's population lives in areas that are at the front line of climate change induced vulnerability and many of them are resource and income poor and are not prepared to deal with the changes that will affect their lives and livelihoods. Rural small holder farmers, farm labourers, fisher folk communities, pastoralists, urban poor and low lying coastal populations are most at risk.

The impacts of climate change that will affect the lives of people (in this century and beyond) are a key issue for social policy, nationally and globally. A major challenge is to articulate the social impacts of climate change and enact appropriate policy and institutional responses.

Climate change adaptations require attention in almost all sectors, from agriculture and food production to infrastructure, health to industrial and energy production, to economic and social policy. Such adaptations should be multi-sectoral and strive for a balance between meeting immediate needs and providing long-term institutional and policy support for sustaining those adaptations.

Among the major social policy related adaptations that demand urgent attention is first national food security, particularly for those countries and vulnerable populations who are most at risk. This is critical because many of the climate change affected countries are food insecure and have large segments of population with limited income. Second is public health preparedness to face new diseases and possible increases in the incidence and severity of existing diseases like malaria, diarrhoea, and tuberculosis. A third interrelated policy area is expanded social protection for climate change affected people. Cash transfers, targeted employment creation and incentives for supporting new carbon neutral production methods in addition to expansion of social protection measures will be important components of the new social protection policy. A fourth new area of social policy is managing displacement and conflict through measures such as orderly migration, increasing the asset base in vulnerable areas (education, skills upgrading, new production options), and the development of policies and institutions to support conflict resolution.

A New Framework for Policy Planners and Administrators

Climate change induced vulnerability requires coordinated responses and adaptation strategies. How prepared are the global community of social policy planners and administrators to face these challenges? Are we going to remain stuck in the welfare and protection framework when we pursue global social policy objectives or will we move beyond this to incorporate fresh thinking on the rights and livelihood issues of hundreds of millions of affected people? Social policy is intricately linked with economic progress and designed to support the ability of society to rebound in the face of adversity. A new framework for social policy in view of the challenges of the twenty-first century, particularly as driven by the profound impact of climate change, would need to incorporate several components, including:

- Conceptual reorientation to include rights, entitlements and concerted public interventions to support an adaptation strategy with focus on disadvantaged sections and social groups. Particularly important are the rights to employment, livelihoods, safe shelter and voice of affected people in new land use and social service planning.

- Governments need to consider seriously changes in food production and distribution mechanisms to ensure that food insecurity does not severely undermine the well-being of their most vulnerable populations. Climate change will trigger scarcity and thus rises in food prices will affect millions of households worldwide and multi-pronged efforts need to be in place to increase production from limited land and devise better nutritional fortification for children, mothers and older persons. Targeted food availability, distribution and fortification must be among the key elements.
- Targeted employment schemes for climate change vulnerable groups, many of whom may lose their livelihoods due to climate change (coastal fisher-folks, rain-fed small holder farmers, farm labour in coastal areas, pastoralists in increasingly arid Africa and South West Asia, etc.). Cash transfers, incentives for supporting new carbon neutral production methods in addition to expanding social protection measures will be important components of the new social protection interventions under the new social policy.
- Refocusing on preventive aspects of primary health care to deal with changed climate induced vector-borne diseases.
- Internal displacement and involuntary migration management. Global warming and sea level rise, reduced flow of freshwater from melting glaciers, and the increasing aridity of Sahel and Asian grasslands will force millions of people from the affected areas to migrate. We need changes in migration and immigration policies, decriminalization of the migration process and conflict mitigation capacity for internally displaced people.
- Multi-sectoral coordination with effective and integrated authority for comprehensive adaptation implementation.
- Advocacy for realignment of planning and budgeting by incorporating the concerns of vulnerable people and their livelihoods.
- Community and citizen engagement in highlighting vulnerability and adaptation.
- Identification of the special needs of social groups and immediately affected people.

Climate change is already being felt, while the severity of future impacts will depend on global mitigation actions and other aspects of climate that are perhaps not yet fully understood. Given the negative impacts already underway considerable adaptation will be necessary to sustain the current level of human well-being, which in itself is not the desired long-term goal. Along with physical planning, technological changes supporting low carbon life, expansion of carbon sinks and economic restructuring, the world needs to reorient social policy responses as well to ensure human well-being is not sacrificed.

Note

From *Global Social Policy*, 10, GSP Forum 2010, copyright © 2010 Sage Publications, by permission of Sage Publications Ltd., conveyed through Copyright Clearance Center.

Basic Income and the Two Dilemmas of the Welfare State

Philippe van Parijs

Can we avoid a social tragedy? Can we help entering the next century with our welfare states in disarray, with labour's hard-won conquests under deadly threat, and with a growing minority of citizens losing all hope of ever getting a decent job and securing a decent standard of living throughout their existence? I believe we can, but also that it won't be easy. We shall badly need intelligence and will, to come to terms with two central dilemmas.

First Dilemma: Fighting Exploitation versus Fighting Exclusion

Improving the incomes and working conditions of the poorest workers – whether directly through a statutory minimum wage and other aspects of labour law or indirectly through improving the levels of the replacement incomes granted to those out of work – has long been a central objective of our welfare states. But because exclusion from paid work is also a major form of deprivation, another central objective must be to fight against unemployment. The tension between these two objectives generates our first dilemma. Under a number of (un-Keynesian) assumptions that have become realistic enough, the more you do to improve the material situation of the poorest among the workers, the scarcer the jobs become, and the more people there are who are deprived of the privilege of having one. Thus the two objectives potentially pull in opposite directions; and as soon as unemployment ceases to be a marginal phenomenon, this leads to an acute dilemma.

This dilemma can be highlighted by starting from the dramatic explosion of inequalities in gross earnings that has been observed in much of the Western world [since the early 1980s]. The exact pattern of causation is disputed. But it is bound to include such factors as worldwide outlet expansion, increased competition on both labour and goods markets and the nature and distribution of the skills made more crucial by the computer revolution. In both the US and Western Europe, the higher gross earnings have risen considerably; but at the bottom end, there is a striking difference. Owing precisely to the better social protection of both the employed and the unemployed, what has led in the US to a sizeable fall in the lower categories of earnings has led in Europe to a considerable permanent increase – across cycles – in the proportion of people excluded from gainful employment. The very success (however partial) of Europe's fight against exploitation is making exclusion the dominant form of social injustice. Is there a way out of this painful dilemma between the fight against exploitation and the fight against exclusion, between our concern with poverty and our concern with unemployment? Yes, there is.

Along with a growing number of people across Western Europe,[1] I have been arguing that any realistic and desirable solution to this dilemma must involve the introduction of a comprehensive minimum income guarantee that takes the form, *not* of a means-tested safety net in which people get stuck – as illustrated by the UK's basic social security, Germany's *Sozialhilfe*, France's *revenu minimum d'insertion*, etc. – but of a genuine unconditional floor. Under various names – basic income, social dividend, *Grundeinkommen, reddito di cittadinanza, allocation universelle*, etc., this idea is being proposed as a key component of the backbone of a positive progressive project for a post-neo-liberal, post-communist Europe. Of course, because of the principled though partial disconnection between labour and income it implies, this proposal calls for some quite radical rethinking – not least in those parties whose very name makes it clear that they regard (paid) labour as central. But contrary to what is sometimes said, it does not rely on some absurdly optimistic assumption of abundance. Nor does it give up the aim of full employment, at any rate in the important sense of trying to give everyone the possibility of doing meaningful paid work. Indeed, something like a basic income is part of any realistic strategy for achieving it.

Ever wider circles of people are beginning to see some sense in this bold claim, as they start realizing the narrow limits of what can be expected from such alternative policies as general working time reduction or active labour market policies, and as they start sharing the following crucial insights. Coupled with a corresponding reduction in all other benefits and in the net minimum wage, basic income can be viewed as an employment subsidy given to the potential worker rather than to the employer, with crucially distinctive implications as to the type of low-productivity job that is thereby made viable. Secondly, because it is given irrespective of employment status, the introduction of a basic income abolishes or reduces the unemployment trap, not only by making more room for a positive income differential between total idleness and some work, but even more by providing the administrative security which will enable many people to take the risk of accepting a job or creating their own. Thirdly, basic income can be viewed as a soft strategy for job-sharing, by providing all with a small unconditional sabbatical pay, and thereby making it more affordable for many either to relinquish their job temporarily in order to get a break, go self-employed or retrain, or to work durably on a more part-time basis.

The combined effect of these three processes should lead to a far more flexible working of the labour market, with significantly more stepping-stone, training-intensive, often part-time jobs. Such jobs must be paid little because they represent a risky investment on the part of the employer in a free human being who could leave at any time; and they could acceptably be paid little because the pay would supplement an income to which the workers are unconditionally entitled and which therefore enables them to filter out the jobs that are not sufficiently attractive in themselves or in terms of the prospects they offer.

Of course, the size of this effect will be very sensitive to the level of the basic income and to the package of labour-market and tax-and-benefit institutional adjustments that will need to accompany its introduction. But if embedded in an appropriate package, even a modest basic income could put a halt to the growing dualization and demoralization of our socio-economic system. Under present conditions, the indignation of the jobless who are morally and legally expected to keep looking for what many know they will never find is matched by the outrage of those who subsidize with their social security contributions the idleness of people who are overtly transgressing the rules of the game. Once it stops being Utopian to believe that all those who wish to work can find a job which earns them (when added to the unconditional part of their income) enough to live on, the conditions attached to supplementary entitlements – typically, unemployment benefits restricted to active job-seekers – can more realistically and more legitimately be expected to be enforced. The introduction of an unconditional basic income would thereby also make it possible to rehabilitate the social insurance aspect of our welfare systems. Consequently, whereas a well-intentioned gradual increase in the real level of the safety net could rightly be feared further to disturb the working of the labour market, a well-embedded gradual lifting of the floor can be expected to address both the poverty and the unemployment problem.

Second Dilemma: Economic Capacity versus Political Capacity

Whether or not one is willing to introduce a basic income and make it a central component of our welfare states, one seems faced with a second dilemma which was neatly, though shockingly, illustrated by a full-page advert published some time ago in Belgian newspapers on behalf of the (socialist) president of the Walloon government. The advert starts with a copy of a number of large cheques made out by various companies which had decided to settle or expand in Wallonia. The headline, and the punch-line of the message, reads: 'What unites us today is no longer charity but business.'

Here is, then, our second dilemma. *Either* you try to formulate and implement your ideal of social justice in one region or in one nation, but then you soon find out that, for a number of mutually reinforcing reasons, the potential mobility of savings, investment, skilled labour and consumer demand is now such in Europe that the only aim you can afford in all areas of policy – social, educational, environmental and so on – is none other than 'business', as the advert put it. The economic constraints are so powerful that you are compelled to run the state as if it were a firm and to make competitiveness your paramount concern. *Or* you try to give yourself some leeway by attempting to formulate and implement your ideal of social justice on a large scale – typically, [. . .] the European Union – but then you are soon faced with the powerful obstacles that stem from a widespread distrust of highly centralized institutions, from a lack of identification and hence of spontaneous solidarity between residents of the various areas, and from the difficulty of generating a common public debate across national and linguistic boundaries about the extent and shape of the solidarity you advocate.

Is there a way out of this second dilemma? Once again, I think there is, and one in which basic income has some role to play. I shall here make no attempt even to sketch the broad outlines of what I believe [would be] an adequate solution. Let me just state two firm convictions to which I have been led by a close observation of the debate around the regional aspect of redistribution in Europe and in my own country [Belgium], whose very existence is contingent upon the preservation of a nationwide social security system. One is that a high level of structural redistribution across the borders of broadly autonomous political entities can be sustained only if it takes the form of an interpersonal transfer system, rather than of grants to the governments of the beneficiary entities. The other conviction is that, especially if the political entities involved are culturally and linguistically very different, such a system can be sustained only if on both the contribution and the benefit sides it can operate using extremely simple and uncontroversial information. Fatal resentment is far less likely to arise, for example, if all that needs checking on the benefit side is whether [particular individuals exist] and how old they are, rather than whether they really need psychiatric treatment or truly are involuntarily unemployed.

Because of the conjunction of these two convictions, I strongly believe not only that basic income does have a central role to play in solving the

first dilemma of our European welfare states, but also that it has a significant role to play in tackling the second one, between the economic
unsustainability of a generous national welfare state and the political
unsustainability of a generous transnational welfare state. The argument
sketched here would need to be elaborated and qualified along many
dimensions. But I predict that as more and more people start realizing the
full extent and exact nature of the two big dilemmas we face, basic income
will be transformed from the pet idea of a handful of cranks who believe
abundance has been reached at long last to a key weapon in the struggle
for the preservation of social solidarity and the promotion of social
justice.[2]

Notes

From *Political Quarterly*, 67, 1, 1996, pp. 63–6, copyright © 2005, John Wiley and
Sons, by permission of John Wiley and Sons, conveyed through Copyright
Clearance Center.

1 The Basic Income European Network, founded in 1988, gathers together
   individuals and organizations from fourteen countries. [. . .]
2 Several aspects of the argument sketched here are developed in Philippe van
   Parijs, *Real Freedom for All: What (if Anything) Can Justify Capitalism?*,
   Oxford, Oxford University Press, 1995.

Emergent Forms

What Adult Worker Model? A Critical Look at Recent Social Policy Reform in Europe from a Gender and Family Perspective

Mary Daly

The adult worker model thesis holds that social policy is increasingly treating women and men as individual (actual or potential) workers. Individual agency – 'choice' in everyday terms – is both valued and assumed and labour market participation is promoted as an expression of this 'choice'. This kind of thinking draws from sociological depictions of change in contemporary society (Beck 2002; Beck-Gernsheim 2002). The underlying argument is about the erosion of tradition, long-standing practices, and venerated institutions. Theorists see the structure, role, and content of family changing as part of a general movement from constraint to choice in the age of 'do-it-yourself biographies', the rise of reflexive modernization, and the growing significance of individualized identities. Individualization is cast especially in terms of independence of agency (Hobson 2004) and is closely related to commodification of personal relations. [. . .]

Lewis (2001) was one of the first to identify the emergence of individualization as a normative model in social policy, advancing the thesis that the new norm in social policy is of an adult worker model and that this involves a set of assumptions about individuals and their work and family lives. [. . .] She identifies a number of empirical elements of the social policy template involved. Of significance is the encouragement of employment on the part of both parents. A second relevant direction of recent policy is 'defamilization', essentially facilitating care to take place outside of the family – Lewis and Giullari (2005) identify this as a commodification of care whereby care is increasingly paid for. A third associated trend is individualization for social security purposes, in particular the granting of more individual rights to children and the fact that among female and male adults the aspect that counts increasingly for the purposes of getting access to benefits, tax allowances, and even services is their relationship to the labour market. All of this is associated with policy reforms that disincentivize one-earner families.

While Lewis used the framework with critical distance, the adult worker model has begun to be quite widely applied, both as a conceptual framework and a characterization of real life. The question has to be posed about how well-equipped the model is for what is being asked of it. I adjudge it to be helpful in several respects. First, it picks up on and identifies emerging trends in social policy. It especially fits with contemporary discourses of choice because it is focused on the extent to which people have options (although it is biased towards the option of employment). In addition, it has a gender subtext in that in a critical usage 'adult' is meant to depict a move to gender neutrality or sameness. However, this is implicit rather than explicit and the term adult could as easily be seen to qualify the term worker rather than depicting a particular gender arrangement. This highlights a relative silence in the formulation about the division of unpaid labour and the family arrangements implied by the adult worker model. The framework, furthermore, gives little or no attention to the broader institutional and other arrangements that underpin the model – family and other institutions are treated as a backdrop to individual functioning. While the focus on individual agency is apposite, the lack of attention to more collective considerations represents a considerable weakness. There is also the fact that the framework lacks nuance – it is not clear what if any variations there are to individualization. This too is a significant weakness, especially when the adult worker model is compared with Lewis's earlier male breadwinner typology in which she described the main variations in the most developed western European welfare states in terms of whether they adhered to a strong, moderate, or weak version of the model (Lewis 1992). In a nutshell, the adult worker characterization is under-specified in its own right and as a comparative approach.

There is work that is more collective in focus. I refer here to the scholarship on the concept of familization/defamilization, which focuses on relationships and the trade-offs involved between work and family especially for women. It also has an analytic line on whether measures prop up or undermine family as an institution and way of life [. . .] (Lister 1994; McLaughlin and Glendinning 1994). [. . .] For Lister, the framework captured the extent to which people can uphold a socially acceptable standard of living independently of family. [. . .] Another conceptualization of familization/defamilization, which has evolved from work on the conservative welfare state model (e.g., Leitner 2003; Leitner, Ostner, and Schmitt 2008; Pfau-Effinger 2005), is much more focused on family as a collective unit. [. . .] When it comes to the analysis of policy, the continental European work utilizes familization to refer especially to the role played by and assigned to the family in regard to care and the extent to which policy reform is delimiting families' care obligations (defamilization) or extending them (refamilization) (Leitner 2003; Ostner 2004). [. . .]

As a conceptual framework, familization/defamilization has both strengths and weaknesses. It too picks up on a real trend in policy, and, especially if used in its more collective sense, recognizes that the individual is not the sole interest or focus of policy. It seems to me, therefore, that familization remains an important pole against which movements in policy should be analysed. I have more of a problem with the contrasting notion of 'defamilization', which tends to reify family. For example moves towards individualization are perceived in negative terms as a 'de'. Furthermore, using both familization and defamilization to capture the universe of variation risks viewing family in relatively static terms – an unproblematic concept of family as the unit against which change is evaluated carries little recognition that family itself may be changing and that family and its societal functions are always constructed, always contingent (Daly and Scheiwe 2010). I thus suggest that individualization is the more appropriate opposing pole to familization for the purpose of the analysis of the gender and family emphases of contemporary social policy reform (Figure 1).

There is, then, the question of which dimensions of variation capture the key movements. I regard the following four dimensions as crucial: the treatment of people as individuals or family members, the favoured location of care and its construction as paid or unpaid, the treatment of family as institution and living arrangement, and the treatment of gender (in)equality and especially how and whether gender inequality is problematized. [. . .]

Individualization -- Familization

←   Treatment of people as individuals or as family members   →

←   Location of care and its treatment as paid or unpaid   →

←   Treatment of family as institution/set of relations   →

←   Problematization of gender (in)equality   →

Figure 1 Conceptualizing change in gender and family models

Analysing the Emphases of Contemporary Policy

Table 1 sets out the main relevant reforms – taking account of reform of benefits, taxation, leaves, and services as they relate to families with children – and locates them in terms of whether they primarily endorse an individualistic or a familistic model. The qualification in the last sentence defers to the fact that policy measures can tend in both directions.

[. . .]

In relation to the first parameter, there are three notable trends that are leading in the direction of individualization. The first is the tendency to grant children some individual rights and thereby to put distance between them and the family. The introduction of a guarantee to each child of a place in childcare in Finland, Germany, Sweden, and the UK can be taken as evidence of the emergence of a rights-based perspective on children. While there are limits on the extension of social rights to children, children are coming to be recognized as political citizens (Lister 2006). [. . .]

A second trend focuses on lone mothers. In the push towards activation, lone mothers have been selected for measures that limit their entitlement to public support and compel them into or strongly encourage employment. While provision varied across Europe, historically lone mothers tended to be granted access to financial assistance on the basis of their maternal status so as to enable them to care for their young children on a full-time basis. They were the beneficiaries of a maternalist orientation, not only in Scandinavia but also in Ireland, The Netherlands, and the UK. These countries are now typically cutting lone mothers' eligibility for stay-at-home support. [. . .] In the UK from 2008 lone parents on benefits (mainly mothers) have been required to seek employment once their child reaches the age of twelve years. [. . .] In The Netherlands, reforms in social assistance in 1996 required lone mothers to seek employment once their child reached the age of four, reduced from a threshold of eighteen years. This is part of a broader trend to promote a worker role and financial independence for mothers. Full-time motherhood for such women is no longer idealized by policy, except for a limited period. [. . .]

A worker role for women is promoted also by a third trend – the downgrading of derived rights. Survivor pensions (most commonly widows' pensions) are, as Saraceno (2004, 73) points out, a most important bulwark of the male breadwinner model, acknowledging both a man's lasting responsibility to support his family and the marriage contract which legitimized a care-based and servicing role for women in exchange for financial support from their husbands. The qualifying condition for such benefits was being the spouse of a person who had pension entitlement (Leitner 2001, 107). Reform is proceeding to phase out such

Table 1 Interpreting significant emphases in contemporary reforms as they relate to family and gender

Focus	Moves towards individualization	Moves towards or continuation of familization
Treatment of people as individuals or as family members for the purposes of social rights	Granting some rights to children Reduction of lone mothers' claims to benefits	
	Promotion of worker role for women, mothers especially Downgrading of derived benefits (pensions especially)	Support for part-time employment role for mothers
Favoured location of care and degree of public compensation for it	Expansion in childcare services outside the home	Extending payments/ subsidies to families around care Extension of rights around care (e.g., granting pension credits for periods spent on caring)
Treatment of family as institution/set of relations	Reduction in subsidies for one-earner families	Continuation of survivor pensions Continuation of marital or couple unit as a basis for benefits and services
Treatment of gender inequality	Daddy leave	Endorsement of maternal childcare (extension of maternity leave and directing parental leaves at mothers)

pensions or render them less generous, especially for people below retirement pension age. They are either being phased out for survivors who have no children under the age of twelve years (as in Sweden), being changed into a shortened period of income replacement (Denmark), or being subjected to income-testing (Belgium, Italy, Germany, The Netherlands). In addition, there is a general move to make the individual the unit of entitlement for the purposes of old age pensions.

Individualization is furthered also by the moves to provide childcare services outside the family and the increasing interest on the part of European welfare states in the availability and range of childcare services. Even countries such as Germany, Ireland, the Netherlands, and the UK (under New Labour) which traditionally treated this as a 'private' matter (for families themselves and/or for the market) have been undertaking reforms to improve the supply and widen the range of providers. Valorizing of childcare outside the home has at least two origins. First, it fits with a social investment approach in that it is oriented to building children's social capital (Jenson 2006; Lister 2006). This means that the new types of services that are emerging are especially oriented to the education of young children rather than (just) their care. Secondly, the provision of services has the aim of facilitating mothers' employment (Daly 2000).

Evidence of a further trend towards individualization is found in the decline in subsidies for one-income households (effectively the housewife bonus). These were long-standing features of European tax systems but are now being eliminated as Europe moves to an individualized taxation system (Dingeldey 2001). France, Germany, and Ireland – where joint taxation still prevails as the majority practice – are the three main exceptions among the countries considered here. Separate treatment of spouses for taxation purposes is the norm in most countries in Europe. France is the only country that maintains mandatory joint taxation (OECD 2007).

A final relevant trend is the emergence in Scandinavia of policies that target men's behaviour as fathers. Starting in Norway in 1993, the 'daddy quota' – whereby a proportion of the parental leave is designated for the father and is lost to the family should he not take it – is proving influential across Northern Europe. The aim is to encourage fathers' involvement in the early life of their young children. While it has a number of roots, including some in father-child bonding, it also has purchase on gender equality. In particular, it draws from a problematization of the unequal distribution of family-related tasks between women and men as one of the sources of women's disadvantage, and a barrier to greater female employment. The Scandinavian countries constitute the pole of high-grade incentivizing for sharing of parental roles. [. . .] Other countries are much more equivocal and as we shall see in the discussion to follow could be said to be familializing childcare by virtue of how they frame their leave policies.

This brings us to counter moves or tendencies which act to create or continue the familization of individuals' entitlements and personal functioning and to support the family as an institution and set of relations. The right-most column in Table 1 sets out the most important developments. A number of these moves are prosecuted under the rubric of 'balancing work and family life'.

Beginning again with the treatment of individuals, and mothers in particular, moves towards individualization are tempered through the support for and promotion of part-time work. [. . .] There are numerous examples of how welfare and other areas of social policy promote a part-time worker role and, while not always gender-specific in language or stated intent, they most typically spell a secondary worker role for women. Many countries have granted parents the right to work part-time without losing benefits – in recent years, these include Austria, Belgium, Germany, and Portugal (Morgan 2009, 41). The promotion of a part-time worker role for women is also implicit, and sometimes explicit, in social policies. In its reform of parental leave in 2001, for example, Germany made it possible to work 30 hours a week (up from 20) while on parental leave (Ostner 2004, 52–3). In France, the *Prestation d'Accueil du Jeune Enfant* encourages mothers on leave to re-enter work on a part-time basis (Morel 2007, 626). [. . .] So, social policy is showing quite considerable tacit if not overt support for a part-time worker role for mothers suggesting that, far from moving to an adult worker model, some form of a one-and-a-half earner family arrangement is now favoured.

Care is another significant domain of familization. Contemporary policy shows a notable propensity to assist and subsidize the family with care-related tasks and/or expenses. [. . .]

These care-related payments or benefits constitute something of a mixed bag, however, comprising, on the one hand, payments or subsidies that target particular types of care (e.g., parental care, purchased care) and, on the other hand, measures that are more oriented to financially assisting families with the costs of childcare regardless of where and by whom the child is cared for. A brief discussion of the two main types is in order, given their significance and their distinctiveness.

The first are cash benefits or financial subsidies paid to parents to assist with the costs of child-rearing and childcare. The UK under New Labour was a leader here. Child tax credits were introduced in 2003 and represent a significant general subsidy to families with children – some 90 per cent of families (in and out of employment) were eligible (Williams 2006). A more instrumentalist working tax credit was introduced in 2003 (payable to parents in employment for a minimum of 16 hours a week) and a childcare tax credit was also introduced, which could cover up to 80 per cent of the costs of paid childcare. While a tax credit implies a move to support employment, the tax credits introduced in the UK under New

Labour were not unequivocally in this direction. Since the credits are paid to the main carer regardless of her/his earning status, they are not promoting employment for the carer as such and one of their effects has been to transfer income from the earner to the main carer, a change that by the 2004–5 tax year was estimated to have increased mothers' incomes by about 10 per cent (Campbell 2008, 462). The fact that this happened without necessitating employment on the part of mothers leads me to regard these as tending in the direction of familization of women.

Other countries are more direct about giving financial support to families to provide childcare at home, either by the parent or through the employment of a home-based childcare worker. Examples of the former include Finland and Norway [. . .] while France is an example of the latter. France has been especially active in promoting variation in how children are cared for and in recent years especially emphasizing parental 'choice'. In 1986 a new benefit, *Allocation de Garde d'enfant à Domicile* (AGED), was created for families who hire a private nanny (who does not need to be licensed or qualified) [. . .] (Morel 2007, 625). Another benefit, *L'aide à la Famille pour l'emploi d'une Assistante Maternelle Agréée* (AFEAMA), was introduced in 1990 to cover the cost of social contributions when parents employ a registered childminder to care for children in the home. A new streamlined benefit was introduced in 2004 – the *Prestation d'Accueil du Jeune Enfant* comprises a birth allowance and a means-tested benefit paid out until the child turns three. [. . .] Spain, too, has a benefit encouraging home care – families with three or more children can reduce social security contributions by 45 per cent if they hire a childminder or domestic worker.

Although they represent at base some commodification of care (Knijn and Ostner 2002; Ungerson 1997), the payments and subsidies are quite complex and have multiple aims. Sometimes they seek to directly influence where and how children are cared for – endorsing a particular type or location of care – and in other cases they function more as another layer of support to parents, especially those on lower incomes and where the second parent may not be in employment (Lister et al. 2007, 130). Caution is therefore advised in reading these provisions as uni-directional. [. . .] The bottom line is that the family is still seen as the appropriate provider of childcare to young children, although not as the sole provider. The latter is a key difference with the past.

Another way in which care-related rights and entitlements are being endorsed is through pension credits for care provided to family members. These have existed for a considerable period of time – indeed during the 1970s and 1980s they were often introduced or expanded in the name of gender equality. If welfare states were seriously promoting individualization, they would start to abolish or cut back on these. That is not happening and so these measures continue to endorse home-based care by mothers. It is the continental European countries – Austria, Belgium, France, Germany, and Luxembourg – that are most likely to recognize care-giving for pension purposes. Most typically, the credits are for child-care, although Finland, Germany, Ireland, and the UK also grant pension recognition for periods spent caring for an elderly, ill, or incapacitated person (Leitner 2001). [. . .]

While it enabled women to gain benefits and gave them certain entitlements to support, marital status as a conduit to rights, benefits, and services has elements that are counter to gender equality. In particular, the practice tends to perpetuate women's secondary status and legitimate a second-order tier of social rights. Survivor pensions served to institutionalize women's secondary status. They still exist in most countries, although as pointed out above they are being curtailed, especially for survivors of working age, and also rendered increasingly subject to means-testing. While they are not the kind of derived right that they once were, their longevity attests to the continued significance of marriage as an institution of maintenance. A similar point can be made in regard to the taxation system in that many countries (Austria, Italy, The Netherlands, and the UK according to Saraceno (2004, 75)) still maintain a tax bonus for married breadwinners where the spouse is not employed.

The decline in marriage as the institutional reference point has not necessarily led to individualization because the partnered couple has replaced the married couple as the reference unit. Several moves are leading in the direction of renewed 'jointism'. This is especially the case for the many parental leaves that have been introduced. In France, the unit of entitlement for the paid parental leave benefit (APE) is the couple and also in Denmark the leave is increasingly constructed as a joint benefit for parents. In Germany too, a partnership model is envisaged in the parental leave reforms that have been put in place. The tax credits introduced in the UK under New Labour are joint in several ways. In fact, their only claim to individualization was that they are paid to one individual – either the person in paid work (in the case of working tax credit) or the main carer (in the case of the child tax credit and the childcare element of working tax credit). A growth in means-testing of benefits may also be indirectly leading to a growth of 'jointism' in that such benefits almost always take the situation of both partners into account.

Finally, the absence of attention to gender equality and the construction of many of the reforms in gender-neutral terms act to endorse familization. In the earlier discussion, we picked out the Daddy quota as an example of moves towards individualization. [. . .] This is not true for the bulk of paternity and parental leaves in place in Europe. These are typically of short duration and unpaid or paid at a low rate (especially the paternity leaves). The most recent evidence (Ray et al. 2010) shows that there is a huge contrast between the leave entitlements of mothers and fathers and that in most countries the leaves are more generous for mothers. Judged in terms of the degree to which change in fathers' behaviour is targeted as norm or practice, the measures are little more than symbolic and constitute but a low-grade incentive as many of the parental and paternal leaves are unpaid or paid at a flat rate. In the context of evaluating whether recent policy reforms tend in the direction of endorsing traditional patterns or change, mention must also be made of the extension of maternity leave. This has happened in the UK where the New Labour government mandated a significant extension of paid maternity leave – from 26 to 39 weeks in 2007 (Daly 2010). The female focus of this should be noted.

Overall, there are certainly some moves in the direction of individualization but there are also tendencies towards familization. [. . .] The point is that policy today at once familializes and individualizes. Parents, therefore, are getting very mixed messages and if mothers want to be in employment on anything other than a short part-time basis they have to put together rather complex care packages (Bettio and Plantenga 2004; Lewis, Campbell, and Huerta 2008). [. . .]

How to Characterize and Explain Developments?

While Jane Lewis viewed it with a critical eye, the adult worker model has started to be quite widely used as a fully-fledged model or characterization of real life. This is unwise. To the extent that it depicts an empirical trend towards individualization, the adult worker model is but a partial characterization of what is happening, as demonstrated by the evidence considered here. Certainly, there is greater recognition of female agency – women are treated as actors with some choices in a context where the 'free choice' rhetoric for women between family and work extends widely. There is a sense in which 'choice' for men has also become more widespread in that men are being given greater options *vis-à-vis* the family. In neither case, however, is the underlying welfare subject the unencumbered individual. While there is no doubt but that the agentic self is valorized by policy nowadays, it is not autonomous agency but a kind of 'weighted' autonomy that is the ideal. The individual with family bonds and familial embeddedness is the ideal social policy subject.

The analyses offered here make clear that for contemporary welfare states in Europe, family has meaning as an institution and collective entity. The over-arching concern about work/family balance issues indicates this with its strong sense of reconciliation of two institutional domains of life. The increased support for familial-based roles and relationships is another example of states' concern to reinforce family as an institution and a factor in social integration. Viewed from the perspective of European welfare states, family life is still characterized by a web of dependencies organized in part anyway according to a gender hierarchy. [. . .] While there is a strong push to increase the availability of out-of-home childcare and children have been given certain entitlements in this regard, these are constructed so that they act as a complement to family care rather than as a substitute for it.

Finally, we turn to how the emerging model should be characterized. If the adult worker model is meant to depict a movement away from both breadwinning and housewifery, it is accurate. Yet measures to encourage 'greater symmetry in male and female roles and lifestyles' (Pfau-Effinger 2005, 338) do not amount to an adult worker model. It seems to me that a *dual earner, gender specialized, family model* is an appropriate characterization of the trends in policy reform that this article has identified. [. . .] This extends the existing work on modelling (Crompton 2006; Lewis 2001; Pfau-Effinger 2005) which has tended to use two main criteria of categorization: the degree of both partners' involvement in employment and the sources or providers of care (e.g., parents, other family members, state, market, or voluntary sector services). I suggest the need to broaden the lens especially to take into account considerations around valuing and supporting the family as societal institution. Some European countries are putting a renewed emphasis on both women and men's parental roles and, rather than moving care fully from the family, are endorsing a model of family life in which care is more widely distributed among individuals within a broader family context and also between family and other institutions. While this serves to change families, it also acts to re-embed the family as a societal institution and to link it more closely to economic and social functioning. This means that our analytic frameworks must, therefore, contain conceptions pertaining to both individuals and families.

Note

References

Beck, U. 2002. 'Interview with Ulrich Beck.' In *Individualization*, eds. Beck, U. and Beck-Gernsheim, E. London: Sage.
Beck-Gernsheim, E. 2002. *Reinventing the Family*. Cambridge: Polity Press.
Bettio, F. and Plantenga, J. 2004. 'Comparing Care Regimes in Europe.' *Feminist Economics*, 10 (1): 85–113.
Campbell, M. 2008. 'Labour's Policy on Money for Parents: Combining Care with Paid Work.' *Social Policy & Society*, 7 (4): 457–70.

Crompton, R. 2006. *Employment and the Family: The Reconfiguration of Work and Family Life in Contemporary Societies.* Cambridge: Cambridge University Press.

Daly, M. 2000. 'A Fine Balance: Women's Labour Market Participation in International Comparison.' In *Welfare and Work in the Open Economy, Vol II Diverse Responses to Common Challenges,* eds. Scharpf, F. W. and Schmidt, V. E., 467–510. Oxford: Oxford University Press.

Daly, M. 2010. 'Shifts in Family Policy in the UK under New Labour.' *Journal of European Social Policy,* 20 (5): 433–43.

Daly, M. and Scheiwe, K. 2010. 'Individualisation and Personal Obligations – Social Policy, Family Policy and Law Reform in Germany and the UK.' *International Journal of Law, Policy and the Family,* 24 (2): 177–97.

Dingeldey, I. 2001. 'European Tax Systems and Their Impact on Women's Employment.' *Journal of Social Policy,* 30 (4): 653–72.

Hobson, B. 2004. 'The Individualised Worker, the Gender Participatory and the Gender Equity Models in Sweden.' *Social Policy & Society,* 3 (1): 75–83.

Jenson, J. 2006. 'The Lego Paradigm and New Social Risks: Consequences for Children.' In *Children, Changing Families and Welfare States,* ed. Lewis, J., 27–50. Cheltenham, UK: Edward Elgar.

Knijn, T. and Ostner, I. 2002. 'Commodification and De-commodification.' In *Contested Concepts in Gender and Social Politics,* eds. Hobson, B., Lewis, J. and Siim, B., 141–69. Cheltenham, UK: Edward Elgar.

Leitner, S. 2001. 'Sex and Gender Discrimination within EU Pension Systems.' *Journal of European Social Policy,* 11 (2): 99–115.

Leitner, S. 2003. 'Varieties of Familialism: The Caring Function of the Family in Comparative Perspective.' *European Societies,* 5 (4): 353–75.

Leitner, S., Ostner, I. and Schmitt, C. 2008. 'Family Policies in Germany.' In *Family Policies in the Context of Family Change: The Nordic Countries in Comparative Perspective,* eds. Ostner, I. and Schmitt, C., 175–202. Wiesbaden, Germany: Verlag für Sozialwissenschaften.

Lewis, J. 1992. 'Gender and the Development of Welfare Regimes.' *Journal of European Social Policy,* 2 (3): 159–73.

Lewis, J. 2001. 'The Decline of the Male Breadwinner Model: Implications for Work and Care.' *Social Politics,* 8 (2): 152–69.

Lewis, J. and Giullari, S. 2005. 'The Adult Worker Model Family, Gender Equality and Care: The Search for New Policy Principles and the Possibilities and Problems of a Capabilities Approach.' *Economy and Society,* 34 (1): 76–104.

Lewis, J., Campbell, M. and Huerta, C. 2008. 'Patterns of Paid and Unpaid Work in Western Europe: Gender, Commodification, Preferences and Implications for Policy.' *Journal of European Social Policy,* 18 (1): 21–37.

Lister, R. 1994. 'She Has Other Duties' – Women, Citizenship and Social Security.' In *Social Security and Social Change: New Challenges to the Beveridge Model,* eds. Baldwin, S. and Falkingham, J., 31–44. Hemel Hempstead, UK: Harvester Wheatsheaf.

Lister, R. 2006. 'Children (but not Women) First: New Labour, Child Welfare and Gender.' *Critical Social Policy,* 26 (2): 315–35.

Lister, R., Williams, F., Anttonen, A., Bussemaker, J., Gerhard, U., Heinen, J. and Johansson, S. et al. 2007. *Gendering Citizenship in Western Europe: New Challenges for Citizenship Research in a Cross-national Context.* Bristol, UK: Policy Press.

McLaughlin, E. and Glendinning, C. 1994. 'Paying for Care in Europe: Is There a Feminist Approach?' In *Family Policy and the Welfare of Women.* Cross-

National Research Papers, Third Series. ed. Hantrais, L. and Mangan, S., 52–69. Loughborough, UK: Cross-National Research Group, European Research Centre.

Morel, N. 2007. 'From Subsidiarity to "Free Choice": Child- and Elder-care Policy Reforms in France, Belgium, Germany and the Netherlands.' *Social Policy & Administration*, 41 (6): 618–37.

Morgan, K. 2009. 'Caring Time Policies in Western Europe: Trends and Implications.' *Comparative European Politics*, 7 (1): 37–55.

OECD. 2007. *Taxing Wages 2005–2006*. Paris: OECD.

Ostner, I. 2004. '"Individualisation" – the Origins of the Concept and Its Impact on German Social Policies.' *Social Policy & Society*, 3 (1): 47–56.

Pfau-Effinger, B. 2005. 'Welfare State Policies and the Development of Care Arrangements.' *European Societies*, 7 (2): 321–47.

Ray, R., Gornick, J. and Schmitt, J. 2010. 'Who Cares? Assessing Generosity and Gender Equality in Parental Leave Policy Designs in 21 Countries.' *Journal of European Social Policy*, 20 (3): 196–216.

Saraceno, C. 2004. 'De-familialization or Re-familialization? Trends in Income-tested Family Benefits.' In *Solidarity Between the Sexes and the Generations: Transformations in Europe*, eds. Knijn, T. and Komter, A., 68–86. Cheltenham, UK: Edward Elgar.

Ungerson, C. 1997. 'Social Politics and the Commodification of Care.' *Social Politics*, 4 (3): 362–81.

Williams, F. 2006. 'New Labour's Family Policy.' In *Social Policy Review 17 Analysis and Debate in Social Policy, 2005*, eds. Powell, M., Bauld, L. and Clarke, K., 289–302. Bristol, UK: Policy Press.

Beyond Modernization? Social Care and the Transformation of Welfare Governance

Janet Newman, Caroline Glendinning and Michael Hughes

Introduction

The 'modernization' of public services is a theme that has permeated UK policy discourse as it has sought the right levers for delivering its promises of public service improvement. Introduced in Labour's first term (Cabinet Office, 1999), it has extended across a range of sectors and services: the civil service, health, criminal justice, local government and others. However, it has also shifted in focus through successive stages of policy reform. [. . .]

The current focus on personalization, independence and choice brings social care to the forefront of the wider modernization agenda and raises two important questions that we address in this article. First, how far do these shifts represent a fundamental change in welfare governance? Second, what are the implications for questions of citizenship? We address these questions in subsequent sections of this article. First, however, we set out some of the distinctive features of adult social care in England and its place in the wider modernization agenda.

The Modernization of Adult Social Care

Adult social care in England and Wales has a number of features that distinguish it from other public services and profoundly affect the dynamics and outcomes of modernization processes. First, the boundaries between public and private care are blurred and unstable. Private citizens make very significant economic contributions to the total volume of adult social care provision through private purchase, co-payments and unpaid care labour. Many people – particularly older people – fund some or all of their social care services from their own resources. This includes people who are above the assets limit for publicly funded residential care and people whose levels of need are not considered severe enough to be eligible for publicly funded services (CSCI, 2006b; Help the Aged, 2007). Means-tested co-payments – 17 per cent of total spending on social care for older people (Comas-Herrera *et al.*, 2004) – constitute further private contributions to the provision of adult social care. Friends and relatives provide by far the biggest volume of adult social care – on a largely unpaid basis. Although its value is marginally offset by a very low social security benefit for some carers, it contributes around £57 billion to adult social care (Carers UK, 2002): equivalent to 75 per cent of the annual budget for the whole National Health Service.

A second distinctive feature of adult social care is that statutory agencies purchase a majority of formal services from an extensive market of charitable, voluntary, non-profit and for-profit providers. The latter, in turn, employ a highly differentiated and often very low-status workforce (Eborall, 2005; CSCI, 2006a). Unlike the NHS, where the purchase of core services from private providers has become significant only in the past few years, public sector funding for the private provision of social care dates back to the massive expansion of residential care in the 1980s (Lunt *et al.*, 1996) and the creation of distinct service markets. Large national and multi-national for-profit organizations increasingly dominate residential and nursing home provision. In contrast, providers of domiciliary and day care services are overwhelmingly small, local organizations. Pay rates are lower than in larger organizations, and problems of recruitment and retention restrict attempts to improve skills and status (Eborall, 2005). The rapid turnover of a significant minority of these agencies (CSCI, 2006a) suggests that some struggle to survive the dual pressures of local authority monopsony and tight labour supply (Laing and Buisson, 2005, quoted in CSCI, 2006a). [. . .]

A third feature of adult social care is simultaneous production and consumption, with users playing active 'co-production' (Baldock, 1997) roles in both activities. Daly and Lewis (2000) argue that care is the product or expression of a social relationship between care-giver and recipient. Writers such as Kittay (1999) have also urged attention to these relational aspects of care. These conceptualizations of care as 'co-production' and 'relationship-generated' are as relevant to the care given informally by close relatives as to the care provided on a paid basis by employed social care workers.

These three features of adult social care in England and Wales – the widespread and unstable blurring of public and private boundaries; the extensive use of market mechanisms and the differentiated nature of the providers within that market; and the role of users in the co-production of social care – have a number of implications for the ambitions of modernization. First, they suggest that simple managerial levers – economic incentives and funding penalties, performance targets and measures – may not be adequate or appropriate for bringing about changes in the patterns or nature of services, at least when used on their own. They also suggest that users and carers may play a distinctive – and potentially more active – role in the dynamics of modernization. This is particularly likely given the active role that service user groups and social movements – of disabled people, mental health service users, people with learning disabilities, carers – have played in challenging professional paternalism and bureaucratic models of service delivery (Campbell and Oliver, 1996; Spandler, 2004; Priestley, 2000). We return later to these themes. First, however, we describe the processes of adult social care modernization, and contrast this with corresponding processes elsewhere in health and local government.

Modernization: Multiple Trajectories of Reform

Official ambitions for social care were set out in two key documents: the 1998 White Paper *Modernising Social Services* (DH, 1998); and the 2005 Green Paper *Independence, Well Being, and Choice* (DH, 2005). The 1998 document identified six main areas for improvement:

- weaknesses in the protection of vulnerable people;
- lack of coordination between services, especially health and housing;
- inflexible services;
- lack of clarity about service objectives and standards;
- lack of consistency between localities in the availability of services;
- inefficiency in the costs of services.

Proposed reforms that aimed to tackle these problems included strengthened inspection systems, improved training, the creation of a registration body for social care workers, better joint working between services and improvements in delivery and efficiency. Related measures included the introduction of National Service Frameworks in mental health (DH, 1999) and older people's services (DH, 2001), and the Fair Access to Care Services guidance (DH, 2002). All these aimed to improve consistency and transparency in access to, and the quality of, services.

The 2005 Green Paper, in contrast, highlighted the goals of helping people to maintain their independence, and giving them greater choice and control over how their needs are met. It emphasized the importance of the outcomes of social care: improved health and quality of life, making positive contributions to families and communities, exercising choice and control, freedom from discrimination, economic well-being and personal dignity (DH, 2005). Issues such as regulation and performance management, workforce development and improving the organization and delivery of services were noted, but only in the context of the higher-order objectives of increasing personalization, choice, control and other outcomes for service users.

These two documents reflect significant shifts in the scope and nature of the modernization agenda within adult social care. First, there is a move away from improving the organization, delivery and efficiency of services themselves and a greater emphasis on enhancing service user control and choice. Although the 1998 White Paper advocated the development of services 'that are more sensitive to individual needs' (DH, 1998: 31), this was to be achieved primarily through the introduction of more flexible commissioning and care management processes. In contrast, the 2005 proposals argue for the greater use of self-assessment, Direct Payments and the piloting of individual budgets (the Cabinet Office Strategy Unit's 2005 report on Improving the Life Chances of Disabled People proposed the latter). There was also a move from concerns over the consistency, organization and efficiency of service inputs towards a greater focus on facilitating individual preferences and outcomes. Although largely a shift in emphasis, it is nevertheless noticeable and marked. The outcomes to which social care is now oriented include:

- fostering independence and control;
- promoting wellbeing and preventing ill health;
- protecting vulnerable adults;
- changing the culture of care;
- modernizing the workforce. (DH, 2005)

These changes are significant in three ways. First, they put service users more clearly in control of their own care and thus centrally position them as active agents in the shifting dynamics of care – it is *their* choices that should increasingly shape future service patterns. Secondly, the emphasis on prevention and wellbeing reflects changing demographic patterns in which active older people become a focus for policy attention in order to prevent or delay future service use (DWP, 2005). This latter emphasis resonates with wider health promotion priorities and with estimates of the considerable savings to be made in future health service expenditure through investment in preventive activities (Wanless, 2002), despite the lack of robust evidence on the effectiveness and cost-effectiveness of preventive measures in social care (Godfrey, 1999; Curry, 2006). Finally, there is greater emphasis on the significance of people – staff, service users and informal carers alike – as key actors in determining the quality of experiences of care. [. . .]

These shifts in the goals of modernization for adult social care have occurred not in isolation but against a backdrop of changes elsewhere in local government and the NHS. In local government the organizational separation of adults' and children's social care services reflected the increasing centrality of children and childcare to Labour's 'social investment' policy agenda, as well as to a number of high-profile child abuse cases, suggesting a characteristic intermingling of proactive and reactive features of modernization. In contrast, services to adults have lacked the same social investment policy focus and have often, consequently, been left behind. Thus increases in NHS funding over the past decade have not been matched by similar increases in social care funding, despite demographic pressures and cost increases above the rate of inflation (Age Concern, 2007). This latter phenomenon is not new; the history of the modern welfare state has been characterized by under-investment in social care, despite major shifts in responsibilities across the NHS-social care boundary (Glendinning and Means, 2004; Lewis, 2001).

[. . .]

Achieving Consistency and Equity

The modernization of adult social care has sought to reduce variations in both the quality of services and the eligibility criteria used by different local authorities. Achieving this standardization has involved increasing comparisons between the performance of different local authorities, elaborating central government guidance in the delivery of social care and reforming regulation and inspection processes. [. . .] Modernization has in this respect been largely effective (Huxley *et al.*, 2006): there have been real gains in equity, coupled with a more effective use of resources (Audit Commission, 2003).

But currently only those with needs assessed as 'critical' or 'substantial' are normally able to access services. This potentially compromises the achievement of other modernization goals by reducing opportunities to pursue preventative work and manage risk in relation to some service user groups: measures that may promote wellbeing and reduce costs in the long term. The study on the protection of vulnerable adults (Penhale *et al.*, 2007) therefore raised concerns about people denied access to safety or risk reduction strategies because their current needs are 'below the threshold'.

Pressures on resources coupled with growing demand are likely to exacerbate the problems faced by care managers with limited capacity to purchase services that could prevent future 'critical' needs by promoting wellbeing or pursuing social inclusion agendas. Such dilemmas produce a proliferation of guidelines that are not well communicated to staff (Lyons, 2007; Newman and Hughes, 2007). The question here, then, is whether such problems should be resolved at a strategic level within local authorities or should be the focus of central government intervention (see Lyons, 2007: 101). [. . .]

Creating Synergies: The Dynamics of Partnership Working

Positive outcomes for service users depend on high levels of service integration at the point of delivery. [. . .] Much has been achieved: the Health Act flexibilities (Phelps and Regen, 2008) provide a robust basis for partnership working that is beneficial both for the organizations concerned and for service users, who are enabled to regain mobility, get prompt access to equipment and experience improved physical and mental health. These outcomes appear universal and highly valued. They also led to users being able to regain independence such that they no longer needed support. This evidence is vitally important, given the preoccupation of much research with the *processes* of partnership working and the dearth of evidence on the *benefits* that partnerships can bring to users (Dowling *et al.*, 2004).

Recent policy initiatives (Payment by Results in the NHS; Direct Payments, personalized and Individual Budgets in social care) may lead to renewed divergence, in terms of whether professionals (NHS) or end users (social care) have command over purchasing resources. In practice, the policy focus on solving problems in the acute health sector has been at the expense of the marginalization of social care within a health paradigm (Huxley *et al.*, 2006; Vick *et al.*, 2006; Phelps *et al.*, 2007; Lathlean *et al.*, 2007; Iliffe *et al.*, 2007) [. . .]. The national policy drives to require collaboration and interdependency between sectors may create significant new instabilities. The focus on the boundary between health and social care may undermine the importance of partnerships across a much wider range of services (LGA, 2005; Petch *et al.*, 2007).

Changing the Style: User Involvement and Engagement

Recent trends across the public sector have placed greater emphasis on user involvement, with some recognition of the flaws of consultative mechanisms and moves towards experimentation in more deliberative forms of engagement (Barnes *et al.*, 2007). Social care has a reputation for having led the way, with innovations in engagement with service user movements serving as models for practice elsewhere. However, social care may begin to lag behind because of the tightening resource framework that is creating a narrowing focus on standards, performance and costs. The user voice here may be squeezed out.

[. . .]

Overall, those strands of modernization focused on service user involvement have produced substantial innovation, but the position of users remains one of 'Now you see them; now you don't'. This raises questions about the capacity of service users to influence the future dynamics of social care; blockages in the system may not be attributed simply to staff resistance or organizational inertia, but may derive from deeper tensions within the modernization agenda. Thus, structural tensions exist between modernizing policies designed to target resources more effectively in order to contain costs and those designed to produce positive outcomes for service users. The 'choice' agenda is at the interface between these imperatives. It cannot, alone, resolve them. [. . .]

Independence, Choice and Control: The Place of Service Users in Modernization

The changing place of service users in the process of modernization has been a consistent theme in adult social care modernization since 1997 and has placed the sector in the vanguard of developments around individualization and personalization. The 1998 White Paper made a commitment to 'more personalized models of care'; the 2005 Green Paper aimed to 'foster independence and control'. These related objectives are underpinned by a major transformation in the role of service users, to become active participants in the construction, production and management of their own social care. Service users are increasingly important actors in the dynamics of modernization, rather than simply its imagined beneficiaries. However, the instabilities and uncertainties associated with this role may further influence future modernization processes.

[. . .] User movements (whether led by service users or by articulate advocates) have been critical in transforming social care. Direct Payments were introduced as the result of disabled people's activism and these groups remain the most frequent users of this option. Access to adequately resourced peer support organizations is a critical factor in the take-up of Direct Payments (Vick *et al.*, 2006; Fernández *et al.*, 2007). The

study of the National Strategy for Carers (Seddon *et al.*, 2007) also identified the importance of adequate financial support to enable voluntary
organizations to support carers and formulate plans for service
improvement.

The introduction and extension of Direct Payments, as an alternative
to social care services in kind, has been widely documented (Leece and
Bornat, 2006; Vick *et al.*, 2006). Research has documented the success of
this option, but has also examined the political, institutional and professional barriers to its wider use (CSCI, 2004; Pearson, 2006; Ellis, 2007;
Fernández *et al.*, 2007). Nevertheless, the 2005 Green Paper argued for
the increased use of Direct Payments and for the introduction of a new
cash-based option, Individual Budgets. Thirteen English local authorities
are piloting Individual Budgets. Meanwhile, personalized budgets, originally introduced for people with learning disabilities, are also available in
an increasing number of English local authorities.

[. . .]

The new roles for service users as active agents in the social care system
carry significant risks: risks that have hitherto been borne by social care
organizations and professionals. One risk involves managing finite public
resources and associated responsibility for maximizing efficiency and
effectiveness in the use of those resources. A second risk arises from
potential shortfalls in the stimulus and maintenance of new forms of
supply in response to the demands expressed by newly empowered users
seeking services and the danger 'that individuals will end up in competition with each other over limited resources, an obvious example being
personal assistants, who are in scarce supply' (Scourfield, 2007: 120).
Hitherto, local authorities have been responsible for stimulating voluntary and independent sector social care provision and ensuring market
stability through their commissioning and contracting arrangements.
Individual purchasers will struggle to exercise similar levels of command
over local provider markets as large local authority purchasers.

Social Care, Welfare Governance and Citizenship

[. . .]

The current emphasis on personalization, independence and choice in
adult social care is now firmly embedded across government discourse,
organizational missions and professional norms of good practice. Yet,
[. . .] these are unevenly inscribed in organizational and professional practice. In policy circles low take-up of initiatives such as Direct Payments

for older people is presented in terms of a kind of battle: one between the forces for good (central government, acting in the interests of the public and on behalf of the social movements that have advocated change) and evil (local authorities who are viewed as slow to adapt, reluctant to change and defenders of entrenched interests inscribed in the block contract). Social care organizations and professional bodies in turn talk of resistance from staff, their reluctance to take risks and their continued reluctance to abandon their paternalist approaches of the past. The result, in both cases, is a temptation to strengthen implementation measures.

Our analysis in this article has, however, highlighted deeper issues of welfare governance that cannot be collapsed into the policy/implementation dynamic. [We mapped] important lines of tension within the social care system: for example, between a tightening of assessment and control systems and the capacity for local leadership and culture change; or between the regulatory framework and the need for flexibility within the service relationship. The trope of 'partnership' is particularly significant in that this not only suggests tensions within the social care system but also between different government priorities, and between different modernization programmes. As we noted earlier, adult social care has been profoundly affected by modernizing changes in the NHS, producing a subordination of social care modernization to other imperatives. In this respect, the past decade has been no different from the entire post-war period, in which developments in health services have consistently driven changes in social care services (Glendinning and Means, 2004). Although willing to engage in broader partnerships, social care services have often remained unduly focused on the difficult challenges of managing boundaries, and controlling costs across the health and social care divide (LGA, 2007). These actions have significant implications for the trust on which effective partnerships depend (Rummery, 2002). The White Paper *Our Health, Our Care, Our Say* (DH, 2006) identifies many positive points of integration between primary health and social care services, opening up opportunities to harness policy and professional concerns with preventing ill health and promoting independence. However, these potential opportunities risk remaining marginal to a service preoccupied with allocating increasingly scarce resources to those in most acute need. Attitudes towards collaboration and partnership with NHS services are also shaped by anxieties about the potential subordination of distinctive social care priorities to high-profile NHS targets. These anxieties are underpinned by the desire to sustain distinctive professional and epistemological paradigms and professional identities: care rather than cure and social rather than medical models (Hudson and Henwood, 2002; Glendinning and Means, 2006). The position of social care at the interface between a highly centralizing government and the rhetoric (and to some extent the practice) of local autonomy and control has compounded these difficulties.

Such issues highlight the importance of the institutional and policy frameworks that constitute welfare governance. But we also want to raise a wider concern about the interaction of different governance regimes. Notions of independence, choice and control imply a shift of power to the service user: what elsewhere one of us has termed as a form of 'self-governance', one of four governance regimes along with hierarchical, managerial and network governance (Newman, 2001). Studies suggest emerging tensions between policy aspirations for self-governance on the part of service users and a continuing dominant emphasis on managerial forms of governance. Self-governance depends, for its success, on longer-term capacity building supported by user-led peer and other community organizations, effective mechanisms for information-sharing and meaningful participation, co-production processes and developing skills for decision-making and management among a wide range of civil society actors. These are time-consuming activities, and require high levels of skill. They are not readily accommodated in neo-Taylorist styles of working and, above all, are not cheap. They also do not currently receive much recognition in performance and regulatory regimes, which inevitably focus on shorter-term delivery of easily measurable targets (Glendinning, 2002; de Bruijn, 2002).

Aspirations for self-governance are also not easily reconciled with hierarchical governance regimes that emphasize consistency, standards, accountability and protection – all issues that are high in the government's list of priorities. How might the tension between these different aspirations produce new dynamics in welfare governance? One possible response is that of government retreating from policy interventions and restructuring initiatives and allowing greater scope for local discretion, but retaining a role as protector of the people (as social care users) in a fragmented and a competitive marketplace. Given the current funding pressures, a distancing of government from local decision-making – and its consequences – seems a strong probability. But it could also be suggested that government, having attempted with only limited success to reform public services, is now turning away from 'top-down' levers that focus on changing structures and systems towards a reliance on service users themselves – as consumers in a new public service marketplace – to lever change through the ways in which they exercise choice. As Direct Payments and Individual Budgets become more firmly established, with groups of service users sharing their resources to purchase services in common or employing personal assistants from beyond the traditional social care workforce, hard questions will need to be asked about the place of standards and the role of regulation in ensuring equity and accountability.

In assessing the interaction between these different governance regimes, it is one thing to highlight tensions between them but another to look at deeper shifts in welfare governance that may be at stake. Here we want to turn to issues of welfare citizenship implied in the increasing stress on self-governance represented by the discourse of independence, choice and control. Much has been made in the policy literature – and academic writing – about the desirability of an 'adult' rather than a 'dependent' conception of citizenship – one that transcends the paternalism associated with bureaucratic and professional power:

> Of course, the individual's own assessment of their needs might conflict with those of their professional assessor. At present, this is too often hidden. The individual's personal assessment must be transparent in this whole process. (DH, 2005, para. 4.16)
>   We will shift the whole system towards the active, engaged citizen in his or her local community and away from monolithic, top-down paternalism. (DH, 2006, para. 1.39)

We do not wish to challenge the importance of such aspirations. Rather, we want to examine a little more closely the concept of citizenship that is implicit in the shift towards self-governance. Underpinning this is a deeper trend that some have termed governmentality: creating citizens and communities as governable subjects (Dean, 1999; Rose, 1999; Clarke, 2005). As Kemshall explains, governmentality is 'displaced to the micro-domain of individual and locale, with the residual role of welfare agencies constituted as facilitating prudential choices through the provision of expert knowledge' (2002: 132). Risks that were previously collectively managed become individualized, with service users expected to manage their own risks as active, responsible and enterprising citizens. Moreover, the poverty, deprivation and social exclusion that many disabled and older people experience (Cabinet Office, 2005) means that the choices open to them may be very limited indeed, particularly if they perceive themselves to be involuntary service users (Ferguson, 2007).

The conception of citizenship underpinning many of these reforms is one in which responsibilities are emphasized (Dwyer, 2006). Disabled people, frail older people, people with learning difficulties and others may therefore be winning citizenship rights just as the meaning of citizenship itself is changing towards more communitarian models. The interaction between liberal, republican and communitarian models of citizenship is of great interest to adult social care. Briefly:

> Liberalism puts a strong emphasis on the individual, and most rights involve liberties that adhere to each and every person. Communitarianism puts strong emphasis on the community (or the society or the nation), whose primary concern is with the cohesive and just functioning of society. Republican theories in both their social and radical variants put emphasis on both individual and group rights and underline the role of conflict and contest in the expansion or construction of such rights. (Isin, 2000: 4–5)

In social care we can trace elements of communitarian models of citizenship in the notions of care – and self-care – as a duty or responsibility, and its contribution to social cohesion and wellbeing. The proliferation of service user involvement and empowerment strategies in recent years can be aligned to a republican model, while notions of choice invoke a liberal model of individual freedoms and entitlements. These are not, however, clear-cut distinctions. The drive for greater choice and control can be attributed to pressure from service user movements, especially those of disabled people, mental health service users and, to a lesser extent, carer organizations, and to alliances between these and radical professionals. There is a clear trace of republican citizenship here. But the dominant framing of such struggles has tended to be in the form of access to a public domain of liberal citizenship. This makes the notion of self-governance through independence, control and choice vulnerable to neo-liberal tendencies in the policy agendas of many 'modernizing' welfare states especially, perhaps, in the UK.

The confluence between these different dynamics – social movement activism, liberal conceptions of citizenship, a communitarian emphasis on responsibilities and neo-liberal agendas of markets and consumer choice – produces a widespread unease. Such unease is traceable in debates about what kinds of choices are of most importance to service users [. . .]. Choice of provider may be important but is not necessarily the key value expressed by service users. Choice of time (when care is provided), of carer (with continuity of care worker), of task (to accommodate variations in daily routines and capacities) and of type of support service are of prime importance, but do not receive the same emphasis in social care policy and practice (Petch *et al.*, 2007). Choice to access the same facilities and services as 'ordinary' citizens – such as going to the cinema, pub or football match – also raises wider questions about the limits of political acceptability in how social care resources are used. It anticipates a direct confrontation between discourses of social inclusion and citizenship and popular conceptions of the lifestyles that it is appropriate for social care resources to support. Unease also pervades the debates on choice that have littered papers in UK social policy journals in recent years, debates that have highlighted the implications for questions of accountability, fairness, equity and other 'public' goods (for example, Clarke *et al.*, 2006, 2007; Needham, 2007).

Conclusion: Policy, Theory and Research

[. . .]

In this article, we have highlighted a number of disjunctures and tensions within the modernization of adult social care. In doing so we have looked beyond the policy-oriented systems model to wider theories of welfare governance. This, we argue, enables us to explore what happens as different regimes of power – hierarchical, network-based, managerial and self-governance – interact. All are present within the social care system in England and Wales. And, it might be argued, all are a necessary component of modernization. But their interaction, and the instabilities these produce, create dilemmas for social care organizations and those who manage or work in them.

Finally, in exploring the dynamics of welfare governance and citizenship, we suggest that social care modernization opens up ambiguous political spaces. 'Progressive' agendas that emerged from social movements, service user and advocacy groups have now taken centre stage in policy discourse, and are actively being pursued through a number of initiatives: Direct Payments, Individual Budgets, personalized services, and the enlargement of choice. However, these may, as we have suggested, also be vulnerable to cooption within neo-liberal imperatives towards individuation and the privatization of public goods. There is currently a remarkable disparity between academic critiques of choice in health and education, on the one hand, and discussions of choice in social care, on the other. This disparity reflects different trajectories of reform and different perceptions of the professional–user relationship in different services. 'Choice' is now such a loaded term that fruitful conversations may not be possible. But a focus on welfare governance and the politics of citizenship perhaps provides a fertile terrain for future cross-disciplinary conversations in and beyond social policy.

Note

From *Journal of Social Policy*, 37(4): 532–6, 540–50, 553, copyright © Cambridge University Press, 2008, by permission of Cambridge University Press and author Janet Newman.

References

Age Concern (2007), *The Age Agenda 2007*, London: Age Concern.
Audit Commission (2003), *All Our Lives – Social Care in England 2002–2003*, London: Audit Commission.
Baldock, J. (1997), 'Social care in old age: more than a funding problem', *Social Policy and Administration*, 31: 1, 73–89.
Barnes, M., Newman, J. and Sullivan, H. (2007), *Power, Participation and Political Renewal*, Bristol: Policy Press.
de Bruijn, H. (2002), *Managing Performance in the Public Sector*, London: Routledge.
Cabinet Office (1999), *Modernising Government*, London: HMSO.

Cabinet Office (2005), *Improving the Life Chances of Disabled People*, London: Cabinet Office.

Campbell, J. and Oliver, M. (1996), *Disability Politics: Understanding our Past, Changing our Future*, London: Routledge.

Carers, UK (2002), *Without us . . .? Calculating the Value of Carers' Support*, London: Carers UK.

Clarke, J. (2005), 'New Labour's citizens: activated, empowered, responsibilized, abandoned?', *Critical Social Policy*, 25: 4, 447–63.

Clarke, J., Smith, N. and Vidler, E. (2006), 'The indeterminacy of choice: political, policy and organisational dilemmas', *Social Policy and Society*, 5: 3, 1–10.

Clarke, J., Newman, J., Smith, N., Vidler, E. and Westmarland, L. (2007), *Creating Citizen-Consumers: Changing Relationships and Identifications*, London: Sage.

Comas-Herrera, A., Wittenberg, R. and Pickard, L. (2004), 'Long-term care for older people in the United Kingdom: structure and challenges', in M. Knapp, D. Challis, J.-L. Fernández and A. Netten (eds), *Long-Term Care: Matching Needs and Resources*, Aldershot: Ashgate.

Commission for Social Care Inspection (CSCI) (2004), *Direct Payments: What Are The Barriers?* London: Commission for Social Care Inspection.

Commission for Social Care Inspection (CSCI) (2006a), *Time to Care*, London: Commission for Social Care Inspection.

Commission for Social Care Inspection (CSCI) (2006b), *State of Social Care in England*, London: Commission for Social Care Inspection.

Curry, N. (2006), *Preventive Social Care: Is It Cost-Effective?* Wanless Social Care Review, London: Kings Fund.

Daly, M. and Lewis, J. (2000), 'The concept of social care and the analysis of contemporary welfare states', *British Journal of Sociology*, 51: 2, 281–98.

Dean, M. (1999), *Governmentality: Power and Rule in Modern Society*, London: Sage.

Department for Work and Pensions (DWP) (2005), *Opportunity Age: Meeting the Challenges of Ageing in the 21st Century*, London: Department for Work and Pensions.

Department of Health (DH) (1998), *Modernising Social Services*, Cm 4169, London: Department of Health.

Department of Health (DH) (1999), *National Service Framework for Mental Health: Modern Standards And Services Models*, London: Department of Health.

Department of Health (DH) (2001), *National Service Framework for Older People*, London: Department of Health.

Department of Health (DH) (2002), *Fair Access to Care Services: Guidelines on Eligibility Criteria for Adult Services* [LAC 2002 (13)], London: Department of Health.

Department of Health (DH) (2005), *Independence, Well-being and Choice*, Cm 6499, London: Department of Health.

Department of Health (DH) (2006), *Our Health, Our Care, Our Say – A New Direction For Community Services*, Cm 6737, London: Department of Health.

Dowling, B., Powell, M. and Glendinning, C. (2004), 'Conceptualising successful partnerships', *Health and Social Care in the Community*, 12: 4, 309–17.

Dwyer, P. (2006), *Understanding Social Citizenship*, Bristol: Policy Press.

Eborall, C. (2005), *The State of the Social Care Workforce 2004*, London: Skills for Care.

Ellis, K. (2007), 'Direct payments and social work practice: the significance of "street-level bureaucracy" in determining eligibility', *British Journal of Social Work*, 37: 405–22.

Fernández, J.-L., Kendall, J., Davey, V. and Knapp, M. (2007), 'Direct payments in England: factors linked to variation in local provision', *Journal of Social Policy*, 36: 1, 97–122.

Ferguson, I. (2007), 'Increasing user choice or privatising risk? The antinomies of personalisation', *British Journal of Social Work*, 37: 387–403.

Glendinning, C. (2002), 'Partnerships between health and social services: developing a framework for evaluation', *Policy and Politics*, 30: 1, 115–27.

Glendinning, C. and Means, R. (2004), 'Rearranging the deckchairs on the Titanic of long-term care – is organisational integration the answer?', *Critical Social Policy*, 24: 4, 435–51.

Glendinning, C. and Means, R. (2006), 'Personal social services: developments in adult social care', in L. Bauld, K. Clarke and T. Maltby (eds), *Social Policy Review 18*, Bristol: Policy Press.

Godfrey, M. (1999), *Preventive Strategies for Older People: Mapping the Literature on Effectiveness and Outcomes*, Oxford: Anchor Housing Research.

Help the Aged (2007), *Undervalued, Underfunded, and Unfit*, London: Help the Aged.

Hudson, B. and Henwood, M. (2002), 'The NHS and Social Care – the final countdown', *Policy and Politics*, 30: 2, 153–66.

Huxley, P., Evans, S., Munroe, M. and Cestari, L. (2006), 'Fair access to care services in integrated mental health teams', MASC website, Birmingham, http://www.masc.bham.ac.uk/Reports/FACS.pdf, accessed 13 July 2007.

Iliffe, S., Kharicha, K., Manthorpe, J., Goodman, C., Harari, D. and Swift, C. (2007), 'Smarter working in social care and health', MASC website, Birmingham, http://www.masc.bham.ac.uk/Reports/SWISH.pdf, accessed 13 July 2007.

Isin, E. (2000), 'Introduction: democracy, citizenship and the city', in E. Isin (ed.), *Democracy, Citizenship and the Global City*, London: Routledge.

Kemshall, H. (2002), *Risk, Social Policy and Welfare*, Buckingham: Open University Press.

Kittay, E. F. (1999), *Love's Labor: Essays on Women, Equality and Dependency*, New York: Routledge.

Laing and Buisson (2005), *Domiciliary Care Markets*, London: Laing & Buisson.

Lathlean, J., Goodship, J. and Jacks, K. with S. Cope and M. Gummerson (2007), 'Modernising adult social care for vulnerable adults: the process and impact of regulation', MASC website, Birmingham, http://www.masc.bham.ac.uk/Reports/RASC.pdf, accessed 13 July 2007.

Leece, J. and Bornat, J. (eds) (2006), *Developments in Direct Payments*, Bristol: Policy Press.

Lewis, J. (2001), 'Older people and the health–social care boundary in the UK: half a century of hidden policy conflict', *Social Policy and Administration*, 35: 4, 343–59.

Local Government Association (LGA) (2005), *The Future of Health and Adult Social Care: A Partnership Approach for Well-being*, London: Local Government Association.

Local Government Association (LGA) (2007), Press release 'New survey on cost shunting', http://www.lga.gov.uk/PressRelease.asp?id=SX14C2-A7841070, released 15 March 2007, accessed 13 July 2007.

Lunt, N., Mannion, P. and Smith, P. (1996), 'Economic discourse and the market: the case of community care', *Public Administration*, 74: 3, 369–91.

376   *Beyond Modernization?*

Lyons, M. (2007), *Place-shaping: A Shared Ambition for the Future of Local Government*, London: Stationery Office.

Moore, J. and Hart, O. D. (1998), *Foundations of Incomplete Contracts*, Harvard Institute of Economic Research Working Papers 1846, Harvard: Institute of Economic Research.

Needham, C. (2007), *The Reform of Public Services under New Labour*, Basingstoke: Palgrave Macmillan.

Newman, J. (2001), *Modernising Governance: New Labour, Policy and Society*, London: Sage.

Newman, J. and Hughes, M. (2007), *Modernising Adult Care – What's Working?* London: Department of Health. [The MASC overview report downloadable from http://www.masc.bham.ac.uk/pdfs/DH_076204.pdf, accessed on 11 July 2007.]

Pearson, C. (ed.) (2006), *Direct Payments and Personalisation of Care*, Edinburgh: Dunedin Academic Press.

Penhale, B., Perkins, N., Pinkney, L., Reid, D., Hussein, S. and Manthorpe, J. (2007), 'Partnership and regulation in adult protection', MASC website, Birmingham, http://www.masc.bham.ac.uk/Reports/PRAP.pdf, http://www.masc.bham.ac.uk/Reports/HAE.pdf, accessed 13 July 2007.

Petch, A., Miller, E. and Cook, A. with Morrison, J., Cooper, A., Hubbard, D. and Alexander, H. (2007), 'Users and carers define effective partnerships in health and social care', MASC website, Birmingham, http://www.masc.bham.ac.uk/Reports/UCDEP.pdf, accessed 13 July 2007.

Phelps, K. and Regen, E. (2008), 'To what extent does the use of Health Act Flexibilities promote effective partnership working and positive outcomes for frail and vulnerable older people?', MASC website, Birmingham, http://www.masc.bham.ac.uk/Reports/HAF.pdf, accessed 13 July 2007.

Priestley, M. (2000), 'Adults only: disability, social policy and the life course', *Journal of Social Policy*, 29: 3, 421–39.

Rose, N. (1999), *Powers of Freedom*, Cambridge: Cambridge University Press.

Rummery, K. (2002), 'Conclusions', in C. Glendinning, M. Powell and K. Rummery (eds), *Partnerships, New Labour and the Governance of Welfare*, Bristol: Policy Press.

Scourfield, P. (2007), 'Social care and the modern citizen: client, consumer, service users, manager and entrepreneur', *British Journal of Social Work*, 37: 107–22.

Seddon, D., Robinson, C., Tommis, Y., Reeves, C., Perry, J., Woods, B., Russell, L., Harper, G., Berry, A., Phillips, J., Cheung, I. and Williams, J. (2007), 'The modernisation of social care services: a study of the effectiveness of the National Strategy for Carers in meeting carer needs', MASC website, Birmingham, http://www.masc.bham.ac.uk/Reports/NCS.pdf, accessed 13 July 2007.

Spandler, H., (2004), 'Friend or foe? Towards a critical assessment of direct payments', *Critical Social Policy*, 24: 2, 187–209.

Vick, N., Tobin, R., Swift, P., Spandler, H., Hill, M., Coldham, T., Towers, C. and Waldock, H. 2006. 'An evaluation of the impact of the modernisation of social care on the implementation of Direct Payments', MASC website, Birmingham, http://www.masc.bham.ac.uk/Reports/DP.pdf, accessed 13 July 2007.

Wanless, D. 2002. *Securing our Future: Taking a Long-term View*. London: HM Treasury.

Waine, B. 2004. 'Regulation and inspection of adult social care services: baseline study', MASC website, Birmingham, http://www.masc.bham.ac.uk/Baseline1.pdf, accessed 13 July 2007.

Assessing the Welfare State: The Politics of Happiness

Alexander Pacek and Benjamin Radcliff

[Welfare state literature tends to] assess the success or failure of the welfare state in terms of its apparent consequences for individual or particular aspects of life. In this paper we follow a different course by attempting to evaluate the practical impact of the welfare state in a more basic and fundamental way – by considering whether, in the end, it tends to make people more satisfied with their lives. Simply put, we ask if an expansive welfare state improves the overall quality of human life, using the extent to which people genuinely enjoy their lives as the appropriate evaluative metric.

This is now possible, given the emergence of an extensive social-scientific literature devoted to studying life satisfaction. With the refinement of the tools necessary to measure with reasonable reliability and validity how people subjectively evaluate the quality of their lives, it has become possible to test theoretically-derived hypotheses about the observable factors that tend to make people more satisfied in some societies than others. In sum, we are capable of measuring subjective quality of life across countries in a rigorous fashion, theorizing about the real-world conditions that determine such differences, and testing the resulting empirical predictions.[1] We thus propose to assess the welfare state by determining whether it has positive or negative consequences for the degree to which people find their lives satisfying.

[. . .]

Subjective Well-Being and the Welfare State

Scholars have long debated the role of the welfare state in creating and distributing well-being. At its core, this debate reduces to the familiar dispute between politics versus markets[2] as manifested in the argument over whether to supplement the presumed inequalities of market distribution with the presumed equality of citizenship rights, i.e., whether to make 'citizen entitlements . . . rather than the market contract' the basis of the allocation of well-being.[3] Those favouring political 'entitlements' ultimately do so because, as Lane puts it, markets are 'indifferent to the fate of individuals.'[4] Esping-Andersen summarizes the argument perfectly when he notes that while capitalism certainly has many positive aspects that doubtless do contribute to quality of life, in the end 'the market becomes to the worker a prison within which it is imperative to behave as a commodity in order to survive.'[5] As it is hardly surprising or even controversial to suggest that human beings do not enjoy being reduced to a commodity to be bought and sold, it seems equally unremarkable to suggest that their lives are likely to be less rewarding the more this metaphor approaches literalness. Indeed, as we discuss presently, it is now commonplace to define the welfare state in terms of its ability to 'decommodify' citizens. If so, the welfare state should contribute to greater well-being to the extent that its defenders are correct in their socio-analysis of markets.[6]

Conversely, if the defenders of unfettered markets are right, we should observe precisely the opposite relationship: 'decommodification' becomes an ideological mask for inefficiency and wastefulness, which will impose itself as costs on the population, so as to lower the general level of happiness. In this view, the state's efforts at redistribution and provision fail because they actually reduce both the 'quantity' and 'quality' of well-being, relative to markets. This is principally because they displace the church and family as sources of qualitatively superior support and, more critically, because it encourages 'collectivization' with deleterious consequences for individual privacy, freedom, and autonomy.[7]

Surprisingly little empirical research has been undertaken to test these contesting points of view.

[. . .]

We attempt to provide a verdict in the analyses that follow.

[. . .]

Analysis

The initial empirical analysis utilizes aggregate data on average life satisfaction for the only sample of countries – eleven member states of the European Union – for which comparable, yearly time-serial data are available, courtesy of the Eurobarometer. These basic results are then confirmed with an analysis of a wider sample of seventeen industrial democracies using data from the World Values Surveys.

The European Union

The most extensive set of comparable time-serial data on subjective well-being are from the Eurobarometer. It contains a standard question commonly used to assess life satisfaction: 'On the whole, are you very satisfied, fairly satisfied, not very satisfied, or not at all satisfied with the life you lead?' We utilize the national mean on this indicator, with the response categories coded so that higher values indicate greater satisfaction. The countries included are Austria, Belgium, Denmark, Finland, France, Germany, Ireland, Italy, the Netherlands, Sweden, and the United Kingdom. The data are from 1975 to 2002.[8] Multiple observations per year are averaged.

The principal independent variables are three alternative measures of the underlying concept of independence from market forces discussed previously. The first is a measure of the degree of decommodification provided by the welfare state, using the time-serial data from Scruggs[9] which follow the original formulation from Esping-Andersen.[10] The second is the conceptually similar index of the social wage[11] defined in terms of income that a typical unemployed worker can expect to receive by status of his citizenship rather than market participation. The third shifts from the welfare state *per se* to the wider political ideology of governments, operationalized as the cumulative share of left-party cabinet seats less those of right-party seats.[12] In each instance higher values indicate a greater commitment to the social democratic project of emancipation from market dependence and should consequently show a positive relationship with life satisfaction.

Two controls are utilized. The first is the unemployment rate, expressed as a percentage, from Armingeon et al.,[13] given a large body of evidence documenting the depressive effect of this phenomenon on satisfaction.[14] We also introduce a set of dummy variables for each country (excepting a reference category) to account for the relatively fixed social, economic, and cultural characteristics of a given country. [. . .] The effect of the dummies is, of course, to fit separate intercepts for each country, thus accounting for the large and sustained differences in satisfaction that one might expect to result from different cultural and institutional contexts. The nation dummies thus account for unmodelled structural difference across countries. [. . .]

Results are in Table 1. As is apparent, each of the three political variables is significant and correctly signed. The implication is obviously that

Assessing the Welfare State

Table 1 The welfare state and life satisfaction, European Union 1975–2002

	(a)	(b)	(c)
Decommodification	.005*	n/a	n/a
	(.003)		
Social wage	n/a	.005***	n/a
		(.001)	
Cumulative left-party score	n/a	n/a	.002*
			(.001)
Unemployment	−.002	−.006*	−.001
	(.002)	(.003)	(.002)
Life satisfaction lag t-1	.620***	.507***	.638***
	(.060)	(.089)	(.059)
Austria	−.057*	−.102**	−.088**
	(.028)	(.036)	(.038)
Belgium	−.050*	−.094**	−.056*
	(.027)	(.037)	(.029)
Denmark	.100***	.049	.084*
	(.041)	(.031)	(.039)
Finland	−.032	−.023	−.063*
	(.027)	(.028)	(.037)
France	−.149***	−.208***	−.101***
	(.031)	(.047)	(.022)
Germany	−.115***	−.139***	−.068***
	(.033)	(.041)	(.020)
Ireland	.008	−.008	.002
	(.013)	(.021)	(.015)
Italy	−.135***	−.113***	−.166***
	(.027)	(.032)	(.036)
Netherlands	.030	−.052*	.056**
	(.034)	(.024)	(.020)
Sweden	.009	.111***	−.055
	(.036)	(.017)	(.064)
Constant	1.077***	1.490***	1.161***
	(.200)	(.270)	(.206)
R-squared	.94	.94	.94
N	242	121	223

Note: Dependent variable is mean life satisfaction (1–4 scale). Estimation is with panel corrected standard errors with a lagged dependent variable to control for autocorrelation. Entries are regression coefficients (standard errors). The United Kingdom is the reference category for fixed effects.
* – significant at .05 level
** – significant at .01 level
*** – significant at .001 level

national levels of satisfaction vary directly with the level of decommodification, the social wage, and left-dominance of government.

Perhaps the most profitable way of interpreting the magnitude of the impact of the political variables on life satisfaction is to compute the expected change in satisfaction when moving between the maximum and minimum observed values of the former variables. Doing so indicates a predicted difference of over three-quarters of a standard deviation in satisfaction for decommodification, one-and-a-quarter standard deviations for the social wage, and six-tenths of a standard deviation for left party dominance. Clearly, then, the degree of market independence a society provides has a substantive as well as statistically significant effect on the degree to which individuals tend, on average, to find their lives satisfying.

While the multivariate models described above are the best way to appraise the relationships between the welfare state variables and subjective well-being (SWB), we can also document the basic patterns through the more intuitive method by illustrating the simple bivariate relationships (using the mean values over time for the welfare state measures and SWB), as provided in Figures 1–3. The patterns are by no means entirely neat (reflecting the fact that there are indeed other determinants of satisfaction beyond the welfare state) but they do illustrate nicely the basic relationships in question.

The Industrial Democracies

The results above can be substantiated using an entirely different data collection covering a wider sample of nations by turning to the several

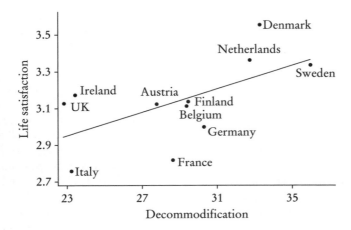

Figure 1 Life satisfaction and decommodification

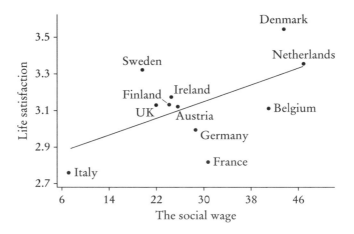

Figure 2 Life satisfaction and the social wage

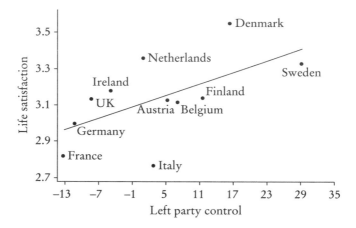

Figure 3 Life satisfaction and party government

waves of the World Values Survey. Our dependent variable is again the national mean of life satisfaction, from the standard question: 'All things considered, how satisfied or dissatisfied are you with your life now?' Higher values, of course, suggest greater satisfaction. We compute national values using all waves of the WVS from 1981 to 2000. The number of observations varies by country but averages 3.1.

The principal independent variables are as before: decommodification, the social wage, and left party control of government. The sample now includes the same eleven West European countries, plus the United

States, Canada, Australia, New Zealand, Norway, Switzerland, and Japan. Given the small number of time points per country, neither panel-corrected standard errors nor dummy variables are appropriate; instead we rely on a GLS random-effects model to account for the pooled structure of the data.[15] Given the absence of country dummies, we include the three control variables commonly used in cross-national studies:[16] a measure of the 'individualism' of national cultures,[17] GDP per capita,[18] and unemployment.[19]

Results are in Table 2. As is apparent, theoretical expectations are once again confirmed: the coefficient of each of the variables of interest is significant and of the correct sign. Interpreting the magnitude of the coefficients (using the same method as earlier) actually suggests a slightly greater overall impact of the political factors on satisfaction: moving across the range of the independent variables in each case suggests a change of more than one full standard deviation in satisfaction.

Table 2 The welfare state and life satisfaction, industrial democracies 1981–2000

	(a)	(b)	(c)
Decommodification	.033[*]	n/a	n/a
	(.015)		
Social wage	n/a	.009[*]	n/a
		(.005)	
Cumulative left-party score	n/a	n/a	.007[*]
			(.004)
Culture	.144[**]	.136[**]	.134[**]
	(.061)	(.060)	(.058)
Real per capita GDP	5.09	5.90	.000
	(9.06)	(9.35)	(9.34)
Unemployment	−.009	−.016	−.012
	(.013)	(.014)	(.014)
Constant	5.50[***]	6.26[***]	6.40[***]
	(.643)	(.513)	(.494)
R-squared	.36	.36	.43
N	55	55	55

Note: Dependent variable is mean life satisfaction (1–10 scale). Estimation is with a GLS random-effects model. Entries are regression coefficients (standard errors).
* – significant at .05 level
** – significant at .01 level
*** – significant at .001 level

In sum, the data analysis clearly and unequivocally confirms the hypothesis that the welfare state contributes to human well-being. Simply stated, the less people are forced 'to behave as commodities in order to survive', the greater their satisfaction with life tends to be.

Discussion

Albert Einstein posed the question 'Why Socialism?' (1949). The answer he provided was that socialism provided the best method available to 'structure society in order to make human life as satisfying as possible'. Much of Einstein's reasoning followed the conventional class-analytical critique of capitalism as a means of production, which we have briefly touched upon above: 'workers' (in the most expansive sense, as Einstein puts it, of 'those who do not share in the ownership of the means of production') become prisoners – commodities – within the system of production, such that their lives are characterized by insecurity. To the extent that the welfare state is the emblematic institution of the modern socialist (or, at least, social democratic) enterprise, the evidence presented here would seem to vindicate Einstein's judgment. Whatever else we might say about the welfare state, it does indeed seem to make important contributions to the project of making 'human life as satisfying as possible'. We thus echo Einstein by concluding that socialism (at least as represented by its social democratic incarnation) provides what is perhaps our best hope for improving the human condition, in so far as we agree that making 'life as satisfying as possible' is the appropriate standard of evaluation.

This is not the most hopeful conclusion to draw given current ideological trends. The welfare state appears to be everywhere in retreat. Across Europe, from Sweden to Germany to the UK, commitment to the idea of social security in general, and to the idea of 'decommodification' in particular, has eroded. In the United States, where the welfare state never coalesced into anything beyond its most minimal and anaemic form, these pressures are more keenly felt than ever. More generally the neo-liberal agenda of unfettered markets, privatization, 'flexible' labour laws, and lower social spending appears to be advancing nearly unopposed everywhere from Scandinavia to 'communist' China, leaving the world to face an ideological hegemony ('the Washington consensus') unknown since capitalism's inception. If the contentions advanced in this article carry any validity at all, it takes no great insight to deduce the implications for the human condition.

Can we find any other basis for a more sanguine view of the future of human happiness? One possibility is that offered by Robert Lane who, like Robert Putnam, stresses not so much the structure of the economy but rather human connections – supportive and nurturing relationships – as the key to satisfying lives.[20] Einstein again provides a convenient starting point for considering this approach. He observes, familiarly, that humans have two primary 'drives'. One is 'private' or 'egoistical'; it encourages one 'to protect his own existence' and 'to satisfy his personal desires'. The other is 'social'; it suggests seeking 'to gain the recognition and affection of [one's] fellow human beings, to share in their pleasures, to comfort them in their sorrows'. Both are always present and necessary, of course, but it is 'their specific combination [that] determines the extent to which an individual can achieve an inner equilibrium' in which he or she lives life to its fullest. The 'relative strength' of these two drives in most persons is in turn determined 'by the structure of society' in which they live. Some institutional arrangements push one or other of the drives to dominate in an unhealthy way over the other. Thus, the extent to which people find the correct 'inner equilibrium' necessary for a good life is greatly influenced 'by the types of organizations that predominate in society'.

Here we come to what Einstein sees as the central problem with capitalism: whatever its many commendable aspects, as an institution it encourages the individual to see society not 'as a positive asset, as an organic tie, as a protective force, but rather as a threat to his natural rights . . . such that the egoistical drives . . . are constantly being accentuated, while his social drives, which are by nature weaker, progressively deteriorate'. This, then, is Einstein's view of 'the real source of evil' in contemporary society: market economies tend to make individuals 'prisoners of their own egotism', so that 'they feel insecure, lonely and deprived of the naïve, simple, and unsophisticated enjoyment of life'.

This is precisely Lane's point: what makes people happy is ultimately freedom from the 'loneliness' that he sees as responsible for the decline in happiness in capitalist societies. Similarly, Einstein's conclusion would please Putnam and the other proponents of social capital: 'Man can find meaning in life . . . only through devoting himself to society.' By this he means simply an emphasis on the 'social drive' so as to build connections and relationships of trust and reciprocity with others, in order to escape being 'a prisoner of egotism'.

The circle closes itself when we consider Einstein's suggested cure. Given that the problems he addresses stem from the structural conditions of the market system, the only solution is to replace that system – or, at a minimum, to supplement it with other countervailing institutions that limit its potential for converting human beings into commodities. As we have seen, this is precisely the goal of the social democratic project. We thus return again to the conclusion that the welfare state is an agent of human well-being.

Notes

From *Perspectives on Politics*, Vol. 6, No. 2, pp. 267–77, copyright © The American Political Science Association, published by Cambridge University Press, 2008, by permission of Cambridge University Press and author Alexander Pacek.

1   For reviews, see Diener and Suh 2000; Frey and Stutzer 2005; Layard 2005.
2   Lindblom 1977.
3   Esping-Andersen 1985, 159.
4   Lane 1978.
5   Esping-Andersen 1990, 36.
6   For a review, see Radcliff 2001.
7   For a discussion of these and other arguments against the welfare state as it relates to happiness, see Veenhoven 2000, 112–19.
8   Austria, Finland, and Sweden have a shorter (1996–2002) time series, given their later entry into the EU. Greece, Luxembourg, Portugal, and Spain are effectively eliminated due to missing data on independent variables.
9   Scruggs 2005.
10   Esping-Andersen 1990.
11   OECD 2004.
12   Following Radcliff 2001, we also attempted to fit a variable for cumulative centre-party seats, but this proved to lack all statistical significance.
13   Armingeon et al. 2005.
14   For a review, see Frey and Stutzer 2005, ch. 5.
15   See Stimson 1985.
16   For a review and a discussion see Radcliff 2001.
17   From Diener, Diener, and Diener 1995.
18   From the Penn World Table, as reported in Huber et al. 2004.
19   From Armingeon et al. 2005.
20   Lane 2000; Putnam 2000.

Alexander C. Pacek is associate professor in the Department of Political Science at Texas A&M University (e339ap@polisci.tamu.edu). Benjamin Radcliff is professor in the Department of Political Science at Notre Dame University (radcliff.1@nd.edu). A previous version of this paper was given at the 2006 Political Studies Association meeting. The authors would like to thank the following who offered valuable advice and assistance: Amy Gille, Rodney Hero, David Nickerson, David Peterson, Benjamin Freeman, Jason Smith, and David Rossbach.

References

Armingeon, Klaus, Phillipp Leimgruber, Michelle Beyeler, and Sarah Menegale. 2005. Comparative Political Data Set 1960–2002. Institute of Berne. Accessed 15 April 2005.
Diener, Ed, Diener, Marissa, and Diener, Carol. 1995. Factors predicting the subjective well-being of nations. *Journal of Personality and Social Psychology* 69: 851–64.
Diener, E., and E. M. Suh, eds. 2000. *Culture and Subjective Well-Being.* Cambridge, MA: MIT Press.
Einstein, Albert. 2002 [1949]. 'Why Socialism?' *Monthly Review* 52 (1): 36–44.
Esping-Andersen, Gosta. 1985. *Politics against Markets: The Social Democratic Road to Power.* Princeton: Princeton University Press.

Esping-Andersen, Gosta. 1990. *The Three Worlds of Welfare Capitalism*. Princeton: Princeton University Press.

Frey, Bruno, and Alois Stutzer. 2005. *Happiness and Economics*. Princeton and Oxford: Princeton University Press.

Huber, Evelyne, Charles Ragin, John D. Stephen, David Brady, and Jason Beckfield. 2004. Comparative Welfare States Data Set, Northwestern University, University of North Carolina, Duke University, and Indiana University. Data available at http://www.lisproject.org/publications/welfaredata/welfareaccess.htm. Accessed 15 April 2005.

Lane, Robert. 1978. Autonomy, felicity, futility. *Journal of Politics* 40: 1–24.

Lane, Robert. 2000. *The Loss of Happiness in Market Democracies*. New Haven, CT: Yale University Press.

Layard, Richard. 2005. *Happiness: Lessons from a New Science*. London: Allen Lane.

Lindblom, Charles. 1977. *Politics and Markets*. New York: Basic Books.

Organisation for Economic Co-operation and Development (OECD). 2004. Social Expenditure Data Set 1980–2001 (SOCX 2004).

Putnam, Robert. 2000. *Bowling Alone: The Collapse and Revival of American Community*. New York: Simon and Schuster.

Radcliff, Benjamin. 2001. Politics, markets, and life satisfaction: The political economy of human happiness. *American Political Science Review* 95 (4): 932–52.

Scruggs, Lyle. 2005. 'Comparative Welfare Entitlements Dataset.' Department of Political Science, University of Connecticut. Accessed 15 April 2005.

Stimson, James. 1985. Regression models in space and time: A statistical essay. *American Journal of Political Science* 29: 914–47.

Veenhoven, Ruut. 2000. Well-being in the welfare state: Level not higher, distribution not more equitable. *Journal of Comparative Policy Analysis* 2: 91–125.

Europe's Post-Democratic Era

Jürgen Habermas

Democratic constitutions [. . .] enter into a new constellation at the European level. Once a constitutional community reaches beyond the boundaries of a single state [. . .] solidarity among citizens who are willing to support each other should expand to keep pace with it, as it were. [. . .] According to the scenario I propose, an extended, though also more abstract and hence comparatively less resilient, civic solidarity would have to include the members of each of the other European peoples – from the German perspective, for example, the Greeks when they are subjected to internationally imposed and socially unbalanced austerity programmes. Only in that case would the EU citizens who elect and control the Parliament in Strasbourg be able to participate in a joint process of democratic will-formation reaching across national borders.[1]

To be sure, the expansion of communication networks and horizons of perception, the liberalization of values and attitudes, an increase in the willingness to include strangers, the strengthening of civil society initiatives and a corresponding transformation of strong identities can at best be stimulated through legal-administrative means. There nevertheless exists a circular, either mutually reinforcing or mutually inhibiting, interaction between political processes and constitutional norms, on the one hand, and the network of shared political and cultural attitudes and convictions, on the other. [. . .] When it comes to the constitutional definition of the boundaries of a political community and its subpopulations or to defining the tiers in a multi-level political system, there are no 'givens'; loyalties evolve and traditions change. Nations, too, just like all other comparable referents, are not natural facts, even if they are generally not merely fictions either (as was the case with many colonial state creations).

Many loyalties overlap in the political life of a citizen, loyalties to which individuals attach quite different weights. Among them are politically relevant ties with one's region of origin, with the state or province of one's domicile, with country or nation, etc. Only in cases of conflict do the weights attached to these loyalties acquire relevance because they have to be balanced against each other. A measure of the strength of an identification with one social unit rather than another is the willingness to make sacrifices based on longer-term relations of reciprocity. With the abolition of universal conscription, the test case of war, and hence the *absolute* claim to sacrifice one's life for the well-being of the nation, has fortunately lost its relevance. But the long shadow cast by nationalism continues to obscure the present. The supranational expansion of civic solidarity depends on learning processes which, as the current crisis leads us to hope, can be stimulated by perceptions of economic and political constraints.

In the meantime, the cunning of economic reason has at least set cross-border communication in train. The European institutions have long since staked out for the enfranchised EU citizens, with their wine-red passports, the virtual space which would have to be filled with life by appropriately extended communication processes within civil society. But this can take on concrete form only as the national public spheres gradually *open themselves up to each other*. The transnationalization of the existing national publics does not call for different news media, but instead for a different practice on the part of the existing leading media. Not only must the latter thematize and address European issues as such, but they must at the same time report on the political positions and controversies which the same topics evoke in other member states. A dangerous asymmetry has developed because until now the European Union has been sustained and monopolized by political elites – an asymmetry between the democratic participation of the *peoples* in what their governments 'obtain' for them on the, as they see it, far-off Brussels stage and the indifference, even apathy, of the *EU citizens* regarding the decisions of their parliament in Strasbourg.

However, this observation does not justify substantializing 'the people' or 'the nation'. The caricature of national macrosubjects shutting themselves off from each other and blocking any cross-border democratic will-formation is now the preserve of right-wing populism. After half a century of labour immigration, even the European peoples, given their growing ethnic, linguistic and religious diversity, can no longer be conceived as culturally homogenous entities.[2] In addition, the internet and mass tourism have rendered national borders porous. Within the vast territories of our nation states, the floating horizon of a shared political lifeworld spanning large distances and complex relations *always* had to be produced and maintained by mass media, and it had to be lent substance by the abstract flows of ideas circulating through the communication networks of civil society. Such a process can acquire a secure foothold only on the basis of a shared political culture, however fluid it may be.

But the more the national populations realize, *and the media help them to realize*, how profoundly the decisions of the European Union pervade their daily lives, the more their interest in making use of their democratic rights also as EU citizens will increase.

The impact factor of the perceived importance of European decisions has become palpable during the euro crisis. A reluctant European Council is being forced to make decisions that have patently unequal impacts on the budgets of the member states. As of 9 May 2009, the European Council has passed a threshold with its decisions on rescue packages and possible debt restructurings and its declarations of intent to bring about harmonization of the national budgets in all fields of relevance for competition – namely, economic, fiscal, labour market and social policy. Once this threshold is crossed, new problems of distributive justice arise. With the transition from 'negative' to 'positive' integration, the balance shifts from output to input legitimation. For the citizens, actively influencing the nature and content of policies and laws becomes all the more important as discontent with public services grows.[3] Thus the logic of this development would imply that national citizens who *have* to accept a redistribution of the burdens across national borders would also *want* to exercise democratic influence in their role as EU citizens over what their heads of government negotiate or agree upon in a legal grey area. Instead of this, we see the governments engaging in delaying tactics and the populations being led by populist sentiment to a wholesale rejection of the European project. The immediate reason for this self-destructive behaviour is that the political elites and the media are reluctant to win over the populations to a common European future.

Under the pressure of the financial markets, it has become an accepted fact that an essential economic precondition for the constitutional project was neglected when the euro was introduced. Analysts agree that the European Union can withstand the financial speculation only if it acquires the necessary political steering capacities to work towards a convergence of the member states' economic and social development in the medium term at least in core Europe, i.e. among the members of the European monetary zone.[4] All of those involved are actually aware that this level of 'increased cooperation' is impossible within the frame of the existing treaties. The conclusion that a joint 'economic government' is necessary, with which even the German federal government is now reconciling itself, would mean that European policies designed to promote the competitiveness of all economies in the euro zone would extend far beyond the financial sector and affect national budgets as a whole, thus encroaching deeply on the budgetary privilege of national parliaments. Hence, if existing law is not to be flouted, the long overdue reform is possible only by transferring further competences from the member states to the Union.

[. . .] On 22 July 2011, Angela Merkel and Nicolas Sarkozy agreed on a compromise, which is vague and certainly in need of interpretation, between German economic liberalism and French etatism which reflects a completely different intention. All signs point to the fact that the two leaders want to expand the executive federalism implicit in the Lisbon Treaty into a form of intergovernmental rule by the European Council, moreover, one which is at odds with the spirit of the treaty. Such a regime of central steering by the European Council would enable them to transfer the imperatives of the markets to the national budgets. This would involve using threats of sanctions and pressure on the disempowered national parliaments to enforce non-transparent and informal agreements. In this way, the heads of government would invert the European project into its opposite. The first transnational democracy would be transformed into an arrangement for exercising a kind of post-democratic, bureaucratic rule.

The alternative is to continue the democratic legal domestication of the European Union in a consistent way. A Europe-wide civic solidarity cannot develop if social inequalities between the member states become permanent structural features, and hence reinforce the fault lines separating rich and poor nations. The Union must guarantee what the Basic Law of the German Federal Republic calls the 'uniformity of living standards' (Art. 106, para. 3). This 'uniformity' refers only to a range of variation in social living conditions which is still acceptable from the perspective of distributive justice, not to the levelling of cultural differences. A political integration backed by social welfare is necessary if the national diversity and the incomparable cultural wealth of the biotope 'old Europe' are to enjoy any protection against becoming levelled in the midst of rapidly progressing globalization.

Notes

From *The Crisis of the European Union: A Response*, Cambridge, Polity, 2012, pp. 45–53, by permission of Polity Press Ltd.

1 Habermas, 'Is the development of a European identity necessary, and is it possible?', in *The Divided West*, Cambridge, Polity, 2006, pp. 67–82.

2 Klaus Eder, 'Europäische Öffentlichkeit und multiple Identitäten – das Ende des Volksbegriffs?', in Claudio Franzius and Ulrich K. Preuß (eds), *Europäische Öffentlichkeit*, Baden-Baden, Nomos, 2004, pp. 61–80.

3 Fritz W. Scharpf, *Governing in Europe: Effective and Democratic?*, Oxford, Oxford University Press, 1999.

4 On the legal possibilities of a European internal differentiation see Daniel Thym, 'Variable Geometrie in der Europäischen Union: Kontrollierte Binnendifferenzierung und Schutz vor unionsexterner Gefährdung', in Stefan Kadelbach (ed.), *60 Jahre Integration in Europa: Variable Geometrien und politische Verfl echtung jenseits der EU*, Baden-Baden, Nomos, 2011, pp. 117–35.

Index